INVESTIGATING THE
FBI

INVESTIGATING THE

F B I

EDITED BY
PAT WATTERS
AND
STEPHEN GILLERS

A Book of the Committee for Public Justice

1973
DOUBLEDAY & COMPANY, INC.
GARDEN CITY, NEW YORK

A slightly different version of "Why I Got Out of It," by Robert Wall, appeared in *The New York Review of Books*, © 1971 by NYREV. Used by permission.

Designed by Marshall Henrichs

ISBN: 0-385-06684-8
Library of Congress Catalog Card Number 72–76219

CONTENTS

ORIGINS AND
ACKNOWLEDGMENTS

Investigating the FBI is based on a conference on the FBI held at Princeton University, October 29 and 30, 1971, sponsored by the Committee for Public Justice and the Woodrow Wilson School of Public and International Affairs. This book contains edited versions of the papers presented at the conference and significant portions of the dialogue and panel discussions that occurred during the thirteen hours of conference time.*

The idea of a conference on the FBI was suggested by Professor H. H. Wilson of Princeton's Politics Department, writing in the February 8, 1971, issue of *The Nation*. He communicated with Professor Norman Dorsen of the New York University Law School, a member of the Executive Council of the Committee for Public Justice (and now its Chairman). From there, the idea grew rapidly. In the following months, committee members and staff members of the Princeton faculty and others worked to bring some fifty lawyers, scholars, journalists and former government officials together for as thorough a study of the FBI as private citizens could hope to undertake. This book is one result of that effort.

There are many people whose energies made the Princeton conference successful. In addition to Professor Dorsen, Duane Lockard, Chairman of the Politics Department at Princeton, and Burke Marshall, deputy Dean of the Yale Law School and a member of the committee, served as Chairmen of the con-

---

* The Call to the Conference and the extensive correspondence with J. Edgar Hoover appear in the Appendix.

ference and were instrumental in its planning. Other committee members who provided substantial assistance prior to and at the conference were Blair Clark, Thomas Brandon, Elinor Gordon, Milton Gordon, Lillian Hellman, Robert B. Silvers and Roger Wilkins. Mr. Wilkins, now on the Editorial Board of the Washington *Post*, was then Chairman of the committee.

Others who provided valuable assistance in the planning and execution of the FBI conference were: John Doar, Jameson W. Doig, John T. Elliff, Thomas I. Emerson, Garrett Epps, Robert Jeffers, Dorothy Landsberg, David Obst, John Strange and William W. Turner. The participants are also grateful to the Field and New World Foundations for their generous contributions to the conference expenses.

Much gratitude is owed to the writers, panelists and participants, whose work constitutes most of this book and who were willing to travel across country—and in the case of C. H. Rolph across the Atlantic—to make the FBI conference possible. Dorothy Waleski of the committee and Princeton's Gloria Mason gave close attention to the conference's myriad details. And credit belongs to two NYU law students—Jack Novik, for his diligence in checking the accuracy of the many citations and quotations, and Rochelle Korman, for her assistance in writing and organizing the final chapter and working with Sheila Rossi in preparing the manuscript for publication.

Finally, much is owed two people in particular: Tom Congdon, our Doubleday editor, for his advice on and confidence in this project; and Glenda H. Watters, for her careful editorial attention. Both helped reduce an unwieldy manuscript to, one hopes, a manageable and useful book.

A note on style: J. Edgar Hoover died on May 2, 1972, after the conference but before this book's publication. His activities and attitudes were often mentioned at the conference and again here. Verb tenses in written articles reflect Mr. Hoover's death, but the editors have not altered the conference dialogue in the same way. The articles were finally prepared for publication after May 2, but the oral assessments were made while the Director lived and the editors believed they should so appear.

Pat Watters
Stephen Gillers

INTRODUCTION

BY TOM WICKER

I

In the fall of 1971 J. Edgar Hoover, the late fabled Director of the Federal Bureau of Investigation, wrote to Duane Lockard of Princeton University that the FBI would not send a representative to a conference at Princeton on the FBI's role in American life.

"The basic facts," wrote Mr. Hoover, "on how the FBI is organized and how it discharges its duties have been so well known for so long, and to so many responsible persons, that they are obvious to all except those who are so blind that they do not wish to see." And those "basic facts," he concluded, "if fully developed and exposed to public view" could only produce a verdict "that the FBI is a lawfully composed and operated public agency, staffed by honest and reasonably intelligent citizens doing a difficult job in the best way they know how and, moreover, doing it quite as well as it could be done by anyone else."

The Director could hardly have given the Committee for Public Justice and cooperating officials at Princeton a more solid justification for going ahead with their conference, of which this book is the core record. There was the Director, after all, stating publicly and blatantly that no inquiry into the FBI was needed, because all the basic facts were known, and those facts showed the Bureau to be doing its job well—when it was the belief of the sponsors that an inquiry was needed precisely because the FBI told the public too few of the "basic facts" about its operations and hence that public had no real way to know how effectively the Bureau functioned.

Was the Bureau, in every sense of the words, "lawfully . . . operated"? And while few doubted that its personnel were generally "honest and reasonably intelligent," were they in fact "doing a difficult job in the best way they know how"? Or were they doing it nowhere near as well "as it could be done by anyone else" if operating under different rules and attitudes, with different priorities?

The Director's lengthy letter even touched upon many of the right questions—though its wording turned them all into conclusions favorable to the FBI. Asserting, for instance, that he and the Bureau he had headed since the Coolidge administration were "not at all a law unto ourselves," Mr. Hoover contended that there were "many who monitor us in some way or other; they are a system of checks and balances on the manner in which we perform our duties."

Then he cited, first, senators and representatives—when the sponsors well knew that the Senate had rarely held hearings on the FBI budget before 1971, and that a House Appropriations subcommittee dependent on FBI agents for its investigatory work had never altered the Director's budget request except twice to give him more money than he had asked for. He cited also the supervision of the Department of Justice, of which the FBI nominally is a part—when one of the major purposes of the Princeton inquiry was to study to what extent the department actually controlled such FBI operations as electronic surveillance, the use of informers and the maintenance and dissemination of political dossiers on persons not charged with any crime and not in public office.

The system of "checks and balances," the Director claimed, included U.S. attorneys, magistrates and judges, who had supervisory authority over FBI cases that found their way into court at whatever level. But is that "supervisory authority" either check or balance on FBI activities that may not surface in any court? Even in court, does evidence presented accu-

to the extent that the FBI was "the lengthened shadow of one man," it remains as necessary as in J. Edgar Hoover's lifetime to study what he did and how he did it, what he achieved and where he failed. The agency he built was no less and perhaps more in need of objective study and appraisal after his death than before it; there would be, after all, a new Director, operating in a new manner, and if one thing was clear it was that no one should again have the unlimited and unexamined license, over so important an agency, that J. Edgar Hoover had achieved in his long and remarkable life of single-minded devotion to the FBI.

II

Many themes were pursued and developed at the Princeton conference but none, it seems to me, more historically important, as well as significant for contemporary American society, than the idea that in its counterespionage mission against Fascist and Communist agents in the 1930s, the FBI found the instrument with which to develop a pervasive system of political surveillance in America. How it was done makes a scary syllogism: it was necessary to conduct surveillance of the agents of Fascist and Communist foreign powers; since Fascism and Communism are evangelistic doctrines, American citizens sympathetic or devoted to them could knowingly or unwittingly become agents of foreign powers; hence it was necessary to conduct surveillance of American citizens.

Once that reasoning could be advanced, the FBI no longer had to worry about the troublesome distinction between foreign espionage and sabotage, on the one hand, and domestic revolutionary or radical activities on the other. If the latter could be viewed as "subversive alien theories and isms," to use one of Mr. Hoover's phrases, they would be as subject to surveillance and counteraction as any Red spy. Thus, even

Attorney General Robert Jackson could say in 1940 that the
FBI had to maintain "steady surveillance over individuals and
groups within the United States who are so sympathetic with
the systems or designs of foreign dictators as to make them a
likely source of federal law violation."

In one of the papers presented at the Princeton conference
and published here in part, John T. Elliff, an assistant professor
of politics at Brandeis University, points out that Attorney
General Jackson had not liked the term "subversive activity,"
because he said there were "no definite standards to determine
what constitutes a 'subversive activity,' such as we have for
murder or larceny." But domestic political activity that appeared or threatened to be linked to promotion of the interest
of a foreign power could override Mr. Jackson's fear; that was
truly subversion!

J. Edgar Hoover apparently got the point early, as Mr. Elliff
relates:

> Discussing the FBI's role with Secretary of State Hull in
> Hoover's presence, [President Franklin] Roosevelt emphasized
> the international character of Communism and Fascism, citing
> reports of movements around the country by a Soviet Em-
> bassy official. However, when Hoover issued instructions to
> FBI field offices in September, 1936, he used language which
> theoretically included purely domestic advocacy of revolu-
> tionary doctrine. The Bureau desired to obtain from all possible
> sources information concerning subversive activities being con-
> ducted in the United States by Communists, Fascists and rep-
> resentatives or advocates of other organizations or groups
> advocating overthrow or replacement of the government by
> illegal methods.

Note how Robert Jackson's desire for "definite standards"
is here surmounted; for how is it possible to know if a radical
political group advocates overthrow or replacement of the government unless you investigate it? How can you know if its

methods are illegal without surveillance? And even if a group under investigation at the moment isn't advocating anything wicked or doing anything illegal in its advocacy, how can you tell what it might do tomorrow or next month unless you keep close track of its development?

So, as Mr. Elliff observes, "real international danger in the Thirties" revived a practice that even the Director had had to give up a decade earlier. When Attorney General Harlan F. Stone curtailed, in 1924, the domestic political surveillance in which the FBI and the young J. Edgar Hoover had been so heavily involved in the years just preceding, Mr. Hoover wrote —with obvious reluctance—that "the activities of Communists and other ultra-radicals have not up to the present time constituted a violation of the federal statutes, and consequently, the Department of Justice, theoretically, has no right to investigate such activities as there has been no violation of the federal laws." In 1936 he still maintained that it was not a federal offense to be a Communist; but if he had the mission to watch the agents of foreign powers, and if American citizens engaged in otherwise legal political activities became or might become foreign agents through such activities, that was all the reason necessary to investigate such persons and keep files on them.

Another such artful expansion of domestic political surveillance followed soon after World War II. As related by Victor Navasky and Nathan Lewin, Attorney General Tom Clark wrote President Truman to remind him that in 1940 President Roosevelt had authorized the use of "listening devices directed to the conversations or other communications of persons suspected of subversive activities against the government of the United States, including suspected spies." Mr. Clark remarked on his own that "in the present troubled period in international affairs, accompanied as it is by an increase in subversive activity here at home, it is as necessary as it was in 1940 to take the investigative measures referred to in President Roosevelt's memorandum."

But Mr. Clark had deleted a sentence from the Roosevelt memo instructing the Justice Department "to limit these investigations so conducted to a minimum and to limit them insofar as possible to aliens." Nor did he convey the concern Mr. Roosevelt had expressed that wiretapping be restricted to foreign activities involving the threat of sabotage. Mr. Clark even *recommended* the use of wiretapping in domestic crime and subversive activities, and when Mr. Truman approved what apparently appeared to him to be little more than an extension of the Roosevelt policy, a significant expansion of domestic surveillance had been given official sanction.

The idea that subversion includes domestic political activity was ultimately embodied in the Smith Act of 1940. Throughout the Cold War era of the 1950s, FBI surveillance of Communist and Communist-front and Communist-maybe and Communist-potential organizations, as well as the Director's jeremiads against them, aided and abetted the hysteria engendered by Joe McCarthy, the House Un-American Activities Committee and their myriad bush-league imitators, until fervent, fearful anti-Communism became a profound article of American faith. What that might have done to the actual course of Soviet-American relations is conjectural, but it plainly was not conducive to *détente*, any more than it encouraged the sensible policy toward Communist China that did not arrive until 1971.

But what, someone may say, is after all wrong with monitoring domestic subversion—with the government trying to protect itself from those who would overthrow it by unlawful means? Well, for one thing, former FBI special agent Bob Wall told the Princeton conference, the whole system makes it too easy to investigate *anybody*, compile a dossier on him and either frighten him in the process or hold the threat of the dossier over his head; to many Americans, the mere fact of an FBI investigation is evidence enough of some degree of guilt.

For instance, Mr. Wall said, the magic term "Cominfil" can lay the most innocuous group open to the full range of FBI surveillance techniques. "Kiwanis, Cominfil," for example, would be the tab on the file of an investigation of the extent of "Communist infiltration" into the Kiwanis Clubs of America. About all that would be required to cause such a file to be opened is a couple of informers who for some reason disliked Kiwanis, or even a left-wing after-dinner speaker—and not too left-wing at that.

If that seems a remote threat, even from the FBI, bear in mind that it is not remote at all to most black, student or "New Left" political groups, and lately even to such organizations as Gay and Women's Liberation and the Harvard law faculty; Cominfil stops at nothing. Frank J. Donner, who heads an ACLU special project on political surveillance at the Yale Law School, contends in a notable paper on FBI informers, that "out of an estimated total of about ten thousand political undercover agents" employed by the FBI, "only a small number are deployed to police the activities of violence-prone groups in order to forestall bombings and related offenses. The rest are used principally as informers against left, liberal, anti-war, racial and ghetto groups and individuals."

Mr. Donner is of the opinion that while this vast informant apparatus actually serves the purpose of gathering information, of whatever reliability, one of its primary purposes is to inhibit or chill political expression by its very existence.

"Surveillance," he writes, "is 'only' an investigation of the 'facts,' we are told; it neither enjoins nor punishes political expression and activities. Yet it can hardly be denied that the self-censorship which it stimulates is far more damaging than many express statutory or administrative restraints. It yields a maximum return of repression for a minimum investment of official power . . . The recruitment of informers is *intended* as a restraint on free expression, as a curb on movements for change."

So informers are kept on for years, turning in worthless repetitious reports; and other informers are paid for reporting on the same oganizations; and each is valued less for information than for being "an intruder who intimidates and demoralizes his targets." How else explain, asks Mr. Donner, "the curious dualism in American infiltration practice: while the identity of the individual informer is concealed, the fact that there is a widespread network of informers in the American left is widely publicized"? What else was the meaning of that FBI report on the New Left, stolen from the Media, Pennsylvania, office and distributed to the press, which suggested that intensive contact with "these subjects and hangers-on" was desirable because "it will enhance the paranoia endemic in these circles and will further serve to get the point across that there is an FBI agent behind every mailbox." Paranoia indeed!

The development of FBI surveillance in racial cases also is instructive. Beginning haltingly in the 1950s, and spurred on by the advent of the Kennedy and then the Johnson administrations with their black supporters, the FBI undertook to report on civil rights demonstrations and the often bloody and violent southern white reaction. From this start, it was an easy jump, after the ghetto riots of 1967, into intensive surveillance of "black extremist" groups, to the point where now virtually every black organization is under the tender care of FBI informants, bugs and taps. Now the FBI has a whole class of informers it refers to as "racial informant-ghetto"—many of whom, one Bureau document said, might be recruited among "taxi drivers, salesmen and distributors of newspapers, food and beverages. Installment collectors might also be considered." In short, everyone is a potential spy on almost anyone else, as the FBI sees it; and instructions to "racial informant-ghetto" in one instance included the following: "Visit Afro-American type bookstores for the purpose of determining if militant extremist literature is available therein and, if so, to identify the owners, operators, and clientele of such stores . . ."

Such a blunt instrument of surveillance in the hands of the Nixon administration is a conjunction of forces that, to some of those at Princeton as well as to many others concerned for the Bill of Rights, is "chilling" indeed. It was, after all, this Administration that pushed for "preventive detention" of people who *might* commit crimes, and that sought the first prior restraint on newspaper publication in American history. It was this Administration's Attorney General who raised to legal doctrine (fortunately rejected by the Supreme Court) the contention that anyone could be tapped and bugged without sanction if the executive branch thought he might be a threat to national security, and who reduced to commonplace the government's reliance upon that most dubious of prosecutorial weapons, the conspiracy charge. It was this Administration that defended FBI interrogation of a Harvard professor for opposing a Supreme Court nominee, began the practice of subpoenaing reporters' notes and turned the FBI loose to investigate critical television correspondents.

In such an atmosphere of carelessness and callousness toward personal liberties, J. Edgar Hoover's FBI seemed clearly to fit; but the deeper question was whether the Director and his men had not, in fact, prepared the conditions from which that atmosphere had been bound to arise.

III

The striking development of the agency that killed Dillinger, and of the Director who personally arrested Alvin Karpis, into a contemporary situation in which—as Mr. Elliff puts it—"by far

the FBI's most important function is gathering intelligence"
was not the only important idea pursued at the Princeton conference. The results are mostly to be found in this book.

They include lengthy discussion, for instance, on the question whether in its emphasis on political intelligence the Bureau
has recently played a very effective role in fighting crime; there
were many witnesses, most tellingly some former agents, to
suggest that it had not. One of them, William W. Turner,
bluntly debunked some of the most cherished Hooverian
myths:

> The famous Lady in Red who put the finger on Dillinger
> was an informant of the Hargrave Secret Service, not the FBI.
> The Lindbergh kidnapper, Bruno Richard Hauptmann, was
> trapped by the insistence of Treasury agents, not the FBI,
> that the ransom packet should contain gold notes. The German
> saboteurs landed by submarine during World War II were be-
> trayed by their own leader and master spy Rudolf Abel by a
> defecting subagent. As for organized crime, Hoover was guilty
> of nonfeasance for the first thirty-seven years of his regime,
> and recent achievements have been dimmed by a continued
> lack of cooperation with the other federal agencies that have
> long borne the brunt of the fight.

Another matter to which much time was devoted at Princeton was the bureaucracy and red tape in which Mr. Hoover
ensnarled the Bureau. Some of the ex-agents' descriptions
of the paper work that bogged them down and frequently laid
them open to the Director's unchecked wrath will startle ad-
mirers of Efrem Zimbalist, Jr.'s, exciting life on television's
version of "The FBI."

On the other hand, a perceptive essay by Walter Pincus details how the Director's skill at the bureaucratic game, at public
relations—and perhaps the collection of dossiers in his control
—kept the Bureau free of the close congressional supervision
that other agencies endure. In J. Edgar Hoover's time, the

Budget Bureau gave the FBI budget but cursory review. That budget was drawn up entirely within the FBI, with Department of Justice officials barely aware of its totals. When appropriated, Bureau funds—$334 million in the 1971 fiscal year, about as much as the State Department got—came in a lump sum to be expended not necessarily as the Director projected to Congress, but as he decided from day to day.

Still another paper, by journalist Robert Sherrill, undertakes an analysis of what he calls "the most successful job of salesmanship in the history of Western bureaucracy"—Mr. Hoover's decision in the Thirties to make himself and the G-man stand as the very symbols of bravery and purity in the enforcement of the law. Aryeh Neier, Executive Director of the ACLU, pursued the Bureau's record in controlling the information it collects and concluded that in the era of the computerized data bank, "the FBI's promiscuous data-dissemination practices have injured millions of people." And he asks, "Could it be that the rising crime rates and the recidivism and the rearrests have something to do with the rising efficiency with which records are distributed? Are people forced into crime by their inability to escape a 'record-prison' of things they have done and things they never did but are alleged to have done?"

All in all, as this overview suggests, the picture of the FBI that emerged from the Princeton conference was not a pretty one—as the Director quite rightly feared it would not be. It was the picture of a law-enforcement body that had made domestic political surveillance in America a vast and ominous fact, despite what most of us have thought were the guarantees of the Bill of Rights. (Read Thomas I. Emerson if you have any doubts about this.) But it was also the picture of a law-enforcement body that had steadily fallen behind in the immense task of coping with crime, organized and otherwise, in America. It was the picture of a sensitive and vital agency that functioned with little if any oversight either from Congress or the executive branch, whose army of agents served virtually at the pleasure of an aging and autocratic Director whose social ideas had been formed early in the century and whose ideological fixations had scarcely changed since he led the raids in the Red Scare days of A. Mitchell Palmer after the First World War. It was the picture of a law-enforcement body whose reputation had been inflated by relentless public relations but whose everyday reality was bureaucracy and red tape.

The consequences in American political life of the Bureau's activities in furtherance of the Director's messianic anti-Communism could only be surmised by the Princeton conferees. Readers of this account of their deliberations may well ask themselves the question that kept occurring to me as I wrote this introduction—if J. Edgar Hoover had retired, full of years and honor, twenty years ago and after his first quarter century at the head of the FBI, might not the history of the Cold War and the development of American political attitudes have been substantially different?

IV

Even so, it would be a mistake to assume that the death of the Director—"If you've seen one FBI Director, you've seen 'em all," quipped a character in the 1971 Gridiron Club show—will necessarily put an end to the things that are wrong with the FBI and emphasize the things—there are many—that are good about it (although it is doubtful that we shall ever see another J. Edgar Hoover, with his combination of social attitudes, bureaucratic skills and public relations talents).

There were anomalies, for instance, in Hoover's career that make one wonder if closer supervision of the Bureau and a more thoughtful concern about its activities, in Congress and the executive, might not at one time have found him receptive. He was the major opponent, for one thing, of the greatest single injustice of his time—the internment of Japanese-Americans in concentration camps during World War II.

He was once also a strong opponent of wiretapping. Navasky and Lewin quote him as telling an appropriations hearing in 1931 that "while [wiretapping] may not be illegal, I think it is unethical, and it is not permitted under the regulations by the Attorney General." As late as 1940 he wrote in the *Harvard Law Review* that wiretapping was an "archaic and inefficient" practice which "has proved a definite handicap or barrier in the development of ethical, scientific and sound investigative techniques"—which sounds like Ramsey Clark today.

So perhaps it is not insignificant that when Mr. Hoover was forced to confess to President Roosevelt that an agent had been caught red-handed installing a tap on Harry Bridges, the President—according to Attorney General Biddle, who was present —"was delighted; and with one of his great grins, intent on every word, slapped Hoover on the back when he had finished. 'By God, Edgar, that's the first time you've been caught with your pants down!'"

If the President saw nothing wrong with wiretapping, was even entertained by it, why should the Director stand out against it? Again and again, the pattern of executive or congressional indulgence recurs—President Truman did not take the time to analyze or have his staff research the Tom Clark letter that gave domestic wiretapping some kind of legal standing; John F. Kennedy made the reappointment of J. Edgar Hoover his first presidential act, out of what some of his closest associates have called the "cold, political" knowledge that firing the Director would have been too unpopular a move for a youthful new President to undertake; Lyndon Johnson saw to it that the Director did not have to retire at the statutory age limit of seventy, and Congress was happy to concur. Until Eugene McCarthy dared in 1968, no presidential candidate had ever criticized the Director; when he was seventy-five years old, Richard Nixon and John Mitchell made it clear that he could remain in office as long as he lived and wanted to.

Similarly, the public—gulled, it is true, by the Bureau's incessant propaganda—until recent years loved it all; and what considerable percentage of voters Washington believed were still devoted to J. Edgar Hoover at his death was suggested by the President's funeral oration and by Congress's decision that his body should lie in state, where Lincoln and John Kennedy had lain. There was little or no outcry when the Director, guardian of liberty, spoke up for Joe McCarthy, called Martin Luther King a liar and for years singlehandedly held up congressional passage of the consular treaty with the Soviet Union. There was always a radio audience for "The FBI in Peace and War" and the G-man movies to which the Director invariably lent "technical assistance" and his seal of approval— as long as they pictured his men on the side of the angels. For decades, his turgid and moralistic articles appeared with the regularity of the seasons in *Reader's Digest* and *American* magazine, and publishers took turns presenting his self-aggrandizing books to the waiting public. If J. Edgar Hoover passed eventually beyond the normal restraints of office, the American public seemed to view the process happily, and with a sense of gratitude.

As a result of this record of public and official indulgence, any plans for "doing something about the FBI" probably ought to start at the elementary level of supervision. Walter Pincus points out that the Attorney General, at the least, could exercise real control over FBI budget-making. The Office of Management and Budget and the relevant congressional committees could give the new Director the same kind of intensive grilling other heads of agencies get. None of them, for instance, has ever really inquired into the exorbitant costs of wiretapping as against the paucity of significant results—much less questioned the FBI's dubious figures on the extent of "national security" wiretapping done without a court order or any shred of sanction from anyone outside the executive branch.

An important section of the 1968 omnibus crime act provided that the successor to Mr. Hoover had to be confirmed by the Senate, as if he were to be an ambassador or a Supreme Court Justice. This ensures that Mr. Nixon, or whoever succeeds him, cannot lightly name a political crony or anyone of dubious reputation or scant qualification and character to the position that—as now constituted—may be the most important in government; because the Senate has shown that no Carswells need apply for jobs that, unlike the Cabinet posts in which a President is generally entitled to have the men he wants, entail responsibilities far beyond the immediate political program and interests of an incumbent administration.

But what if a President should nominate an FBI Director in the mold of William H. Rehnquist—that is, an able man, technically qualified, unblemished ethically, but holding such social and ideological views—liberal or conservative—as to make him unacceptable and frightening to a large segment of the population? As in the case of Mr. Rehnquist, that would still devolve into the most unpleasant kind of confirmation fight, in which the issue would be basically the politics of the nominee; that also would be the toughest kind of fight for opponents of the nominee to win.

Thus, the need for Senate confirmation is by no means a guarantee against a Director who might reproduce some of the worst features of the long Hoover regime—or, for instance, one who, unlike Mr. Hoover, might prove so weak that the Bureau could become a partisan political instrument or the obedient tool of some determined and highly partisan or ideological President or Attorney General. This possibility leads some to suggest that subsequent Directors should serve for a definite term—perhaps six or ten years—after which they would have to win renomination and reconfirmation.

There are obvious ways, however, in which the necessity or the desire to hang on to his job might lead a Director into more nefarious or subservient activities than any charged to Mr. Hoover. And if, as has also been suggested, the office of Director were to be downgraded—say to the status of an assistant attorney general—in an effort to give the Attorney General more control of the FBI, it has to be asked whether control by a politically appointed official is always to be desired. For one thing, as Walter Pincus put it at Princeton: "The FBI has responsibilities for undertaking investigations that reach into the highest levels of government—inquiries that should not be subject to review by higher authorities or Congress because these individuals may in fact be involved. This is the gravest type of responsibility and one that must be vested wholly within the Bureau."

One suggestion that came from several participants in the Princeton conference was that the functions of gathering intelligence, whether on domestic subversives or foreign spies, be separated from that of criminal law enforcement. "On the face of it," writes Mr. Turner, "counterespionage and criminal investigation are as immiscible as oil and water. They demand different approaches, different degrees of sophistication, different techniques." Moreover, separation of the two functions ought to make it easier to oversee and control the one—counterespionage—and for the Bureau to pursue and combat the other—crime. Mr. Elliff even suggests that serious consideration be given to separating foreign counterespionage from domestic intelligence; in fact, as he points out, "the controversy over FBI 'political surveillance' may get in the way of effective counterespionage contacts," the necessity for which few would deny.

Serious consideration, several other participants suggested, ought also to be given to the idea of a permanent independent oversight body—something like the Foreign Intelligence Advisory Board that has substantial authority to keep tabs on, and rein in, the activities of the Central Intelligence Agency. With that body as a precedent, even J. Edgar Hoover might have found it hard to argue convincingly against the proposition that the FBI, too, ought to have some independent supervision from a body of capable but disinterested and public-spirited citizens; but the temporary Director, Patrick Gray, already has opposed this idea.

Perhaps the best hope lies in the possibility that Mr. Nixon or the next President might appoint a blue-ribbon panel that would do an in-depth study of the whole "national security" apparatus, domestic as well as foreign, and make recommendations on how best to proceed and what reforms are necessary. This study, properly undertaken and supported, could cover everything from the Army's *opéra bouffe* efforts in the field of domestic surveillance to the complex questions of electronic surveillance in national security matters, and who—if anyone— ought to conduct it, under what controls.

We know that such presidentially commissioned studies can do superior work—witness President Johnson's Advisory Commission on Civil Disorders, whose report is still an essential text on racial problems in America. We know such commissions can even get things done—witness the Ash Commission, whose recommendations led Mr. Nixon to establish the Office of Management and Budget and the Domestic Council, and to propose the unhappily named "New American Revolution." There is no inherent reason why such a commission, adequately led, staffed and supported, could not produce significant recommendations in those fields in which the FBI and J. Edgar Hoover were most controversial.

If such a commission ever is appointed its work might well start with a perusal of the proceedings of that Princeton conference in which the Director so loftily refused to participate. In any case, readers of this book will have the benefits of that group's work, and if there are enough of them who care, they just might be able to force some necessary action.

WRITERS AND PANELISTS*

WRITERS:

Fred J. Cook is the author of twenty-seven books, including *The FBI Nobody Knows*, and hundreds of magazine articles. A former journalist, now a free-lance writer, he received three Page One Awards from the New York Newspaper Guild and a Sidney Hillman Foundation Award for his article "Gambling Inc." in *The Nation*.

Vern Countryman is a professor of law at Harvard Law School and is the former Dean of the University of New Mexico Law School. He was a law clerk to Supreme Court Justice William O. Douglas.

Frank Donner is a constitutional lawyer who has argued and briefed a number of cases before the United States Supreme Court. He is the Director of an ACLU project on political surveillance and is currently writing a book on that topic.

John T. Elliff is an assistant professor of politics at Brandeis University. He is the author of "Aspects of Federal Civil Rights Enforcement: The Justice Department and the FBI, 1939–1964," published in *Perspectives in American History* (vol. 5, 1971), and of the forthcoming book *Crime, Dissent, and the Attorney General*.

Thomas I. Emerson is Lines Professor of Law at Yale Law School. He is the author of *Toward a General Theory of the First Amendment* and *The System of Freedom of Expression*.

Nathan Lewin is a former deputy assistant attorney general of the United States and served as law clerk to Supreme Court Justice John Harlan. He is now in private practice in Washington, D.C.

Victor Navasky is the author of the recently published book *Kennedy Justice*, which deals with the attorney generalship of Robert

* Conference participants who were not writers or on a panel are identified when their names first appear.

Kennedy and particularly his relationship with the FBI. He is a graduate of the Yale Law School and was an editor of the New York *Times Magazine* until recently, when he resigned to begin another book.

Aryeh Neier has been a member of the staff of the American Civil Liberties Union since 1963. In 1970 he was appointed to his present post as Executive Director of the ACLU.

Walter Pincus is a journalist who has written for the Washington *Post,* the Washington *Star* and has directed two Special Investigations for the Senate Foreign Relations Committee. He is currently an associate editor of *The New Republic.*

C. H. Rolph is a former official in British law enforcement and is currently a writer and frequent contributor to the magazine *The New Statesman.*

Arlie Schardt, a former reporter for *Time,* based in Atlanta, is the national legislative representative of the ACLU, in its Washington, D.C., office.

Robert Sherrill is the Washington correspondent for *The Nation,* an author and a regular contributor to the New York *Times Magazine.*

William W. Turner was an FBI agent from 1951 to 1961. He is the writer of, among other books, *The Police Establishment* and *Hoover's FBI: The Men and The Myth.*

Robert Wall is a former FBI agent now at work on a book about his experience in the Bureau.

PANEL OF FORMER JUSTICE DEPARTMENT OFFICIALS:

William Bittman is a former special assistant to the Attorney General.

William Hundley is a former chief of the Organized Crime Section of the Department of Justice.

Robert Owen is a former deputy assistant attorney general in the Civil Rights Division of the Justice Department.

Roger Wilkins is the former Director of the Community Relations

Section of the Justice Department and was the Chairman of the Committee for Public Justice until February 1, 1972. He is now on the editorial board of the Washington *Post*.

PANEL OF FORMER SPECIAL AGENTS:

John Shaw, William W. Turner and *Robert Wall* are all former special agents of the FBI.

PANEL ON FBI RELATIONS WITH LOCAL POLICE:

James Ahern is the former Police Commissioner of New Haven.

Vincent Broderick is the former Police Commissioner of New York City.

Terrell Glenn is a former United States attorney in South Carolina.

James Vorenberg is a professor of law at Harvard University and was Executive Director of the President's Commission on Law Enforcement and the Administration of Justice.

Andrew Young is former executive secretary of the Southern Christian Leadership Conference and is active in the civil rights movement in the South.

EDITORS:

Pat Watters, author of *Down to Now: Reflections on the Southern Civil Rights Movement; The South and the Nation;* and other books, is a former newspaperman who has been Director of Information for the Southern Regional Council since 1963.

Stephen Gillers is a lawyer and the author of *Getting Justice: The Rights of People.* He is the Director of the Committee for Public Justice.

PART I
BACKGROUNDING
THE BUREAU

CHAPTER ONE

THE SELLING OF THE FBI

BY ROBERT SHERRILL

DRAFT J. EDGAR HOOVER FOR PRESIDENT
HEIGHT: *Tall in the Eyes of Free Men*
BUILD: *Great in Stature*
WEIGHT: *Heavy for Liberty and Justice*
HAIR: *Covers a Wealth of Knowledge*
EYES: *Sees the Threat to Our Freedom*
RACE: *To Victory Without Compromise*
NATIONALITY: *All American*
COMPLEXION: *Fair to All*
OCCUPATION: *Protector of Our Constitution**

The youth of the Seventies may wonder how grass-roots Mom and Dad could have ignored reality for so long and still have seen John Edgar Hoover as the same wonderful, wonderful man who protected us from gangsters and un-American gremlins those many years. What youth does not understand is that a mature awareness of the Perfect Image for more than three decades is well-nigh impossible to erase from the mind.

Fiftyish Father who belonged to the Post Toasties' Detectives in the 1930s and learned the secret whistle (two shorts and a long) and how to take fingerprints with white flour

---

* Brochure sent out by the National Grass Roots Movement to Draft Loyal Americans for America.

could not easily come to discredit the man whose gangbusting reputation once merited the highest accolade of childhood: two boxtops and a dime.

And then there were the years when the ex-junior G-man was in the armed services and knew that the war he won on foreign soil would not be lost at home because—a veritable deluge of magazine articles and movies convinced him of it— J. Edgar Hoover and his clean-cut men were wise to every move the saboteur rats were trying to make.

And then came the 1950s. Some of us let down our guard; we were tired of the international tension and were willing to come to terms with our conscience; we were willing to tolerate the dangerous radicals in our midst, excusing their perfidious ideologies in the name of freedom of speech. Not J. Edgar Hoover. Not the FBI. They knew it was no time to relax. They knew that that was what the international conspirators wanted us to do. And so through the untiring vigilance of Hoover and his men, Americans made it safely into the 1960s and even, despite the startling coddling of the Red Chinese in some high offices, into the 1970s.

Let youth view him as cynically as youth is inclined to view all sacred traditions. Mom and Dad know J. Edgar Hoover was really and truly tall in the eyes of free men, great in stature, heavy for liberty and justice . . .

I: A Cop Goes Public

Scholars of FBI lore say the building of that image and the selling of it to the American public—the most successful job of salesmanship in the history of Western bureaucracy— were decided on as a result of two bloody events that occurred on June 17, 1933, and July 22, 1934.

June 17, 1933. Frank Nash, a mail robber who had escaped from Leavenworth only to be recaptured three years later, arrived in Kansas City under heavy guard. It was supposed to be the last lap of his trip back to prison.

From the train terminal, a flying wedge of FBI agents and local cops took Nash across the street, stuffed him inside an auto and climbed in beside and behind him. A second car with two officers was parked to the rear. They never left the curbside. Three journeymen gangsters, Verne Miller, Charles ("Pretty Boy") Floyd and Adam Ricchetti, "materialized as if they had popped up out of the pavement" and began demolishing both cars and their occupants with submachine gun fire. Five died.

July 22, 1934. At the Biograph Theatre in East Chicago it was *Manhattan Melodrama,* a gangster flick starring Clark Gable and William Powell. The feature ended at 10:30 P.M. and a few minutes later out strolled John Dillinger, the most notorious outlaw of the 1930s, and two women friends, one of whom had tipped the federal agents to Dillinger's whereabouts.

Fifteen FBI men were waiting for him. Sensing that something was amiss, Dillinger broke for the alley and as he ran he attempted to draw his gun. Before he could aim or pull the trigger, he was dead, one bullet through his side and another through his head.

Neither of those episodes could be considered a smashing success for the underworld, inasmuch as the three gangsters who set out to free Nash wound up killing him in their fusillade and inasmuch as Dillinger showed himself to be neither fleet of foot nor wise in his choice of girl friends. Yet many people made other judgments. The boldness of the daytime Kansas City massacre was such as to catch the public's fancy. In those days of bread lines and mortgage foreclosures, it was not difficult for large segments of the public to sympathize with men who violently opposed the established order of society or, if sympathy was out of the question, at least to be titillated by their gory escapades. Floundering in the Great Depression, the general public had little love for bankers or for people who possessed such riches that their kinfolk were worth kidnapping. Vicious the gangsters might be, but what they did at least brightened days otherwise dampened by WPA jobs, and they did what they did in such a style as to indicate that the individual (if he chose to be violent enough) could, so long as his luck held out against the markmanship of the police, still shape his own destiny. It was no small attraction to people on the government dole.

And it was the era of the anti-hero, an era when the hokey biographies of badmen filled the 10-cent movie houses. The fantasy of the "good crook" even afflicted some solid citizens. After the FBI ambushed John Dillinger, a Virginia newspaper editor called it a dastardly deed. "Any brave man," he wrote, "would have walked down the aisle and arrested Dillinger [in the movie house] . . . Why were there so many cowards afraid of this one man? The answer is that the federal agents are mostly cowards."

It was this kind of response to the Kansas City massacre and to the Dillinger ambush, writes Don Whitehead in *The FBI Story*, the authorized history of the Bureau, that made Hoover decide to sell himself and his agency to the public. He determined to beat the crooks at the public relations game, for although "the vast weight of public opinion was on the side of Hoover and the FBI," nevertheless "the sympathy poured out for the dead gangsters and the criticism of the FBI outraged J. Edgar Hoover's Presbyterian concept of right and wrong."

Throughout his previous career, Hoover had shown the usual reticence of a cop. The only time he happily opened his mouth in public was to sing in the church choir. But now, having decided to go public, he also decided to go all the way and in every way: through magazine articles, books, comic strips, rotogravure sections, movies. Pick up a newspaper and there he was, eating a "G-man sandwich" at Toots Shor's, or sitting at his desk with America's other favorite, Shirley Temple, or pinning medals on Girl Scouts, or taking some target practice with a submachine gun.

Writers who flattered him were flattered in return; and in those early *quid pro quo* days it wasn't difficult to get a Hoover introduction to a book on the Bureau—as did four authors. Hoover, too, or his ghost writer, was busy. Between February, 1935, and August, 1936, *American magazine* alone carried sixteen articles under the Hoover by-line.

Very much a middle American himself, Hoover usually had an accurate feel for the kind of propaganda that would be effective with most Americans. In the 1930s his own favorite comic strips (in addition to *Tarzan*) were *Dick Tracy, Secret Agent X-9* and *War on Crime*. He considered these to be highly valuable allies in the promotion of law and order. Rex Collier, creator of the *War on Crime* strip, was a friend of Hoover's and got steady cooperation from the FBI in writing it. Pulp magazines—highly popular in the 1930s—were not too humble to catch Hoover's eye, and when they carried flattering stories of FBI manhunts, no matter how ridiculously exaggerated, the editors could look forward to a letter of praise from the FBI Director himself.

In fact, when one surveys FBI propaganda, it appears Hoover was most successful in that which "built for the future" by appealing to youngsters, not only in comic strips and pulp magazines and simplistic movies but also in the highly successful radio show "The FBI in Peace and War," which for several years recruited members to fan clubs called "The Junior G-Men." This may also be the age level aimed at by the currently popular television series "The FBI"; but in television it is not easy to tell just who the target audience is.

In those delicate beginnings of self-aggrandizing, it was essential that Hoover maintain some semblance of modesty, so none of the articles that appeared under his name in the first years contained autobiographical material. This approach was left to others and the FBI cooperated fully in shoveling out information to those writers who wanted to concentrate on Hoover the man. Of the twenty-eight magazine pieces written outside the Bureau between December, 1934, and January, 1939, eighteen were strictly biographical.

In the judgment of Jack Alexander (whose Hoover profile in *The New Yorker* of September 25, 1937, was singular in that era for its balance), Hoover came out of the closet and exposed his life to the biographers because he thought this was for the good of the Bureau. "Someone had to become a symbol of the [anti-crime] crusade," wrote Alexander, "and the Director decided that, because of his position, it was plainly up to him."

Not only up to him, but to him alone. When Melvin Purvis gained international notoriety as the special agent who directed the ambush of Dillinger, and when Purvis subsequently quit the FBI and marketed his reputation for print and movies and radio, Hoover was enraged.

His rage was triggered again in 1938 at what he considered the defection of Leon G. Turrou, who singlehandedly uncovered some of the clumsier German espionage agents. For this he became so famous that when J. David Stern, publisher of the New York *Post* and Philadelphia *Record*, offered to pay him $40,000 to write a series of spy articles, Turrou (who was earning $4,600 as a top G-man) decided the life of a writer was for him. He sent a letter of resignation to Hoover, signed on with Stern and the next day the *Post* carried promotional ads alerting its readers to the upcoming series that would tell of the GERMAN CONSPIRACY TO PARALYZE UNITED STATES.

When Hoover saw the ad, he fired Turrou "with prejudice."

It's kind of hard to fire a man ten days after he quit, but Hoover managed to do it, charging Turrou with violating the FBI "oath" not to disclose service information. Turrou responded that there was no such oath but merely a supplementary order that Hoover had issued hurriedly at the time Purvis was writing his Dillinger articles. "After Purvis resigned and wrote stuff, Hoover became jealous," Turrou said. "Unlike Mr. Hoover, I decided to step completely out of the service before attempting to write a word for publication."

By the end of the decade, Hoover had sacrificed his privacy with such wholesale selflessness that he was being scolded as a publicity fiend.

"Do you want to know something about Mr. Hoover?" Westbrook Pegler asked rhetorically in his August 8, 1938, column. "He is spoiled. The American press has treated him as a sacred cow . . . He has been praised in proportion to the very fine feats of detection which his Bureau has achieved, and a little beyond, for the G-men have received entire credit for some jobs in which other agencies took part. He is a great personal press agent, and he has pet writers, or stooges, with access to big newspapers and magazine circulation, who scratch his back in return for material that glorifies Edgar Hoover and the G's."

Two years later Senator George Norris was even more brutal. He described Hoover as "the greatest publicity hound on the American continent today." Norris warned that unless Hoover was discouraged from pumping out the thriller stories to every magazine and book writer who drifted by, "there will be a spy behind every stump and a detective in every closet."

II: The Themes: From Gangbuster to Ideologue

Bureau literary efforts in the 1930s were largely aimed at convincing the public (1) what nasty people criminals were

("Errand Boy of Crime," "The Meanest Man I Ever Knew," "Buzzard in Disguise," "King of Bandits" etc.) and at the same time (2) how attractively clever and scientific the FBI was ("Brains Against Bullets," "Science at the Scene of the Crime," "Tales the Bullet Tells" etc.).

The first objective was not at all difficult to achieve, given the brutish quality of underworld life (about the most appealing thing that could be said of Dillinger, for example, was that gravy was his favorite dish), but the second goal—spreading an aura of omniscience around the Bureau—took a bit of doing. The problem, simply put, was that the Bureau contained its share of bunglers. A study by the Brookings Institute covering the years 1935–36 showed that the FBI's record for building cases into convictions was lower than the achievement records of the Narcotics Bureau, the Secret Service Division, the Alcohol Tax Unit, the Post Office Inspection Service and the Internal Revenue Bureau. In fact, the only federal agency that the FBI could boast superiority over was the Customs Bureau, which never had been famous for the quality of its sleuths.

In his latest book, *Hoover's FBI: The Men and the Myth*, William W. Turner tells how the agents sometimes bungled grotesquely, as when they "recovered" the wrong baby in the Lindbergh kidnapping. Former agent Turner quotes another agent on this: "'Naturally, all of us on the Lindbergh Squad took special pains to keep these blunderings out of reach of the reporters. The FBI was still struggling for recognition and respect, and couldn't afford the public's horse laughs.'"

As for the FBI's laboratory wizardry, that was easier to write about, usually in gee-whiz tones, because criminal science was still pretty much in its infancy and the public was easily impressed. (For that matter, it sometimes seemed that all mechanics were in their infancy; FBI agents set out in five autos to capture the Dillinger gang at Little Bohemia—in

the wilds of Wisconsin—but three of the cars broke down
en route and their federal passengers had to travel the rest
of the way on the running boards of the remaining two cars.)
Ballistics was still a rudimentary science, as was fingerprinting
and wirephoto and many other devices that every rube cop
today looks upon as no more exceptional than handcuffs. The
FBI fingerprint file was still only a trifling mishmash when
Hoover wrote his first article on the subject in 1937 ("Fingerprint Everybody? Yes," for *The Rotarian*).

The ease with which Hoover captured the magazine and
book markets was nothing compared with the way he took over
Hollywood. Having become somewhat weary of its usual Hell's
Kitchen approach to the topic of crime, the town was eager
to receive any new (salable) perspective on this subject.
Hoover's public relations office was ready to oblige by supplying "consultants" and by opening its files for movie plots.
Harry Warner and his brothers were especially receptive, turning their No. 1 hoodlum actor, James Cagney, into a sometime
federal agent. Universal was also hospitable. But Hoover took
no chances. From the beginning, Hollywood's productions—
such as the early *G-Men* at Warner Brothers and *You Can't
Get Away with It* at Universal—were supervised all the way by
FBI agents.

Throughout World War II, the articles Hoover's ghost writers turned out, and this was also true of the articles produced
by non-Bureau writers, concentrated on the FBI's success in
frustrating spies ("How the Nazi Spy Invasion Was
Smashed"). Then, with the end of the war, in fact almost
before it had ended, the FBI was pumping out the kind of
propaganda that has sustained it ever since, on a topic that
was unknown before the war—"crime waves." This guaranteed
budget inflater was a favorite topic of the late 1940s: "Postwar
Crime Wave Unless—," in the April, 1945, *Rotarian*; "Crime
Wave We Now Face," in the April 21, 1946, New York *Times*

Magazine; "Rising Crime Wave," in the March, 1946, *American*
magazine; and a half-dozen allied articles such as "How Safe
Is Your Daughter?" and "Mothers, Our Only Hope," scattered
around the magazine marketplace. Always the FBI was presented as being steadfastly, dependably on call.

Came the 1950s, and the departure of foreign spies and the
non-arrival of the crime wave. At that point, Hoover had a
choice. He could go after big-time organized crime, or he
could become an ideologue cop. He did the latter. Hoover
was right in there with Senator Joseph McCarthy grinding out
his warnings. He launched himself into print as an ideologue
cop in the December, 1950, *Coronet* ("Underground Tactics
of the Communists"), and he continued in that vein to the
end of his life. But over the years there has been a range, as
might be expected, in the sophistication of these articles. At
first the emphasis was on the spy under the bed (for example,
"Red Spy Masters in America," August, 1952, *Reader's Digest,*
and "Communists Are After Our Minds," in the October, 1954,
American). Later Hoover's articles played down the spooky
and played up the crafty. The emphasis was not so much on
Communists as spies as on Communists as persuasive con men
("Why Reds Make Friends with U. S. Businessmen," May,
1962, *Nation's Business*).

Significantly, throughout the 1950s and 1960s Hoover
seemed unable to spell Mafia. So far as I can discover, during
that twenty-year period only one article ("The Inside Story
of Organized Crime and How You Can Help Smash It," *Parade,*
September 15, 1963) tentatively approached this most basic
crime problem. Hoover had so many outlets that it is likely
he addressed himself to organized crime more often than I
was able to discover, but it is accurate to say that this never
became one of his favorite literary topics just as it never was
accepted as one of the crucial targets for his Bureau.

The same predictable transition found in the magazine articles is even more apparent in the FBI's use of the cinema, as illustrated in several of the most representative films between 1945 and 1959: *The House on 92nd Street*, 1945; *Walk a Crooked Mile*, 1948; *I Was a Communist for the FBI*, 1951; *Walk East on Beacon*, 1952; *The FBI Story*, 1959.

Although these films were distributed under the aegis of major studios—20th Century-Fox, Columbia, Warner Brothers —they were quite literally FBI productions, in the sense that everything in the script and the manner of acting had to be approved by the FBI; coaching often preceded the approval. Far from attempting to pretend that the hand of the FBI had not been felt, the producers invariably capitalized on the Bureau's presence. Typically, *The House on 92nd Street* carried the credit: "This story is adapted from cases in the espionage files of the Federal Bureau of Investigation. Produced with the FBI's complete cooperation . . . with the exception of the leading players, all FBI personnel in the picture are members of the Federal Bureau of Investigation."

The supervision of the film work was made all the easier for Hoover to demand because of a federal law passed in 1954, at his request, prohibiting the use of the FBI name, or its files, without specific authorization from Hoover.

Henry Hathaway, who was the director for *House*, readily acknowledged in an interview with Garrett Epps of the *Harvard Crimson* that as many as fifteen agents from the New York office were assigned to act in some scenes, that an FBI monitor was on the set at all times "not for censorship but to make sure that we didn't exaggerate anything or say that someone was guilty when he was innocent or innocent when he was guilty" and that "we worked very closely with Mr. Hoover and we welcomed his enthusiasm. We thought it was a good thing to show the American people what was being done with their gasoline tax money."

The plots shifted from the spying of Nazi hirelings to the

sabotage of Communist dupes, but the interwoven themes never varied: (1) the FBI is the final and most important dike that stands between foreign totalitarianism and the American people; and the old standbys, (2) FBI agents are mighty clever fellows, and (3) the FBI has such overpoweringly scientific equipment that it virtually amounts to witchcraft.

Usually the totalitarianism is communistic. In *The House on 92nd Street* it was Nazi, but in any case the credit to the FBI was just as total: "Vigilant, tireless, implacable—the most silent service of the United States in peace or war is the Federal Bureau of Investigation. The Bureau went to war against Germany long before hostilities began. No word or picture could then make public the crucial war service of the FBI. But now it can be told."

When referring to the brilliance of the FBI agents and the niftiness of their equipment, the announcer [most of these movies are pseudo-documentaries] is just as direct. In *Walk East on Beacon:* "Fighting in the front lines of the FBI offensive against the forces of treason are alert and highly trained special agents."

The illustrations of the "highly trained" qualities of the agents may have often left viewers more amused than impressed. At one point in *Walk East on Beacon,* G-men were trying to trace down a woman who was last seen carrying a shoulder bag and walking with a peculiar gait. The announcer confides to the movie audience: "From Philadelphia to Seattle police already knew many suspected Communists with shoulder bags. Some of these had distinctive walks."

The FBI Story illustrates what Hoover considered friendly adjustments of history. At one point the film deals with the famous episode at Little Bohemia, where FBI agents converged on a tavern in an effort to corner Dillinger. It was night, and as it actually happened, the agents who tried to sneak up on the place got tangled in a fence and made so much noise the dogs began to bark. This rattled the agents and when five men came out the front door—three tipsy customers and two bartenders, curious about the dogs' barking—the agents jumped to the conclusion that this must be the Dillinger gang, and they opened fire on them. One customer was killed and two were wounded. This is not mentioned in the film; it was also left out of Don Whitehead's book, from which the film was taken.

III: Television Image: "Zimmy"

Hoover's adventures as the author of full-length works would best be forgotten. Only the sales are impressive. *A Study of Communism* (New York: Holt, Rinehart & Winston, 1962) reportedly sold 125,000 copies and *J. Edgar Hoover on Communism* (New York: Random House, 1964) supposedly sold 40,000 copies. They are such heavy going that one cannot help but be skeptical about these figures or about whether buyers were readers. His best-known book, *Masters of Deceit* (New York: Holt, 1958), supposedly sold 250,000 copies. It is nobby with such thoughts as "If communists can be inspired from error, falsehood, and hate, just think what we could do with truth, justice, and love! I thrill to think of the even greater wonders America could fashion from its rich, glorious, and deep tradition. All we need is faith, *real faith.*"

The book is also full of descriptions of Communist underground activities of stealth and "reckless abandon" (Hoover's phrase) that at best will remind ex-Post Toasties' Detectives of their own mail-order instructions in how to be tricky and at worst will convince readers that Red agents act, on instruction, as erratically as other residents in this hyped-up country act by nature. For example, Hoover disclosed that a "few of the tactics employed by communists to determine if they are being followed" include "driving alternately at high and low rates of speed" and "waiting until the last minute, then making a sharp left turn in front of oncoming traffic." With those actions as criteria, a drive through any city will certainly persuade the reader that this country is swarming with spies.

Some say that while the thoughts were the thoughts of Hoover, the hands that set them down were the hands of special agents Charles Moore and Fern Stukenbroker. This raises the interesting question: if Hoover farmed out the work, did he also farm out the profits? Or did he pocket them? In his May 11, 1971, column, Jack Anderson concluded that it must have been the latter. He wrote, "That tireless guardian of the nation's morals, J. Edgar Hoover, has collected more than $250,000 in royalties from three books researched and ghost-written for him by FBI agents on government time. This is an offense, if it had been committed by some other government official, that the FBI might have been asked to investigate. For the money rightfully should have gone to the taxpayers, who paid the salaries of the FBI researchers and writers." Hoover responded via a leak, through William Rusher, publisher of the *National Review,* who reported that he had learned from the FBI that Hoover kept some of his profits, but split up the rest between the FBI recreational fund and the FBI employees who actually did the writing.

Booty aside, the fate of *Masters of Deceit* was important only in that a payoff to Hoover for the movie rights to the book may have led to the most important propaganda effort now being conducted by the Bureau. Anderson suggests, with good logic, that it was Warner Brothers' $50,000 price for these rights (no movie was made from it) that put it in position to become the producer of the television series "The FBI." Although the book was published in 1958, Warner Brothers did not plunk down the $50,000 until 1964; the next year they got the nod.

Which brings us to Efrem Zimbalist, Jr. In the last four years, the job of selling the FBI has depended very heavily on him. When one considers that during that period an estimated 45 million Americans have watched each edition of the weekly television thriller in which he stars, one must acknowledge, with Professor Arthur Miller, that Zimbalist has "probably contributed as much to the image of the FBI as Mr. Hoover," at least in shaping the minds of those 45 million Americans.

Inasmuch as the program is prefabricated by the FBI, and inasmuch as Zimbalist is not only permitted to play the key role but promoted for continued stardom by the FBI, this television show makes a good case study of what goes into the preparation and application of FBI propaganda.

The Bureau does not make such moves frivolously. There is deliberation. In this case, there were eight years of deliberation. The Bureau and Warner Brothers started negotiating on details of the television series in 1957. It was much sought after by others as well. During these seven years the FBI also considered, and rejected, six hundred other requests from various radio and television producers to do shows based on real-life FBI situations.

There were at least two reasons why the FBI decided that 1965 was a good time to corner a part of the TV public. For one thing, the Bureau needed to convey the image of youthfulness and activity to offset the Director's turning seventy-one that year—going into the first year beyond what is normally the required retirement age for federal employees. A considerable amount of criticism was directed at the Johnson administration and especially at the FBI for this acquiescence to senior citizenship. Zimbalist was no chick himself—he does not disclose his age, nor do the public relations men who surround him. But at the time the series went into production he was believed to be pushing fifty. But since he keeps in shape with early morning tennis and plenty of California sun his well-conditioned middle age has fuzzed over Hoover's older image.

Secondly, the FBI had been taking a great deal of criticism for its handling of civil rights violations in the South. This reason for launching the FBI program was acknowledged by Cartha D. (Deke) DeLoach, then assistant director of the FBI. On announcing the Bureau's decision to do business with Warner Brothers, DeLoach explained, "We finally decided that the time is propitious to clarify for the public what the FBI does. We're simply an investigative agency. We don't evaluate or prosecute. We can't protect people—like civil rights workers, for instance. There's some confusion about what we do and I hope this program will show people how we really work."

While there has been some pretense on the part of the Bureau that it does not run "The FBI," it doesn't push this pretense very far because all of the evidence lies in the other direction. The FBI supplies the rough plots; these are farmed out to scriptwriters, and after they get through fashioning the material for television, the scripts are sent back to Washington for a final reading and approval by either the Director or one of his two assistant directors (the level at which the script reading is done gives some idea what value Hoover put on the show).

Testimony given before Senator Sam Ervin's Subcommittee on Constitutional Rights shows how the FBI guides the plots away from sensitive political areas. David W. Rintels, Chairman of the Committee on Censorship of the Writers Guild of America, told the subcommittee that when he was asked to write an episode for the series on a subject of his own choosing, he suggested using a plot about four black girls being killed when a racist bomber destroyed a church in Birmingham—in other words, he wanted to use a real-life tragedy.

This said Rintels, is what happened next: "The producer

checked with the sponsor, the Ford Motor Company, and with the FBI—every proposed show is cleared sequentially through the producing company, QM; the Federal Bureau of Investigation; the network, ABC; and the sponsor, Ford, and any of the four can veto any show for any reason, which it need not disclose—and reported back that they would be delighted to have me write about a church bombing subject only to these stipulations: *the church must be in the North, there could be no Negroes involved, and the bombing could have nothing at all to do with civil rights."*

Among the first lessons learned by scriptwriters for this show, says Rintels, is: no plots about anti-trust, wiretapping, or police brutality. And don't offend Italians by calling the Mafia by its real name; just call it the Organization.

From his own experience and from the experiences of a number of other writer alumni of this series, Rintels concluded that the Bureau has found that the best way to avoid controversy is to avoid reality. While the producers of the series used to claim that the programs were based on real cases, they eventually stopped pulling that line and began saying that the programs are only "inspired" by real FBI cases; but even in that claim, says Rintels, they are usually engaging in deceit— deceit helped along by such trappings as a narrator who opens the show by giving the date of the crime and ends the show by announcing the prison terms handed out. The air of authenticity is heightened by filling the screen with the great seal of the FBI; and then comes a statement of thanks to the FBI and to Mr. Hoover for their cooperation.

Obviously, the public is supposed to infer that it has just been made privy to something right out of the FBI files. Actually, says Rintels, when he was hired he was told to go sit in a corner and dream up some plots, and never mind the dossiers.

An FBI agent is permanently assigned to the set as a technical adviser. One television critic, Marvin Kitman, has suggested that the agent-adviser's most serious duties probably come down to the level of guarding "against some Communist-liberal extra covertly making an obscene gesture in a crowd scene." Actually, Kitman in jest is not far wide of what *is* guarded against. A press agent for the show told Ken Michaels of the Washington *Star,* "Zimbalist likes to wear his coat unbuttoned. The guy [FBI technical adviser] makes him button the coat. When everybody's hair started growing long, Zimbalist let his grow a little longer, too. The story is that J. Edgar Hoover saw a show, and next day the order came down that Zimbalist had to get a haircut. Before that, it was gum-chewing. Zimbalist loves to chew. Right away they caught that. Now before every scene, Zimbalist parks the gum."

Julius Duscha, who did one of the earliest studies of the show's production for the Washington *Post,* reported that the agent-adviser "is concerned with the language used by Zimmy [the nickname for Zimbalist] and other actors portraying FBI agents, the tone of their voices and the way they look. Zimbalist, for instance, has only four suits to choose from in the shows because most agents can only afford to have about four suits on their $200-a-week salaries."

Of special concern to the agent-adviser is the manner of arrest. No ungentlemanly language, if you please, no shouting or pushing. "The FBI should approach people in a business-like, friendly way and an agent should say, 'Pardon me, FBI,' or something like that."

Both Michaels and Duscha came away with the distinct understanding that the agent-adviser knows he is under the Director's scrutiny at all times and that he had better not make a clumsy decision. The FBI acknowledges what will surprise nobody, that it ran a security check on all the leading actors to make sure they had the kind of character and patriotism that would survive public cynicism.

Before "The FBI," Quinn Martin, the producer, was best

known to Hoover as the producer of "The Untouchables," a now defunct show about the war between government agents and the underworld in the 1920s and early 1930s. Apparently Hoover was untroubled by the fact that Martin's reputation had been somewhat smudged in 1962 during an investigation by the Senate Juvenile Delinquency Subcommittee into the excessive violence of some shows on TV. The subcommittee had singled out Martin's shows as some of the worst in this repect; it released an interoffice memo (dated January 19, 1960) from Martin to his subordinates in which he had complained about the lack of imagination in some of the mayhem on "The Untouchables." He wrote: "I wish we could come up with a different device than running the man down with a car, as we have done this now in three different shows. I like the idea of the sadism, but I hope we can come up with another approach for it."

Martin has paid for that candor. Just about every reporter who has written at length of his work on "The FBI" has referred to the 1960 memo. There probably isn't all that justification for doing it, inasmuch as "The FBI" reveals much more banality than sadism. The absence of violence is the result of Hoover's intervention. Martin says that when Senator John Pastore got to raising a stink about violence on television, Hoover called him and asked him to get rid of some of the violence. Martin didn't agree, but he obeyed. "It's not a real blood-and-guts show," he said, "but to be honest with you, we made an adjustment and I don't think it affected the show— our ratings went up, in fact."

Much more significant than the hiring of Martin, however, was the casting of Zimbalist. Indeed, Hoover was so enchanted with Zimbalist that there were times when he hinted that he would have liked life to follow art, rather than the other way around—that he measured his agents against the perfection of Zimbalist rather than holding Zimmy up to the standards of the Bureau. In testimony before a House Appropriations subcommittee, Hoover said, "I am not looking for the 'collar ad' type [to serve as FBI special agents], but I am looking for men who are clean-cut, mature, and who will measure up to the image which I think the American people feel an FBI man should be. In this regard, we cooperate with a weekly TV show . . . *Efrem Zimbalist, Jr., is the inspector in the show. In other words, there is an image that people have of the FBI. I want our special agents to live up to that image.*" (Emphasis added.)

Martin says that the idea for casting Zimbalist in the key role was his own, and that "I presented his name to Mr. Hoover along with three or four back-up names." Before getting the job, Zimbalist had to spend a week in Washington, being thoroughly scrutinized by the FBI hierarchy, including the Director. Zimbalist says Hoover and he "discussed about thirty subjects, covered four decades and three continents." Considering subsequent remarks made by Zimbalist, it is not difficult to see why they hit it off so well.

Addressing an FBI Academy graduation class, Zimbalist spoke the language of Hoover, regretting the growing tendency toward "liberty without obedience," denouncing "permissive court decisions and penal leniency." This is not an attitude he adopted with the beginning of the TV series; in 1964 he had spoken in favor of Barry Goldwater's candidacy, and had in fact done so with such violent phrases that the Goldwater staff induced him to shut up and stop "helping" them.

IV: A Propaganda Machine

Let us now make a final survey of propaganda devices adroitly used by Hoover.

Magazines Revisited. The burst of creativity that launched

Hoover into the newsstands of the 1930s continued unabated. By his death he had written well over a hundred articles for the major magazines—that is, magazines indexed by Reader's Guide—not to mention probably an equal number of articles in magazines of lesser repute and circulation.

Over the years, Hoover maintained extremely close ties with several magazines—*U.S. News & World Report* and *Reader's Digest* being perhaps the closest. Of these, none was so useful to Hoover as an outlet and none was considered such an intimate part of his personal life as the *Digest*. He loved it. He is known to have called one of the Washington editors of the *Digest* to ask why his home copy hadn't arrived.

Sometimes Hoover made his magazine friends privy to special information. During the period when Hoover was leaking information about the Martin Luther King hotel room tapes, a group of editors from a well-known pro-Hoover magazine visited him in Washington and he entertained them not only with a rendition of the hotel tapes but also with tapes of Mrs. King's reaction. (The FBI, which had sent her a copy of the tapes, was apparently able to record the reaction via a bug.)

But Hoover showed no snobbishness. He also wrote articles for, and permitted the Bureau to cooperate with, such lesser-known journals as *Listen* (American Temperance Society magazine), the *Disabled American Veterans'* magazine, *Junior Review, Ave Maria, Parade, The Elks* magazine, *Christianity Today, Catholic Action* and *Decision*, the magazine published by the Billy Graham Evangelistic Association.

Of course, writing for a small journal was not exactly a modest act on his part; he must have known that if he said anything at all worth repeating, no matter how hidden the original article, it would inevitably be picked up and reprinted in the national press.

Fodder for Others. Hoover got a great deal of reprint mileage out of statements he made in the monthly *FBI Law Enforce-*

ment Bulletin, especially in the summer months when columnists, ready to go on vacation, were looking around for "guests."
Victor Riesel's anti-labor column, for example, often used
Hooverana in this way. It is impossible to say how much encouragement the Bureau gives some organizations in their reprint mania. Probably they don't give any encouragement at all
in many instances; they don't have to. But in any event there
are some ad hoc patriotic groups (such as the Committee for
Constitutional Government, Inc.) that practically survive for
the purpose of circulating Bureau stuff.

The most controversial fodder supplied to the press by
Hoover was his crime statistics. In Washington it was taken as
a matter of natural law that Hoover monkeyed around with
these statistics. Scorned as they sometimes were, however,
Hoover's statistics made headlines—and, most comforting of all
to him, no doubt, they were almost impossible to disprove.

Usually Hoover used his crime statistics for money, to show
that the criminals were taking over the country and that the
only hope was in giving him a bigger budget to fight them; or
for ideological reasons, to show that the blacks and the hippies
were a bigger nuisance than Gus Hall and the Communist
Party U.S.A.

As of 1971, however, something historically memorable began to happen; Attorney General John Mitchell decided it was
time to put a different twist to the FBI's crime statistics, and
for the first time in four decades Hoover was deprived of sole
control of the numbers.

To use a crime boom for promoting the budget was all very
well, but sometimes there are more important things than
money; when an administration that came into office in 1968
promising a crackdown on crime approaches reelection time,
crime booms must be made to fade. And so it came to pass, as
Fred Graham of the New York *Times* wrote, "as a result of the
interpretations placed on the crime situation by Mr. Mitchell's

partment of State causes immediate cries of pain), nor is it anything new for the FBI to respond in this way. For a generation, Hoover made the bitterest sort of rebuttal to his critics, slandering their patriotism and their intelligence. His defense was not only organized but actually built into the Bureau and supported by tax money; as James Phelan reported:

> The FBI Crime Records division relentlessly keeps tabs on books and articles critical of Hoover and of the Bureau. Within hours of a news magazine's recent story that Hoover had failed to write a note of condolence to Robert Kennedy on the death of John F. Kennedy, the division had dug out, photocopied, and distributed copies of Hoover's note of condolence. The division can spot the source of an unfavorable story—and often produce a rebuttal—within a matter of minutes. "That's from the Cookbook," an agent will say, referring to Fred Cook's derogatory *The FBI Nobody Knows* and reaching for a telephone. "Let me get an agent in here who knows all the *facts* about the incident." The writer is shortly provided with an entirely contradictory version of the event.

As an example of Hoover's acid, James Phelan told of his response to New York *Herald Tribune* columnist John Crosby's criticism of Hoover for flinching from the fight against organized crime. In a letter to Crosby's editor, Hoover said the column was "degrading to the code of the journalistic profession" and suggested that Crosby probably "had an ulterior purpose in mind."

Hoover used letter writing with great effectiveness, often seizing upon some celebrated act of another's to ride into print piggyback. For instance, when A. B. Chandler, former governor of Kentucky, poked a hippie in the nose, Hoover at once dispatched a letter of congratulations to him—and inevitably the letter found its way into the newspapers.

Hoover was also capable of hanging on to a quarrel for so long that the sheer volume of his letters became newsworthy.

Almost two entire pages of the July 5, 1971, issue of *The National Observer* were taken up by an exchange of letters between Hoover and the *Observer*'s editors.

The Hoover propaganda machine was indeed impressive when one considers its every aspect—letters, speeches by, speeches about, articles by, articles about, radio shows, television shows, books by, books about—and when one considers its effects on the public and the government—not the least of which was a downright revulsion on the part of many people to any criticism of the Bureau, let alone exercise of the responsibility to control it.

V: Conference Discussion

MR. REBER BOULT:† It sounds like the problem is not the FBI selling itself at all, but a Hollywood that eats up these rather ridiculous plots, puts them out, and people believe them.

MR. SHERRILL: Yes, that's my point.

MR. ARTHUR SCHLESINGER:‡ The real problem isn't the propaganda effort on the part of the FBI, but the extent to which the Director succeeded in stopping criticism. I recall that as late as 1934 or so Ray Tucker could write a piece in *Collier's* called "Washington's Number One Snoop." It was a very funny, rather derisive piece. But somewhere in the next few years it became impossible to write pieces about J. Edgar Hoover as Washington's No. 1 snoop. By the Forties and Fifties, except for a few journalists like Jimmy Wechsler and Izzy Stone, the press had stopped saying anything critical at all. The great figures of American journalism have been as silent as everybody else.

Take the New York *Times*. I think you can search the New York *Times* for years and find nothing critical of J. Edgar

† Attorney with the Institute for Southern Studies, Atlanta, Georgia.
‡ Professor of History and holder of Albert Schweitzer Chair in the Humanities, City University of New York, Graduate Center.

Hoover. I think the reason for that wasn't the success of the mechanisms which Mr. Sherrill so well described, but something deeper, and I'd be interested in a comment on that.

MR. BURKE MARSHALL:* I think that we should always remember that a great deal of what is attributed to the Bureau shouldn't be attributed to the Bureau alone. It's part of the whole political climate in the country, participated in by Presidents, Attorneys General, the Congress of the United States and newspapers.

I wanted to ask another question. The [CBS-TV] program on "The Selling of the Pentagon" suggested an enormous and, I guess, improper expenditure of funds from the military budget for publicity. As I listened to Mr. Sherrill, I didn't hear any suggestion of that kind with respect to the Bureau, and I wanted to know whether he considered that point.

MR. SHERRILL: As far as I know, it doesn't exist. Warner Brothers and 20th Century and the others were more than happy to pay the cost of producing the movies. The most you could dock Hoover for, in most instances, would be supplying a special agent for the set as an adviser and giving up his own time or his assistant's in reading scripts. And although he has agents talk to Kiwanis clubs and schools and so forth, just as the Pentagon sends around colonels, I don't think the expenditures are even nearly the same, even in terms of their respective budgets.

MR. I. F. STONE:† I think a very important point hasn't been covered. It is very difficult for the executive to control a secret agency. We now have twelve known secret agencies. Is it good public policy to permit an agency to engage in expensive self-glorification? Doesn't it make it very hard for a President or an Attorney General to control the FBI when its Director is

---

* Deputy Dean of the Yale Law School, former Assistant Attorney General of the United States and one of the conference chairmen.
† Washington writer and contributing editor to *The New York Review of Books*.

allowed to become a public character, a kind of matinee idol? I think it's improper and unwise and should be stopped. I think the indoctrination and propagation of ideological views by FBI speakers is open to the same objections Senator Fulbright made to the indoctrination courses of the Army. The FBI's job is the investigation of crime, not indoctrination of the public. It's been engaging in brainwashing and self-glorification and this makes it difficult to control.

MR. SHERRILL: That's because you read the speeches one way and people who agree with them read them another way. I don't think, if you considered most of the speeches FBI speakers give to schools and clubs, you could fault the general thrust of them.

MR. STONE: Wouldn't you agree that every Attorney General for a good many years has had trouble controlling the FBI?

MR. SHERRILL: Well, I guess so.

MR. STONE: And isn't one reason the fact that Hoover has built himself up as a public hero?

MR. SHERRILL: Sure.

MR. STONE: He's a law unto himself and the Bureau does what it pleases.

MR. SHERRILL: But, are you suggesting that he not be allowed to write magazine pieces?

MR. STONE: Yes. I don't think it's his business to write for magazines. I don't know of any other free society where the head of the intelligence service is permitted to abandon anonymity for self-glorification. We're the only one I know.‡

MR. PINCUS: I'd like to raise the issue of the "selling" of the Martin Luther King tape material. That was a publicity cam-

‡ Mr. Sherrill later elaborated on his position: "There is logic in saying that the taxpayer should not be required to subsidize his own brainwashing. But the larger and more important question of freedom of speech and freedom of the press remains, and it hardly seems that libertarians will be winning a point if, by overreacting to Hoover the propagandist, they refuse to grant him the full freedoms that they accuse him of trying to deprive them of."

paign. Agents around the country did go out and did go to newspaper editors and did offer them an opportunity to see the substance of the tapes. They were specifically offered to a number of papers in Washington. I know for a fact that the substance of them was specifically offered to Gene Patterson, who at the time was running the Atlanta *Constitution,* and he refused to look at it.

But the point I'm trying to make is about the manner in which the press operates or fails to operate. The story wasn't the tapes or what was on the tapes, but the fact that the Bureau was offering them. The Bureau itself was peddling this material. This says something about what's going on within that agency. Had one newspaper written that story, Hoover would have stopped pretty quickly and it would have been a long time before he'd do it again. But nobody reported it. Newspaper editors are just as fearful as congressmen and, as a result, he keeps going and I'm sure his successor will do the same if he operates within the same mold. This, then, is an example of the press failing to meet its responsibilities.

MR. NAVASKY: I'd like to respond to Burke Marshall's comments on "The Selling of the Pentagon." The fact that the Bureau says it doesn't have a public relations operation, of course, doesn't mean that it doesn't. I'm told the Crime Records Office is the *de facto* equivalent of the Public Information Office in other agencies. Now, I think a lot of the things the Crime Records Office does are worth doing, but if you look at its budget, it might prove quite substantial. You might then have to weigh its job against other priorities.

This office publishes, for example, the Uniform Crime Statistics, which I think are useful. It also puts out the *Law Enforcement Bulletins,* which may or may not be useful. These contain a monthly editorial from Mr. Hoover. They're not made available to private citizens, like me, who've asked for them, although you can get to see them. They're not classified documents. The Crime Records Office also puts out press releases. It also conducts the most popular tour in Washington, D.C. There are millions of Americans who every year come down there to go through the FBI building. In addition, it runs a kind of reverse public relations campaign which no one has ever attempted to determine the cost of. For many years, it has monitored radio, television and magazines, and Mr. Hoover responds to statements about the FBI. Somebody takes the time to help him do that. I know Station WMCA in New York, in the early Sixties, had an editorial by Peter Straus in which he criticized the FBI for letting Robert Soblen escape the country. There was an agent on the telephone a half hour later to say that wasn't the FBI's responsibility.

All these things probably make a heavy dent in the Bureau's budget and help to sell it.

CHAPTER TWO

THE HISTORY OF THE FBI: DEMOCRACY'S DEVELOPMENT OF A SECRET POLICE

BY VERN COUNTRYMAN

I: Birth of the Bureau

When Charles Bonaparte, grandnephew of Emperor Napoleon I and Attorney General of the United States under President Theodore Roosevelt, sought funds in 1907 and 1908 for a permanent detective force in the Department of Justice, reaction was hostile and fierce in the House Appropriations subcommittee.

Subcommittee member Sherley was the most blunt:

> Now, it does not strike some if us as being in accord with the American ideas of government to undertake, by a system of spying on men and prying into what would ordinarily be designated as their private affairs, to determine whether or not a crime has been committed and to make the efficiency of a Department depend . . . upon the nosings of secret-service men. There seems to be a growing tendency to look to the employment of special agents whose chief attribute is their ability to spy.

Subcommitteeman Smith joined in this condemnation of the "spy system" and proclaimed his opposition to "a general system of espionage . . . conducted by the General Government." Chairman Tawney opposed any detective force "in any Department of Government" except the narrowly curtailed Secret

Service Division of the Treasury. Congressman Fitzgerald expressed fears about a "Federal secret police," and Representative Sherley reiterated his views:

> Now, I deny it is the business of the Secretary of the Navy, or the Secretary of War, or any other Secretary, to employ secret-service men to dig up the private scandals of men . . . I do not believe the country has reached a point where it needs that sort of supervision over men's conduct by Government and by secret-service methods.

A lesser man than Attorney General Bonaparte might have given up. But he persisted, and his eventual success was to be marked in June, 1972, by the sixty-fourth birthday of the Federal Bureau of Investigation.

Bonaparte had begun his quest because he felt it unseemly that Justice, lacking such a permanent detective force, was obliged from time to time to borrow Secret Service agents from the Treasury Department on a per diem plus expenses basis. (Although the 1870 statute creating the Department of Justice gave him ample authority to create his own force, he had to go to the subcommittee for funding; he had earlier presented the case for his force in his 1907 annual report to Congress.) But the Secret Service Division itself was not regarded with great favor by all members of Congress. Much earlier one of its agents, on hire to the Navy, had been involved in an investigation of the amorous adventures of a Navy officer on leave. Even worse, the Secret Service had aired unsubstantiated charges that a congressman had tampered with an appropriation bill.

Consequently, the division had for some time been limited to detection of counterfeiting and violations of the federal pay and bounty laws. Protection of the person of the President was added in 1907. Some subcommittee members could thus argue that the Justice Department's use of Secret Service agents to do what they could not do for the Secret Service violated the spirit if not the letter of the limitations. Appropriations Committee Chairman Tawney finally proposed forbidding other departments to use funds appropriated for fiscal 1909 to pay Secret Service agents, and the Sixtieth Congress approved his measure in May, 1908.

Thus, Bonaparte found himself worse off than when he began, but undaunted. Within one month after Congress adjourned and before the beginning of fiscal 1909 he hired nine Secret Service agents on a permanent basis, using a "miscellaneous expense" fund appropriated that year. He reported to Congress that this was both "necessary" and "involuntary," since he could no longer hire the agents on a temporary basis, and such a force was "absolutely indispensable to the proper discharge of the duties of this department."

But there was no cause for alarm. The special agents were required to make daily reports, and summaries of these were submitted daily to him so that "the Attorney-General knows of, or ought to know, at all times what they are doing and at what cost. Under these circumstances he may be justly held responsible for the efficiency and economy of the service rendered." He also reported a further need for a special accounting force "if the Congress shall not see fit to indicate its disapproval . . ." Finally, he suggested to the House subcommittee that "it might tend to clearness" in its work if the appropriation for miscellaneous expenses were merged with "the appropriation for prevention and detection of crime . . . and a new title given to it."

Before the House subcommittee met to consider Bonaparte's actions and proposals, President Roosevelt delivered a message to Congress which may have been calculated to influence that consideration:

> It is not too much to say that [the restriction on use of Secret Service agents] has been of benefit only to the criminal classes

. . . The chief argument in favor of the provision was that the Congressmen did not themselves wish to be investigated by Secret Service men. Very little of such investigation has been done in the past; but it is true that the work of the Secret Service agents was partly responsible for the indictment and conviction of a Senator and a Congressman for land frauds in Oregon. I do not believe that it is in the public interest to protect criminals in any branch of the public service, and exactly as we have again and again . . . prosecuted and convicted such criminals who were in the executive branch . . . , so in my belief we should be given ample means to prosecute them if found in the legislative branch. But if this is not considered desirable a special exception could be made in the law prohibiting the use of the Secret Service force in investigating members of the Congress . . .

When Bonaparte next appeared before the appropriations subcommittee he found its members irritated, but not prepared to challenge his action. The congressmen were still concerned about a "spy system" or a "system of espionage" that keeps department heads "thoroughly informed of the actions and habits and whereabouts of every employee." When they pressed Bonaparte for safeguards against abuse he returned to his system of departmental accountability based on his daily reading of the summaries of his special agents' activities ("of course it is a good deal of a bore to read these things all over"). Any restriction in advance on the use to which his detectives (now twenty permanent and eighteen temporary) might be put would "tend to the advantage of lawbreakers." The Congress must be content with "a centralized and accurately ascertained authority and responsibility" and "such a system of record as will enable the legislative branches of the Government, the head executive, and possibly the courts, to fix the responsibility for anything that goes wrong."

But he did concede that there should not be a "secret political service" or a detective force "for the ascertainment of mere matters of scandal and gossip that could affect only a man's purely private life." And he stated that he had no objection to having the work of his detectives confined to "frauds and crimes and the like against the Government." Accordingly, the committee limited the use of his funds to "detection and prosecution of crimes against the United States" and the Congress enacted the limitation without the special exception for the benefit of congressmen mentioned by the President.

Even this modest limitation had a short life. In the very next year (1910) Congress added authorization for funds to be used "for such other investigations regarding official matters under the control of the Department of Justice as may be directed by the Attorney General."

Thus was born what Bonaparte's successor, Attorney General Wickersham, designated the Bureau of Investigation. Congress, in a 1935 appropriation act, redesignated it the Federal Bureau of Investigation.

II: Combating Crime

At first, the Bureau's work was largely confined to antitrust, revenue and postal law violations, and to land frauds. But it was soon plunged into investigations of "matters of scandal." In 1910 Congress had enacted the Mann Act, making it a crime to transport a woman in interstate or foreign commerce or within any federal territory "for the purpose of prostitution, or for any other immoral purpose."

This legislation had been presented as designed "solely to prevent panderers and procurers from compelling thousands of women and girls against their will and desire to enter and continue in a life of prostitution" and not to regulate "immorality in general." It was officially entitled the White-Slave Traffic Act. But the Justice Department promptly took the position that it also applied to private conduct where no commercial element was involved, enabling it to convict, among others, heavyweight champion Jack Johnson. The Supreme Court in 1917 sustained the department's interpretation.

After that, the FBI policed unsanctified sexual activities with gusto. In 1932 it reported 431 convictions under the Mann Act, more than any other federal crime save interstate theft of motor vehicles. Seven years later it reported that since 1922 it had investigated over 54,780 Mann Act cases and had raised its yearly conviction total to 524.

This work was not without its embarrassments. A garbled wiretap of the telephone of a Maryland state legislator led to a spectacular raid of ten brothels in Baltimore in 1937 on the erroneous assumption that their residents were destined for an interstate trip to Washington to entertain federal legislators. Their true destination was the Maryland state capital. Another raid in 1940 in Miami during the height of the tourist season was not well received. In 1941 the FBI reported its enforcement of the Mann Act as one aimed at "commercialized vice." Subsequent reports suggest that a heavy proportion of the prior convictions must have represented non-commercial dalliance, or that commercial vice has been on the decline, or that the FBI has been losing interest in the subject. Mann Act convictions declined to 202 in 1951, 169 in 1961 and have been less than 100 in every year since 1965.

The federal commerce power was employed again in the Dyer Act of 1919 to send the FBI after interstate transportation of stolen motor vehicles. This act promptly provided a heavy grist of cases, and in 1970 the FBI reported that it had "recovered" 30,599 stolen autos. (Many of these were doubtless delivered to it by state and local police.) Its reported 3,694 Dyer Act convictions that year led the list of federal convictions and constituted 28 per cent of the total. Presumably the pursuit of hot cars did not consume 28 per cent of the Bureau's appropriation of almost $232 million for that year.

Between 1932 and 1934 the Congress enacted a series of

criminal statutes forbidding the transportation of kidnapped persons in interstate commerce, extortion by means of threats sent through the mails or interstate commerce, theft from interstate shipments, traveling in interstate commerce to avoid state prosecution, robbery of national banks, transportation of stolen property in interstate commerce, transportation of unregistered firearms in interstate commerce and extortion "in any way or in any respect affecting" interstate commerce. Bank robberies, interstate transportation of stolen property and thefts from interstate shipments accounted for more than 25 per cent of all federal convictions reported by the FBI in 1970.

In 1934, also, the Congress authorized FBI agents to carry firearms. Then followed the Bonnie and Clyde era—the 1934-35 period of shoot-outs between FBI agents and gangs of bank robbers with well-known names—John Dillinger, "Baby Face" Nelson and "Ma" Barker. Out of that brief flurry of gunfire was born the FBI's "gangbuster" image.

Shortly after the Supreme Court decided *Brown* v. *Board of Education* in 1954 the FBI reported 1,275 "preliminary investigations" under then extant civil rights acts, resulting in only four convictions. Even the report's treatment of the subject was gingerly:

> In its investigations of civil rights complaints against law enforcement officers or personnel of other public agencies, the FBI meticulously avoids interfering with the orderly operation of the agency concerned. At the outset, the FBI contacts the head of the agency—and the governor if a state agency is involved—and apprises him of the allegations against the employee and the FBI's responsibility to investigate. These investigations, like all others handled by the FBI, are conducted in a thorough, factual and impartial manner.

Passage of more recent civil rights laws resulted in increased criminal reactions to civil rights activities. And, beginning in 1961, the number of reported preliminary investigations "handled" by the FBI increased—from 1,813 in 1961 to 3,340 in 1964, to more than 5,000 in every year since 1966. But the annual convictions recorded since 1961 ranged from 0 to 9 until a new high of 18 was reported for 1970.

III: Combating Subversion

Even the FBI's official historian admits that the Bureau under its first chief, Stanley W. Finch (1908–12), and its second, A. Bruce Bielaski (1912–19), "was far from being prepared for the test" of World War I. In 1916 Bielaski reported the number of Mann Act investigations had increased slightly over the previous year "despite the fact that the energies of the agents of this service were to a very unusual degree devoted to investigations of matters affecting the neutrality of the United States in the European war." In 1917 Attorney General Gregory explained that the drop in Mann Act indictments from 494 to 327 was "due in large part to the fact that . . . many investigations arising out of the war have required such immediate attention as to seriously interfere with the normal work of the department."

By this time the Bureau had four hundred agents. Bielaski considered this number inadequate, and began recruiting volunteer private assistants (who labeled themselves the American Protective League) to aid the Bureau in detecting spies and saboteurs. Violence, including murder, was used against those suspected of treasonable thoughts. Whether the perpetrators were Bureau agents, APL members working with them or unrecruited patriots was never established. But it is a matter of record that the Bureau directed a force of 35 of its own agents, 2,000 APL members, 2,350 soldiers and sailors and several hundred local policemen in massive draft raids in New York and Newark over a three-day period in September, 1918. Tens of thousands of men who could not establish their right to be abroad in civilian dress were arrested. Newspapers reported that only 1 out of every 200 arrested was found to be a draft evader. Bielaski's final report asserted that 1,505 men had been inducted into service as a consequence of the raids.

Earlier vigilante acts had prompted protests. The draft raids provoked an uproar. President Wilson asked for a full report. Attorney General Gregory's report got quickly to the heart of the matter. Bonaparte's principle of departmental account-ability had broken down. The Bureau's agents had acted "contrary to my express instructions." And apparently he had not read daily summaries of their activities so as to detect the infractions. Bielaski soon resigned, and a new Attorney General, A. Mitchell Palmer, appointed William J. Flynn, former chief of the Secret Service, to replace him.

Shortly thereafter, in May and June, 1919, the country suffered a bomb scare. Authorities discovered and defused two dozen bombs deposited in a New York post office for mailing to their intended victims, but with insufficient postage. A mailed bomb reached the home of ex-Senator Hardwick of Georgia: his wife and maid were injured. Bombings occurred in eight other cities. A watchman was killed by one in New York. Another in front of Attorney General Palmer's residence in Washington killed two men, apparently the bombers.

The bombings were widely assumed to be the work of "radicals" and in August, 1919, a new General Intelligence Division was set up to "deal with radicalism." Bureau Director Flynn complained that the paucity of federal legislation applicable to "persons of American citizenship engaged in radical agitation" would make it necessary for the GID to focus efforts on "alien agitators." The head of the new division was J. Edgar Hoover, who had entered the department's alien registration section two years earlier, fresh out of George Washington University Law School.

The bombers were never apprehended. But on November 7,

1919, the Bureau, working with the Immigration Service, staged simultaneous raids in eleven cities on meetings of the Federation of the Union of Russian Workers. The number arrested has never been established. But 249 of them were swiftly found by the Immigration Service to be subject to a 1918 statute providing for deportation of aliens who were "anarchists" or "members of or affiliated with any organization that entertains a belief in, teaches, or advocates the overthrow by force and violence of the government of the United States." They were all deported to Russia on a single army transport (dubbed the "Soviet Ark") which sailed on December 21, 1919. The cases against two of the deportees, Emma Goldman and Alexander Berkman, were presented "by young J. Edgar Hoover" and he and Bureau Director Flynn were at dockside when the "Soviet Ark" sailed.

Prior to the November raid the Senate had adopted a resolution requesting the Attorney General to report whether the Department of Justice had taken legal proceedings, "and if not, why not," to arrest and punish persons attempting to overthrow the government and preaching "anarchy" and "defiance of law and authority," and also whether it had taken legal proceedings, "and if not, why not," for the arrest and deportation of aliens who "have committed the acts aforesaid." One week after the raid, Attorney General Palmer responded that he lacked federal legislation applicable to "the present radical activities" of citizens. As for aliens, administration of the deportation laws was "entirely within the jurisdiction of the Department of Labor" with whom he had "cooperated . . . to the fullest extent" in the raids a week before. And, he reported, since the organization of the radical division, "a more or less complete history of over 60,000 radically inclined individuals has been gathered together and classified, and a foundation for action laid either under the deportation statutes or legislation to be enacted by the Congress."

On January 2, 1920, the combined forces of the Bureau and the Immigration Service struck again—at members of the Communist party and the Communist Labor party. Simultaneous nighttime raids occurred in thirty-three cities across the country. Elaborate advance plans had been laid, with thousands of arrest warrants issued by the Immigration Service. Bureau agents received written instructions to telephone "to Mr. Hoover any matters of vital importance or interest" arising out of the arrests and to forward lists of those arrested to the Bureau marked "Attention of Mr. Hoover." In all, in the raids, 3,000 arrests were officially reported. Some 760 of those arrested were finally ordered deported after hearings in the Immigration Service.

But the second "Red Raid" was not as well received as the first. A group arrested in Boston filed petitions for habeas corpus, and a federal district court, in the celebrated case of *Colyer* v. *Skeffington,* ordered them released. In four of the cases, the court held that insufficient evidence had been presented to show that the Communist party to which defendants belonged advocated forcible overthrow of the government (a point on which the court was later reversed on appeal). The court also held (in a ruling the government did not appeal) that the others had been denied due process of law in the deportation hearings. After a detailed description of the Immigration Service's abdication and the Bureau's usurpation of authority to administer the deportation laws, of the lawless searches that had been made without search warrants and of the miserable conditions under which arrestees were held incommunicado, the court also passed judgment on the entire operation:

I refrain from any extended comment on the lawlessness of these proceedings by our supposedly law-enforcing officials

. . . It may, however, fitly be observed that a mob is a mob,
whether made up of government officials acting under instructions from the Department of Justice, or of criminals, loafers,
and the vicious classes.

In March, 1920, Assistant Secretary of Labor Louis F. Post
took over the decisions on deportation in the department. While
he considered himself bound by an earlier ruling of the Secretary that a member of the Communist party was deportable
under the 1918 statute, he required strict proof that the alien
was a member of the party. Moreover, he concluded, and the
Secretary concurred in his conclusion, that members of the
Communist Labor party did not come within the statute. (The
January raids had been conducted on the theory that they
did.) And he took the position that merely labeling oneself an
"anarchist" did not mean guilt within the meaning of the statute, which he read to require opposition to all forms of government.

In May, 1920, the National Popular Government League
published a *Report Upon the Illegal Practices of the United
States Department of Justice,* signed by twelve lawyers, including Zechariah Chafee, Roscoe Pound, Ernest Freund and
Felix Frankfurter. Focusing on the "Red Raids," but not exclusively, they charged the department with violating the constitutional rights of citizens and aliens alike by making searches
and arrests without warrants, by coercing evidence in violation
of the privilege against self-incrimination and by imposing
cruel and unusual punishments. They also charged the department with the use of *agents provocateurs* and with attempting
to influence the press in its favor. Later, a similarly critical report was published by the Federal Council of the Churches of
Christ in America.

But in the House of Representatives, Louis Post was called
before a committee for a hearing on a resolution that he be

impeached. Post impressively defended his actions and the impeachment effort collapsed.

In the course of the hearing, Post and his attorney charged Department of Justice agents with recruiting aliens into the Communist party so that they could be deported, with making illegal arrests and searches without warrants, with forging an alien's signature to a confession, with demanding excessive bail in deportation cases, with dictating deportation decisions and with usurping the authority of the Labor Department in deportation matters.

The committee invited Attorney General Palmer to respond to the charges and he did so. Again it appeared that Bonaparte's principle of departmental accountability had broken down. It was "obvious," Palmer said, "that I cannot have personal knowledge of all the facts with reference to the conduct of the large body of agents and other subordinates of the department . . . I accept responsibility for such conduct of my subordinates as is in line with the general instructions issued under my direction; as to conduct of the officers of the department evidently outside those instructions, I have caused a complete investigation to be made and it is upon the basis of such investigation that I declare these charges are outrageous and unconscionable falsehood."

It was the "friends of the anarchists" who criticized the Department of Justice. And it was "not surprising that Mr. Post, when the opportunity has presented itself in an official way to render a service to those who advocate force and violence, should employ it to the limit. He has always been sympathetic to that sort of thing. In 1907 and 1908 he and his wife were the editors of a so-called 'liberal' magazine, *The Public* . . ."

Palmer went on to assure the committee that he had now found the time to take "personal pains to inquire and satisfy

myself as to the character [and] ability . . . of every one of
the so-called under-cover agents of the Department of Justice." And he found them "men of splendid character, of unusual intellectual attainments and of physical courage," in
short, "a splendid brigade for the enforcement of the law in the
United States." Finally, Palmer concluded that although he
had received "vilification, abuse, and ridicule" from the "ultra-
radicals," he proposed to continue to do his duty "to the end,
without fear or favor, and without pain or prejudice." On that
note the hearings ended. There were no other witnesses and
there was no further action.

But a subcommittee of the Senate Judiciary Committee held
hearings in early 1921 on the charges made by the twelve
lawyers against the Justice Department. The accusing lawyers
and others presented their evidence. Palmer and Hoover appeared, but Palmer did most of the talking. Hoover did make
one contribution which indicated a further erosion in the concept of departmental responsibility. Palmer was asked about
written instructions given Bureau agents in the alien raids.
(These said that "meeting places and residences of the members should be thoroughly searched," and left it entirely to
the agents' discretion "as to the method by which you should
gain access to such places." They directed the obtaining of
search warrants if "due to the local conditions in your territory, you find that it is absolutely necessary.")

Palmer referred the questions to Hoover. In sparse answers,
volunteering nothing, the young Hoover testified that he had
no knowledge of the number of search warrants issued because
local agents handled that, and that he did not know how many
searches were made without warrants, and, indeed, that he
did not know if any had been.

Hoover was similarly unhelpful on the matter of arrests
without warrant:

Hoover: Most of the [arrest] warrants issued by the Department of Labor, at the instance of the Department of Justice, were issued upon sworn affidavits.

Sen. Walsh: Beforehand?

Hoover: Beforehand.

Sen. Walsh: That is, all the warrants that were issued were issued upon these affidavits.

Hoover: I would not say all . . .

The person whose "investigation" had enabled Palmer a year earlier to label Post's charges of illegal arrests and searches without warrant "outrageous and unconscionable falsehood" did not appear. And so it went. Palmer now admitted he had "never interviewed a single agent who had anything to do with these arrests." He admitted that "undoubtedly persons were arrested who were not named in the warrants," and that it "was bound to happen . . . that citizens would be taken." And he admitted that persons arrested without warrants "were held awaiting the result of a telegraphic request for a warrant, and if the warrant did not come they were released."

He reiterated his pleas that "the supervisory officers in the Department of Justice cannot know all that is being done by their agents," and that "Mr. Hoover, who was in charge of this in the bureau of investigation, is more familiar with the history of it than I am." But, save as indicated above, Hoover was not interrogated about the conduct of the raids.

When the hearing was concluded, Senator Walsh wrote a report which would have condemned the "essential lawlessness" of the raids. It would have said that "those who conceived the procedure here criticized were oblivious of the letter and wholly unappreciative of the spirit of the Bill of Rights."

This did not meet with the approval of the subcommittee

Chairman, Senator Sterling of South Dakota, who prepared another report. It would have completely exonerated the Justice Department and would have pointed out that Felix Frankfurter, Ernest Freund and one other of the twelve lawyers making the charges were members of the American Civil Liberties Union, "a supporter of all subversive movements." It also would have said that "although it does not appear that [Zechariah Chafee] is member of the Civil Liberties Union, Mr. Chafee has written a book in which he declares that there should be no law against sedition and anarchy."

Only Senators Ashurst, Borah and Norris favored the Walsh report and the full committee would not accept either report. Almost two years later, Senator Walsh had both reports printed in the Congressional Record, and there the matter ended. There ended also the FBI's closest brush with a congressional investigation.

Meanwhile Warren G. Harding had come to the White House and Harry M. Daugherty had become Attorney General. Daugherty, in August, 1921, replaced Bureau Director Flynn with his boyhood friend William J. Burns, president of the detective agency which bore his name. Hoover became assistant director of the Bureau.

By this time the General Intelligence Division boasted "index cards numbering approximately 450,000 covering both activities and subjects." Like his predecessors, Burns reported that action against ultra-radicalism was limited by law to aliens. But many of the states had sedition laws and the Bureau "frequently not only cooperates with the state . . . officials but in many instances has furnished information upon which individuals have been successfully prosecuted." According to affidavits submitted by two former Bureau agents, one such instance was the case of Sacco and Vanzetti.

As one step in the effort to clean up the corrupt mess he inherited on the death of Harding, President Coolidge early

in 1924 replaced Attorney General Daugherty with Harlan
F. Stone. Stone promptly accepted the resignation of Bureau
Director Burns and made Hoover, then twenty-nine years old,
first acting director and then in December, 1924, Director of
the Bureau.

During the first fifteen of his almost forty-eight years in
office as Director, Hoover was preoccupied primarily with
improving the efficiency of the Bureau and enforcing the
various federal laws on interstate crime. But in June, 1939,
President Roosevelt by executive order put the FBI in charge
of "the investigation of all espionage and cognate matters,"
and by another order in September, 1939, requested all other
enforcement officers to turn over to the FBI "any information
obtained by them relating to espionage, counterespionage,
sabotage, subversive activities and violations of the neutrality
laws."

One great sabotage case occurred during World War II.
In June, 1942, four agents of Nazi Germany bent on sabotage
were landed by submarine on a beach on Long Island and
four more were landed in Florida. Within ten days all eight
were apprehended, and each promptly confessed his plans.
They were tried by a special military commission and, after
the Supreme Court had approved this procedure, they were
convicted. Six were electrocuted, one received a life sentence
and one a sentence of thirty years. The FBI claimed credit
for the captures.

Actually, the landing on Long Island was observed by a
patrolling Coast Guardsman, and the Coast Guard discovered
explosives buried on the beach and other evidence which
enabled the New York City police to identify one of the would-
be saboteurs before the case was turned over to the FBI.
William Turner has related another aspect of the case: One
of the saboteurs, George John Dasch, was anti-Nazi and
tipped off the FBI. Rather than permit him to become a hero,

the FBI brought about his conviction and in 1948 spirited him out of the country to Germany without the knowledge of his wife or attorney. When *Newsweek* tried to tell the true story, Hoover managed to have it rewritten to conform to the FBI version.

Until the end of World War II, Hoover reported that the FBI was rendering full protection against espionage, sabotage and related activities. The relatively small number of espionage convictions was easily explained:

> Effectiveness of intelligence work cannot be judged entirely by the number of arrests or convictions as in the case of kidnapings, bank robberies and other types of crimes. The FBI since the inception of the emergency in 1939, has followed the policy of ascertaining the identities of enemies within the country, their sources of information and methods of communication. Thus it has been possible in many instances to gain control of sources of information and communications completely, immobilizing groups of foreign agents.

The wartime Fuchs-Gold-Rosenberg spy ring involving theft of atomic secrets was not uncovered until 1949. The disclosures came first from British authorities but, according to Hoover, they were acting on "information furnished by the FBI." In the same year, the FBI nabbed another spy very close to home. Judith Coplon, an employee of the alien registration section of the Department of Justice, was seized in New York in the company of an employee of the Russian delegation to the United Nations and with summaries of FBI reports in her handbag. She was convicted in Washington for stealing the information and in New York for attempting to pass it on to her Russian confederate. Both convictions were reversed on appeal—in Washington because the FBI had illegally tapped her telephone and listened in on conversations with her lawyer before and during the trial and in New

York because FBI agents had illegally arrested her without a warrant.

The FBI has continued to claim "primary responsibility" for protecting "internal security" under President Roosevelt's order of September, 1939. Congress and the President have provided the Bureau with a variety of avenues through which to exercise that responsibility.

The Smith Act of 1940 makes it a crime to advocate forcible overthrow of the government, to organize a group so to advocate, or to be a member of such a group with knowledge of its purpose. The wartime conviction under this act of eighteen members of the Socialist Workers party for conspiracy to advocate forcible overthrow received little attention from a nation otherwise preoccupied. But in 1949 eleven national leaders of the Communist party were convicted pursuant to a postwar program "of further prosecution of Communist party leaders under the Smith Act on the basis of investigative reports prepared by the FBI." Their convictions, for conspiracy to advocate and to organize a party to advocate forcible overthrow, were upheld by the Supreme Court.

Thereafter Hoover reported that, while the "open activities" of the party had been "considerably circumscribed" as a result of the convictions, the party nonetheless "posed one of the major threats to the internal security of the country" and that prosecutions of lesser party functionaries were proceeding apace. After 1954 a few of these prosecutions were based on the membership clause of the Smith Act. By mid-1957 there had been a total of 108 convictions of party members.

But in that year the Supreme Court began to find obstacles. Reviewing the convictions of "second-string" party leaders, it held that the statute of limitations had run on prosecutions for conspiracy to organize the party. It also held that their convictions for conspiracy to advocate forcible overthrow must be reversed because the jury had not been instructed that it must find a conspiracy calculated to incite action rather than to advocate abstract doctrine. It found the evidence so inadequate against some defendants that it directed their acquittal and remanded other cases for new trial.

Two years later Hoover reported that of 109 Smith Act convictions of Communist party members, 70 had been reversed. Of these, 26 defendants were ordered acquitted. Of the remaining 44 reversals remanded for new trial, "the government subsequently instituted action to dismiss the indictments against a number of these persons."

In 1960 Hoover summed up the net effect of a twelve-year program under the Smith Act: 27 convicted defendants had completed serving their sentences, 2 were still in prison, 10 were convicted but out on bail pending sentencing or appeal, and 13 indictments were outstanding. No further Smith Act convictions have been reported.

But by this time executive orders had the FBI heavily engaged in other efforts affecting many more people. As established by President Truman's order of 1947 and continued by President Eisenhower's order of 1953, the loyalty program for federal executive employees required an FBI check for all incumbent employees and for all applicants for employment, and required a "full field investigation" whenever "derogatory information" was disclosed. The Attorney General was also directed to compile a list of subversive organizations so that evidence of employees' or applicants' "membership in, affiliation with or sympathetic association with" such organizations could be taken as evidence of disloyalty.

This program has been expended to cover the private employees of those who contract with various agencies and departments of the federal government. A careful estimate in 1958 put the number of people subject to some sort of loyalty program, federal, state or local, at more than 13 million, or one fifth of the national labor force. Probably more than 16 million are subject today.

Although much of preliminary investigation under the program was transferred to the Civil Service Commission in 1952, the FBI remains heavily involved in spying on and prying into "private affairs" and "mere matters of scandal and gossip," and in "keeping the heads of the departments thoroughly informed of the actions and habits and whereabouts of every employee," the very activities members of Congress had feared at the outset.

The Internal Security Act of 1950 added further to the Bureau's authority to pursue subversion. Title I of that act created the Subversive Activities Control Board and authorized it, in cases presented by the Attorney General, to label groups as "Communist-action" or "Communist-front" groups (a third category, "Communist-infiltrated" groups, was added by 1954 amendment). Organizations so designated were required to register with the board, to give the names and addresses of their officers (and, in the case of Communist-action organizations, of their members), an accounting of their receipts and expenses and (by 1954 amendment) an inventory of their printing presses and duplicating equipment.

The Attorney General began with proceedings to have the Communist party labeled a Communist-action group. "It was necessary for the FBI to obtain and make available witnesses who could present evidence necessary to establish the government's case. A total of 22 government witnesses, some of whom were confidential informants of the FBI, were presented." The board eventually made the desired finding but the Supreme Court reversed its determination on the ground that three of the witnesses obtained by the FBI were perjurers. When the board expunged the testimony of these three witnesses from the record and then reiterated its findings, the Supreme Court affirmed the board's action. But the court later held that the registration provisions of the act ran afoul of the Fifth Amendment's privilege against self-incrimination. Congress in 1968 tried to patch up the old statute, but constitutional infirmities remained, and the five board positions, at $36,000 per year, have long constituted some of the most remarkable sinecures in Washington.

In July, 1971, President Nixon transferred to the board the not very onerous task of keeping up to date the list of subversive organizations compiled by the Attorney General for use under the federal loyalty program.

Title II of the Internal Security Act of 1950 provided that the President could declare an "Internal Security Emergency" in the event of an invasion of the United States or its possessions, a declaration of war by Congress or "insurrection within the United States in aid of a foreign enemy." Upon such declaration, the Attorney General was authorized to apprehend and incarcerate "each person as to whom there was reasonable ground to believe that such person probably will engage in, or probably will conspire with others to engage in, acts of espionage or sabotage."

These provisions have never been invoked although the government for a time maintained detention facilities on a stand-by basis. In September, 1971, Title II was repealed. But in the past twenty-one years any prudent Attorney General must have maintained a list of those he considered ripe for detention. And that list was doubtless based largely upon "facts" supplied by the FBI.

Thus, the Bureau found itself in late 1971 with only shreds of ostensible authority for its war on subversion. Only the federal loyalty program remained as its warrant for inquiring into our beliefs, utterances and associations.

IV: Records

In the course of its long history the FBI has compiled millions of records and dossiers on individuals and organizations. Before the Bureau was created, the Department of Justice maintained fingerprint records of all those passing through federal prisons. In 1923 they were moved from the U.S. penitentiary in Leavenworth, Kansas, to Washington and combined, in the Bureau, with a collection of prints contributed by the International Association of Chiefs of Police. In 1930 Hoover reported that the prints of all persons arrested by U.S. marshals were being added to the collection; by the following year he reported that "[p]ractically all Federal agencies receiving such information now forward the same to the Bureau." This included the Civil Service Commission, and when the Selective Service System became a contributor in 1939 the Federal input into the collection was virtually complete. Contributions are also made by state and local police and licensing officials and by those touring FBI headquarters who are persuaded to leave their prints. Since 1932 there has also been an international exchange with foreign police officials which now extends to "82 friendly non-communist countries."

By March 1, 1971, the FBI had a collection of more than 200 million prints which, because of duplications, were estimated to cover more than 86 million persons. Less than one third of these prints were in the "criminal file."

In addition to its Identification Division, the FBI in 1967 established a National Crime Information Center, a computerized collection of other information in its files relating to crime. Hoover recently categorized the information in his computer as relating to stolen securities (32 per cent), stolen cars (25 per cent), other stolen articles (18 per cent), stolen license plates (7 per cent), wanted persons (3 per cent) and boats (3 per cent). At the same time he reported that the computer was tied to 104 control terminals serving the fifty states and Canada, and to some 60 FBI field offices. In addition, forty state and metropolitan computer systems are tied into the FBI computer, thus enabling "an estimated 4,000 local law enforcement agencies to enter their own records into the [FBI computer] and make inquiries directly from terminals located on their premises." The FBI is trying to develop a method for computerizing its fingerprint collection, and is now working with state and local authorities to develop a "Computerized Criminal History System."

In 1930 the FBI took over from the International Association of Chiefs of Police the work of collecting and compiling uniform crime statistics for the nation. Seven years later a Brookings Institution study found the statistics so deficient that "we are unable to tell whether crime is increasing or decreasing, except in a few categories, and there only roughly." That study also recommended that, "since crime statistics should be used to locate areas of efficiency and inefficiency and to evaluate agencies," the "functions of collection, compilation, and dissemination should not be assigned to one of the several crime-control units." The FBI continues to perform the function and the statistics remain deficient.

Apart from its compilations on crime, there remain as "the heart of FBI operations" all the other files containing "the data which this Bureau gathers as a result of its investigative and auxiliary responsibilities" and which, "among other things, enables the FBI to carry out its assignment of coordinating and disseminating security and intelligence data to authorized federal sources. A total of 2,567,373 name checks were processed during the fiscal year 1970." In 1970 these files totaled over 5,958,000 and were supplemented by 55,739,000 index cards.

A long-standing Justice Department directive provides that, "except upon a specific authorization of the Attorney General, no officer or employee shall forward to any person outside the Department of Justice . . . any information obtained from the Federal Bureau of Investigation . . ." But there are manifold exceptions, as subsequent chapters reveal. The use the FBI makes of its records and dossiers is really unknown—unknown to the Attorney General, to the President, to the Congress and to the American public.

V: *The Bureau*

Under Hoover the FBI, which had 20 full-time "special agents" in 1908, had 7,837 in 1971 operating fifty-nine major Bureau offices and five hundred resident agency offices. It had 10,639 other employees, who are referred to in the FBI's annual reports as "clerical, stenographic, and technical personnel" and in Hoover's annual presentation to the House Appropriations subcommittee simply as "clerks."

Hoover's predecessor, William J. Burns, initiated a training school for special agents. Eight years later Hoover reported that the school had been "perfected." It has since grown into the FBI National Academy, "often termed the 'West Point of Law Enforcement,'" which offers not only a fourteen-week training course and refresher courses for FBI agents but also a twelve-week training course for two hundred state and local police officers each year. The number of state and local officers to be trained annually will increase to two thousand, with shorter, special courses for another thousand each year, upon completion of new $24 million Academy facilities in Quantico, Virginia.

The FBI also meticulously counts and annually reports to Congress the total number of persons who go on the tour of FBI headquarters. The House subcommittee is alert to this activity also. In 1969 Chairman Rooney detected a drop in attendance (from 590,097 persons in 1968 to 572,290 in 1969) and sought an explanation. Hoover explained that this was "due to the riots in the spring of 1968" which kept many tourists away from Washington, but assured the subcommittee that, "[a]t present there is a tremendous increase in the number of tourists."

To a man who admired both, "Hoover *is* the FBI." Even
one who admired neither must concede that this was not
much of an exaggeration. Certainly Hoover's word was law
within the Bureau. All positions in the FBI are exempted
from civil service and no FBI employee has any legal protection against dismissal unless some should in the future be
found in the Constitution itself. As Congress belatedly recognized in 1966, "the Director of the Federal Bureau of Investigation is the head of the Federal Bureau of Investigation."

Unfortunately, Hoover seemed also to be largely unaccount-
able to his ostensible superiors without the Bureau. According
to Hoover's recollection, both he and Attorney General Stone
were agreed when he took the job as Director that he should
"be responsible only to the Attorney General." The experience
of subsequent Attorneys General is well summed up by the
statement of a long-time Justice Department official, reported
in a recent study, identifying as the "greatest single problem"
confronting an Attorney General "the control and management of J. Edgar Hoover." That same study reveals that an
Attorney General whose brother was simultaneously the President of the United States met with only limited success in
his efforts to do so.

As Attorney General Bonaparte's principle of departmental
accountability broke down in the failure of his successors to
control the Director, so did his further suggestion of congressional review break down in the failure of Congress to
attempt any such review.

VI: *The Bureau Perspective*

Given Hoover's virtually uncontrolled authority over the
policies and practices of the FBI, his views of the Bureau's
main preoccupations—crime and subversion—are of major importance to its future history, despite his death. First, some of
his views on crime:

Causes of Crime: In the final analysis our high rates of crime today are traceable primarily to the following two conditions:

1. There has been an unfortunate spread of moral deterioration among growing segments of our population. We find this not merely in the rise of bank robberies, crimes of violence, and other types of underworld activity, but also in the willingness of many law-abiding Americans to compromise their ideals if an easy dollar can be made. This tragic fact underlies the recent scandals which have been exposed in the entertainment world, the television industry in particular.

2. Public apathy toward crime and other dangerous conditions has been on the rise in far too many American communities. Such apathy is really a sickness. It attacks man's sensitivity to the difference between right and wrong. Its symptoms are lethargy, self-indulgence and adherence to the principle of pleasure before duty.

Other factors also have contributed to the aggravated crime problem confronting the Nation today. The overprotective attitude which exists in some areas toward vicious young offenders, delays in the administration of justice, legal technicalities, and pressures exerted by outsiders to thwart honest and impartial enforcement of the law—these are conditions which encourage the growth of crime and hamper the cause of decency. No amount of efficient law enforcement can compensate for basic weaknesses in our moral armor, such as those which I have just cited.

Juvenile Delinquency: We are allowing a group of disrespectful young people who have no sense of moral responsibility to develop into hardened criminals. This is true because these children are being allowed to just grow up, rather than receiving proper home training. They are being neglected and denied the love, care, and guidance in the home necessary to proper development as good, law-abiding citizens.

. . . There must be a line drawn between the mischievous pranks of young people, which may indeed be called juvenile delinquency, and the depraved deeds of teenage thugs who rope, rape, and kill . . .

I am a firm believer in fitting the punishment to the crime. To excuse a willful murder, rape, or robbery committed by a young man, merely because he has not reached his 18th birth-

day, defies all sane logic. Such action can only encourage
greater disrespect for law and order.

There are other great serious causes of the moral decay which
is taking place among the children of our Nation. I speak of
those depraved individuals who seek out our young people of
this country as customers for all forms of obscene material,
narcotics, and intoxicating beverages. Many of the crimes of
violence committed by juveniles result from the use of drugs or
intoxicants or exposure to obscene movies or literature.

Even the various entertainment media must share their part
of the blame for weakening the morals of our young people.
Many movies, television shows, and theatrical productions have
overstepped the bounds of decency. Likewise, these media
have flooded the land with scenes of violence which cannot
avoid [sic] affecting young minds.

Probation and Parole: Be assured, law enforcement is trying,
and trying hard. Despite intensified training efforts and heroic
dedication to duty, amidst frequent public apathy and commonplace open derision and hostility from anarchistic elements
of all types and by certain jackals of the news media, and notwithstanding increased physical assaults, often fatal, from fanatical predators, dedicated law enforcement officers are striving desperately to maintain the public peace . . .

Unfortunately, compounding the crisis today are unrealistic
and unworkable parole, probation, and related leniency policies
which all too frequently, as can be readily noted from reading
the daily press, result in new tragedy and sorrow to innocent,
law-abiding citizens . . .

Now Hoover's views on the perennial threat of subversion:

Communist Party: The Communist Party–USA is under the
complete control and domination of the Soviet Union and as
such poses a menace to the security of our country. The Communist Party–USA is a tool which the Soviets attempt to use
to neutralize U.S. efforts directed at preventing further expansion of Soviet-imposed control in various parts of the world.

Gus Hall, general secretary of the Communist Party–USA,
has been the dominant figure of the American Communist

Party for the past 11 years. He has been called by the Soviets the most outstanding Marxist-Leninist outside the Soviet Union because of his unceasing support of Soviet positions at conferences of the international communist movement.

Hall, as recently as February 1971, has stated there are approximately 15,000 dues-paying members in the Communist Party—USA. Through the years, leading Party officials have estimated that there are at least ten sympathizers for every Party member.

Currently, Hall and the Party are riding the crest of optimism. They visualize many opportunities to exploit the current unsettled conditions in this country. They believe the problems of unemployment, racial strife, and anti-Vietnam discord offer the Party a chance to make impressive gains in this country and the Party has embarked upon ambitious programs to take advantage of the situation . . .

To take advantage of all these situations and as an indication of Party optimism, the National Committee meeting of the Party in New York City on November 21–23, 1970, announced a Party recruiting drive which is expected to recruit approximately 1,300 members during the coming year.

New Left: During 1968 the New Left movement in the United States continued to reveal itself as a firmly established subversive force dedicated to the complete destruction of our traditional democratic values and the principles of free government. This movement represents the militant, nihilistic and anarchistic forces which have become entrenched, for the most part, on college campuses and which threaten the orderly process of education as the forerunner of a more determined effort to destroy our economic, social, and political structures.

The discontent expressed by the movement in this country is also found in other countries. As a result, the New Left movement is a new specter haunting the Western World. It is a movement that is united to some degree by common issues, such as the Vietnam war, civil rights matters, so-called capitalist corruption, and a so-called archaic university system.

Combined Menace: Although activities of old line Communist organizations in the United States have been overshadowed by the militancy of the New Left and racial disorders, the threat of communism has certainly not diminished.

It flows from the Communist Party—USA, with its blind obedience to the Soviet Union and from various Communist splin-
ter groups such as the Progressive Labor Party . . . , which,
in addition to stepped-up efforts to extend its influence on college campuses, has made a concerted effort to take over the
national leadership of the Students for a Democratic Society,
the militant, pro-Marxist, anarchistic, campus-based New Left
group; the Socialist Workers Party; the Workers World Party;
and their affiliates. These organizations seek to transform this
country into a Communist state but differ on the plans to be
followed.

The turbulence generated by the New Left stimulated all
these organizations into moving toward increased militancy
themselves. Seizing any pretext as the foundation for a protest demonstration, leaders of these organizations seek to proliferate [sic] each demonstration into a massive confrontation with the authorities to generate disrespect for law and
order.

VII: Conference Discussion

MR. ROBERT SILVERS:* Mr. Countryman, can you suggest
specific limits on the functions of a federal agency of this
kind?

MR. COUNTRYMAN: It should be, in my judgment, confined
to the enforcement of criminal statutes. The thing that most
concerns me about the FBI is its compilation of political
information. This is largely, and perhaps today almost entirely,
a consequence of the federal loyalty program.

MR. HARRY RANSOM:† I would like to ask Professor Countryman what observations he can make on what I think may
be the fundamental issue of this conference. That is, in our
delicately balanced mechanism of national government, with
power divided among the President, Congress and the courts,

* Editor, *The New York Review of Books;* member of Executive Council,
Committee for Public Justice.
† Chairman, Department of Political Science, Vanderbilt University.

we are trying to identify the methods of control of a governmental police agency. I wonder if he could give us his observations, from studying the history of the FBI, on whether the fundamental problem has been not so much in defining the jurisdiction and role of the Bureau as in defining the role of the presidency, the Congress and the courts in controlling the FBI.

MR. COUNTRYMAN: I think that is the fundamental question, all right. I tried to advert to the fact that there has not been enough responsibility taken by the Department of Justice itself. I think Victor Navasky's book, which most of you have read, illustrates very clearly that this has been true even when the Attorney General had his brother in the White House as President: Attorney General Kennedy was not able to bring the Bureau under control.

There is no congressional supervision of the operation at all. I mentioned that the only thing that ever resembled a congressional investigation of the FBI took place in the aftermath of the Palmer raids, and it came to nothing. No committee report was submitted after that investigation. The only time Congress gets an official look at the FBI is when Hoover makes his annual appearance before the House Appropriations subcommittee, and the way the members of that committee fawn over "the great man" is pitiful. They never ask him a critical question. So there is virtually no one in a position to control Hoover. That, I think, is the basic difficulty. The FBI does what Hoover decides it will do. It doesn't do what he decides it won't do.

CHAPTER THREE

THE BUREAU'S BUDGET: A SOURCE OF POWER

BY WALTER PINCUS

I: *Lack of Normal Controls*

The Federal Bureau of Investigation's budget—like the organization itself—stands unique within the federal government.

It is drawn up and approved, and the resultant federal funds are disbursed and even audited, not only within the Bureau itself but within just one division of it.

The funds appropriated to the Bureau come in one lump sum, to be expended not necessarily as the Director said they would during his congressional appearances, but as he wishes.

While other government agencies are tied down because their appropriations are divided among various named or line items, the FBI has only four legally binding requirements in its appropriations: the number of new and replacement automobiles (including each year "one armored vehicle," the fabled Hoover limousine, which in 1970 cost $30,000); $10,000 for taxicab hire, a historic item; a $70,000 contingency fund "to meet unforeseen emergencies of a confidential character," but not including "payment of rewards"; and finally $42,500 as "compensation of the director . . . so long as the position is held by the present incumbent."

The outside budget review systems that apply to other agencies and departments do not apply to the Bureau, thanks either to statute or to tradition. The Department of Justice has not in the past held in-house hearings on the FBI budget. A former top Justice Department administrator, when asked recently how the FBI budget is integrated into the department's, replied succinctly, "With a stapler."

Those who have participated in the Office of Management and Budget's half-day review of the FBI budget say it is superficial. One former official could recall only one question being raised over an eight-year period—and it was directed to the number of cars the Bureau sought.

Congress and particularly the Appropriations committees have given special treatment to the Bureau budget. The Director himself noted in testimony that "I can frankly say we have seldom been denied funds by the House Subcommittee on Appropriations . . . The Bureau of the Budget and the Congress . . . have always been most considerate of our needs." In his own modest way, Hoover was saying that over the past twenty years he got all that he asked for and on two occasions, even more—a record no other government department or agency can equal.

If the FBI were a small agency or if its activities were non-controversial, the budgetary short cuts and special treatment would be understandable if not totally acceptable. But the Bureau is big and growing bigger. The $334 million it received for the 1971 fiscal year makes it nearly as large in terms of budget and personnel as the Department of State. And this figure is almost double the FBI budget of just four years ago. By the end of fiscal 1972 there will be a programmed 8,900 special agents, an increase of 30 per cent over the number just three years ago.

In short, after almost twenty years of slow steady growth, the FBI still employs the secrecy in management and allocation of funds that it practiced when it was a relatively small elite agency run by younger men.

An agency with the Bureau's over-all mission must maintain

some special rights in contrast to the normal budget process. The FBI—along with the CIA and the National Security Agency in the intelligence area—should be able to undertake activities that by their nature must remain secret. The limits of that secrecy, however, should be clearly defined and should permit some outside albeit protected review, by both the executive and legislative branches.

II: Controls from Within

Discussing the manner in which the Bureau puts together its budget is difficult—impossible, in fact, without the cooperation of those within the FBI with budgetary responsibilities. I have been unable to get that cooperation.

Thus, the picture one can draw of the process itself is of necessity limited. Two things are certain. John P. Mohr, a thirty-year veteran of the FBI and now assistant to the director, is the key budgetary figure, and the process itself is run by the Bureau's Division 3, the administrative division.

Unlike other agencies, the FBI assistant directors for operational activities—general investigative or domestic intelligence, for example—do not have budgetary responsibility. They do not take part in formulation of the budget and they do not allocate funds after the budget is approved. Instead they formulate programs which are passed on to the Director for approval. Such programs may require additional agents or special equipment—but the cost factors are not included as a part of the input to the Director.

"You always would assume that if the program was approved, money would be available," a former official told me. "And with a budget that was always going up, funds were never a problem."

Cost may, according to one former assistant director, have been part of Hoover's decision whether to approve or disapprove a program. But once a program was approved, it was Mohr's job to come up with the money.

On the operational level, budgeting is the responsibility of the special agents in charge of field offices (SACs). A SAC must make the allocations and seek the finances to perform the tasks assigned to him by the various assistant directors back in Washington.

The SAC's performance is judged by the statistics he generates while using the assets at hand. The Bureau does undertake case level studies that determine whether an office, based on the number of investigative matters handled, deserves to have additional agents. Thus, in the game of Bureau politics, it becomes reasonable for the SACs to turn their assets toward those matters that will generate the most statistics. And not surprisingly, according to former officials, the assistant directors push for approval of broad programs that generate those same statistics. In this process, the well-publicized mandatory unpaid agent overtime figures are built in for later use before the Congress.

The primary asset is agents, and each agent is a generalist. The number in any field office assigned to internal security, bank robberies or car thefts can vary from day to day and is controlled not by Washington but by the local SAC. "The successful SAC is the one who reads the pressures from Washington," one official suggested in discussing how funds are allocated and statistics developed.

In only one situation, according to a former top official, did the Bureau assign from Washington a set number of agents to a national program, and that was to the loyalty program during the 1950s.

In years past, Hoover always took the position that he would undertake new tasks or responsibilities with everyone working harder. "He would always absorb the additional effort for a few months after Congress passed additional laws within the

Bureau's purview," recalled a former official. "Then he would come in with a budget request to cover a full year's operational increase." His request would talk in terms of a number of new agents per program, but the figure would not represent the actual number of agents that in fact would be so assigned. It was just a compilation of agent hours applied to that program from hundreds of agents around the country.

In 1963, when President Lyndon Johnson wanted Hoover to step up his work in the civil rights field, the Director responded that every agent he had was fully allocated; to undertake that task he would need funds adequate to hire an additional two hundred agents.

"That was just a way to add to the Bureau," one former Justice official said in discussing the matter. "A good manager could reallocate" from less important tasks, he suggested, and pointed initially to the agents involved in car theft and interstate payment cases that generate impressive numbers and dollar-recovery figures—both of which are used before Congress.

It took several years but Hoover did get additional funds sufficient to hire one hundred new agents, supposedly for civil rights cases. In his last budgets, he sought and received funds for one thousand new agents to handle organized crime, aircraft hijacking and "extremist" matters. Whether one thousand agents are ever assigned to such cases will be known only within the Bureau's administration division.

Using the backup material Hoover provided in the budget and supplied to Congress, one may make the following estimates on how his funds were allocated:

Close to 80 per cent of the Bureau's expenditures are for personnel salaries and "other personnel compensation." Almost 75 per cent of the FBI's budget is devoted to field investigations. The fingerprint identification activity costs more than $25 million; the FBI lab more than $7 million. One has difficulties going beyond that, although it is clear that the Bureau itself maintains extremely tight budget controls within its own house. For example, Hoover was able to tell the Congress that the Kent State inquiry, which involved 302 special agents at the peak, cost an estimated $274,100 not including "6,316 hours of overtime for which [the agents] received no compensation."

The first level for review of the Bureau's budget would normally be the Department of Justice and its Assistant Attorney General for Administration. Past practice was that the Justice Department official played no role in drawing up the budget. He was permitted to sit in when Clyde Tolson, Hoover's chief deputy, spent an afternoon before the Office of Management and Budget going over the Bureau's figures. The Budget agency has a reputation for looking closely and refusing funds for most agencies, but, asked in June, 1971, at a Senate hearing whether the Budget Bureau had ever denied him any funds, Hoover replied, "The Budget Bureau frequently rounds off sums which we calculate as accurately as we can. They also set limitations on the total amounts we can request in a particular year and they frequently require us to absorb unforeseen costs which may arise from time to time. As an example, the FBI was required to absorb $670,000 during the fiscal year 1971 resulting from increased statutory health benefit costs."

What Hoover didn't add to that illustration, though he had told the House committee about it, was that rather than "absorbing" the costs, he used funds Congress had already given him in a supplemental appropriation for salaries, and deferred the hiring of one hundred new agents and seventy clerks until the beginning of the next fiscal year. In other words, he exercised his right of reaching in and taking money he had for one purpose and used it for another.

General Accounting Office audits undertaken of FBI expenditures are normally spot checks which determine if the disbursing office has a voucher behind each payment. For this type of bookkeeping the Bureau gets high marks, not just from the GAO but from the Budget Bureau as well. But that type of auditing does not measure the workings of a program nor the employment of assets—a type of audit that GAO often undertakes within other executive branch agencies.

The manner in which the Bureau uses its confidential funds, informant payments and reward money is tightly held—as it should be. The CIA has similar funds, but it makes an outside top-secret accounting to a White House control committee. The Bureau apparently tells no one.

III: Congressional Review

The FBI's unique budgetary situation must be attributed to a number of factors, not the least of which is the Bureau's almost sacrosanct status in the halls of Congress. Until 1971 Director Hoover rarely found it necessary to appear before more than one Appropriations Committee. Every other department or agency director—including the CIA most years—had to put in an appearance before both the House and Senate Appropriations Committees. But Hoover took the position that since the House had always granted him all the funds requested, he had no reason to appear before the Senate committee.

Senator John McClellan became Chairman in 1961 of the Senate subcommittee which handles the over-all Justice Department budget including that of the FBI, and pressed for a Hoover appearance that year. According to both FBI and Hill sources, the Director declined and eventually the matter was settled amicably over lunch with an understanding that the Director would not be "invited" to appear and thus not placed in the position of "refusing."

In June, 1971, both an NBC television program and a newspaper series on the FBI made the point of Hoover's non-appearance before the Senate committee. On June 24, weeks after this criticism, Hoover made his first appearance before McClellan's subcommittee at a special closed afternoon session that followed immediately after the appearance of Attorney General John Mitchell.

The congressional committees with legislative (as opposed to appropriation) authority over the Bureau—specifically the House and Senate Judiciary Committees—have shown no interest in inquiring into the Bureau. So the only congressional review of the Bureau for the past twenty years, with minor exceptions, has been that undertaken by the House Appropriations Committee's subcommittee which handles the FBI budget.

The Bureau has maintained another unique relationship to Congress, and particularly to the House Appropriations Committee. Since 1959 FBI personnel on loan to the committee have acted as full-time directors of all surveys and investigations run by the committee. Although the committee has used investigators from other agencies, the overwhelming number of its investigators are loaned FBI agents. In fact, almost two thirds of the House committee's $1 million investigations budget for fiscal 1971 went to reimburse the FBI for loaned agents.

Not only does this arrangement cement relations between the FBI and the committee, it also gives the Bureau a special status among other government departments. What other executive agency serves at the direction of both the legislative and executive branches?

For his part, Hoover understood the importance of his Hill connections and their value to the Bureau. The FBI agent chosen to serve as one of the committee's three full-time investigators—on loan, of course—was carefully chosen. For example, FBI inspector Paul J. Mohr, who recently concluded an unusual four-year term with the committee, is the brother of John P. Mohr, until recently No. 4 man in the Bureau hierarchy and responsible for the budget.

The Bureau's involvement with the House Appropriations Committee was institutionalized in 1959 when the late Representative Clarence Cannon was Chairman. Cannon developed the system of using executive branch investigators as a means of saving money and asked Hoover to loan him some agents for full-time work. When George Mahon took over the committee in 1964 he decided to continue the system. Not surprisingly, a *Congressional Quarterly* survey of ten committee members (out of fifty-five) found a general lack of knowledge about the committee's investigating system. All knew that FBI agents did investigative work for the committee, but only three knew the extent to which FBI men were used.

It is also not surprising, based more on the committee's view of the Bureau than on the presence of the agents on its staff, to find that there has been no investigation of the FBI by the committee in the last twenty years, according to the present committee staff director, Paul Wilson.

Representative John J. Rooney, the New York Democrat who now chairs the Appropriations subcommittee which handles the FBI budget, recently defended the practice of using FBI investigators in a speech on the House floor. Rooney declared: "The surveys and investigations staff has never been requested to conduct any studies directly involving an appropriations request of the FBI. The FBI's request is closely studied and independently evaluated by the regular staff of the committee—which has no FBI personnel assigned—prior to being considered by the members of the subcommittee of which I have the honor to serve as Chairman."

What Rooney failed to point out was that although the regular committee "has no FBI personnel assigned," his own subcommittee staff assistant, Jay B. Howe, the man on the regular staff most directly involved with the FBI budget, is himself a former FBI agent.

A less direct connection exists between the Bureau and the Senate Appropriations Committee. In the mid-1940s, according to one Bureau official, the former Senate Appropriations Committee Chairman, Carl Hayden, asked Hoover to recommend someone to work on the staff. Hoover suggested a special agent who had caught his notice named Thomas J. Scott. Today Scott, the former FBI agent, is staff director of the Senate Appropriations Committee.

Hoover's congressional testimony hardly varied in his last ten years. It reflected not only the Director's manner of operation, but also the interests of Congressman Rooney. Rooney's own words in an NBC interview earlier this year best characterized his approach to the FBI and its Director: "There have been very few other agencies in government that have been so efficiently run and with such results to the taxpayers' benefit as the Federal Bureau of Investigation . . . without a doubt Mr. Hoover is the greatest administrator we have in government, in any part of the government."

The outline of Hoover's testimony was predictable year after year and made for dismal reading to those who sought some enlightenment on the Bureau's activities. The Director's prime emphasis was constantly on the dangers that faced the country rather than on details of what the Bureau was doing with its assets. In the 1950s the stress essentially was on Communist subversion from within and Soviet spies from without. In the late 1950s Hoover picked up the theme of crime, with emphasis on youthful offenders and repeaters. The black and radical movements began to appear in his testimony in the early 1960s, and in 1971 they dominated along with an appropriate exposition on "parole, probation and clemency abuses" and an extensive paper on "major prosecutive efforts directed against organized crime."

Surrounding these dramatic readings of the dangers we face were the statistics and dollar figures so dear to the hearts of both the Director and Mr. Rooney. The Director invariably opened his testimony with a direct statement on the increases being sought, along with a line of description—"The remaining 398 full-year employees (all clerks) for FBI headquarters are for the fingerprint operation where 95 will be used for current work increases, 29 will be involved with preparation work for the automation of identification records and 274 will work on a long-term project to consolidate our civil fingerprinting file." Those details were further embellished by an array of tables and comparison charts that would bore the most intense Bureau follower.

Hoover also occasionally lightened matters by throwing in statements that reflected a shrewd assessment of what Congress wanted to hear. For example, in telling Rooney in March, 1971, about his major increase in agents—one thousand new ones or an over-all agent growth of 12 per cent at an annual cost of more than $10 million—Hoover stated, "The committee will be interested in knowing that of 1,000 agents which were requested by the President and implemented by the Bureau, 67 per cent or 667 of those men have had military experience, many at the rank of captain and above. That experience is a great asset because they are in fine physical shape and have the discipline needed as an agent. They have the ability to make prompt decisions, having served in leadership positions during the Vietnam era." (These are hardly the credentials needed to do objective investigative work among the peace groups and new student radicals, however.)

Among the regular statistics of 1970 delivered by Mr. Hoover in 1971—as in the past—were:

—Fingerprint receipts and, normally, how they reached record numbers. In 1971, however, there was a falling off, so

Hoover introduced a new statistic, "correspondence, forms and name checks received." Needless to say that 1970 carried the asterisk for all-time high.

—Laboratory examinations, which as usual were at an all-time high.

—Fugitives located were at 30,318—"a new high and an increase of 18 percent over the locations in 1969."

—Automobile recoveries "increased 5 percent in 1970 as compared to 1969 to reach a new record high of 30,599."

—Investigative matters received continued to grow along with another figure, average assignment per agent. Hoover stressed he "prefers to see" an average of eighteen matters. But the average assignment per agent reported for 1970 to the House subcommittee was thirty-one matters and Hoover pointed out that the 1,036 agents to be added during the coming two fiscal years "would have little impact upon this average work assignment . . ." Just three months later in his testimony before the Senate committee Hoover noted, "The average assignment per agent is now twenty-nine investigative matters." In the intervening three months, according to the presentations, only seventy-four new agents had been added to the rolls. What caused the drop of two matters per agent was not disclosed.

One of Hoover's proudest charts was labeled "FBI accomplishments and appropriations." It showed how each year, despite the Bureau's ever-growing budget, the fines, savings and recoveries stemming from the Bureau's activities rose at an even greater rate. "This accomplishment represents an average return of $1.60 for each $1 of direct funds appropriated to the FBI in the 1970 fiscal year," the Director said as he handed Rooney his five-year chart.

Taken alone, these statistics appear ludicrous when ranged against the more serious problems that Hoover said the country faced—organized crime and espionage, for example—and which should have been a prime focus for the assets he received. Yet interviews with past and present Bureau officials confirm that a substantial amount of agent time across the country is devoted to the tasks that result in providing these statistics, rather than toward investigations that require large numbers of agents and long periods of time and may not produce any dollar statistics at all.

When the House subcommittee members ask any questions, they are most likely to be of the character that were posed in March, 1971. Representative Neal Smith, a Democrat from Iowa, asked if the Director had fingerprints for all members of Congress on file. Hoover, still stung by accusations that he had bugged Capitol Hill telephones, automatically responded, "No, sir. I would like to add, also, we have never tapped a telephone of any Congressman or any Senator since I have been Director of the Bureau."

Smith, who himself didn't want to be misunderstood, quickly responded that he "was thinking in terms of it being a good thing to have the fingerprints of all Members for the protection of the Members in the case of accident."

Representative Elford A. Cederberg raised the question of Ramsey Clark's knowledge and approval of wiretaps while he was Attorney General. Cederberg and Hoover then entered into a colloquy on Clark during which the congressman quoted a section of Clark's previous testimony before the same subcommittee in which he praised the FBI. Cederberg remarked he had brought it up because "I thought it might not be a bad idea to place on the record the statements of the former Attorney General in his last testimony before our Committee in regard to the FBI. I am delighted, in light of the facts that are being put out in public print, to know that he did, in writing, authorize the use of electronic surveillances by the FBI."

Chairman Rooney then asked, "What do we know about this

Bernadette Devlin?" and Hoover's brief reply included the statement, "I don't know why the State Department granted the Visa for her to come over here, but it did."

Representative Robert Sikes did close by asking about "the purchase of armored cars for the FBI . . . Are they for your use?"

Hoover responded that two were kept in Washington, one in New York and one in Los Angeles, but rather than calling them his own, preferred to describe them merely as being "used for protective purposes." It fell to Clyde Tolson, sitting beside Hoover, to tell Sikes that "during the calendar year 1970, Mr. Hoover received twenty-six threats on his life and so far this year, he has received another sixteen threats. It is necessary for security reasons for Mr. Hoover to be transported in these vehicles."

The questioning—if that is what it can be called—clearly shows that the lack of substance in Hoover's testimony before the subcommittee was not solely of his own doing. The congressmen themselves did not want to get into substance.

A close study of Hoover's testimony over the past fifteen years, however, discloses a number of areas worth congressional questioning—from the approach of Bureau investigative work, such as use of informants and wiretaps, to the allocation of agent resources to produce statistics.

For example, although the number of FBI agents has increased from 6,005 in fiscal 1957 to 8,482 in fiscal 1971, Congress has actually provided funds over the past fourteen years for a total of 8,976 agents. Thus, Hoover received money enough to hire more than he actually had.

In February 1967 Hoover testified he had 6,532 agents, and, with the additional funds he sought, he would add another 106 agents. This, he told Congress, would give him a total of 6,638 agents in fiscal 1968. He got the money he wanted, but the next year, the Director was back saying he had only 6,590 agents—and the subcommittee never asked why this was 48 fewer than he said he would have one year earlier.

Hoover's biggest agent gap took place between 1957, when he said he had 6,005 agents, and 1962, when he said he had 5,985. In the interim, he had sought and received funds from Congress to add no fewer than 287 agents.

When asked about the "missing" agents, FBI spokesman Thomas Bishop at first said the new agent funds were to fill slots vacated by retiring agents. He later revised that to say it might refer to authorized rather than actual agents on duty. Finally he said he had no answer.

Apparently, however, the funds involved were used for other Bureau expenses. But by asking for money for new agents, Hoover was always assured he would get his request. The FBI budget is appropriated in one lump sum, so there is nothing legally wrong in what Hoover did—but it does show a bureaucrat's ability to use figures to get what he wants.

IV: *The Future*

Clearly if the FBI is to be reintegrated into the government, one of the first steps would be for the Attorney General and his top staff to play a role in the FBI's budgeting and the programming that stems from it. The U.S. attorneys and the department's Criminal Division in particular should be aware of FBI future planning as a guide to their own activities. As a former Justice official understated it recently, "The FBI budget planning can in the long run have an impact on caseloads and the courts."

The measure of FBI performance should be changed so as to put less stress on the statistics that prove its "efficiency" and more on meeting the most pressing of the problems it faces. In short, assets probably should be reallocated. But that judgment can only be made with a clear understanding of what the distribution is today.

It will fall to the congressional committees that review the FBI budget to apply the kinds of policy controls many feel are now lacking. They have a broad enough makeup and separation from executive responsibility to raise the controversial questions that never seem to get asked within an administration's family. Only the attitude of the members on the Hill need to change; the opportunity is already there.

Almost every year Hoover provided a brief statistical report in the area of civil rights and the FBI. He told the Rooney subcommittee that the FBI in 1970 handled 934 investigations under the Civil Rights Act of 1964 and that cases in this area "often are of a controversial nature." In order to provide a figure on agent participation, Hoover linked the work in civil rights with "that required in connection with racial disturbances and keeping abreast of the activities of extremist and hate groups" and came up with a figure of "an average of 2,139 agents each month." The Media, Pennsylvania, documents showed that the Bureau undertook a vast investigation into all black student groups—an undertaking that one would hardly class as falling within the civil rights area, though Hoover's testimony indicated that he did. No congressman present, however, raised any questions.

Hoover often referred to the publications produced by the Bureau and their costs, but no one asked him about his office of criminal records or costs of his publicity activities.

Each year Hoover reported on informants in a few paragraphs. But there never was a question about the varieties of informant activity; the committee limited its concern to the two areas Hoover cited—location of fugitives and recovery of stolen goods.

Handling of derogatory arrest information by the FBI was raised before both the House and Senate committees in 1971 through a question and answer insert provided by the Bureau. Only Senator Roman Hruska followed up with a few questions.

The Director each year provided information on the number of Bureau electronic surveillances as of the day of his testimony. The only substantial discussion on the subject in both committees in 1971 was to criticize newspaper articles which discussed FBI wiretapping.

Hoover provided both committees with extensive prepared papers on the FBI and organized crime.

Thus, there was hardly an area of public controversy or concern that Hoover himself did not raise in his congressional appearances. In the future, perhaps someone on the pertinent subcommittees will have the sense of responsibility to follow through with questions to the Director that the public deserves to have answered.

The Bureau must be opened up for within-government review and coordination, as well as congressional inquiry for the public benefit. But this does not mean that *everything* the FBI does should be subject to executive or public review. The FBI has responsibilities for undertaking investigations that reach the highest levels of government—inquiries that should not be subject to review by higher authorities or Congress because those individuals may in fact be involved. This is the gravest type of responsibility and one that must be vested wholly within the Bureau. In some areas at some times the FBI must be an agency unto itself—and it must be so structured and run by men of the highest caliber to perform such tasks.

This country needs an agency of quality and public standing to perform the tasks assigned by law to the FBI. Time and practice have made it today a totally separate power. It needs to be brought back into government, but with the limited special status required to protect all the people and not just the few who run it now.

V: Conference Discussion

MR. ELLIFF: First, Ken Clausen of the Washington *Post* has done some good work on informants and he comes up with this: "The Justice Department of Attorney General John Mitchell does not know how much money the FBI actually spends for informants. The funds are hidden in the Bureau's $300 million plus budget, and the figure is jealously guarded." However, recently, Representative Rooney said, "The FBI informant fund is the same as the Bureau of Narcotics and Dangerous Drugs, which is 3.7 million dollars for informants, at least this year."

Second, in 1943, when Clarence Cannon became Chairman of the House Appropriations Committee, he asked for FBI agents to help and in the Roosevelt papers I found this memo from Francis Biddle, the Attorney General, to Roosevelt:

> Congressman Cannon has requested that Hoover assign FBI agents to investigate needs of the various departments requesting appropriations so that the Committee may determine in any particular case whether additional personnel is needed, whether there is waste and so forth.

The Biddle memo goes on:

> I am strongly opposed to the plan. It would put the Department of Justice in the impossible position of investigating other departments, including the Army and Navy, and passing on their needs.

And he says to the President, "I thought that I should report the matter to you since you might wish to indicate what you think should be done." And Roosevelt notes, "You are absolutely right." So under the Roosevelt administration, no FBI agents were assigned to the Appropriations Committee. That, of course, was changed, as you report in your paper.

MR. PINCUS: Yes, I think two things. One, Cannon wanted to do it because he wanted to save money and he went ahead and did it anyway. It didn't matter what Biddle said. It started back in the Forties; he had not only Bureau agents, but a variety of other executive agency people working for him.

Second, my own personal feeling is that it really shouldn't be allowed. Any committee can put together its own staff and in many ways do a much better job than the Bureau is capable of doing. But you can't at the same time serve both the legislative and the executive branches.

MR. RANSOM: I have a question for Mr. Pincus. To what extent on Capitol Hill is the fear of a secret dossier in the Bureau a deterrent to a more aggressive questioning of its present Director? I realize you can only have an impression about this, but I wonder if you have one.

MR. PINCUS: I think it fits into the same category as every civil rights leader's feeling that his phone is tapped. A politician can't afford certain kinds of exposure or doesn't think he can afford it. Politicians have a certain number of battles that they can fight; they usually want to fight ones that they can win. It is almost impossible to beat the Bureau. Nobody has really been willing to make the fight. Part of it is the fear of the secret dossier, and I'm sure at times there have been actual uses or at least threats made.

I've asked the same question of people who have worked in the Justice Department. How often are they willing to take the extra step to confront Mr. Hoover or the Bureau on some question? Most people are willing to win some and lose some, but never try to fight the whole battle. Much of the power that has been accumulated by the Bureau has been weaned away from other agencies and institutions over a period of time because they haven't been willing to call a halt at some point.

MR. HUNDLEY: My question ties in with what you just said. I can understand why politicians and even people in the Department of Justice, including Attorneys General, have had some reluctance to deal directly with a person as powerful as Mr. Hoover. I also agree, as you said earlier, that the press, until quite recently, has dealt very tenderly with him. I wonder how you would explain that.

MR. PINCUS: To go into my theories of the press would take a long time. The simplest one is that newspapers, and television to a greater degree, are dependent upon official sources for news. It is not news if I say something happens; it is news if Mr. Hoover does. And so, if you want to go after the Bureau, you're not going to get anybody to talk to you about the Bureau. You've got to go find it out yourself, and then you've got to bring those facts forward and say, "This is what I uncovered." That's a difficult job. It's much easier to use your assets as a newspaper in covering press conferences, where you can quote well-known people.

There have been, over a period of time, pieces about the Bureau, but not very many. The lack is a result of the difficulty in developing stories without help and a result of Mr. Hoover's ability to give reporters access to files that can make them look very good.

Let me give an example. When I first started out, I did a piece about his armored cars. I was doing a piece about everybody's limousines and somebody at GSA gave me the bid for Hoover's. At the time, it was just a $20,000 car. I wrote about it. The fellow who gave me the contract, which was a public record, was transferred. My paper got all sorts of letters from Hoover, and finally said, "Well, you know, we have no control over things like that." It's not worth it for them.

CHAPTER FOUR

THE INSIDE STORY:
AN AGENT'S DILEMMAS

BY WILLIAM W. TURNER

The career of Nelson H. (Skip) Gibbons illuminates most of the faults of Bureau personnel policies and their crippling effect on FBI performance. Assigned to the Detroit office, Gibbons had an outstanding record in criminal investigation and a bureau-wide reputation for having discovered a Soviet spy. The spy had come to a small Michigan community to obtain a copy of a baptismal certificate to create an identity, since he had entered the country clandestinely as an "illegal." The circumstances aroused Gibbons' suspicions and, despite scoffing by his superiors, he kept the man under surveillance through several states.

It turned out the man was Kaarlo Rudolph Tuomi, whom New York agents finally pressured into becoming a double agent. Some five years later Gibbons' perspicacity and perseverance paid off handsomely for the Bureau as headlines proclaimed: FBI SMASHES SOVIET SPY RING. Among those under arrest were a husband and wife team who had appropriated the identities of a Catholic priest and a Connecticut housewife.

But by this time, Gibbons was long gone from the Bureau. He had become a victim of the weight program. Hoover had decided to reduce, and he ruled that his agents, too, had to conform to strict standards. The powerfully built Gibbons had been a boxer in the Marine Corps and a football lineman at St. Bonaventure University. When he took his annual physical, the military doctor noted his weight as "medically proper." But a superior in the Detroit office consulted Hoover's chart and commanded, "Lose five pounds."

When Gibbons did not, he was threatened with a charge of insubordination. When he retained an attorney, his judgment was rated "unsatisfactory." Then he was put "on the bicycle" —a rapid series of transfers designed to force resignation. On the headquarters copy of his transfer to Mobile, Alabama, Associate Director Clyde Tolson scrawled: "Transfer O.C. in November," and promptly in November he was sent packing to Oklahoma City.

Gibbons hung tough. Ordinarily, he would have been fired. But, like me, he was a veteran of World War II, which meant that, although the Bureau is free of civil service, he had the protection of the Veterans Preference Act of 1944. The act permits employees who are fired or suspended more than thirty days to appeal outside the FBI. To circumvent the law, the Bureau handed Gibbons three suspensions without pay in rapid-fire order, all of them for less than thirty days.

Now it is unwritten law that a suspended agent address a letter to the Director expressing his regret at having transgressed and promising never to do so again. He is then expected to volunteer to report to the office and perform menial tasks in atonement. As Hoover has written, "Offenders are often compelled to perform special 'disciplinary chores' to 'earn their way back,' to show through hard work, devotion, and acknowledging the supremacy of the [Bureau] that they should be readmitted to favor . . . In most instances the more menial the task the better. In [Bureau] eyes, a member who has gone through this self-abasement becomes a better [agent] because of it. All thought of resistance is pounded out and he becomes a viable [Bureau] tool. He can be reprimanded, criticized, treated in a brutally unfair manner, yet he'll keep on working."

Of course, this passage is from Hoover's chapter on "Communist Discipline" in *Masters of Deceit,* and I have substituted "Bureau" for "Party" and "agent" for "comrade," but the underlying philosophy is the same.

Instead of purging himself, Gibbons simply left town during the periods of suspension. He was exiled to Butte, Montana, and then to Anchorage, Alaska. A year later, fed up with the hounding, he disappeared. Inspectors found him back in Michigan. But rather than fire him and submit its shabby conduct to outside review, the FBI pensioned him out as "nervous." Today he is the only officially nervous, government-subsidized ski instructor in the world.

I: Obsession with Image

It is impossible to ponder the organization without sizing up the late Director. His father was a federal employee and his mother a strict religious fundamentalist, factors which seem to have vectored his career. The twin traits of bureaucratic aptitude and theological anti-Communism emerged at the beginning of Hoover's career and persisted. Another factor was important. When he became Director in 1924, he was at the disadvantage of never having investigated a case in the field. Over the years, his only touch with the realities of investigation was the vicarious one of reading the reports flowing across his desk. I believe that this detachment explains in large measure the Bureau's excessively bureaucratic and priggish ways.

In the early phase of Hoover's directorship, his principal and most publicized accomplishment was cleaning up an agency ridden with hacks and rogues. So much has been made of this, however, that belief in FBI incorruptibility has reached legendary proportions. In its cover story on May 10, 1971, *Newsweek* repeated the myth in saying of FBI agents: "They tend, like Hoover, to be incorruptible as well: of all the blizzard of statistics the bureau likes to quote about itself, none is more impressive than its count of agents charged with crimes during Hoover's half-century: zero." Like most facets of the FBI legend, this one is literally true simply because the Bureau has been able to cover up its internal problems. Consider these incidents:

—Several years ago the wife of a special agent in charge of an FBI office reported to the local sheriff's office that her husband had severely beaten her. The report was suppressed by the sheriff, who is a former FBI agent.

—In 1961 in the New York office, an agent stole another agent's paycheck and cashed it. Forgery of government securities is a crime under the jurisdiction of the Secret Service. But FBI officials quietly prevailed upon an assistant U.S. attorney to decline prosecution and just as quietly allowed the agent to resign.

—Not long ago an inspector went to Phoenix, Arizona to deliver a speech. He got so drunk, a substitute had to appear for him. Still drunk, he drove a car through three red lights on the wrong side of the road. A drunk driving charge was fixed by FBI officials, much to the disgust of the police.

—According to current FBI agents, one high-ranking official is an alcoholic, and has been involved in many drunken scenes, including one in Toots Shor's in New York City and others on airline flights and in many field offices. On one occasion he demanded that two prostitutes be provided by the Chicago office. He also forced the Chicago FBI to buy him an engine for his personal boat at a cost of about $1,000. This was covered by phony vouchers in the office fund for confidential informant payments.

These episodes are typical. But the point is not that venality and misconduct are widespread in the FBI. They are not.

What is important to note is the diligence with which the Bureau shields its imperfection. This illustrates how obsessed it is with its image.

This obsession, which bears so directly on the socialization of agents, is manifest in the effort to portray the FBI's investigative endeavors as an unbroken chain of success. Toward this end, Bureau propagandists have simply rewritten history at practically every turn. The famous Lady in Red who put the finger on Dillinger was an informant of the Hargrave Secret Service, not the FBI. The Lindbergh kidnapper, Bruno Richard Hauptmann, was trapped by the insistence of Treasury agents, not the FBI, that the ransom packet should contain gold notes. The German saboteurs landed by submarine during World War II were betrayed by their own leader, and master spy Rudolf Abel by a defecting sub-agent. As for organized crime, Hoover was guilty of non-feasance for the first thirty-seven years of his regime, and recent achievements have been dimmed by a continued lack of cooperation with the other federal agencies that have long borne the brunt of the fight.

This fixation on image has spawned serious problems. For one thing the public has been lulled into a false sense of security. For another, the mass acceptance of the mythology has created a megalomania in the leadership, reflected in internal aberrations. The cardinal sin in the FBI is anything that detracts from the image. It is called "embarrassment to the Bureau."

The phrase is often heard inside the FBI. In April, 1961, while still an agent, I wrote to Representative Emanuel Celler, Chairman of the House Judiciary Committee: "It is indeed frustrating to work under conditions where every action (or lack of action) is predicated upon the potentiality of embarrassment to the Bureau." A decade later agent John F. Shaw declared in a letter intended only for the eyes of his college instructor: "There is a haunting phrase that echoes throughout the Bureau. 'Do not embarrass the Director.'"

The shibboleth overrides even matters of justice. In 1959 Wesley Grapp, then the agent in charge of the Oklahoma City office, recommended that an FBI laboratory report tending to exculpate Mrs. Kathryn Kelly, imprisoned for twenty-five years as an accomplice of her husband "Machine Gun" Kelly, not be furnished to the U.S. attorney because of potential "embarrassment to the Bureau."

Penalties for embarrassment are invariably harsh. A young agent in the Chicago office accidentally shot himself in the foot and was taken to the hospital. Unfortunately for him, the incident was reported in the local newspaper. The agent was denied advance sick leave, censured, put on probation and transferred to Oklahoma City, an unpopular post, considered a disciplinary office. Then there was James P. Hosty, Jr., of the Dallas office, who had the ill fortune of having been assigned the security case on Lee Harvey Oswald, subsequently accused of assassinating President Kennedy. The Warren Commission faulted the FBI for not advising the Secret Service about Oswald's background. Before the commission, Hoover stoutly defended his minion, arguing that there "was nothing up to the time of the assassination that gave any indication this man [Oswald] was a dangerous character . . ." Yet a few months later, when the public was no longer looking, Hoover suspended Hosty without pay for thirty days and transferred him to the disciplinary office at Kansas City.

Every agent realized that he could run afoul of the Director simply by doing his job. In 1969 three New York City agents furnished affidavits to U. S. Attorney Robert M. Morgenthau that were material to his prosecution of Roy Cohn, the late Senator Joseph McCarthy's chief counsel. Cohn retained a friendship with Hoover dating from the witch-hunt days. When word got to the Director, the transfers read Lousiville, Pittsburgh and St. Louis. When Morgenthau protested to John Malone, New York agent in charge, the three agents were given only thirty-six hours to get out of town.

II: *Bureaucratic Bullying and Bungling*

Incidents of this sort, which make the rounds as "horror stories," happen so frequently that the Bureau has become virtually a paranoiac society. In fact, it would appear that FBI officials want it that way. I recall that our new agents' class was told a horror story by Assistant Director Hugh Clegg, then head of the Training and Inspection Division. It was about the rookie whose locked car had been broken into and his FBI manual stolen. The Washington Metropolitan Police caught the thief and had the pleasure of returning the manual. Declared Clegg gravely, "That agent is no longer with us."

Agents in training during the 1940s remember a different horror story as their introduction. An agent assigned to the Butte office, a bachelor, was dating a young lady, and she admitted to her mother that they had had sexual relations. The mother called the sheriff. Unable to mollify her, the sheriff notified the FBI. An inspector was sent out from Washington, and, despite the fact that the couple intended to marry, prevailed on the local district attorney to prosecute the agent for rape. I am sure that no rookie in those classes missed the point that the wayward agent was sentenced to fifty years in the penitentiary.

Contributing to the paranoia is the fact that any agent privy to a rules violation is expected under pain of equal penalty to report it to his superiors. Most "submarines," as the tattlers are termed, have their periscopes showing, but occasionally an agent is unexpectedly "torpedoed."

Jack Shaw was one. Shaw had had second thoughts about

his partly critical letter to the college professor and had torn it up and dropped it in the wastebasket in the steno pool. But while it was being typed, an agent had peered over the shoulder of the typist and caught some of the heretical passages. Ten agents descended on the pool, retrieved the pieces and assembled the letter. Although Shaw argued that he was "entitled to the privacy of my thoughts," the bumptious John Malone retorted, "You're an FBI agent from the top of your head to the tip of your toes and anything you write belongs to the FBI."

Even non-agent personnel are expected to be informers. In 1965 a fellow employee of clerk Thomas H. Carter tipped off headquarters that a young lady had spent two nights in his apartment. Carter freely conceded the fact, but maintained that she was merely visting from his home town in Oklahoma and nothing improper had taken place. Fired for "conduct unbecoming an employee," Carter was ordered reinstated by the courts.

Enforcement of the codes is carried out by the Internal Inspection Division, until recently headed by W. Mark Felt. Each office is inspected at least once a year. The inspectors' arrival is supposed to be a surprise, but the field offices generally find out ahead of time. Most special agents in charge (SACs) prepare by means of a self-inspection. Investigative activities slow to a crawl as agents polish their desk tops and clean the drawers, pore over daily records for the previous months to weed out errors, and review case files for errors of commission and omission. Once I was "written up" because an item not on the approved list was in my desk—an airline brochure. The offense cost me a meritorious pay raise that had been in order for outstanding performance.

Not all of the inspectors who pass judgment on the agents are top investigators in their own right. During an inspection of the Seattle office a waspish little man named Marlin Johnson chewed out several agents he deemed unproductive in developing informants—"jellyfish," he labeled them. I checked, and the word was that Johnson hadn't developed a single confidential informant himself at his last post as an agent. Yet he was on the way up, and a stint on the inspection staff is one step on the ladder. Today he is a SAC in a major office.

Sometimes an inspection team arrives with the intent of "getting" a SAC, often for whimsical reason. Several years ago Chief Inspector Gale disapproved of pictures on the office wall of the San Francisco SAC, thus setting off write-ups of agents for everything from scuffed shoes to dirty cars. The office was put on probation, and the SAC demoted to a small office.

On the other hand, some inspections are predetermined to be whitewashes, especially when a politically wired SAC is involved. For the seven-odd years that Richard A. Auerbach was SAC at Seattle, he was able to boast that his agents had not received a single letter of censure. Auerbach had been secretary to the late Senator Styles Bridges of New Hampshire and close to Edgar Eisenhower, the late President's brother. Another untouchable was SAC Wesley Grapp of Los Angeles; his political godfather was Senator Karl Mundt of South Dakota.

In a 1968 letter to the Attorney General, Los Angeles agents contended that myriad allegations against their SAC would have been easy to confirm. The letter continued: "Hoover sent a top aide, Mark Felt, out here and Felt turned up dozens of serious derelictions but he, too, is afraid of Grapp. Felt did something unknown in F.B.I. inspections—he turned the damaging allegations back to Grapp to handle, to the bitter disgust of all of us here." Before Hoover's death, Felt was promoted to the No. 3 spot behind Hoover and Tolson, and there was speculation that he might be the heir apparent.

An inspection team seeking to find fault with an individual or an office has not only the surfeit of rules and regulations to exploit, but a morass of forms and documents that invite mistakes and errors. It is hard to imagine a bureaucracy more paper-bound than the FBI. Some of the forms had legitimate origins, but the proliferation of paper work mirrors Hoover's distrust of his agents and how they spend their time.

Exhibit 1 is FD-256, better known as the No. 3 card, because it follows the No. 1 and No. 2 sign-in and sign-out registers, the Bureau equivalents of the time clock. In the distant past the 3 card was a guide to where the agent might be located in case of emergency. It has columns for the times he enters the office, leaves, probable time of return, the file numbers of cases he expects to work on, destinations (name, address and telephone numbers) and the precise times he calls in as recorded by the switchboard operator. All times are expressed to the minute. The advent of the radio car made the 3 card obsolete. But it was not abandoned.

Down at the bottom are a row of tabulations to be calculated from data on the card: VOT, TIO, ATIO, TOPCI, TOPSI, TOPRI. VOT is Voluntary Overtime. It represents the excess over regular business hours. The bureau-wide total is computed each year. Hoover proffered these hundreds of thousands of hours to the Appropriations subcommittee as a direct savings to the taxpayer: they obviate the need to hire so many additional agents at so many millions of dollars.

In the field there is nothing spontaneous or voluntary about VOT. The offices tabulate an office average on a monthly basis. Agents who are below the average, even by a few minutes, are hauled on the carpet for "not sharing the workload." No matter that some agents are simply more efficient than others: the time's the thing. So foot-dragging and padding have become a way of life. A number of agents have been caught altering 3 cards and registers. Claiming VOT while eating supper, bowling, going to the movies and having a few in a bar is not uncommon.

TIO stands for Time in Office. Theoretically, cases are not solved in the office; so the Bureau has set an arbitrary maximum of 15 per cent. But the proliferation of paperwork has made this figure unrealistic for all but the most facile at dictation and administration. Some agents head over to the public library or other retreat to fight the paper war, while others resort to phonying the figures. Some TIO is obligatory: conferences, special projects and so forth. It is permissible to subtract this time, the net being shown as Adjusted Time in Office in the ATIO space.

TOPCI is Time on Potential Criminal Informants; TOPSI is for Security Informants. Informants are the primary investigative technique. Lately there has been a third category, TOPRI, for Racial Informants. Woe betide the agent deemed not putting in sufficient hours in the cultivation of informants.

Predictably, the accent on time for its own sake spawns duplicity and mendacity. A guileless young Detroit agent at in-service training in Washington in 1959 was interviewed by John Malone. Was there anything on his mind? Well, yes, there was. It was a shame, the agent ventured, that those who padded their VOT received raises while those who didn't, didn't. And did *he* pad *his*? Yes. The agent was instantly fired and the Detroit office subjected to an inspection that resulted in the demotion and transfer of the SAC and several supervisors.

III: *Personnel Policies and the Conservative Profile*

Why do agents join up to begin with? And why do so many stay to retirement? A couple of decades ago the romantic image of the FBI attracted applicants in droves. The salary was—and still is—the highest in federal law enforcement, nearly double the Secret Service and Bureau of Narcotics. Once in, and struck with the realization that the emperor wore no clothes, the agent had a choice: he could stay long enough to let the prestige rub off, or he could adjust himself to the environment.

Those who opt for the latter point toward retirement benefits unexcelled in government: after twenty years, one third pay, and after thirty, two thirds. Since a senior agent can make, without assuming administrative responsibilities, in the neighborhood of $20,000 a year, it is easy to understand why 50 per cent of the agent corps has over ten years' service.

The most serious indictment of FBI personnel policies is the turnover among those with little time invested. It reached a point in 1961 where recruits were required to sign an agreement to stay at least three years. Fewer applicants appeared, forcing the Bureau to recruit aggressively and set up quotas for each office.

One of the most durable components of the FBI myth is that all agents are lawyers or accountants. This has not been true since the 1930s, when the agency was much smaller. The FBI's own statistics reveal that in 1960 only 30.3 per cent of the agents held law degrees and 12.6 were accountants; by 1970 the percentages had slipped to 22.3 and 9.1 respectively.

The educational prerequisites have been steadily broadened. In 1960 the Bureau began proselytizing science graduates. In 1961 it went after insurance adjusters, ex-military investigators and persons "in private industry in a substantial capacity." At the time headquarters warned the field offices: "As these qualifications are temporary, there should be no publicity nor public announcements." A decade later the "temporary" situation had become more acute, with schoolteachers and former Vietnam military officers the particular targets of recruitment.

To be hired, an applicant must survive a written test, personal interview and penetrating background investigation. The decision rests with Washington, and the criteria applied over the years were those of an overwhelmingly white Christian agent staff. In my estimation the two largest blocs were Protestants from southern and midwestern universities and Irish Catholics from Fordham, Boston College and similar sectarian institutions. The Ivy League had only token representation. The Mormon complement far exceeded its population ratio. As a group, the agents were what is now called Middle American—firmly anti-Communist, politically conservative, illiberal regarding subcultures and minorities and slightly anti-intellectual.

There were few Jews in the FBI, even in the clerical departments. I don't recall ever encountering an Oriental employee. But the Bureau's discrimination was most notorious in the dearth of blacks. In five field offices and a number of trips to Washington, I never encountered a black employee; month after month through the pages of the house organ *The Investigator* hardly a black face appeared. There were a half-dozen black "agents," but this was showcasing, since none had been through the FBI Academy like the rest of us and all were assigned the simplest of cases.

Robert Kennedy brought at least token integration to the FBI. Kennedy was the first Attorney General to try to lay down the law to Hoover, and hiring policy was part of it. Faced with the inevitable, the Bureau chief displayed his remarkable ability to turn defeat into victory. First, the personable Harvey Foster, then SAC at New York, went to work on a fellow Notre Dame alumnus, Aubrey C. Lewis. Lewis was black, a football All-American who had gone on to the Chicago Bears. Next a reporter for *Ebony* was invited to headquarters and afforded one of those rare interviews with the Director. *Ebony* fell for it. In the issue of September,

1962, it ran a feature story "The Negro in the FBI." Photos depicted Lewis at the FBI Academy studying, on the shooting range, at dinner.

"The newest Negro fledgling," the article called him, "one of the most promising men recruited for action." Unmentioned was the fact that Lewis was the first black agent to go through the Academy since it had opened a quarter century before.

Where were other black agents assigned? "On cases in every part of the country," Hoover temporized. How many were there? Can't disclose the "tricks of the trade," he parried. *Ebony* apparently didn't detect the cynicism; it played the story straight and allowed the impression to remain that the FBI was an equal opportunity employer.

Recently columnist Carl Rowan put pressure on the Department of Justice to release FBI minority employment statistics. They had been as hard to come by as Kremlin secrets. On November 25, 1970, Rowan repeated what Hoover himself said he told Robert Kennedy: "Now, Bobby, I have no prejudices. The FBI has Negro agents, Indian agents, Chinese agents, and all kinds of other agents. Anyone who can meet the qualifications can have a job." The implication was that not many blacks possessed the educational qualifications, prompting Rowan to ask, "How many white FBI agents do not have law or accounting degrees?" The FBI declined to state, and Justice would only say that "about 1400 blacks are employed by the FBI."

Rowan kept at it, with the result that on January 9, 1971, Justice gave out the figures. There were fifty-one black *agents*, less than half of 1 per cent. There were three Indians. Of the total work force, agent and clerical, less than 10 per cent belonged to minority groups. Tokenism still prevailed.

Lately charges of sex discrimination have been raised because there are no female agents. Indeed, the Bureau has been a bastion of male chauvinism. When a woman was absolutely required on a surveillance, one of the senior stenographers would be pressed into service. The status quo has been challenged by twenty-eight-year-old Sandra Rothenberg of Denver, Colorado, a lawyer married to a psychiatrist. Her first application for the agent position, filed in 1968, was bemusedly sidetracked with the query, "How fast can you type?"

In 1970 her interest was renewed by reading that women were becoming U. S. Treasury enforcement agents and sky marshals. This seemed to repudiate the FBI's excuses that women were unacceptable because of the "hazardous nature" and "strenuous physical exertion" involved. Rebuffed once again, Mrs. Rothenberg filed suit in U.S. district court in Washington charging sex discrimination.

Once accepted, employees had to adhere not only to Hoover's puritanical behavior codes but to outmoded standards of appearance. In a *Time* magazine interview on December 14, 1970, the Director observed, "You won't find long hair or sideburns à la [Joe] Namath here. There are no hippies. The public has an image of what an FBI agent should look like."

When I was in the agency, instructors drummed into us that we must dress and act "like young businessmen." Once I was told to get rid of a brush cut; another time I was criticized for wearing a sports coat to the office; on several occasions I was admonished to wear a fedora.

Violators are landed on heavily. One time the Director spotted a news photo of an agent with a cigarette dangling from his lips and handed out a letter of censure and transfer. In 1971 Hoover noticed that agent John F. Mullen of the Richmond office, who was photographed escorting an airplane hijack suspect, had sideburns even with the bottom of his ear. Mullen was shipped to Indianapolis.

The conservatism applies to politics. Liberals are not an FBI commodity, as the case of two young ladies from Mississippi and Virginia attests. Both were safely apolitical when recruited as fingerprint clerks, but they metamorphosized into peace advocates while working in the nation's capital. Linda Janca and Janice Bush both spent off-duty hours as volunteers for the National Peace Action Coalition, and their employer got wind of it.

Interrogated by their supervisor about their political views —"He was kind of cold," Miss Janca remembers—they were ordered to cease peace activities or resign. Both chose the latter, Miss Janca writing "Peace" as her reason for leaving. The ACLU instituted a suit on their behalf in the hope of preventing Hoover from interfering with off-the-job activities of others.

On the face of it Hoover's insistence that agents appear in the image and likeness of Efrem Zimbalist, Jr., would seem to have impaired the agency's investigative aims. For example, agents of the Federal Bureau of Narcotics and Dangerous Drugs are such a heterogeneous lot that they have been able to meld with the European and American underworlds to score signal successes. Police departments deploy their men in undercover roles. But the FBI's college fraternity types can't pass for anything except G-men.

The difference is that the FBI relies on informants—persons who themselves are part of the criminal or "subversive" milieu and are willing, for one motive or another, to feed back information. Informant payments are made from confidential "blue slip" funds, the total being one of the FBI's best-kept secrets. By purchasing information rather than obtaining it through other investigative techniques, the FBI gains a measure of protection against "embarrassment to the Bureau"; should a case backfire the informant can be piously disowned.

IV: *The Loyal Alumni*

There are, roughly, ten thousand ex-agents. Many have moved over to other government bureaus such as the IRS, the CIA and the Secret Service, whose chief, James Rowley, is a onetime Hoover underling. Others remain "in the business" by joining the security departments of large corporations. Ford and Sears, Roebuck are prime job markets for resigned or superannuated FBI men, Sears by virtue of Hoover's affinity for the late General Robert E. Wood, a Sears chairman active in right-wing councils, and Ford through Henry Ford, a Bureau friend who needed little persuasion to pick up the sponsorship of "The FBI" on television.

Many alumni become private investigators. Fidelifacts is a nationwide franchise operation that exploits the FBI name. Private eye Vincent Gillen gained notoriety as the sleuth hired by General Motors to spy on Ralph Nader. The Wackenhut Corporation, a Florida outfit headed by George Wackenhut, a former agent, made news a few years ago as what some called Governor Claude Kirk's "private gestapo."

Local law enforcement is liberally sprinkled with conservative ex-FBIers. Joseph I. Woods is the Matt Dillon sheriff of Cook County, Illinois. Peter Pitchess heads the nation's largest law-enforcement body, the Los Angeles County sheriff's office. Advertising executive Emmett C. McGaughey is a Los Angeles police commissioner. Former Los Angeles District Attorney Evelle Younger is now California's attorney general. The list goes on.

Politics has attracted alumni. Younger aspires to be governor of California. William T. Cahill is governor of New Jersey. A sizable congressional delegation is led by H. Allen Smith of California, an ultraconservative who not long ago introduced a bill requiring that the next FBI Director be appointed from the inside. Robert E. Lee sits among the FCC commissioners critical of television news reporting.

The landscape of ideological politics is dotted with former agents. Alan Belemont, who led the Domestic Intelligence Division is with the rightist Hoover Institute on War, Revolution and Peace at Stanford. W. Cleon Skousen, once a John Birch Society functionary, travels the right-wing lecture circuit. Dan Smoot broadcasts the right-wing line. John W. Fisher and several other former agents run the American Security Council, a lobbying and propaganda group that promotes the Cold War and the military establishment.

Executive suites are occupied: Harold M. Perry is president of the huge CIT Financial Corporation; John D. Steward is a vice-president of American Express; George V. Myers is a vice-president of Standard Oil of Indiana and Kenneth M. Piper is personnel director of Motorola—to name a few.

About half the alumni have seen fit to join the New York-based Society of Former Special Agents of the FBI. The society has local chapters and holds an annual convention. The 1971 affair was addressed by Spiro Agnew. On the practical side, it has an "Executive Services" committee, in effect a placement bureau that recently reported having "placed 39 Society members with an average salary of $19,750."

The society has made a fetish of Hoover artifacts, distributing a desk-top bust of The Man and selling at reduced prices an anthology called *J. Edgar Hoover on Communism* (New York: Random House, 1969). The society defends the legend with crusading zeal. For example, in 1964 when *Life* hinted it might be time for Hoover to step down, then-president Emmett McGaughey replied, "The amalgam that binds the agents of the FBI to the bureau is Mr. Hoover and his leadership. He is also the amalgam that binds the 4,600 members of our organization together in our devotion to each other, to the Federal Bureau of Investigation, and to

Mr. Hoover, whose life is the fulfillment of the motto of the
FBI: fidelity, bravery, integrity."

This kind of stuff obviously borders on the fanatic, which
makes the penetration of society members into the corridors
of American power all the more disturbing.

So the paradox of the FBI goes on. Its public image is one
of brisk effectiveness, of up-to-the-minute techniques. In reality it is one of the most reactionary bureaus in government,
riding the momentum of long ago.

Its executives are mostly senescent, in outlook as well as
age. Hoover died at seventy-seven, an anachronism. His alter
ego Clyde Tolson, an ailing seventy-one, needed a presidential
waiver to stay on past the mandatory retirement age of
seventy, but could never have passed the physical such a
waiver requires. So Hoover bypassed the law by retiring him,
then rehiring him under a legal proviso allowing employment
of retired personnel on a temporary basis to complete projects they had been working on. Ten others past seventy have
lingered on by the use of this ploy. At fifty-nine, Mark Felt,
an important official, is a relative youngster.

What the FBI needs is not more Mark Felts who have
inched their way up Hoover's promotional ladder, but a massive transfusion of new blood with fresh ideas and new approaches—outsiders not tied to the legend, able to bridge
the age and culture gaps. For the FBI's own attitudinal
weaknesses have rendered it obsolete in a rapidly changing
environment.

V: Conference Discussion by Panel of Former Agents

Mr. Blair Clark:* I would like to get two things out of
this dialogue. One is some notion of your own experience in
the Bureau, in order to shed some light on how the Bureau

* Member of the Executive Council, Committee for Public Justice.

actually operates. Second, I would like your own ideas and notions of how you could have operated more effectively given the purposes the Bureau was set up to fulfill. I think I'll start by asking you, Bob Wall, to tell your own history of roughly five years in the FBI in about three or four minutes.

MR. WALL: That's a big order in a short time. But, briefly, I spent most of my time in the field of what we call internal security or national security and I worked in the Washington field office, which was a clearinghouse for many of the national investigations of such organizations as anti-war groups and the draft card burners.

I went into the Bureau with a very naïve outlook. I was completely apolitical; I had a very conservative family background. But, unfortunately, I never stopped asking questions and this eventually led to my leaving the Bureau.

When I was working in internal security, we were called upon to cover demonstrations. We went out and photographed people who were there, took license numbers, tried to identify people and copied down what the speaker said.

I began to ask, "Why are we covering this demonstration?" And inevitably someone would respond that the Communist party is attempting to infiltrate the peace movement or attempting to infiltrate the civil rights movement and we're here to find the hidden Communist infiltrators and thereby protect the organization and protect America. But it didn't take the agents on the street too long to realize that here really wasn't much of a Communist menace in the sense that Mr. Hoover was speaking of it.

Nevertheless, the Bureau's rationale carried over to all of the people who were involved. It wasn't possible to go back to the office and simply report on one person whom we saw at this large demonstration and who was, according to Bureau records, a Communist. Rather, we were bringing in each and every person we could photograph or whose license number we could get. We were opening investigations and compiling dossiers on people whose sole interest in the rally was the fact that the war was going on and they wanted to see it end.

I personally was beginning to become very much disturbed by this shotgun approach. We had it in the anti-war movement and we certainly had it in the racial field. It was a kind of predetermined bias that anyone who would be so rash as to go out there and say something against the American war policy was a bad guy who had to be watched and watched closely.

The chilling effect that we heard spoken of this morning is a very real thing in the FBI investigations. You can't walk up to a relative or an employer or a friend or a neighbor of a person and tell them you're an FBI agent investigating their neighbor or employee or friend or relative and convince them that you're not doing it because a guy really needs an investigation. In other words, the agent leaves a very strong impression that somehow or other this guy is really a bad guy and you should watch out for him too.

The crushing of human relationships that results was more than I could take and I attempted on a number of occasions to find out some specific guidelines. Unfortunately, you don't get answers to your questions despite Mr. Hoover's statement that he's open to criticism and answers criticisms and comments. I never received any answer.

I think one story I'll relate tells a lot about the way the Bureau operates. It pertains to a school. We received directions, and I was unfortunate enough to get the case assigned to me, to investigate the school. It was run by former associates or friends or relatives of Black Panthers. There was, in any event, some relationship between the individuals running the school and Black Panthers. And I was understandably concerned because the FBI had made the Black Panther party into a real national menace, although I don't think it warranted that label on its own.

But I spent a considerable amount of time doing this investigation. I had no less than six informants working, two under my direct control and four others assigned to other agents. But we had these six informants infiltrate the school because a supervisor at the Bureau stated that this school was being used as a base for training guerrillas, for making Molotov cocktails, for instructing the young blacks in the neighborhood in how to go about destroying things and bombing things.

In addition to the informant coverage, we also had intensive surveillance, physical surveillance by myself and other agents, at all hours of the day and night. We set up stationary lookouts. We had movable lookouts. We went so far as to request, but were refused, permission to install technical surveillance.

At any rate at the end of a six-month investigation I compiled a report in which I said the school is a school, and we should cease our investigation. Three days later I received what we call a "green weanie," which is a special Bureau directive. It's on green paper and it means either something very good or something very bad. It was so brief I knew it couldn't be good. It said, simply, in three paragraphs, either the agent is naïve, he doesn't know how to handle informants or the informants are deluding him.

That was the straw that broke the camel's back, if you will, and shortly after that I resigned. I found out later that the Bureau ordered an intensive reinvestigation of the whole thing with more manpower assigned, more informants, and agreed to some technical surveillance.

So that's the trouble with the Bureau. It needs some help. It needs somebody to draw lines so that they know where they're going, who they are investigating and why they're investigating. Those lines don't exist now.

MR. SHAW: I'd like to bring up one point about criticism. I think every agent walks away from the Bureau with a feeling of great ambivalence no matter what circumstances he leaves under. And the reason for that ambivalence is that the Bureau, to its credit, to the Director's credit, has established a wonderful public image, a public image which, I believe, is much deserved. But it's not a perfect organization and the thesis of my letter was, and the thesis of my remarks today is, that any human organization, within the context of an academic argument at any rate, can be described as an imperfect institution. And arguing ideally, within an academic context, we would hope that we would be able to discuss certain imperfections, certain means of improving this system.

Mr. Hoover came into power on the basis of a reform program. He was known as a great reformer and a great innovator. I think that if there's one thing lacking in the FBI today, it is innovation; it is lack of reforms in certain key areas. I notice in Mr. Hoover's letter, addressed to the conference, that even he believed the FBI deserves some criticism, though he also believed it deserves an acquittal.

Mr. Hoover recently wrote an article about turmoil on campuses and disunity and dissension among the youth of this country. Mr. Hoover in that article addressed himself to the business community, the businessmen of the United States, and he asked them, he remonstrated with them, to take a closer look at themselves and their practices and to reform their businesses. He urged them to do away with the malpractice and the dishonesty and the white-collar crime and the other things that led the younger generation to believe businessmen were hypocrites. Mr. Hoover said in that article that any organization that is not willing to take a long look at itself, to critically appraise itself and to reset its directions has died.

I remember one sentence in my letter of censure, my letter

of criticism, which I received after the facts of my case were reviewed and before I left the Bureau. The only violation, the only charge brought against me, was that I had prepared a communication for a person outside the Bureau which contained criticisms of the Bureau, and that I had failed to report criticism by a person outside the Bureau to my FBI superiors.

I have a difficult time analyzing and accepting either of those pronouncements on criticism. Consequently, I'll leave it up to further discussion. But this is the crisis within the Bureau today. The agents are not about to abandon their organization. It's a fine, worthy organization. I think they are struggling with the same slogan that we see on bumper stickers: "America, love it or leave it."

I think that within the Bureau, the alternatives should not be that extreme. But the difficulty is that any agent who desires to voice change or to discuss openly, or perhaps not openly, some areas of criticism based on his own experience, based on his own investigation and based on the intransigence which he sees around him, that agent becomes immediately marked for administrative difficulties and perhaps dismissal from the service.

MR. CLARK: What is it that you felt you should have been doing rather than some of the trivia that Bill Turner has written about and the others have discussed, and on which there's quite a literature? In other words, did you feel that the petty bureaucratic routine, as it's been described, frustrated you from doing an effective job at what you were supposed to be doing, namely investigating and enforcing the law?

MR. TURNER: One of the criticisms I had of the Bureau when I wrote to Congress in 1961 was a certain amount of looking the other way with regard to organized crime. I felt that this kind of nonfeasance against the really top hoodlums, as opposed to the car thief who happens to wander across a state line and become a Bureau statistic, was an aberration of the law-enforcement mission. And I said so. Since during most of my career I was in criminal work, I was oriented that way.

MR. WILKINS: What are the possibilities for change within the Bureau if there is a new Director?

MR. TURNER: The Bureau has been created in the image and likeness of J. Edgar Hoover and reflects to an extraordinary degree the man's own personal prejudices, strong points, weak points, whims and fancies. I think the important thing now is an overhaul, after some forty-eight years of one-man rule, and a complete reevaluation of the Bureau.

I would like to speculate on possible successors. I think that if Mr. Nixon is in we would get one type of Director, just as we get one type of Supreme Court nominee. And if a Democratic administration is in, perhaps we'll get a different type of Director.

I'm awfully afraid that Mr. Nixon would appoint somebody who was a high executive in the Bureau for many years but is no longer there. For example, Cartha DeLoach, who retired from the Bureau at age fifty, has for the last year been at PepsiCo, which happens to be headed by Donald M. Kendall, one of Mr. Nixon's financial angels. DeLoach could be appointed as both an outside business official and a man with an intimate knowledge of the Bureau. This would appease two factions, and, I think, is a very Nixonian thing to do.

But I would like to see someone appointed who has not had a long association with Mr. Hoover in the higher councils of the Bureau.

MR. WILKINS: Could a genuine outsider change the institution?

MR. TURNER: I think so. I think, to Hoover's vast credit, the Bureau is virtually self-functioning; it goes of its own momentum. Therefore, I think if there is a man with the right philosophy who sets policy at the top, change could be very rapid.

Mr. Richard Wright:† Mr. Wall has already indicated that he is an ideologically disaffected agent, so I won't direct this question to him. I would like to ask Mr. Turner and Mr. Shaw —I presume their interest is in constructive criticism of the FBI, in improving the FBI's ability to combat crime and revolutionary terrorism—if either of them has any substantial disagreement with any of the papers presented here? Do you think, for instance, there is ever any need to photograph people or record their license plate numbers at political meetings?

Mr. Turner: I think you should direct that question to Jack Shaw. I don't have substantial disagreement. I've written for such subversive magazines as *The Nation* and *The Progressive*. So maybe Jack had better answer that.

Mr. Wright: Well, you have answered the question then.

Mr. Shaw: I didn't work those cases. I certainly worked espionage cases and I feel that the mode of investigation you suggest can be defended. I assume this could also be justified in other types of cases. It depends on the substance of the case and the nature of the allegation. I think the Bureau does a great job where it can devote its personnel to a Ku Klux Klan case or whatever.

But your question was how to make the Bureau more effective. The problem is that in the broad day-to-day operations of the Bureau, programs get established, empires are built. And when empires are built, one begins, after a while, to justify his own existence by creating squads within squads within his empire, however small.

At the same time, the Bureau has been given more to do today than ever before. This is not necessarily the fault of the Bureau, but it raises problems. There are 180 separate violations for which the FBI has responsibility and the Bureau can pick and choose its areas of emphasis. It can choose to ignore civil rights violations and concentrate on solving minor

† Associate Executive Director, Americans for Effective Law Enforcement.

or relatively petty thefts from interstate commerce because there are more convictions there.

What I am suggesting and what I was arguing for when I was an agent is a review of the Bureau's programs and the best use of its available personnel. How can these men be best utilized in the twentieth-century world of crime and crime fighting? How can we maximize their investigative ingenuity and their abilities? These are questions the Bureau must answer.

PART II
LESS THAN PERFECT
PERFORMANCE

CHAPTER FIVE

THE FBI AND OTHER POLICE FORCES

BY WILLIAM W. TURNER

I: Counterespionage and Criminal Law Enforcement

One internal difficulty of the Bureau that has been little noted is the strain of the dual role of law enforcement and counterespionage. The latter drains off energies that ought to be applied to the former. It contributes to the Bureau's debilitating feuds with other intelligence-gathering agencies and is a reason for the Bureau's difficulties with other law-enforcement agencies.

The United States is the only major power vesting counterespionage and criminal responsibilities under one roof. On the face of it, counterespionage and criminal investigation are as immiscible as oil and water. They demand different approaches, different degrees of sophistication, different techniques. The FBI is not capable of doing both competently. It should not be expected to.

In fact, the FBI became saddled with counterespionage work on top of its criminal jurisdiction through the circumstances of the time. Until war clouds began to gather in the 1930s, the United States was a vulnerable innocent in what has been called the Secret War. There was no civilian agency carrying on either espionage or counterespionage.

During World War I the Secret Service had stepped into the breach to oppose the Kaiser's spies, with some success. But between the wars military agencies, the Office of Naval Intelligence (ONI) and the Army's G-2 and Counterintelligence Corps (CIC), were engaged in the field, while the State Department had a small security group. Since their concern was primarily with military intelligence, espionage and counterespionage of a political, industrial, diplomatic and economic nature were lacking.

There was considerable sentiment that "black operations" were not befitting a democracy. But it also became patent that espionage directed at the United States was under way. The efforts of Soviet spies Nicholas Dozenberg, William Gregory Burton, Alfred Tilton and Valentine Markin can be traced as far back as the mid-1920s. In September of 1938 one Mikhail Nicholas Gorin forgot to remove stolen ONI documents from a suit he sent to the cleaners, which resulted in his exposure as an agent for GRU (Red Army intelligence). He was the first Soviet operative to be prosecuted. During the mid-1930s the Nazis began to set up espionage networks, while on the West Coast Japanese spying became perceptible.

In 1939 President Roosevelt entrusted Hoover with domestic security, including counterespionage, rather than openly establishing an agency capable of specializing in such work.

The need for wartime propaganda victories was instrumental in burnishing the Bureau's spy-catching reputation. The biggest coup was the capture of eight saboteurs landed by submarine on Long Island, and the FBI's role was exaggerated. Similarly overblown was the FBI's Special Intelligence Service (SIS), created to check German moves in South America. It was upon the legend of SIS that Hoover made his postwar bid for overseas power. With the wartime Office of Strategic Services (OSS) disbanded, there was a vacuum. But President Harry Truman, evidently wary of Hoover's ambitions, established the Central Intelligence Agency (CIA) instead. The FBI was limited to counterespionage within the United States.

Typically, the FBI has been portrayed to the American people as the infallible counterspy, a fable fed as much by the so-called Atom Spies case as was its criminal image by the Dillinger affair. In his pro-FBI book, *The FBI Story*, Don Whitehead describes the charged moment when, in September, 1949, Hoover was informed that the Soviets had pulled off an espionage coup. "Hoover reached for the intercom telephone. He gave a series of orders to his key subordinates and soon the vast machinery of the FBI was in high gear. In essence, Hoover's orders were 'The secret of the atomic bomb has been stolen. Find the thieves!'"

Find the thieves, indeed. The object of counterespionage is to thwart espionage, and in this case the thefts had occurred more than five years earlier.

What is remarkable about the subsequent belated FBI probe is that it took so long to resolve. The main purveyor of information was a physicist, Klaus Fuchs, whose name had been in a notebook taken from the Soviet Embassy safe in Canada by a defector and turned over to the FBI in 1945. The courier, Harry Gold, was brought before a federal grand jury in 1947 and admitted being "on the fringe of espionage"; yet we are regaled with tales of FBI doggedness in checking long lists of chemists to identify him. And Julius Rosenberg, who was fingered by Gold, had been questioned by the FBI in 1945 and ousted as a "security risk" from his government job.

So Julius and Ethel Rosenberg, minor cogs at best, were tried and executed in the apex of McCarthy era "justice." That wrapped it up. "Nine months after J. Edgar Hoover flashed the warning that atomic secrets had been stolen by agents of a foreign power," *The FBI Story* bragged, "the whole wretched story of espionage was known to the FBI."

The Bureau had briefly questioned sometime friends of the Rosenbergs, Morris and Lona Cohen. As it turned out the Cohens were the real professionals, but the FBI didn't recognize the fact. After the questioning, the Cohens slipped out of the United States and, in 1961, as Mr. and Mrs. Peter Kroger, were arrested by British counterespionage authorities as belonging to a ring stealing secrets of nuclear-powered submarines.

Also in the British net was Conon Molody, alias Gordon Lonsdale, another Soviet professional. What makes this doubly damning to the FBI is that Molody had operated undetected in the United States from 1950 to 1955. His superior: the vaunted Colonel Rudolf I. Abel, later exchanged for U-2 pilot Francis Gary Powers. Abel himself had operated unmolested in the United States for nine years and might still be here were it not for a bibulous subagent who defected to the CIA in Paris. When FBI agents, acting on the defector's information, searched Abel's New York apartment, they found a photograph of the Cohens, alias Krogers.

The front-page spy stories that recount how the Bureau uncloaked yet another ring are, almost without exception, the product of surveillance of "legals"—diplomatic and commercial attachés who enter the country overtly under their own names. They are easy to find. It is the "illegal," the highly trained professional who slips across the border or enters under a false identity, who poses the greatest challenge. The quintessential spy Colonel Abel was an illegal: he entered surreptitiously from Canada in 1948 and set up a cover as Emil Goldfus, photographer. But Abel was an accidental catch. To my knowledge the only time the FBI ferreted out an illegal strictly through its own prowess was the unmasking of Kaarlo Tuomi by Nelson Gibbons.

One problem is the intense rivalry with the CIA. Theoretically, the CIA plays an offensive role abroad and the FBI a defensive one at home, but as the Abel case illustrates, these functions can overlap. Each agency has poached on the other's turf. Through agents posted as "legal attachés" to U.S. embassies, the Bureau has carried on its own foreign intelligence; last year, with the addition of six new "liaison posts," operations were extended to seventeen countries. For its part, the CIA has widespread domestic operations.

Each resents the other's encroachments, with the result that exchange of information is not as free as it might be. Compounding the problem was Hoover's long-smoldering resentment that the CIA even exists. Several years ago he bitterly complained that it was luring away many of his agents (most were merely escaping his punitive policies). After the Bay of Pigs, he spread the word around official Washington that the FBI should take over the bumbling CIA. At Langley, Hoover was known as "that cop," while at 9th and Pennsylvania the CIA Director Richard Helms is disparaged as "Princeton Ought-Ought" and his brain trust as "high-domed theoreticians."

This cop-versus-intellectual distinction points up another FBI lack in the counterespionage field. Hoover's views were essentially those of a cop—he oversimplified and failed to comprehend nuances and subtleties. In my experience, most FBI agents are not only unsuited to counterespionage, they don't want it. The Bureau made its mark early in criminal detection and the agency's recruiting and training programs are heavily loaded in that direction. Nor did Hoover tolerate the kind of unorthodox, semi-Bohemian, perhaps long-haired individual who traditionally has made the best counterspy. Such types are, however, welcomed by the CIA.

The imperative is clear. The FBI should be divested of its counterespionage responsibilities, which are incompatible with the Bureau's essentially criminal investigative nature. However, I would not recommend that they be turned over to the CIA; that agency is already too large and without effective control. Rather, create a separate division within the Department of Justice that will function under the statutory authority of the Espionage Act and National Security Act. Staff it with imaginative men, and appoint a director willing to operate in obscurity. Call it descriptively the Division of Counterespionage (DCE). And let there be no television series "The DCE." Counterespionage is best conducted backstage, without theatrics.

II: Relationship Between the FBI and Local Police

Despite a public façade of normality, relations between the FBI and local police departments have also been tense for years. It is only natural that the police seethe under the Bureau's air of superiority and the way the Bureau is pampered by Congress and the public. Police repeatedly complain that exchange of information is a "one-way street," and that in cases mutually investigated the G-men have a habit of hogging the credit. There is also the matter of the FBI's "cooperative services"—the central fingerprint file, computer storage and retrieval hookup, laboratory and training programs. They all have strings attached.

As in everything FBI, the Bureau-police relationship has been dominated by the looming personality of Hoover. The police seemed to regard their celebrated colleague with mixed emotions. When the FBI chief spoke, the nation listened, and his utterances have been the police cant down the line: court decisions have handcuffed law enforcement, judges and rehabilitation authorities are soft on criminals, a Red conspiracy lurks behind militant movements and civil disturbances.

But any policeman who harbored a distaste for Hoover and the FBI must consider the lesson of William H. Parker. Dour, tough-minded Bill Parker was chief of the Los Angeles police for seventeen years until his death in 1968. Ultraconservative politically, he ran a mechanically proficient, relatively uncorrupt department. Parker's fault, insofar as the FBI was concerned, was that he bowed to no one. Somehow he became embroiled in a feud with Hoover. And for all the years that Parker was chief, not one Los Angeles officer was admitted to the FBI National Academy at Quantico, Virginia. "The FBI would say quotas were filled," Inspector Vernon Hoy, Parker's administrative aide, told me. "But neighboring cities were having men go. We finally got the message and just stopped applying." After Parker's death, Los Angeles officers were again admitted.

Parker suffered other indignities at Hoover's hand. In 1959 he was nominated to become a vice-president of the International Association of Chiefs of Police, from whence he would escalate automatically to the presidency. It was an honor that Parker richly deserved. But when it came to a vote, the name of Chief Philip Purcell of Newton, Massachusetts, was unexpectedly entered from the floor. Purcell was virtually unknown; his principal asset seems to have been his graduation from the FBI National Academy. Purcell won, 319 to 109. Now retired, Purcell confirms that FBI lobbyists blocked the Los Angeles chief. "Oh, yes," he says. "Hoover poisoned Parker."

Parker was again shut off during the December, 1963, investigation of the kidnapping of Frank Sinatra, Jr. Young Sinatra was abducted from a Lake Tahoe motel, but the scene quickly shifted when ransom calls were traced to the Los Angeles area. The case was cracked when one of the kidnappers got cold feet; but for days, as Sinatra's life hung in the balance, the FBI blacked out the Los Angeles Police Department. Parker complained, "This is the first time that we were faced with a problem where there was criminal activity in the City of Los Angeles that was known to a law enforcement agency where we were not permitted to participate."

When President Nixon called a White House meeting of police officials to discuss what might be done about the rash of attacks on officers, Hoover was put in charge of the guest list. Conspicuous by their absence were two key police executives,

Quinn Tamm, executive director of the International Association of Chiefs of Police, and Patrick V. Murphy, New York's commissioner, two of whose men, ironically, had just been shot to death without warning.

Neither had been invited; both were long-time adversaries of the Bureau chief. Tamm, a former FBI assistant director, had quit after a run-in with Hoover. In his IACP post, he had resisted Bureau domination of police affairs. Murphy is a progressive chief whose philosophy was anathema to Hoover.

Hoover's personal prejudices didn't always interfere with law-enforcement concert. During the Hoover-Parker cold war, agents worked quietly with the Los Angeles Police Department. In fact, when I reviewed the organized crime status during an inspection of that office in 1959, practically all of the FBI intelligence and hard data on top hoodlums in the area had come from the files of the police intelligence division.

As long as I can remember, most police departments have made their files available to the Bureau. On a daily basis agents and special employees (a semi-investigative position) simply walk in and help themselves to the records. The FBI does not reciprocate in kind. Information from Bureau files is closed to the police, although some agents quietly and selectively break the rule.

The FBI's failure to cooperate in united Bureau-police drives against organized crime is notorious. On another front, Murray Gross, a New York City assistant district attorney, told a Senate committee on June 9, 1971, that the FBI was not among the cooperative federal agencies trying to cope with the growing problem of securities thefts. Relations with the Secret Service, never too good, worsened recently when the Bureau tried to abort the prosecution of an FBI informant whom the Secret Service had arrested and charged with trying to sell $86,000 worth of stolen government securities.

The FBI's domineering attitude is epitomized in its involvement with the IACP. In 1948 then-Assistant Director Hugh N. Clegg told an IACP convention that the ideal police chief was a man "who cooperates with the FBI in such a generous manner that he has earned our undying gratitude." Such a chief, said Clegg, sends fingerprints to the FBI, sends his "laboratory problems" to the FBI and has his men trained by the FBI. The IACP would respond to this patronizing approach by passing unanimous resolutions (usually drafted by FBI personnel) praising Hoover and his Bureau.

The first step toward liberation of the IACP was the ill-fated Parker for President drive in 1959. The second was the hiring of Quinn Tamm, who in a 1962 debut speech to the membership signaled the end of FBI ascendancy by asserting that the IACP president "must be the spokesman for law enforcement in this country." Eventually the struggle revolved around police training, for which federal funds became available in 1968 through the Law Enforcement Assistance Administration (LEAA).

The FBI lobbied to make its training a condition precedent for any department to obtain LEAA funding. There was a certain presumptiveness in this since the detective squad of a big city department handles more violent, heinous crime in a week than the entire FBI in a year, and police patrols must constantly make instant decisions while the FBI proceeds at a more leisurely pace. Tamm fought the FBI bid, backed by Attorney General Ramsey Clark. Both warned that centralizing police training with the FBI might set the stage for a national police.

Hoover contacted the IACP board of governors and sought Tamm's ouster. The board instead delivered Tamm an overwhelming vote of confidence. Then Hoover had his men lobby at the IACP convention for amendments that would transfer power from Tamm to the group's president, the pro-Hoover Thomas Cahill of San Francisco. Again, Hoover was rebuffed.

But he nevertheless went ahead with grandiose plans for police training, among them a tenfold expansion of the FBI National Academy to accommodate two thousand officers a year. Since graduates of the Academy are expected to act as FBI pipelines, the FBI's influence over the nation's police will be increased exponentially. As Tamm and Clark have suggested, we seem headed in the direction of a *de facto* national police, impelled by the late Mr. Hoover's policies and thirst for power.

I would recommend that police training be left to the police, who could be guided by uniform standards and helped by federal monies. I would propose that the central fingerprint file be turned over to the police, who use it some 99 per cent of the time anyway. I would suggest that the National Crime Information Center, the computerized data bank primarily of assistance to the police, be put under their direction. All these functions could be administered by an organization such as the IACP, with federal assistance.

The dispersal of police powers was an early American premise. It is time to return to that premise.

III: Conference Discussion by Panel on FBI Relations with Local Police

MR. VORENBERG: The major topic to start with is cooperation between the FBI and state and local police. I hope we will have time to look at the question of the role of the FBI in police training, and more broadly, in setting standards for police at the state and local level. I think I'll ask Mr. Glenn if he wants to kick off discussion on this question of cooperation.

MR. GLENN: Before getting into cooperation, there are two comments I'd like to make on training.

There are two examples where the FBI provided a fine service in giving information to local police. First, the Bureau had conferences, in which members of the Department of

Justice or of the United States attorneys' offices participated, to explain to local policemen the meaning of the public accommodations section of the 1964 Civil Rights Act. This may not seem significant, since the local police had no responsibility for the act's enforcement; but it was the local police to whom the corner restaurateur went with questions about the act. I think that making that advice available was a significant contribution. And, second, the FBI did the same thing after the *Miranda* decision. Respect for the FBI is what brought the local police to these training conferences.

Moving on to cooperation, in my judgment there has been too much cooperation. This is particularly true in the civil rights area. In cases where there were allegations of police brutality, for example, it is difficult for me to believe that the FBI's investigations were always impartial. The same thing was true in investigations of harassment of civil rights workers.

There was, for example, a person in South Carolina who was constantly charging harassment by citizens and by local sheriff and other law-enforcement personnel. Each time there would be a request for investigation, and each time the same special agent went back to investigate. And that special agent was very, very close to the sheriff, the man he was investigating.

The worst example, in my judgment, came in February, 1968, at South Carolina State, when the Bureau investigated the role of the South Carolina Highway Patrol in the demonstrations at Orangeburg. The FBI agents were in close company with the very people whom they were called upon to investigate. This inevitably casts doubt on the impartiality of the investigation.

This to me is the prime danger that exists in too close a relationship with local law enforcement; you may someday be called upon to investigate those very people.

MR. VORENBERG: Mr. Young, do you want to comment on

the problem of either too great or too little cooperation in the South?

MR. YOUNG: I would certainly agree that there was too much cooperation. One incident I remember occurred in Winona, Mississippi, when Fannie Lou Hamer and others were taken off a Greyhound bus and beaten in jail. When we went there to get them out of jail, the FBI agent was calmly joking with the police chief in charge. It was obvious that they were very good friends, if not relatives. The agent took the depositions of the persons beaten but he never made an effort to intercede on their behalf, though they were unjustly arrested for using a public bus station. This was some two years after the ICC ruling prohibiting discrimination in the station. I later heard that this same agent was subsequently elected sheriff of that county.

I remember Sheriff Jim Clark saying that his handling of the demonstration in 1965 in Selma, with tear gas and horses, was standard riot control procedure he learned somewhere. He attempted to show, in federal court, certain films which advocated massive use of force in such a situation. But what it proved was an inability to distinguish between a peaceful nonviolent demonstration and a riot. I don't know who was responsible for that training, but you did get the impression that there was a military approach toward persons who were peacefully exercising their constitutional rights.

I think in all these things the FBI was closely involved, and though I can't say that they were responsible for the tactics, they certainly did nothing to prevent them.

MR. VORENBERG: I'd like to broaden the discussion somewhat and look at the role of the Bureau in dealing with the chiefs of police and other top people in major cities. Let's start with you, Vin, what have your experiences been?

MR. BRODERICK: I think an important thing to consider here is the difference between the FBI's responsibilities and the requirements of local law enforcement. There is a basic difference. The FBI has no competence with much of what local police do on a daily basis. The local police officer's job is primarily a job of preventing crime. This means, as a practical matter, that a lot of the crime the local police officer runs into is crime that happens on the street, in his presence. He has to move to deal with it at that point. He has a tremendous amount of discretion. Professor Wilson has pointed this out in his book on varieties of police behavior.

The FBI agent, generally, is dealing with acts after they occur. His job is investigation and detection. He has a different timetable and he has, because of the composition of the Bureau, very little discretion. So when we talk about relationships between the police and the FBI, we really have to consider that their functions are different.

Now there is an overlap. The police force also has a detective function, an after-the-fact detection and investigation function. The FBI has that function, but generally in different sorts of crimes, so there is only a partial overlap. I think that relationships between the FBI and local police, looked at in this context, don't lend themselves to generalization. You have basic policies, written or unwritten, within the Bureau. Those policies say cooperate with the local police. But that cooperation, I think, as a matter of policy, is a one-way street. Get all the information that you can from the local police, but, generally, don't give them information, because it may get into the wrong hands. This arrangement would be unworkable if you didn't have in, I imagine, every city, certainly in New York, personal relationships between FBI people on the scene and the police on the scene. The police do get information when they need it from the FBI, but on a personal rather than an official basis.

This may not be a tragedy, because there are so few areas where cooperation is really important. There is very little that the FBI has to do that overlaps what the police have to do.

Two exceptions are detection and investigation, and intelligence. And in intelligence there does tend to be some exchange of information, at least on the personal level.

In a large city like New York, and I presume this is true elsewhere, the FBI has a mechanism for getting information from the police department and has free access to the police department's files. Obviously, the police do not have this sort of access to FBI files; they get what an agent is prepared to show them, or, occasionally, what is officially submitted to the chief by the special agent in charge.

I think the functional difference between the FBI agent and the police officer is important in the training area also. I really don't think the nature of the FBI lends itself to training local police officers. The police officer has a tremendous amount of discretion; he has to make decisions about things that happen in front of him. The FBI agent does not have this discretion because he works in an after-the-fact detection context most of the time. In addition, the requirements within the Bureau of reporting and constant checking further limit his discretion.

MR. VORENBERG: Jim, do you want to pick up on that?

MR. AHERN: I agree with Commissioner Broderick that the functions are totally different. Police departments, although they are crime-fighting units, spend 80 per cent of their time attempting to solve social problems. This is something that is of absolutely no interest to a federal agency that is primarily investigative.

A city's police department is the cutting edge of city government. It handles the neighborhood disputes, the tense domestic situations, the potential riot situations. The total job function is so different and so unrelated to what the FBI does that there's no comparison. If you add to this the state of the art, the degree of unsophistication and problems of corruption—I think you can see why the FBI does or does not cooperate from one city to the other. We have forty thousand police departments in this country and some have been called worse than those in the most underdeveloped nations in the world. It's an understatement to say that they're not geared to give the kind of service that is necessary.

The problem of cooperation with local police departments has always been a testy one. We all know Commissioner Parker in Los Angeles had absolutely no relationship with the FBI. That department grew better in a professional sense during his tenure, perhaps in some measure because the FBI ignored its training program and related activities. In the area of technical assistance, the FBI can really play a valid role, in terms of lab facilities, fingerprints and similar things. But in assisting the training of local police officers, the FBI is so far afield that it's ludicrous to give them any money whatsoever.

We send men to the FBI's National Academy for ten to twelve weeks, but the Bureau doesn't teach solutions to urban police problems. An FBI agent has absolutely no feel for the urban scene. He has no feel for the problem of corruption in a local police department. He has no feel for the problems of political interference. The Bureau has been spared all this and that's why its agents are the professionals the public thinks they are. But they have no way of dealing with the need for change in local police departments. I think if the Bureau is to be castigated, it's because of its failure, having once assumed the mantle of leadership, to implement change and to push police departments towards institutional reform.

Mr. VORENBERG: You could either put it that way or you could say that they should have made it clear what they were not doing.

It seems to me that the real problem is that for the last ten years the large departments have had the sense that they are dealing with different, and very often more difficult, problems than those which confront the Bureau. Yet the Bureau is still seen by most people in this country as the top police agency, setting the standards.

Look at the FBI's role and relate it to the role of the IACP, now led by Quinn Tamm. Which of those organizations is generally seen, within the police field, as the standard setter? Which is seen as the place that one looks for advice, standards, training, solutions to community relations problems? Or maybe the answer is neither one.

MR. AHERN: I think the answer is neither one. The International Association of Chiefs of Police is bound by its own constituency. It's made up of chiefs from almost every city, town and borough in America. I think the membership is over forty thousand. The quality, the caliber of police leadership, if it exists at all, is low. Each chief has an equal vote in the IACP, so it's a very conservative group. It does technical things, mostly research. It does very little in terms of training.

Police have the most complex training problem of any institution in the country. They deal with the most complicated forms of human behavior. But nobody has spent any significant money to attempt to train them. In recruiting people, even at the highest levels, the requirement in most cities is at best only a high school degree. The vast majority of cities require even less.

We send these people out with guns. We give them absolutely no training on their major responsibilities, neither from the IACP nor the FBI. The police literally have no training. There has been no substantial research done on this problem; there has been little or no money spent on it. Local police cannot look to either the FBI or the IACP at this time to set professional standards.

MR. VORENBERG: Where can they look?

MR. AHERN: I think it has to be done on the basis of model forces. I think enlightened police administrators around the country, with enlightened political leaders, can begin to move in the right direction. Once a city has demonstrated some success, there will be a great deal of spin-off and copying in the police field. But today we still respond to crises in terms of scooters rather than in terms of human behavior.

That's where the Law Enforcement Assistance Administration has really missed the opportunity to create institutional reform. They have squandered literally millions of dollars to perpetuate the same kind of garbage training programs that we've had for years and years.

I really don't see very much hope for law enforcement in the next decade. I think it's slipped back since your commission, Mr. Vorenberg. The civil rights movement was an impetus for change. It revealed a lot of the failings of the police departments for the first time, much as the failings of the FBI are now being revealed. That's not an unhealthy thing. But whatever impetus there was for change as a result of these revelations has certainly faltered badly because of the political situation and for other reasons.

Mr. Vorenberg: But it is really rather ironic that now, when for the first time there are enormous sums of money available to the police under the Law Enforcement Assistance Administration, there is so little in the way of models or standards or really enlightened leadership within the field saying: Here is how you should use these new opportunities.

Mr. Ahern: Can we expect otherwise? I don't think anybody really thought money was going to solve the problem. We recruit from the high school level and we expect to draw from that chiefs, administrators, trainers, computer people, planners, budget people. No one is taught management training, the nature of the police problem, a philosophy of law enforcement and similar principles. The millions of dollars funneled into police departments through grants—usually applied for by a city's board of education because its police department lacks the expertise—is going to go for equipment and nothing else.

MR. VORENBERG: Let me just ask one more question along this line. If you look at another agency of the federal government, the Federal Bureau of Prisons, it has, to some extent over the last ten or fifteen years, tried to play a leadership role by experimenting with release programs and taking responsibility for disseminating information.

In your first comments, Jim, were you suggesting that this was a possible role for the FBI? Is it your belief that the head of the Bureau ought to see it as part of his job to disseminate information and to set standards? Or are you suggesting that, because the problems the Bureau deals with are so different from the problems local agencies deal with, we'd be better off if they would frankly state that they're going to stay out of it?

MR. AHERN: They should frankly state that they are going to stay out of it. In the Thirties and Forties they did push for some institutional reforms in police departments. They were the main impetus for creation of the few training programs we now have. This was done specifically at the behest and urging of the FBI.

I don't think the Bureau should have assumed this leadership. They failed very badly at it. But I think, given the state of the art in those years, they did make an attempt to do something useful, but it didn't work.

We need a professional organization that goes far beyond the scope of either the IACP or the FBI and deals specifically with the problems of urban policing, with some concern for regional cooperation of police. We can no longer have forty thousand police departments hire kids out of the eighth grade to deal with sophisticated legal problems, to make judgments that affect your life, literally affect your life. We can't deal with those problems any more on the same basis.

MR. BRODERICK: I agree with everything I've heard you say. I would like to make a couple of points, though. I'm not nearly as pessimistic as you.

MR. AHERN: That's because you've been out of it longer.

MR. BRODERICK: It seems to me the approaches Commissioner Murphy is taking in New York make the future of police work brighter. He's exchanging his own people with people in other large departments with both similar and different problems. This sort of cross-fertilization, it seems to me, is very useful. He's regionalizing the police activities. This is another approach we ought to consider today.

It is almost doctrine in this country that we should not have a national police force, that policing is a local problem, not a national one. The leading spokesman for this position has always been J. Edgar Hoover. This is nineteenth-century talk. Today we must think in terms of police law-enforcement powers that cross state lines.

Just last week, in New York, there was a cooperative effort in the entire metropolitan region that apparently was quite successful. This practice should be expanded. We should be asking whether, in certain areas at least, we shouldn't nationalize our policing effort. We certainly don't and can't do it through the FBI because the FBI's law-enforcement powers are limited. And if you try to draw the Bureau into cooperation with local police and other federal law-enforcement agencies, you've got to drag them along, kicking and screaming. The only person in the last twenty years who was able to drag the FBI kicking and screaming anywhere was Bobby Kennedy. And he's gone now.

MR. VORENBERG: I'd like to ask to what extent the federal-local relations problems are a result of the particular personality and background of Mr. Hoover and to what extent they are built into the organization of the Bureau. We all, understandably, have a picture of the FBI and its relationship with local police based on forty-seven years of one kind of leadership. I suppose the question is—one of the purposes of this conference is—to look ahead and ask what the FBI could be, what it should be, in the future. One part of that question is the kind of relationship we would like the Bureau to have with localities in the future.

MR. BRODERICK: It seems to me, in this two-day conference, we have personalized our consideration much too much. Our problem is an institutional problem, not the problem of an individual. They are related, of course, because the basic problem with the FBI today is that there has been no infusion of new thought, new talent, new initiative for the last fifty years.

This is also a problem with our local police departments. It's why I think that Commissioner Murphy's exchange with other police departments is a good and an innovative thing. It's why I think his bringing new people into the police department at various levels is good. No institution that fails to grow, remains insulated and has no infusion of new personnel and talent can remain viable. I think that is a problem with the FBI today. I think it is also a problem with most of our police departments.

MR. GLENN: Much of this conference has concerned itself with what the FBI is doing. I think that there's reason to be upset about what the FBI is not doing. The FBI, after all, besides internal security functions, must enforce federal criminal statutes. I think we should consider whether it is doing that job.

I think there's great room for improvement and cooperation among federal investigative agencies. For example, in prosecuting a major criminal conspiracy case, you may suddenly be confronted with an accounting problem. You can call a special investigator or special agent of the Internal Revenue Service and he'll be down there helping you. Or you can call the postal inspector and he'll come around and help you. But if you're prosecuting a tax evasion case and you'd like to have some help from the Bureau, that's not going to produce an impressive statistic for the Bureau.

Now I throw out this question. Organized crime investigations do not yield the same amount of statistics per agent-hour as, say, finding stolen cars. Is this one of the reasons we're not making greater progress against organized crime?

MR. AHERN: Speaking of statistics, I'd like to talk about the FBI and crime statistics for a moment.

First, how does the FBI tabulate them? I think the Bureau got carried away with statistics as a budgetary device to convince Congress that they were doing great work. That's not uncommon in law-enforcement circles.

Second, crime statistics are kept on the local level. They're voluntary and unaudited. How reliable are they? Crime statistics are traditionally used in political ways. It is not uncommon for a chief of police, in an off year, at budget time, to have a crime increase; he can ask for more money and more manpower to meet his needs. It's also not uncommon, during a political year, to see a sudden decrease in crime. City after city all of a sudden stems the increase in crime or decreases it.

Then, to make a statistical comparison from city to city, given the different problems of each city, is totally ludicrous. I contend that not just the FBI's own statistics, kept internally, but crime statistics in general mislead the public; they are deceptive and don't tell us about the nature of crime. We have no real idea how much exists. Consequently, we have a lot of empty political rhetoric on the issue. I don't think anybody can make the case that we've had a solid increase in crime. Many of the things we consider crime today were not considered crime fifteen or twenty years ago.

MR. VORENBERG: I think the FBI's role in the statistics field has been a mixed one.

On the one hand, it really brought some sort of order, comparability and honesty into the reporting of figures. In fact my sense is that this has been one of the areas where its standards for local agencies have really made sense. On the other hand, its own use of the figures, as you suggest, has been enormously misleading and distorting. Every three months the FBI comes out with a new quarterly report, showing the increase or, now, occasionally, a decrease. It also issues an annual report. The public is assailed with statistics purporting to measure what is happening.

MR. STONE: I'd like to ask Commissioner Broderick and Chief Ahern whether during their incumbency their respective cities had a Red Squad. And whether the operation of these Red Squads is not an exception to Commissioner Broderick's very illuminating analysis of the distinctly different functions of the local police and the FBI. Don't they really give us a national political police network since there is very close cooperation between the Red Squads and the FBI in the collection and dissemination of political information?

MR. BRODERICK: You'll excuse me if I change the terminology; we had a Bureau of Special Services. And the answer to your second question is yes, that is an exception.

I was generalizing on basic functions. Certainly, on the intelligence level, there was a more direct relationship between the FBI and the Bureau of Special Services.

MR. AHERN: In New Haven we had an intelligence division, which was primarily interested in organized crime and not particularly in Communists. We collected very little political data; we were not interested in it. Local police departments don't have the sophistication to gather political information. And they wouldn't know what to do with it if they got it. If they pass it on, it's generally useless. Anybody who would listen to their ideas about who's politically dangerous would have to be crazier than *they* are most of the time.

MR. ADAM YARMOLINSKY:* I would like to ask the panel what alternatives they see for control of the central computerized data bank, which, I take it, is really essential to a variety of police services. Other than control by the FBI, could it, for example, be controlled by an organization that represented local or state police forces? Should it be controlled by an in-

---

* Professor of Law, Harvard University, at the time of the FBI conference; now Ralph Waldo Emerson Professor at the University of Massachusetts.

dependent agency which is set up with appropriate safeguards to protect individual rights and liberties? Or is there some fourth alternative that comes to mind? I believe this issue is really central to the future of the national role in police work. The person who controls the computer is the person who controls the organization.

MR. AHERN: Doesn't that really depend on what's in the computer? If it's straight criminal records or wanted persons or warrants or stolen cars, is that really a threat to anybody's liberty? If it's political information and dossiers, then we're talking about something else.

MR. VORENBERG: There's a middle ground, Jim, as the records begin to build up and other kinds of personal information, like probation and prison records, get fed in. Mr. Yarmolinsky will remember that when he and I were on the Science and Technology Task Force of the Crime Commission we were trying to figure out where this computer was going to be. We had very strong feelings that it ought to be somewhere other than with the FBI, partly because it became clear that there was going to be non-police-type information in it.

Many of us even had some concern about having the Bureau controlling police information. We also, I think, had a sinking feeling because the FBI was just then starting the National Crime Information Center. My own sense is that it ought to be in some independent agency with non-police representatives on the governing board. But I don't see any sign of that on the horizon.

MR. NEIER: I don't know that it matters terribly much which agency controls the information. I just think it's worth pointing out that the critical battles are being fought right now over the kind of information that is going to be disseminated. There are major cases dealing with this issue in the courts right now. There are bills in Congress right now which would try to restore to the FBI the functions which were partially limited by one of the cases.

This, in my view, is the single most damaging function the FBI has played in the last several years, this promiscuous dissemination of data. The FBI sees it as providing criminal records, but in fact, it includes the dissemination of an immense amount of material which is not criminal but only contains allegations of criminal records, such as arrest information, even juvenile arrest. And even when it's sent to law-enforcement agencies, it's used for a lot more than law-enforcement purposes. I think that now is the time to see to it that the congressional and legal battles impose very severe controls on this practice.

MR. PINCUS: The question is no longer who is going to control the computer. The decision has been made that the FBI will control it. Mr. Hoover will transmit information from the new computer in the same way he handles fingerprints, which he exchanges with other agencies that provide information.

The decision to give the FBI this power is the kind people tend to forget about. It was done very quietly last December and announced by the Attorney General about four days after the decision was made. I remember, particularly, four months later, somewhere in April, one of the Washington newspapers had a story that the decision still hadn't been made.

MR. JOHN DOAR:† There's something the panelists have said that bothers me very much. There is a kind of regional or centralist syndrome in the room. The opposite point of view ought to be stated. In my view, the people of Bedford-Stuyvesant, a city of 450,000 members of minority races, don't need a regional police force. They don't need a regional criminal process. They do need a Bedford-Stuyvesant police force. They do need Bedford-Stuyvesant criminal courts. I mention that point because I think it is applicable to the FBI as well.

I can never understand why the FBI agents in New York City are all located up on East Sixty-third Street. Here is a

† Former assistant attorney general in charge of the Civil Rights Division.

supercity of 8 million people. It just doesn't seem to me to make any sense, from the standpoint of performance, that all those agents are located up on the East Side.

If they were assigned to offices in Brooklyn and the lower Bronx and Queens, and if they lived in those areas as well, I think it would be a very healthy situation. The same is true with the local New York City police. Too many of them live out on the Island and up in Putnam or Westchester County.

My theme is, and my thesis is, that problems get more difficult to solve when they get beyond the range of your natural vision, and, so, I'm a decentralist. And I'm a decentralist too with the FBI and the large city police.

MR. MARSHALL: My mind was running along the same lines. I thought that Vincent Broderick's suggestion was a radical one. I wanted to hear more of an explanation of it, what he meant by law enforcement, which I take it does not just mean investigation but some sort of direct law-enforcement activity on at least an interstate and perhaps a national level.

It doesn't seem to me that our experience with the Bureau, in its role as a national law-enforcement agency, suggests that centralization would be a good thing. I would like to hear more of what he has in mind, maybe related directly to the law-enforcement problems of New York City. Then I would like to hear what Mr. Vorenberg or other people think about that.

MR. BRODERICK: I don't think what I suggested was inconsistent with what Mr. Doar said. I don't suggest that we do away with local police. I suggest that we even consider further decentralization. But I do think that we have some law-enforcement problems, some crime problems, that cross state lines, and we should have a tool to deal with them. But we don't today. We don't have the FBI because the FBI either has no power in the area or drags its feet.

We have experience, Burke, with other national police efforts besides the FBI's. I think if we are considering effectiveness, we should consider those as well. Customs, Secret Service, postal inspection, narcotics.

I'm not necessarily endorsing this as something we should adopt. I say we have had no dialogue about the possibility of a national police effort and I think we should have that dialogue. We have not had the dialogue because the FBI has taken the position that there should be no national police, that this is fascistic and unpatriotic, and so there has been no consideration of it at all. It seems to me it is perfectly consistent to consider the possibilities of further decentralization of local crime-preventive efforts and, at the same time, the regionalization or the nationalization of efforts in certain other areas.

MR. VORENBERG: I think my sense is the same as Mr. Doar's and Mr. Marshall's. I have serious doubts about the desirability of more centralization. I think it's rather striking that the area in which the FBI has made its greatest mark is one that is very much a local function. That is automobile theft, where the FBI's role, as I understand it, is simply to take the cars from the local police, who recovered them, and then take the credit.

My own sense is that with very few exceptions, but I do think there are exceptions, a real thrust should be made to build up local neighborhood policing efforts. And I think the FBI can be of very little help with that.

The trouble is you start with an organization that has enormous influence and control, and I really mean control, over police departments around the country. The FBI has quietly, in the last four or five years, built up the national crime information system, hooking in more and more agencies. It has the centralized criminal files. It has enormous influence over how federal money is made available under the Law Enforcement Assistance Administration. It controls the statistics operation for the police on a national basis. And perhaps, most important of all, it is the model police agency for people in the country. That's why I put the question as a policy question at the beginning.

Do we want the next Director of the FBI to be somebody who, building on what I have just described, tries to play more of a national role, to provide leadership in training, leadership and standards? Or do we want him to be somebody who seeks to dismantle some of that, to ask the questions, very much as Pat Murphy's asking them in New York, about how much of this can be given back to the local level? What's the minimum that we need to keep on a centralized basis?

MR. AHERN: I get the sense that we are dangerously close to saying that the only way to protect ourselves from the police is to keep them inefficient and ignorant. I don't think anybody here has recommended a national police force, but I think we have to admit there are certain problems, certain crimes, that can only be handled on the national level.

For example, narcotics and organized crime. Those two cannot be handled by local police departments. Nor can you ever get the degree of cooperation necessary between the myriad federal agencies and the forty thousand local police departments, to effectively launch a war, for instance, on narcotics. Once narcotics hit New York, believe me, it directly affected my operations in New Haven. Once it got off that car, that boat, in New York City, it came in by bus, by car, by foot and by train. The railroad station was the best place to grab traffickers. But you collect maybe 10 per cent of it; it's a ridiculous effort. It cannot be handled on the local level.

I think we can maintain local identity of police departments, local control of police departments, and still have regionalization of standards and record-keeping systems, of communications systems and of crime labs. There can be investigative specialists who are available on a regional basis. But we can no longer expect suburban towns to hire ten guys out of high school and have a police department.

CHAPTER SIX

ORGANIZED CRIME: THE STRANGE RELUCTANCE

BY FRED J. COOK

I: Organization of Organized Crime

J. Edgar Hoover and the FBI on the one hand, and the Mafia on the other, grew and prospered together, neither causing the other the slightest anguish. This has been the greatest, most obvious and most inexplicable failure of the FBI. For decades the Bureau and its Director made no move to combat the underworld crime cartels; in fact, Hoover himself insisted that the menace didn't even exist, that the Mafia was a figment of journalistic imagination. Yet from as far back as 1930 "the invisible government" of crime has been operating, with gang lords reaping literally billions of dollars in revenues from rackets stretching from New York to California.

Pick up any of the self-glorifying FBI books that bear the Director's imprimatur, the most popular undoubtedly being Don Whitehead's *The FBI Story*. Check the index. What names of master criminals appear? John Dillinger. "Pretty Boy" Floyd. "Machine Gun" Kelly. Alvin Karpis. "Baby Face" Nelson. But where—oh, where—are names like Charles (Lucky) Luciano, Frank Costello, Joe Adonis, Albert Anastasia, Bugsy Siegel, Tony Accardo, Meyer Lansky, Vito Genovese? Where—oh, where—is the Mafia? There is not a single mention. In this supposedly definitive account, such names do not exist.

The Director's own emphasis and the achievements in which he gloried have featured the desperadoes and stumblebums of crime. This is no accident. In the 1930s, as Prohibition was coming to an end, Hoover and Homer Cummings, Franklin Roosevelt's first Attorney General and a man whom Hoover greatly influenced, came up with a novel and completely erroneous idea of the nature of the crime menace.

As everyone realized, Prohibition had been the greatest boon ever to befall the underworld. With repeal in the offing, it was obvious that American gangdom would be deprived of its major source of revenue. It would have to develop a new racket. But what? "Kidnapping!" cried Hoover and Cummings.

There was, indeed, a lot of kidnapping and a lot of highly visible, violent crime. But it was obvious to many that the headline desperadoes did not represent the real crime menace of the day. The Federal Bureau of Narcotics, some local police and a number of investigative journalists, both then and throughout the following decades, had a much clearer perception of the real danger. The attitude of the Director becomes the more baffling and mysterious as one traces the developments which obviously demonstrated that there was, indeed, a Mafia; that there was, indeed, a national organization of crime sometimes called the Combination or the Syndicate, and that this organized, underworld system was far more important than the kidnappers and bank robbers whom Hoover had magnified into a national menace.

In 1928 Cleveland police stumbled upon what later became known as the first Grand Council meeting of the Mafia. On December 5, 1928, patrolman Frank Osowski spotted a group of men entering Cleveland's Hotel Statler at the unusual hour of 4:30 A.M. "They looked both ways and pulled their hats down as they entered the hotel," Osowski later testified.

Police raided the hotel and rounded up twenty-three Mafiosi. All were well supplied with folding money, and thirteen had guns. (Several, like Joseph Profaci of Brooklyn, head of one of the five Mafia families of New York, were to turn up nearly thirty years later at the much more highly publicized Mafia conclave at Apalachin.)

The Cleveland raid made quite a splash in the newspapers. The twenty-three Mafiosi were held on various charges, tried and given suspended sentences with the proviso that they get out of Cleveland—and stay out. Since the FBI religiously reads the newspapers, one might have thought that this peculiar rallying of Mafia dons from all sections of the nation would have pricked its curiosity. But there is no evidence that it did. Nor is there any evidence that the Bureau or the Director was interested in the slightest when a second Mafia conference—the most important ever held in America—took place just a few months later with so little secrecy and in surroundings so conspicuous that it sparked speculation in national news magazines.

This second conference perfected the organization of what came to be called the national syndicate of crime. It was held in the President Hotel on the Atlantic City boardwalk in late April, 1929. Seated around a long conference table was probably the greatest collection of powerful mobsters ever assembled in one spot. From Chicago came Scarface Al Capone, accompanied by his bodyguard, Frank Cline, and his leading henchman, Frank (The Enforcer) Nitti and Jake (Greasy Thumb) Guzik. The eastern delegates included a trio soon to become the most powerful in the American underworld: Frank Costello, Lucky Luciano and Joe Adonis.

Costello is generally believed to have been the brains behind this Atlantic City gathering of the clans. At the time, he was a third-echelon figure—the consigliere, or counselor, in the New York Mafia family of Joe (The Boss) Masseria, whose right-hand man was Lucky Luciano. But Costello was widely respected for his wiliness and wisdom, and he had amassed a fortune as one of the kingpins of the East Coast rum-running cartel known as the Big Seven. He represented a rising new breed. He saw that bloody gang wars in the streets, with innocent bystanders, including children, killed or wounded, were doing infinite harm to the profession. He had come to believe that the self-interest of all the mobs and their leaders would be served by the development of a businesslike organization.

This was the motivation for the Atlantic City conference, and the decisions made there were fundamental. The Federal Bureau of Narcotics, after years of checking and cross-checking accounts of informers, concluded:

1. The conference established a national crime syndicate. Delegates reportedly took a map of the United States and carved the nation up into specific territories. Gang bosses who had established their rule and demonstrated their efficiency were confirmed in their control of specified areas and particular rackets. The most important were named to a national board or commission of crime.

2. The hierarchy was to be protected. No top-level boss could be executed unless the national commission judged him guilty of unpardonable offenses against the organization. Lowly button men (or soldiers) were not to be executed without a hearing before the underboss or lieutenant in their particular family. In effect, a system of kangaroo courts was established, providing gangland with its own judicial system.

3. Emissaries were appointed to deal with politicians and police on a nationwide basis. According to some informants, arrangements were made to establish a multi-million-dollar slush fund to bribe law-enforcement officials and to ensure the election of complaisant politicians to important offices.

4. Another slush fund, an "educational fund," was to be established to further the careers of promising young gang

members, guaranteeing them the education and proper veneer
to serve the organization as front men or future executives.

Such was the vision of a "more perfect" criminal organization. Like a lot of new ideas it encountered the opposition of
the old order. The older Mafia leaders—the Mustache Petes or
Greasers, as they were called—wanted to go their own free-
wheeling ways. This could not be permitted; the old order
would have to go.

Lucky Luciano masterminded the plot with ruthless efficiency and September 11, 1931, went down in history as the
"Purge Day of the Greasers." On that day and the next, in
precisely timed executions in New York and other key cities,
leaders of the old order were eliminated. Estimates of the
precise number of slayings vary; former Attorney General
Ramsey Clark puts the figure at forty. Whatever the number,
the methodical precision in the executions was a graphic and
gory demonstration of the existence of an underworld organization capable of acting on a national scale.

Yet this demonstration made no impact on the Director or
the Bureau. Despite it, as the 1930s rolled on, Hoover and
Cummings ignored the reality of syndicated crime and pursued their headline wars against bank robbers and kidnappers.
It was patently ridiculous, and two of the more perceptive
journalists of the day branded it so.

Milton S. Mayer wrote in *The Forum* in September, 1935:

> Kidnaping is largely an amateur sport. Unlike bootlegging, it
> is desperate and dangerous. It attracts two kinds of men: nuts
> and the kind of person who shoots up banks. It does not attract
> the kind of man who peddles illicit goods or murders fellow
> hoodlums for hire under the tolerant eye of both police and
> public. "Good" criminals, the foundation blocks of the under-
> world, avoid it because it's a one-shot racket; kidnaping is easier
> to solve than any other major crime; the life of a "kidnaping
> gang" has never been shown to be more than one kidnaping.

William Seagle in *Harper's Magazine* expressed the same thought.

Time has proved the accuracy of their analyses. The famous kidnappers were not the big names of the underworld. Bruno Richard Hauptmann, the kidnapper of the Lindbergh baby, was an impoverished carpenter; Angelo John LaMarca, executed for the kidnap-murder of the Weinberger baby on Long Island in the late 1950s, was an impecunious laborer driven to the border of insanity by debts.

Organized crime events, at times so public they made eight-column headlines, continued, while the FBI pursued bank robbers and kidnappers, and the Director padded his records with reports of stolen cars recovered and continued to insist that crime was a local problem. The explosive Murder Incorporated probe in Brooklyn in 1940 put into official court records a welter of details documenting the existence of the Syndicate and the practices of its enforcement arm, but the FBI was uninterested. Nor was it interested when Abe (Kid Twist) Reles began to talk—a break that led others to do the same. Reles provided details far more specific than anything the much-publicized Joseph Valachi was able to tell the Senate's McClellan Committee nearly a quarter century later. Reles was gifted with a photographic memory; he recalled minute details of some eight hundred murders that had taken place across the nation. He exposed the workings of a murder-for-hire band of killers who functioned as the official enforcers for mob bosses across the nation. Albert Anastasia, sometimes called the Lord High Executioner, directed the activities of this squad of ghouls. Above him, one safe step removed from messy involvement, was Joe Adonis, the close associate of Frank Costello.

Assistant District Attorney Burton B. Turkus used Reles' revelations to send seven mob killers to the electric chair—an unprecedented feat. He later quoted Reles: "We are out to get

America by the pocketbook . . . the whole Syndicate." And: "We got connections. It wasn't easy at the start. But now we are like this (holding up two fingers close together) with the Purple Mob (in Detroit). We work with Bugsy Siegel in California, and with Lepke (Louis Buchalter) and the troops he's got. We are with Charlie Lucky. With the Jersey troop, too, and Chicago and Cleveland."

II: *Flagrant Interstate Organized Crime*

The Murder Incorporated exposé was a sensation in its time, but its time was short. America was soon involved in World War II; the FBI was preoccupied with hunting German spies and "guaranteeing" internal security. But the Syndicate was still there.

The war-stimulated prosperity fed the Syndicate's take from gambling, which had been given priority at another Mafia Grand Council meeting in 1933. Mayor Fiorello H. La Guardia had made New York too hot for the mob; the crime lords transferred their operations across the George Washington Bridge into Bergen County in northern New Jersey. Here they developed—and operated brazenly for more than ten years—a flourishing criminal empire so obviously interstate in character that it clamored for the FBI's attention.

The big bookmaking play from New York and its environs involved, according to best estimates at the time, a total "handle" (money that was bet and re-bet) of $5 billion a year. This fantastic volume was funneled into Frank Erickson's bookmaking headquarters in Bergen County. Joe Adonis, who had been chased out of Brooklyn, established a string of gambling casinos that spangled the Bergen County countryside. A fleet of chauffeur-driven Cadillacs ferried a nightly stream of high rollers from their New York residences and hotels to Adonis' houses of chance. Gasoline-rationing restrictions of World War II did not crimp this highly visible traffic and agents of the Office of Defense Transportation tailed the Cadillac livery service to the doors of some of Adonis' gambling halls.

This is no figment of journalistic imagination. It is the only instance of which I am aware in which authorities established so positively what might be described as a daily Apalachin. The functioning of Adonis' Council of Crime was traced in investigations by both District Attorney Frank S. Hogan in New York and the Federal Bureau of Narcotics. In 1953 two of Hogan's aides—his chief assistant, Vincent A. G. O'Connor, and Assistant District Attorney Andrew J. Seidler—spelled out for me in detail the manner in which Adonis and his criminal council operated. Subsequently, while working on a book on the structure of the Mafia, I had access to some of the daily working memoranda filed by agents of the Federal Bureau of Narcotics, and a chance to examine formal statements they had gathered from informers about Adonis' operation. What follows is compiled from these two official sources.

Adonis' headquarters were established in a dingy-looking tavern known as Duke's, almost opposite the entrance of the Palisades Amusement Park. Top-level conferences were held there every Tuesday. Frank Costello came over from New York. Meyer Lansky would drop in from Saratoga Springs or Florida, where he was masterminding the mob's gambling casinos. Abner (Longie) Zwillman, the Newark bootleg king of Prohibition days and a master political manipulator who, it was said, hadn't guessed wrong on a New Jersey election in twenty years, would join the brain trust. So, on occasion, would two lesser-known figures who were to come to wield enormous power: Vincent (Jimmy Blue Eyes) Alo, a dock and gambling czar, sometimes known as Costello's "right bower"; and Gerardo (Jerry) Catena, a New Jersey mob boss with close ties to Zwillman and, in recent years, since the death of Vito Genovese, the reputed ruler of one wing of Genovese's Mafia family.

This illustrates how obvious—to law-enforcement agencies that really looked—was the fact of syndicated crime, operating on an interstate and, indeed, on a national level. The Kefauver probe of 1951 picked up many of New York County District Attorney Frank S. Hogan's discoveries of Adonis' operations and gave the nation a vivid demonstration of how organized crime operated in city after city across the nation. Still the FBI remained indifferent; the Director, the national hero of wars against crime, didn't stir a hair.

Apologists for the FBI sometimes argue that the Bureau had no jurisdiction. It had authority to pursue kidnappers and car thieves and hijackers when they crossed state lines, the rationalization goes, but not to investigate organized crime. But, as William Turner has pointed out, a spate of legislation during the Roosevelt years had made the FBI the most important watchdog of interstate crime. If the Director had willed, the Bureau could have hit the Syndicate on nearly a score of fronts. Turner listed these opportunities:

> Among the statutes under the FBI's wing were acts relating to the kickback rackets, extortion, anti-racketeering, labor-management relations, unauthorized publication or use of communications, obstruction of justice, bankruptcy (the sham has long been a favorite Cosa Nostra fraud), the white slave traffic, perjury, misprison of [i.e. helping to conceal] a felony, trust formation, interstate transportation of stolen property, interstate transportation of gambling devices, lottery tickets and wagering data, hijacking, bribery, fraud by wire, and federal firearms control. This amounted to considerable firepower, but it had never been used in any concerted way.

Not only that, but the Director and the Bureau threw roadblocks in the path of anyone else who tried to do the job.

This became especially clear after the Apalachin conference—the most publicized and most disastrous Grand Council in the history of the American wing of the Mafia.

III: *Apalachin and Continuing Reluctance*

Mafia dons from all sections of the nation gathered on November 14, 1957, at the hilltop home of Joseph Barbara, a wealthy merchant whose firm controlled much of the distribution of beer and soft drinks in the Binghamton, New York, area. Sergeant Edgar Croswell, of the New York State Police, who had long suspected Barbara of Mafia ties, discovered the gathering and began to set up a roadblock below Barbara's $150,000 mansion. Observing this, sixty of the Mafia chieftains jumped in their cars and roared down the road, hoping to get away, but all were caught and identified. On the persons of the sixty, police found some $300,000 in cash.

Some of Barbara's guests were so prominent that their names guaranteed instant headlines: Vito Genovese, who had catapulted himself into the supreme position in the eastern Mafia through a series of gangland executions; Joseph Profaci, head of a powerful Mafia family in Brooklyn and one of the delegates to the original Grand Council in Cleveland; Joseph Bonanno, boss of yet another Mafia family with power in New York and Tucson, Arizona. Others among the sixty had come from as far away as California, Florida, Texas and Cuba. Two had even come from Italy where they were reported to have had recent contacts with the deported Lucky Luciano.

Federal agencies learned later that the gathering had been much larger; informers, whose stories cross-checked, put the number of conferees at around one hundred. Some hid out in Barbara's cellar for days until they could slip away; others made their escape through the surrounding woods.

Sergeant Croswell's dramatic coup made an enormous impact on the public and in law-enforcement circles. Here was the reality. Here Mafia dons had been caught assembling to legislate and adjudicate the affairs of crime. The New York *Herald Tribune* called Apalachin a demonstration of "the invisible government," and it called for all-out war by the FBI. If the FBI did not have sufficient powers, let Hoover ask Congress for them; Congress had never denied him anything he had asked before.

The *Herald Tribune* was eminently correct about that. All the more curious, then, was Hoover's conduct after Apalachin. Despite the headlines, despite editorial exhortations to him to lead the charge against what Frederic Sondern, Jr., later called "The Brotherhood of Evil," the Director and the FBI continued to concentrate on recovery of stolen cars.

Others, however, felt that Apalachin required some kind of authoritative response. One with this naïve idea was Eisenhower's Attorney General, William P. Rogers, later Secretary of State. Rogers created what he called the Special Group on Organized Crime, and named Milton R. Wessel, a former United States attorney, to probe the Apalachin gathering and launch an all-out attack on the Syndicate.

Wessel quickly discovered that there was not on any level a clearinghouse for information on organized crime. The efforts of federal agencies and local police departments were splintered into thousands of fragments. The FBI had long boasted about the rapidity with which fingerprints could be identified in its files, but no effort had been made to gather and correlate information about the activities of multi-millionaire mobsters. If alert local police knew that the most eminent Mafioso in town was flying out on some mysterious mission, if similar sudden departures for destinations unknown were observed in a score of cities at the same time, there was still no law-enforcement agency on any level that could put the threads together and discover a Mafia Grand Council meeting in the making.

Unfortunate—because despite the fiasco at Apalachin, the Mafia went right on holding such meetings, immune from interference. Indeed, a larger-than-Apalachin conclave was held in Worcester, Massachusetts, on December 8, 1959. Attorney General Edward J. McCormack of Massachusetts later told the New York State Commission of Investigation that 150 delegates had met in fifteen rented rooms in a Worcester hotel. They had burned the telephone wires between Worcester and New York in night-long discussions and then departed, their beds unused, before authorities learned of their presence. McCormack testified that his subsequent investigation convinced him that at least two murders—one in Hartford, Connecticut, another in Youngstown, Ohio—stemmed from decisions made at this meeting.

Milton Wessel, directing his Special Group, leaned over backward to avoid collision with the all-powerful Director of the FBI. He quickly learned that whatever information the FBI had, it reserved for the FBI; it shared with no one. But Wessel believed that this was only normal bureaucratic infighting. "I always felt that we had to prove ourselves first," Wessel has repeatedly said, "and, in the end, after we had, we did get a lot of cooperation from Hoover."

Some of Wessel's subordinates have been less diplomatic. Gerard L. Goettel, one of Wessel's deputies, later wrote that the Special Group had to fight not only the mob, but investigative bureaucracies that balked at cooperating. "The FBI was the coolest agency of all," Goettel declared. "J. Edgar Hoover, at a national meeting of United States Attorneys, decried the need of 'special groups' to fight organized crime." Goettel added that, when the Special Group tried to follow up on Apalachin, they found everywhere they went the FBI had been there before them. But when the Special Group tried to learn what the FBI had discovered, "the G-men acted as if they had never heard of Apalachin . . ."

Equally outspoken was Richard B. Ogilvie, the head of Wessel's midwestern office, subsequently governor of Illinois. (Ogilvie engineered the first successful prosecution of Tony Accardo, the Chicago successor of Al Capone. Though the conviction was later overthrown on technical grounds, it did much to deactivate Accardo.)

> Hoover was very cool to the whole idea of the Attorney General's Special Group. He ordered the FBI files, containing the very information we needed on organized crime, closed to us . . . Criticizing Hoover is a very dangerous thing for anyone to do. But honesty compels me to say that Hoover's ideas are sadly behind the times . . . The FBI is still organized to fight a crime pattern of the 20's and 30's. It is not set up to do battle with the criminal syndicate—the organized conspiracy that drains $22 billion a year from the United States.

Wessel's Special Group lasted two years before it was quietly strangled. Wessel himself wanted to return to the private practice of law, but he was still concerned about that gaping hole in law enforcement—the lack of a central clearinghouse for information on organized crime. He recommended creation within the Justice Department of a small, permanent special unit which would be the repository of information gathered by law-enforcement agencies across the nation. The idea gained wide support.

The issue came to a head at the annual convention of the International Association of Chiefs of Police in Washington in October, 1960, before the Ogilvie-Goettel revelations. A special committee, headed by Santa Ana, California, Police Chief Edward J. Allen (in the past one of Hoover's favorites), sponsored a resolution calling for a federal nerve center on organized crime. Many police chiefs were sympathetic and inclined to the view expressed by Captain James E. Hamilton of the Los Angeles Police Department, that "the definite lack has been on a Federal level in furnishing local departments information as to the movements of national figures." Hoover reacted at once—and strongly. He told the convention he saw in the proposal the specter of a national police force—a "Gestapo that might rob all of us of our liberties." He went on:

> The persons who endorse these grandiose schemes have lost sight of some very basic facts. America's compact network of state and local enforcement agencies traditionally has been the nation's first line of defense against crime. Nothing could be more dangerous to our democratic ideals than the establishment of an all-powerful police agency on the Federal scene. The truth of these words is clearly demonstrated in the experience of nations ruled by ruthless tyrants both here in the Western Hemisphere and abroad.

The master had spoken, and FBI propagandists, circulating widely at the convention, pointed out to the assembled police chiefs the clear path of duty. They saw and did it. Allen's recommendation was shelved, and Allen, who had been a devout Hoover worshiper, was virtually read out of the lodge. He offered to resign as Chairman of the committee on organized crime, but urged that it continue its work under someone else. Even this was not enough. The board of officers of the IACP met on December 12, 1960, and disbanded the too active committee that had drawn Hoover's ire.

After the subsequent Ogilvie-Goettel blasts about the FBI's foot-dragging in organized crime investigations, Hoover swatted at his critics in an acid statement that emphasized his continuing reluctance to move in the organized crime field. The occasion was his 1961 appearance before the House Appropriations subcommittee headed by his old friend, Congressman Rooney. Rooney asked him the ideal leading question.

Would the Director like to comment about the performance of the Wessel Special Group? The Director would, indeed.

Criticism of the FBI had been "unwarranted and unfair," he said, and: "My only conclusion is that some individuals . . . look at TV too frequently and absorb some fantastic panaceas as to how to solve *local crimes*." (Italics added.) The Wessel group, he said, had indicated by its activities that "their chief preoccupation is nest-feathering publicity." They had asked the FBI to assign special agents to the group "to be used on 'fishing expeditions,'" but "obviously, we have neither the manpower nor the time to waste on such speculative ventures."

Former Agent Turner later wrote:

The "fishing expedition" passage struck me as wryly amusing in the light of an unforgettable scene that had taken place about the time the Special Group was pleading for help. Senior FBI agents had moved up and down the ranks of automobiles in the parking lot of the Seattle-Tacoma International Airport, occasionally jotting down a license number. Their mission was part of a nation-wide drive, but it wasn't aimed at organized crime. The agents were recording out-of-state license numbers on the random chance of finding a stolen car that had been taken interstate. If one was found, they would be able to claim a double statistic: one car recovered, plus the recovery value of the car (to be added to the Fines, Savings, and Recoveries category). It would go into the statistical hopper that enables Hoover each year to boast of "new peaks of achievement."

IV: The Dragon Stirs

Has the FBI ever touched a major crime figure? The answer is: yes, a couple of times, in a kind of hit-and-run effort.

In 1929 Al Capone failed to appear in court to answer a subpoena as a witness in a Prohibition case. He sent a doctor's certificate indicating he was too ill. The FBI discovered that while supposedly bedridden, he had been enjoying himself at the races and had even flown to the Bahamas. The contempt of court charge that resulted jailed Capone for six months.

Then there was the Louis (Lepke) Buchalter case. Lepke was a dread name in New York. He was deeply involved in narcotics, industrial extortion—and murder. He sat on the board of the national Syndicate. When Thomas E. Dewey began his rackets-busting career in the late 1930s, Lepke's was one of the prize scalps he went after. Unwilling to oblige, Lepke went into hiding, and the City of New York put a $25,000 price on his head. The suspicion was that Lepke had fled the state. Actually, he was holed up in Brooklyn most of the time, protected by Albert Anastasia, but this supposed flight across state boundaries gave the FBI an opening wedge into the much-headlined manhunt. The Bureau proclaimed that it, too, would pay a $25,000 reward for Lepke—but only if it got Lepke *first*.

The heat finally became too great for the mob. According to Burton Turkus, Hoover "sent a flat fiat to Joey Adonis and Frank Costello" warning that unless Lepke surrendered to the FBI "every Italian mobster in the country would be picked up." Supposedly, that did it; Lepke was told he would have to surrender for the good of the cause.

One thing he wanted to avoid at all costs was winding up in Dewey's hands. The Federal Bureau of Narcotics had built a case against him—the only federal agency that *did* have a case—and Lepke reasoned that a narcotics rap was much preferable to conviction for murder. At this juncture, columnist Walter Winchell, long a Hoover partisan, made a radio plea to Lepke to surrender. Lepke got in touch with Winchell, and on the night of August 24, 1939, delivered himself to the columnist at a designated rendezvous. Winchell then drove Lepke four blocks to Fifth Avenue and Twenty-eighth Street where Hoover was waiting to receive the prearranged surrender. It was a great publicity coup for the Director and the Bureau, but little more than that. Lepke was turned over to narcotics agents and was later surrendered to Dewey on a murder indictment that finally sent him to the electric chair.

This was the record of the Bureau when Robert F. Kennedy became Attorney General. In the immediate aftermath of Apalachin, the Bureau had made a hasty reassessment of its position. One prosecutor told this writer that he had seen a fat two-volume Bureau study that acknowledged there was, indeed, a Mafia; but this confession of past error was such a closely guarded, high-level secret that the study was whisked out of the prosecutor's hands, into which it had inadvertently fallen, before he could read more than its conclusion. The Bureau's immediate reaction to Apalachin was its Top Hoodlum Program, which called upon every field office to identify and investigate the ten top hoods in its area. This produced no startling results, and more than two years after Apalachin, at the time of the Worcester conclave, the Bureau had only four agents in the New York office assigned to organized crime, while more than four hundred devoted their energies to the Communist menace.

Robert Kennedy had different ideas about the nature of the real menace to the nation—and his brother, John F. Kennedy, was President. As a result of their service with the McClellan rackets committee—John as a committee member, Robert as the committee counsel—both Kennedys had obtained a clear insight into the workings of syndicated crime. They had toyed with the idea of creating a National Crime Commission, a proposal that Estes Kefauver also had favored. But Hoover's adamant opposition doomed the project. So Robert Kennedy established what amounted to a Wessel-like Special Group by beefing up the Organized Crime and Racketeering Section in the Justice Department. He assigned sixty attorneys to the effort and established field offices in New York, Chicago, Miami and Los Angeles. Within the section, he organized an intelligence unit to serve as a central clearinghouse for information about organized crime. He also began to ride herd on the FBI.

The new Attorney General visited Justice Department branches and FBI field offices. "He thinks the FBI is part of the department and in he goes," a Kennedy intimate recalled. He sometimes even gave direct orders to FBI agents. And when he called a strategy conference on organized crime in New York, he demanded the FBI's full participation. Harvey Foster was then the SAC of the New York office, and Kennedy snapped, "I want Harvey Foster to attend."

Impatient with what he considered a dearth of information and lack of progress, Kennedy took one of the most controversial actions of his tenure as Attorney General. At a conference in his fifth-floor office in mid-1961, he told agent Courtney A. Evans, Hoover's liaison man, that the FBI should use more "technical equipment" to fight organized crime. Everyone knew what "technical equipment" meant, according to Edward Silberling, who then headed the Organized Crime and Racketeering Section. It meant wiretapping and bugging. Evans reported the suggestions to his boss in a memorandum dated July 7, 1961, and the FBI quickly plunged into widespread electronic surveillance of mob leaders.

Kennedy's clearance for a bugging-wiretapping operation fitted the needs of the Bureau in more ways than one. In the first place, Hoover's autocratic ukases about the appearance of FBI agents—and the type of agents he selects—make it impossible for FBI agents to do the kind of undercover work federal narcotics agents regularly do. Sometimes they stand out too much even for successful surveillance. But bugging and wiretapping fit the Bureau's vaunted scientific capabilities. And they provided a means for the FBI to gather a lot of information quickly and bring itself up to date on organized crime. Among the results were thousands of pages of transcripts, recently placed in court records, of bugged conversations in the offices of New Jersey mobsters Samuel (Sam the Plumber) De Cavalcante, boss of a small Mafia family, and Angelo (the Gyp) DeCarlo, a Mafia capo in Newark. The Bureau recently disclosed it has another 76,000 pages of transcripts resulting from the bugging of a Buffalo funeral home operated by Stefano Maggadino, seventy-nine-year-old Mafia boss of upstate New York and Ontario.

This indiscriminate eavesdropping produced a lot of scandal and rumor, and a lot of titillating insights into life within the Mafia and the Mafia's political connections. But neither the bugging nor the much-publicized testimony of Mafia informer Joseph Valachi in 1963 achieved very much in the way of prosecutions. Ramsey Clark has written that "the FBI itself denies that a single conviction was obtained on the basis of information from its bugs," and added acidly, "Perhaps a great deal was learned by electronic surveillance. Certainly a lot of time was wasted."

Clark made the point that the hard evidence on which court cases were built had to be assembled by old-fashioned, painstaking detective work—the kind the FBI had always been reluctant to perform in this field. He concluded:

As he [Robert Kennedy] took center stage, the FBI stepped aside, and remained on the periphery until 1965. The conflict between Attorney General Kennedy and the FBI arose from the unwillingness of the Bureau to participate on an equal eted personal credit that it will sacrifice even effective crime control before it will share the glory of its exploits. This has been a petty and costly characteristic caused by the domination of a single person, J. Edgar Hoover, and his self-centered concern for his reputation and that of the FBI.

Despite halfhearted gestures by the FBI, the federal effort mounted. From 19 indictments of organized crime figures in 1960, a negligible record, it climbed steadily to 687 in fiscal 1964. Then it leveled off and declined temporarily before reaching 1,107 in fiscal 1967 and 1,166 in fiscal 1968.

At his death, Hoover still seemed less excited about the menace of organized crime than he did about longhairs at anti-war rallies. But FBI activity against organized crime has increased since another action by the Kennedys. Hoover's claim that he did not have authority disappeared when the Kennedy administration obtained passage in Congress of legislation greatly broadening the Bureau's jurisdiction and giving it specific powers in such fields as interstate gambling and bookmaking. The FBI began to develop cases in these areas, but after President Kennedy's assassination in Dallas in November, 1963, it seemed less eager. "Within a month the FBI men in the field wouldn't tell us anything. We started running out of gas," an organized crime section lawyer told Fred Graham of the New York *Times*. Hoover roared back that if there was any falling off, it was only because so many agents were assigned to investigating the assassination. But in succeeding years the FBI continued to show itself less than wholly enthusiastic about fighting the crime menace.

Early in 1967 Ramsey Clark began putting together special "strike forces" against organized crime, a policy that has been continued by his successor, John N. Mitchell. The idea was to pool all federal investigative talents and hit hard in major cities. Strike forces consisted of Justice Department lawyers, U.S. attorneys and investigators from the Internal Revenue Service, the Secret Service, the Customs Bureau, the Narcotics Bureau and other federal agencies. Only the FBI refused to assign agents to the strike forces and, as *The Wall Street Journal* reported, "There are strong feelings [in the Justice

Department] that Mr. Hoover's independence is rendering the effort far less effective than it could be."

The situation has continued. Columnist Jack Anderson reported in September, 1971: "The FBI has plenty of agents to search for stolen cars, infiltrate antiwar rallies, keep files on Congressmen and polish J. Edgar Hoover's image. But it has assigned only four to the Justice Department's vital, 17-city drive against the Mafia." Other federal agencies had provided 224 detectives, he wrote. The FBI responded that it was helping out with information without the direct assignment of agents, and that it was conducting its own Mafia-hunt. Anderson conceded that this was "partly true," but he made the point that such peripheral cooperation represented something less than full-scale commitment to the drive against organized crime.

The increased federal activity is reflected in almost daily headlines. Hoover repeatedly announced the smashing of bookmaking rings doing multi-million-dollar-a-year business, and the Justice Department has initiated a number of highly successful prosecutions. Officials in Newark and Jersey City, several of whom were accused of having mob ties, have been convicted for a variety of offenses, including bribery and extortion, and a number of top-ranking mobsters—most notably Gerardo (Jerry) Catena, reputedly the most powerful Mafia chieftain in the state following the death of Vito Genovese—have been jailed.

Some crime experts, like Ralph Salerno, former New York City detective supervisor and nationally known crime consultant, believe that "it is now a new ball game." Salerno cites as evidence the case of Meyer Lansky, who for decades was the Mafia's gambling czar and money manager. Lansky, certainly one of the wiliest minds the underworld has produced, has sought sanctuary in Israel. Salerno theorizes that Lansky would not have taken flight had he not recognized the handwriting on the wall and decided that Mafia rule and Mafia immunity were breaking down.

But there have been exposés and headline prosecutions in the past—notably after the Kefauver probe of 1950–51 and again after Apalachin in 1957—and the damage done to the criminal syndicates has been relatively minimal and temporary. It has been a case of "The King is dead; long live the King." For every mob chief who has been deposed, a new and sometimes more menacing figure has arisen. It remains a fact that, despite the FBI's heralded gambling raids, despite the Justice Department's successful prosecutions, it is still almost as easy to place a bet with a bookie as it ever was; and brash young gangsters will tell you, "Sure, we're hurting at the moment, but it will pass. We got it here"—and they tap their wallets significantly.

V: Why?

Such, then, is the record of the Bureau in fighting organized crime during the decades of its greatest glory. The question remains: why? Why did Hoover and the FBI ignore so completely and so persistently the greatest crime menace facing the nation?

It is impossible to give any definitive answer. Professor Donald R. Cressey in his *Theft of the Nation* suggests a number of hypotheses, but thinks the most likely explanation is that, until the legislation of the Kennedy years, Hoover simply did not have the power. But this does not explain why Hoover, never a bashful or reticent man, did not clamor for the power. Or why, instead, he went to the opposite extreme and persisted in denying the very existence of the Mafia.

Others have suggested that part of the explanation probably lies in Hoover's lifelong love affair with statistics. He has built the myth of perfectibility on the claim that the FBI gets from 96 to 98 per cent convictions, and on the ever mounting totals of crimes solved and property reclaimed. As William Turner and others have pointed out, these are totals that can be jacked up by crusades against stumblebums and the stupid crimes they commit. A car thief may say to himself, "Oh, well, the FBI got me; I might as well plead guilty." But the masterminds of crime do not react that way. They cover their tracks with infinite care; they can be cornered only after a heavy investment of time and effort; then they hire the best lawyers money can buy. Concentrating on such adversaries could well dilute both Hoover's prized statistics and the image of the infallible Bureau they have helped him create.

Added to this, just possibly, is another vital consideration—corruption and the political power it buys. The President's Crime Commission in 1967 estimated the net income of syndicated crime at between $6 and $7 billion annually; other sources, including Hoover himself, have placed its gross income at between $20 and $22 billion a year. Milton Wessel, after his experience with the first Special Group on Organized Crime, estimated that the underworld reaps about $9 billion from gambling rackets alone. But, he pointed out, this is not all clear profit. "Fully half the syndicates' income from gambling," he insisted, "is earmarked for protection money paid to police and politicians."

It is not, perhaps, too cynical to suggest that such billions, in their subtle and devious ways, manage to court considerable influence in Congress. And J. Edgar Hoover's relations with Congress were always most cordial. Would such cozy relationships have been jeopardized if the Director had recognized the reality of the Mafia and clamored for the powers to hunt it down? It seems at least possible. It may simply add up to the fact that to the Director, who was the most powerful and long-lived bureaucrat in Washington, the stakes seemed too high.

VI: *Conference Discussion*

MR. VORENBERG: I want to ask Mr. Hundley a question about one of the suggestions in Mr. Cook's paper.

One of the reasons Mr. Cook suggests for the FBI's slowness to get into this field is the possibility that organized crime had connections with leading politicians, and the FBI did not want to cut into its own political capital. I'm just wondering, from your point of view, during the time you were in office, did you see any evidence—in the handling and selection of cases, in where the FBI put its energies and where it didn't—that would support that speculation or possibility?

MR. HUNDLEY: I think there's some validity to it. This is a personal opinion based on experience in the field.

In some political prosecutions that I was personally involved in, the Bureau, although they would investigate, were very sensitive to the consequences. You really have to understand the Bureau's operation. If you're investigating a congressman or a judge, the agents, because of the internal workings of the FBI, are much more cautious than they are when they're investigating a top Communist. Criticism from the Hill on some slight mistake that an agent might make, whether the criticism is justified or not, may, in that type of case, result in the transfer of the agent.

I don't believe it's a complete answer. But there was always a feeling in the department, when I was there, that if you had to investigate a political figure, you always tried to get the Internal Revenue Service in the case somehow. We didn't want to put a lot of agents we liked on the spot.

I think Mr. Hoover was, as Mr. Navasky says, a complete bureaucrat. I don't use that term in a derogatory sense. He was very effective at it. He liked to pick areas of investigation and prosecution where he had the greatest amount of popular support and political support.

I think he had a sincere belief in the danger of domestic Communism. I don't think there's anything phony about his feeling. But he was also smart enough to realize that that was a very popular field to investigate. That's why, initially, I could not understand his reluctance to get into the field of organized crime. Most Americans are against that too.

One of the reasons given for Mr. Hoover's reluctance to bring the Bureau into the organized crime fight was some type of bureaucratic infighting between Hoover and Harry Anslinger, who, like Mr. Hoover, was a very strong bureau director—head of the Bureau of Narcotics. Mr. Anslinger perhaps overemphasized the importance of organized crime. So that may also have been a factor. Mr. Cook, have you ever heard that this was one reason for the Bureau's avoidance of the area?

Mr. Cook: I think, Mr. Hundley, that there is no question that that animosity existed. But Anslinger's jurisdiction was narrowly limited to narcotics. The FBI's jurisdiction is far broader than that. I don't think, if Hoover had really wanted power to fight organized crime, that Anslinger could have been a threat to him.

For example, the Valachi case is, I think, a perfect example of this. When Valachi decided to testify, he talked to a federal narcotics agent who was the man that he had known and whom he thought he could trust. But the Federal Narcotics Bureau's jurisdiction was limited to narcotics. The Attorney General's office turned it over to the FBI, which had far broader jurisdiction. I think there would have been the same result if Hoover had wanted to move into the field. I think there was a continuing struggle because Anslinger emphasized the Mafia and Hoover said no Mafia. But I think if Hoover had wanted to move he could have moved.

Mr. Hundley: I don't have any doubt he could have. He could have had all the public support he has today in that field.

I came to the department when Bill Rogers was Attorney General, and I concluded that the inability to build statistics in organized crime was a factor in the Bureau's reluctance to enter the area. But I thought that he and the other policy makers would be smart enough to realize, as they do today, that even though they might have difficulty making prosecutable cases against the really big people in organized crime, they could still just make gambling cases, over and over, and cite them very effectively for statistical purposes. This is what happens today.

Mr. Cook: I don't know, Mr. Hundley. I'm not satisfied with any of the explanations that have been given why he did not move. You know, I have had no really satisfactory explanation myself from anybody I talk to. We have theories, but no hard and fast answer why it wasn't done. It only exists in the mind of one man, and, of course, we can't read his mind.

Mr. Turner: In 1957 when the Apalachin conclave took place, the Bureau, along with other federal law-enforcement agencies, was severely embarrassed. The FBI started up what they called the Top Hoodlum Program. We were instructed not to divulge its existence outside the Bureau, not even to other law-enforcement agencies. It was strictly an intelligence-gathering effort. Each office, whether it was New York City or Butte, Montana, was supposed to designate five top hoodlums and concentrate on learning everything possible about them. And so we did. Up to that point, all references to the Mafia or to organized crime or to syndicated activity was dropped into a general catchall file called the GIIF, the General Investigative Intelligence File.

Now, in 1959, which was about two years after the institution of this program, I went down to Los Angeles as an inspector's aide, on an inspection of the Los Angeles office. One of my tasks was to write an evaluation of any progress that the Los Angeles office may have made in the field of organized crime. They still didn't call it organized crime. It was still the Top Hoodlum Program. I found that most of the progress was simply a result of the generosity of the Los Angeles Police Department Intelligence Division in furnishing information from their files. Some of this information eventually led to federal prosecutions.

Other information had come from the installation of technical surveillance devices, on such crime figures in Los Angeles as Mickey Cohen.

So, again, when Apalachin happened, the FBI had not yet recognized the fact that organized crime was a federal problem. I think that by the time Bobby Kennedy became Attorney General, the Top Hoodlum Program had fallen of its own weight. It wasn't a statistics-producing program. It wasn't one that resulted in quick headlines for the Bureau. By the time Robert Kennedy became Attorney General, I believe the program was mostly functioning *pro forma.*

MR. HUNDLEY: It was 1958 or 1959 that the bugs started going in, at least on a selective basis. I mean I know they did. When the Bureau realized that Robert Kennedy was going to take office, and that he had these strong feelings about a more effective federal effort in the field of organized crime, it was simply a case of increasing the number of bugs. I always thought it was somewhat similar to the situation John Doar had down in Mississippi. It was a little late in coming. But when it came, it came *en masse.* And, of course, I know from personal experience that it was the urging of Attorney General Kennedy. But it was also the fact that they knew he was going to come in and push in this area and they had to catch up in a hurry.

MR. COOK: You were on the inside of the Justice Department, and it may be that they started to move before this. But I think the great move came after Kennedy became Attorney General.

CHAPTER SEVEN

CIVIL RIGHTS: TOO MUCH, TOO LATE*

BY ARLIE SCHARDT

I: The Bureau's Ambivalence Toward Civil Rights Enforcement

In March, 1956, with racial tensions intensifying throughout the South in the wake of the school desegregation decision, Attorney General Herbert Brownell proposed to President Eisenhower's Cabinet a civil rights legislative program designed to protect voting rights and remedy other violations of constitutional rights. Hoover took part in the briefing, where he presented an extraordinary paper entitled "Racial Tensions and Civil Rights."

Hoover began by explaining why the South (i.e., whites) opposed integration. There had been "a lack of objectivity by press, and . . . intermeddling." There was bound to be "a clash of culture when the protection of racial purity is a rule of life ingrained deeply as the basic truth." Southerners (i.e., whites) claimed Negroes were inferior as seen in their home life, morals, health, intellectual development and crime rates. The South's "paternalistic spirit" realized the need to provide more opportunity for Negroes "but does not yet consider that mixed education is the best means whereby the races can best be

* The conference paper on this topic, by John Doar and Dorothy Landsberg, was not available for publication in this collection. Instead, the editors asked Mr. Schardt, who attended the conference, to prepare this paper and include in it the conference discussion of the activity of the FBI in the civil rights area.

served. And behind this stalks the specter of interracial mar-
riages." Hoover added, "The Southerners advance the view
that the more Negroes who leave the South, the better, since
this will distribute the 'race problem' more evenly across the
country and . . . make for less tension in the South."

Hoover's only quotations from NAACP leaders were inflam-
matory statements, and most of his analysis of civil rights
organizations focused on the role of the Communist Party. For
example:

> The Communist Party has intensified its efforts to infiltrate
> the NAACP, particularly at local levels . . .
> The Communist Party has ordered each district to start a
> program of agitation designed "to put the heat on Federal
> authorities" and to demand that the Federal Government by
> immediate action support the Supreme Court decision on the
> desegregation issue.

Why Hoover found it suspicious that an organization planned
to urge the government to enforce its own laws was not made
clear.

On the other hand, Hoover continued, "in no instance have
we been advised that any of the so-called Citizens Councils
advocate violence." Mississippi Senator Eastland had advised
Citizens Councils against violence. The membership of the Citizens Councils reflected "bankers, lawyers, doctors, state legislators and industrialists." In short, their membership included
many of the leading citizens of the South.

While accurate as far as it went, this characterization of
Citizens Councils definitely did not ring true to newsmen covering the South. They knew the councils served as "white-
collar Klans" that stopped short of publicly advocating violence,
but used intimidation and economic coercion to thwart desegregation and block blacks from voting and other political
activities. Since their members did indeed represent the power

structure in communities, and since they invariably knew who were the people committing the actual violence, their permissiveness was taken as encouragement—and their failure to enforce the law provided sanction—for those who would beat, bomb and kill in the name of protecting "a way of life."

As analyzed by John Elliff, a scholar given to careful understatement, "Hoover's picture of civil rights activity could hardly have been less favorable." The increasing signals of widespread violence might have led the Cabinet to determine that the government should intervene to protect civil rights, concluded Elliff, had not Hoover made that final false point—that the integrationist groups were either extremist or Communist-influenced, while segregationist groups were composed of the South's leading citizens.

The notion that organizations dedicated to the protection of constitutional guarantees, or to opening the doors of opportunity to all citizens, must somehow be Communist-inspired had long been an unfortunate aberration in the thinking of millions of Americans. Not only did this belief enable demagogues to hamper social progress—at an unknown cost to the peace and progress of all—it actually insulted the very persons who supported it, since it relied on the ironic assumption that the bedrock foundations of American democracy, such as the right to vote, were broadened only as the result of pressure from Communists. Southern Negroes needed no "Communist" to tell them they were being systematically cheated of their basic rights. They already knew this—just by being alive every day.

Whether Hoover's statement to the Cabinet in 1956 was actually nothing more than a diversionary tactic to discourage legislation which would have added new tasks to the FBI; whether it may have been based on incomplete or misleading information from the field; or whether it represented his true feelings was an open question. In any case, it supported those who would see him as an opponent of civil rights.

Controversy about FBI performance grew as the civil rights movement expanded, and today remains far from resolution. The crux of the problem was rooted in a scene repeated so often throughout the South that it virtually became a playlet.

Scene: A long line of Negroes stands outside the Dallas County Courthouse in Selma, Alabama, seeking to register to vote.

Time: October, 1963.

Action: Sheriff Jim Clark spots three SNCC workers standing across the street on the steps of the federal courthouse, quietly holding aloft voter registration signs. Clark and three deputies stride quickly up the steps, past two Justice Department attorneys and two FBI agents. They grab the three youths, arrest them for "unlawful assembly" and shove them into a police car. Although Sheriff Clark has no jurisdiction on federal property, and has clearly infringed on the right to vote and the rights of freedom of assembly and speech, the federal men do nothing.

There were hundreds of variations on that "living theater" but many had an added dimension: violence. Time after time, civil rights workers or local Negroes were beaten, often with the tacit approval and even participation of the police, while FBI agents limited themselves to standing by and taking notes.

The best-known example took place in 1961 when the "Freedom Riders," seeking to desegregate public transportation throughout the South with busloads of integrated passengers, arrived at the bus terminal in Montgomery, Alabama. There they were promptly set upon by a mob of a thousand club-wielding thugs who beat them viciously while Montgomery police, fully aware of what was happening, remained discreetly out of sight. One victim of the assault was John Seigenthaler, who was not a Freedom Rider but a special assistant to

Attorney General Robert Kennedy, acting as an observer and as the President's representative. Clubbed from behind as he attempted to help an injured Negro girl into a car, Seigenthaler lay unconscious and unaided in the gutter for twenty-five minutes. An FBI agent standing a few yards away witnessed the entire episode, but never deviated from his assignment, the taking of notes.

Since civic leaders and law-enforcement officials unfailingly bemoan incidents where private citizens refuse to aid someone being set upon by an attacker, scenes like this repeated throughout the South did not exactly enhance the image of the FBI in the eyes of those in the struggle for equal rights.

But the agents who stood by and only took notes were obeying orders, as summed up concisely in an FBI memo:

> The agents are present for the specific purpose of observing and reporting the facts to the Department of Justice in order that the Department will have the benefit of objective observations. If the Agent should become personally involved in the action, he would be deserting his assigned task and would be unable to fulfill his primary responsibility of making objective observations.

This restraint was a key source of confusion, bitterness and mistrust. Black people frequently questioned, as did Dr. King in an article in *The Nation* in 1964, why the richest and most powerful country on earth was apparently unable to enforce its most basic constitutional guarantees, for its own citizens, within its own boundaries. The feeling was expressed in a sign in the Jackson office of COFO (Council of Federated Organizations), the group that coordinated the massive "Freedom Summer" voting rights drive in Mississippi in 1964:

> There is a place in Mississippi called Liberty
> There is a department in Washington called Justice

The sarcasm was doubly biting since Liberty, Mississippi, was the scene of an unpunished racial murder.

Individual Negroes, fearing beatings or even death because of activities in the civil rights movement, understandably, if naïvely, believed that the FBI or *someone* had the duty to protect them. Some civil rights leaders realized, with frustration, that this was not technically the case. They knew the FBI was supposed to be the investigative arm of the Justice Department, digging out the facts so lawyers could effectively pursue the matter in court. But their complaint about the FBI was that the Bureau was not protecting the *rights* of Negroes, through its failure wholeheartedly to investigate crimes against federal law and the U. S. Constitution.

The Reverend C. T. Vivian, who directed affiliate operations for Dr. King's Southern Christian Leadership Conference, tolerantly expressed the doubts created by this failure:

"It's difficult to know who's to blame, for instance, when an assault against a Negro trying to vote or to peacefully assemble goes unpunished. No one with any sense would say it's all the FBI's fault. They write a report and the Justice Department gets it. Then we don't know what happens to it. Now a source of information close to the Department told me that many reports are written in such a way that the lawyer reading them doesn't get the total picture. It's one thing to say simply that a man is beaten; it's another if you show the beating is part of a pattern to deprive him of his rights.

"What does seem strange to me is that when a case gets national attention, the FBI seems able to do an impressive job. The murder of Lemuel Penn outside Athens, Georgia, let's say, or the murders of the three SNCC workers in Mississippi. But the day-by-day violations that don't make headlines, that's where we get disillusioned."

That disillusionment most often centered around the FBI's failure to make on-the-spot arrests. NAACP Director Roy Wilkins said, "All we ask is the kind of diligence the FBI shows in solving kidnappings and bank robberies," where of course agents quickly abandon their investigative roles and make on-the-spot arrests—widely publicized at that—whenever possible. Dr. King once remarked, "You can't explain to a Negro how it is that a plane can be bombed and its pieces scattered for miles and the crime can be solved, but they can't find out who bombed a church." Dr. King's example might be labeled hyperbole, since not many plane bombings are solved either, but the feeling of disillusionment is nonetheless real and the let-down is due in no small measure to the Bureau's own self-advertised image of infallibility.

The question of protection goes beyond the FBI, however, to a gray chasm in the statutes which has left administrators wide latitude in interpreting their responsibilities. The result has been that no agency or person can be said unmistakably to be responsible for seeing to it that the government fully respects the dictum of Article VI of the Constitution, which says "the laws of the United States . . . shall be the supreme law of the land." As noted by the U. S. Commission on Civil Rights in its exhaustive 1965 report on federal law enforcement in civil rights, "Severe self-limitations have been imposed on the scope of Federal protective action. Except where court orders have been previously obtained, the Department of Justice will not directly protect persons exercising Federal rights." The report also cited an FBI memo which stated that neither FBI agents nor United States marshals would arrest persons for offenses committed in their presence, or perform patrolling or other preventive duties in communities where there has been substantial racial violence.

A variety of reasons have been offered through the years by various Justice Department officials to justify the tight limits placed on federal protection. Some have said that providing a federal protective force in the absence of a court order would raise the most critical constitutional questions; yet there is a substantial body of legal thought that finds support for such actions, and in any case the department has on occasion taken them anyway, if indirectly.

Another contention, invoked by officials, including Attorney General Robert Kennedy and Hoover, who used it frequently, is that such use of force would violate the principles of federalism and lead to creation of a national police force. Proponents of broader federal action responded that the controls placed on such activities would be so strict as to safeguard any such possibility, that no ongoing national force could sustain itself, that such a force could never become national because it would be confined to very limited and specific geographic areas where local law enforcement had become grossly derelict and that its powers would be clearly limited and its numbers too small for any national impact. They noted, for example, that the total manpower of the FBI was less than one fourth that of the New York City police.

Another argument opposing federal protection activities is that they would discourage local authorities from carrying out their duties. Yet it is precisely *when* local authorities turn away that the need for federal protection arises. Moreover, where such presence was introduced, local authorities tended to assume, not abandon, their responsibilities. This was borne out not only by the general improvement of performance by Mississippi authorities in the wake of what they described as the FBI "invasion" in 1964, but on a smaller scale in Greenwood, Mississippi, in 1963 and Bogalusa, Louisiana, in 1965.

A final argument raised against use of federal protection is the serious concern that there could be a violent confrontation between federal and local officials. But as the Civil Rights Commission's 1965 report points out, this did not prove to be the case when federal forces were employed to enforce court orders in Little Rock, Montgomery, Oxford, Tuscaloosa, Selma and, on a smaller scale, on some thirty other occasions. In all of these cases, local authorities either stood aside or cooperated. If they had not, of course, the federal government would have had to use sufficient force to prevail.

A substantial body of legal opinion exists which denies that the government is anywhere near so statutorily limited in protecting citizens' civil rights, and suggests that alleged FBI (and Justice Department) restraint is simply a matter of choice.

Proponents of more vigorous federal action assert, first of all, that the Fourteenth Amendment clearly provides that states have no license to work their will, unchecked, on their residents without possible intervention by the federal government.

Professor Howard Zinn, in his study of the Student Nonviolent Coordinating Committee, offers an explicit authority for federal protection, a federal statute. Section 333, Title 10, of the U. S. Code says:

> The President, by using militia or the armed forces, or both, *or by any other means* shall take such measures as he considers necessary to suppress, in a State, any . . . domestic violence, unlawful combination, or conspiracy, if it . . . opposes or obstructs the execution of the laws of the United States or impedes the course of justice under those laws . . .

Analyzing Section 333 in its report on equal protection in the South, the U. S. Civil Rights Commission noted that although Section 333 has never been interpreted in the courts, the primary evil Congress sought to correct with its passage "was widespread violence by private citizens which went unchecked by local law enforcement officials."

Another seemingly explicit authority for federal protection is Section 3052, Title 18, of the U. S. Code, which gives agents the power to make arrests without a warrant "for any offense against the United States committed in their presence." This includes misdemeanors and felonies, and can even be used when agents "have reasonable grounds to believe" that a felony has been committed.

The FBI, thus sanctioned, has often gone far beyond mere note-taking. Indeed, agents have sought out fugitives and shot them to death on the spot. FBI literature celebrates the gunning down of John Dillinger, and FBI history is crammed with impressive instances of agents apprehending bank robbers at the scene of the crime. During the wave of airplane hijackings in the early 1970s FBI agents blazed away several times at hijacked planes parked for refueling.

On December 31, 1971, agents in Odessa, Florida, shot and killed a young black man who had been accused of slaying a Black Panther party member in New York. And on July 27, 1971, four FBI agents in Jacksonville, Florida, shot to death a twenty-three-year-old Negro, William Cox III, who they said slashed at them with a knife when they tried to arrest him. The local NAACP sought suspension of one of the agents, claiming Cox was "shot once and got the second slug while trying to get up." Mr. Hoover replied that his personal review found the agents had "acted with restraint."

But such actions, and the apparent statutory authorizations for on-the-spot arrests, have rarely been taken in regard to civil rights crimes.

Two other federal statutes go to the very heart of the civil rights enforcement question. They are Sections 242 and 241 of Title 18 of the U. S. Code.

Section 242 addresses itself to the problem of violence, brutality or other unlawful action by law-enforcement officials. It says:

Whoever, under color of any law, statute, ordinance, regulation, or custom, wilfully subjects, or causes to be subjected, any inhabitant of any State, Territory, or District to the deprivation of any rights, privileges, or immunities secured or protected by the Constitution and laws of the United States . . . shall be fined not more than $1,000 or imprisoned not more than one year, or both.†

Considerable difficulty in gaining convictions under 242 resulted from a landmark Supreme Court ruling in 1945, *Screws* v. *United States*, 325 U. S. 91 (1945). Sheriff Claude Screws and two other officers publicly beat to death a handcuffed young Negro father, Bobby Hall, in an open area near the center of the town of Newton, Georgia. When no state or local prosecution was commenced, Screws was charged under 242. He was freed when the Supreme Court ruled on the narrow ground that Screws and his companions had not murdered Hall with the "specific intent" of depriving him of his constitutional rights. Screws went on to win election to the Georgia State Senate in 1958, while the decision which bears his name has left an enduring haziness around the interpretation, and subsequent use, of 242.

Section 241, directed against racial violence by private persons, makes it a crime when "two or more persons conspire to injure, oppress, threaten, or intimidate any citizen in the free exercise or enjoyment of any right or privilege secured to him by the Constitution or laws of the United States."

Effectiveness of 241 has also been blunted by court rulings which give the government the burden of proving that the purpose of the conspiracy was to interfere with the free exercise of some right, and not merely to harm someone through malice.

Proponents of stronger federal action have nonetheless advocated much greater use of these statutes, both to seek clearer and broader rulings from the courts, and because the very fact that offenders are constantly prosecuted would in itself deter

† Amended in 1968 to add ". . . and if death results shall be subject to imprisonment for any term of years or for life."

violence and thus protect potential victims of civil rights crimes. But those with the power to prosecute under Sections 241 and 242 have generally accepted the limited view.

On a 1970 CBS program the Reverend Andrew Young, who had been Dr. King's top aide, and former Attorney General Nicholas Katzenbach summed up the contrasting attitudes:

> YOUNG: I think that our experience with the FBI, from '60 to '65 especially, was that no matter what kind of violence, no matter what kind of brutality . . . all the FBI agents did was stand over on the corner and take notes.
>
> KATZENBACH: Dr. King wanted the FBI to do things that the FBI did not want to do, did not feel it should do, did not feel it had the authority to do. And I think to a large extent the Bureau was right and Dr. King was wrong.

Obviously, Young and Katzenbach each viewed the situation in terms of his own experience and training. Civil rights workers were frustrated by the government's apparent unwillingness to protect them when they knew that every day, working amid conditions of blatant injustice, their very lives were on the line. Government officials realized this, but they operated within a context of caution shaped by careful legal training, respect for precedent, bureaucratic reluctance to experiment and administrative considerations that serve to limit bold initiatives. Also, literally every man in a position of power was white, and it was difficult, even for the most well-meaning among them, to approach these problems as other than abstractions.

The U. S. Civil Rights Commission, after two intensive studies of the legal avenues available to the Justice Department (1961 and 1965), stated: "The limitations on Federal action expressed by the Department of Justice . . . are limitations of policy." The Commission found two types of situations where the federal government was not exercising its full authority:

First, where persons seeking to exercise specific rights have been subjected to violent interference by mobs which were not controlled by local authorities, and second, where widespread violence was unconnected with the assertion of any particular right but deterred Negroes from attempting to exercise rights.

Those two areas comprise an enormous proportion of the action which constituted the segregationists' effort to deprive Negroes of their rights.

If there was ambivalence over the FBI's jurisdiction in civil rights, and in Hoover's back-and-forth statements about Communists in the movement, civil rights advocates saw at least three other, more clear-cut reasons for the FBI's reluctance to take the initiative.

First, Hoover wanted no part of any action that would alienate the powerful bloc of southern congressmen who, by reason of longevity, chaired most major committees, dominated Congress and controlled his budget. Second, there was his passion for championship statistics; he wanted the Bureau to work on cases that would result in convictions, an unlikely prospect in a region where Negro targets of white violence were treated as suspects, not as victims. Third, Hoover was traditionally anxious not to offend local police, whose cooperation the Bureau often needed when investigating other categories of crime. A complicated set of investigative procedures for police brutality complaints tended to keep the FBI out of such cases, leaving the investigation in the hands of the very authorities accused of the offense.

The FBI's relationship to local police, indeed, was one of the main sources of mistrust by blacks and civil rights workers. The movement endured hundreds, undoubtedly thousands, of incidents of police brutality, virtually all unpunished. It was understandable that Negroes came to think of the all-white

FBI they saw in the South as just another component of the all-white system of discriminatory southern justice.

This feeling overlooked the fact that on many occasions events would have been even worse had it not been for FBI presence. But the feeling had more than enough reality behind it: the beating and fatal shooting of Jimmy Lee Jackson, Negro, by Alabama State Troopers in Marion; the fatal shooting of unarmed Rev. Jonathan Daniels, white, by Deputy Thomas Coleman in Hayneville, Alabama; the kicking, clubbing and gassing of men, women and children by Mississippi State Highway Patrolmen in Canton during the Meredith March; the shoving and jabbing with electric cattle prods of would-be voters in Selma, where Sheriff Jim Clark and his posse later trampled marchers with horses at the Pettus Bridges. These and other examples of unpunished police behavior constituted the grassroots view of a pattern the FBI seemed to do little to combat.

FBI and Justice Department policies further aggravated the problem. The FBI insisted on notifying local authorities, in advance, whenever one of their officers was about to be investigated. This not only gave the officer time to prepare an alibi, it made victims and witnesses reluctant to file complaints with the FBI in the first place, fearing the police would learn who had complained and might take revenge after the investigation ended.

This particular fear was dramatically borne out by the case of Louis Allen, a Negro witness to a racial murder in Liberty, Mississippi, in September, 1961. Civil rights workers helped Allen get word to the Justice Department that he wanted to testify to a grand jury, which he did. The killer was exonerated anyway, but six months later Allen suffered a broken jaw when a deputy sheriff hit him with a flashlight, telling him he knew Allen had told his story to the FBI. Allen was slain in 1964; no arrests were ever made.

The close relationship of FBI agents with local authorities

often made them appear part of the white power structure, which "kept Negroes in their place," and sympathetic to its cause.

A special U. S. Civil Rights Commission report on Mississippi stated:

> Whatever the reason, the fact that police officers are rarely tried on civil rights charges has led the public to believe that few serious charges are ever made, and has reinforced the belief among offending peace officers that they may mistreat Negroes as their whims direct them.

An earlier Commission report (1961) had already observed that this problem was exacerbated by such department and FBI policies as requiring signed complaints despite the fact that many individuals were unaware of their rights or afraid to press them, as well as:

> . . . a tendency to close some cases without complete investigation; and deference to State authorities which results in withholding any investigation pending State action even at the risk of allowing the evidence to grow stale.

It was not surprising that when local policemen were accused of violating federal laws, FBI agents, who often worked closely with them on other cases, were loath to investigate. A stark example of this occurred in Orangeburg, South Carolina, where on the night of February 8, 1968, South Carolina State Police opened fire from three sides on a crowd of unarmed black students at South Carolina State College. Three students were killed and twenty-eight wounded, all but three shot from the rear or side, some even in the soles of their feet while crawling away. No evidence was ever produced that any of the hundreds of officers and guardsmen in the area had been fired upon. No officers were convicted for the action, and indeed most of those known to have fired their weapons were later promoted.

The FBI's role in this tragedy was painstakingly documented by two white, southern-born reporters, Jack Nelson and Jack Bass, in their book *The Orangeburg Massacre*. The authors learned that two days after the FBI began its investigation, the FBI agent in charge, Charles DeFord, was sharing the same motel room with Chief J. P. Strom, the top state police official on the scene at the time of the shooting, and the man whose actions should have been subject to the most thorough investigation by the FBI.

Even more astonishing, two of three FBI agents who witnessed the shooting—DeFord was one of them—told an attorney from the Civil Rights Division of the Justice Department that they had *not* been present when it happened. It was not until nearly three months later that the Justice Department, trying to develop a case, finally learned that the three were actually eyewitnesses.

When authors Nelson and Bass later asked agent DeFord why he had not disclosed his presence, DeFord replied, "I don't want to say a damn thing about it. I don't want to get in a pissing match with the civil-rights attorneys."

The authors also learned that state agents participated in a largely unsuccessful FBI search for evidence on the campus the morning after the shooting. Three months later, Civil Rights Division attorneys—not FBI agents—learned that a black free-lance photographer had found a dozen shotgun shells at the scene early that morning.

Finally, an agent who had been stationed in South Carolina for eleven years and had helped train the state riot patrol squads on duty at Orangeburg testified that he heard gunfire coming from the campus just prior to the time the patrol opened fire. No other evidence of shots from the campus was ever presented.

The sum total of these discoveries led Nelson and Bass to conclude:

> Regardless of the motive, the FBI had, at the very least, hampered an important Justice Department investigation. If the department had known FBI agents were eyewitnesses, its attorneys quickly could have established some of the pertinent facts, instead of having to grope for an understanding of what had happened. The FBI even submitted a written report of its investigation to the civil rights division two months after the shooting without mentioning that agents had been witnesses.

Hoover responded to the book with a letter denying that any agents were at the scene of the shooting (although three agents had given eyewitness testimony at the trial) and denying all the other assertions regarding the FBI. Later, in response to reporters' questions, Hoover referred to Nelson as "a skunk."

II: Mississippi: The Anomaly

Almost constant tension between the FBI and the Civil Rights Division of the Justice Department grew out of the FBI's reluctance to investigate civil rights cases, especially those involving police violence. There was one period, however, when that reluctance appeared to soften. It began in the spring of 1964 when, in response to national outrage over the breakdown of law and order in Mississippi, President Johnson ordered Hoover to open a field office in Jackson.

John Doar, a tall, slender, serious young attorney, a key member of the Civil Rights Division from 1960–67, regarded by all sides as one of the most conscientious and diligent figures on the southern scene, discussed the change in FBI performance during his appearance at the Princeton conference.

Doar doubted if Hoover had actually known what poor work his agents had been doing in Mississippi. Discussing voting discrimination against Negroes, Doar stated, "The Bureau didn't know the first thing about its job, and made very little attempt to learn about it."

Civil Rights Division lawyers began doing the exhaustive job of records analysis which rightfully belonged to the Bureau. Why? "Because we knew that if the Bureau didn't want to do the work we wouldn't get good performance." Sometimes division lawyers, determined that the FBI would do a complete job, drafted investigative requests in exhaustive detail. Doar recalled one 1962 memo "which went on in the most minute detail for 174 pages, explaining, anticipating, cautioning and coaching the Bureau agents." The memo was "typical of many sent in those years."

In cases of voter intimidation, such as the circulation of lists of names of black people who had sought to register, Doar found FBI investigations "superficial." Division lawyers had to come down and conduct the investigations themselves because the agents "just weren't geared up to their assignment in any way, shape or form." The attorneys also had to conduct most of the interviews with black people, while the FBI interviewed the whites.

Finally, in what amounted to a challenge to Hoover, Attorney General Robert Kennedy dispatched to Mississippi in the spring of 1964 a crack team of twenty Justice Department lawyers fresh from the case of Jimmy Hoffa, under the direction of Walter Sheridan. President Johnson also sent the CIA's Allen Dulles to appraise the situation.

As a result, in July, 1964, Hoover opened a field office in Jackson, Mississippi, "and from that time on in Mississippi the Bureau really performed," said Doar.

The occasion of the opening itself, however, was not particularly heartening to Mississippi Negroes and civil rights workers who had been enduring an unprecedented wave of economic intimidation, bombings, burnings, fires, shootings, beatings and murder. Hoover, who had come to Jackson to dedicate the new office, took the opportunity to assert that the FBI "most certainly" would not offer protection to civil rights workers. Coming some three weeks after the disappearance of three civil rights workers in Neshoba County, the remark seemed at least unnecessary. Mr. Hoover went on to introduce Governor Paul Johnson as "a man I have long admired from a distance"; many Americans, recalling that during his campaign Governor Johnson had used the shibboleth "alligators, apes, coons and possums" in referring to the NAACP, did not share this admiration.

Nonetheless, the FBI went on to perform in Mississippi in an exceptionally positive way. It secured arrests after the dismembered bodies of two Negroes were found in a river; it solved a 1963 Natchez civil rights beating; and it helped apprehend ten men who had bombed sixteen Negro churches and homes in McComb. (A Mississippi circuit judge named J. W. Watkins let the bombers off with suspended sentences on the ground they had been "provoked" and that they were mainly "young men starting out in life"—one was forty-four, and four others were in their thirties.) The very threat of FBI intervention restrained both hostile police and terrorists. The FBI infiltrated the Ku Klux Klan and gradually sapped the menace of an indigenous Mississippi Klan called the White Knights, which had dedicated itself to terrorism. Hoover could boast with justifiable pride, "There are 480 Klansmen in Mississippi . . . I had our agents interview every member of the Klan there, just to let them know we know who they are." Ironically it was just such seemingly simple tactics—being very visible and letting lawbreakers know they were being watched —which in good measure constituted the very protection civil rights workers had sought, and which Hoover had opposed, for so many years. Such a federal presence—delayed for so long on the ground that it would violate the principles of federalism or even, as some claimed, set off a second Civil War—would not have stopped every terrorist act, but would surely have been an exceedingly strong deterrent. It would also have given more courage to many whites of good will who were afraid to speak out, creating a silence that gave added license to the violence-prone.

III: Racial Policies Within the Bureau

FBI reluctance to protect civil rights workers also spurred wide discussion of Mr. Hoover's, *ergo* the Bureau's, attitude toward minorities. Civil rights leaders constantly prodded the Bureau over its lack of any black agents in the South, and over Hoover's refusal to reveal how many black agents the Bureau had anywhere else.

When Congressman Don Edwards (himself a former agent) of the House Judiciary Committee asked all federal agencies in 1967 how many Negro employees they had in Mississippi, all of the departments answered "courteously and in detail," he said, except Hoover. He responded:

> Dear Mr. Congressman: I have your letter of September 25th in which you inquired about the accuracy of several reports that there are no Negroes in Mississippi offices of the Department of Justice. While I cannot speak for the Department of Justice as a whole, insofar as the FBI is concerned, I wish to advise that our employees are assigned wherever the need for them is greatest. Sincerely yours, John Edgar Hoover.

Hoover's repeated remarks that he would not lower FBI standards to increase minority employment—when it turned out the standards (the myth that all agents are lawyers or accountants) were deceptive to begin with—caused further questions about the FBI's impartiality. Such questions apparently never fazed Hoover. In 1964, in the midst of controversy over the FBI in the South, Hoover told *Newsweek* he was a "states' righter" and blamed civil rights troubles on the "harsh approach to the Mississippi situation by the authorities here in Washington." He chose December, 1970, in the wake of revelations about FBI hiring policies, to tell *Time* magazine that Bobby Kennedy ". . . wanted me to lower our qualifications and to hire more Negro agents. I said, 'Bobby, that's not going to be done as long as I'm Director of this Bureau.'"

Black faces among the ranks of FBI agents during the southern civil rights crisis would have countered much of the distrust felt by civil rights advocates. One excuse for their absence was that stationing black agents in the South would have been an exercise in futility from the pure law-enforcement point of view. Yet the city of Atlanta had desegregated its police in the 1940s, and by 1968 the force was 20 per cent black. Dozens of other southern cities added black policemen during the 1960s, but as far as can be learned, there were still no black FBI agents—or at most one—in the South in 1971.

In the instances of lack of black agents and general unwillingness to protect civil rights, the FBI was criticized during the early movement years for sins of omission. But another part of the deterioration of what in the beginning had been a strong faith in the FBI among Negro Southerners involved increasing criticism of the agency for sins of commission. As in many other areas, complaints about the agency not acting were joined by complaints about how it operated when it did act. Eventually many blacks, other minorities and dissidents came to regard the FBI as an instrument of oppression, and the building of this feeling can be traced through the treatment of various individuals and groups in a series of situations through the 1960s and continuing today.

By far the most spectacular—and most publicized—episode

concerning Hoover and racial matters was his statement on November 18, 1964, that Dr. King was "the most notorious liar in the country." The remark stemmed from King's 1962 charge that FBI agents in Albany, Georgia, were all southern-born and were incapable of viewing Negroes impartially. King's specific mention of the Albany office happened to be inaccurate; four of the five agents there were northern-born. But the feeling that the FBI was not in sympathy with the Negro was expressed many times before and after King's 1962 charge.

Promptly after Hoover's blast, King requested a meeting with the Director in Washington. King and three of his aides were closeted with Hoover for fifty minutes, after which King took off for Sweden to accept the Nobel Peace Prize. King never again publicly criticized Hoover. This created speculation that Hoover had "blackmailed" King by threatening to expose details of his alleged extramarital sex life. The three King aides who were there have persistently denied this, saying the meeting was cordial.

What actually took place cannot be known until the FBI releases a transcript, but considerable fuel was added to the blackmail theory when FBI agents began approaching various reporters with details of King's personal life supposedly from Bureau files. The controversy reached a new, even more serious dimension when it was revealed, during FBI testimony in the draft trial of Muhammad Ali, that the FBI had both wire-tapped and bugged Dr. King for several years. This led to charges that Hoover was out to smear King. That controversy continued long after Dr. King's assassination. *The National Observer* of April 12, 1971, for example, quoted a former Justice Department official as saying, "You couldn't spend 30 minutes with Mr. Hoover without his bringing up the sex thing about Dr. King."

That same day, columnist Jack Anderson reported that he

had been shown an FBI memo sent to ex-President Johnson, dated February 20, 1968, which detailed the private life of Dr. King. This prompted William Buckley, long a champion of the FBI, to write on April 27, 1971, that if the column were true, "I consider this the most serious charge leveled against the FBI, inasmuch as Dr. King was not a government employee, and assaults on his privacy, if they do not bear remotely on the security of the nation against crime or subversion, are inexcusable."

When Hoover told *Time* magazine, in December, 1970, "I held him [Dr. King] in complete contempt because of the things he said and because of his conduct," the issue was closed for many people. In that same remarkable interview, Hoover added that Dr. King "was the last one in the world" who should have received the Nobel Peace Prize. He cast considerable doubt on the idea that his famous 1964 meeting with King had been cordial when he also told *Time:*

> First I felt I shouldn't see him, but then I thought he might become a martyr if I didn't. King was very suave and smooth. I said 'if you ever say anything that's a lie again, I'll brand you a liar again.' Strange to say, he never attacked the Bureau again for as long as he lived.

Growing minority distrust of the FBI may have been irrevocably set by the events in the Albany, Georgia, civil rights campaigns of 1962–63. Once famous as the center of the slave-trading market for southwest Georgia, Albany is located in an area blacks regarded as the meanest in the state.

The civil rights drives were met by tenacious resistance, marked by shocking instances of police brutality. C. B. King, the only Negro attorney in Albany and a civil rights activist, was beaten badly with a walking stick by the Dougherty County sheriff. His brother's wife, five months pregnant and carrying a three-year-old child, was visiting some youngsters in the Camilla jail when a deputy knocked her to the ground; her baby was born dead. Police arrested a sixteen-year-old girl for trying to enter a bowling alley, then dragged her down stone steps and kicked her repeatedly in the back and side.

While these incredible incidents of police brutality piled up, some 2,000 non-violent demonstrators were arrested at various times. Yet the one case the federal government chose to prosecute was that of nine civil rights workers arrested for picketing the grocery store of a white man. The grocer had been part of a jury that exonerated a sheriff who had shot a Negro prisoner in the neck while the Negro sat handcuffed in the sheriff's car. The demonstrators claimed they had picketed not to "obstruct justice" by intimidating a juror, but because of the man's racist hiring policies.

While much of the blame for this federal behavior clearly belonged to the Justice Department, the FBI's enthusiasm, reflected through the manpower it assigned to the investigation, was not lost on civil rights workers. Various estimates held that the FBI assigned from thirty to eighty-six men to investigate the case of the pickets (eight of the nine were convicted by a jury from which the United States excluded all Negroes by peremptory challenge), while exactly one man— the resident agent who had lived several years in the white community of Albany—investigated the beatings of C. B. King and his sister-in-law. No action was ever taken.

In Texas, where blacks and Mexican-Americans had long been victims of discrimination, a Houston mother told the U. S. Commission on Civil Rights of her efforts to enroll her child in a white public school in 1967. Having failed through normal channels, she wrote to the FBI in Houston for help. She testified that three days later:

. . . I got a call from the FBI in Houston to come to the office and I was questioned for about 3 hours. Well, he wanted to know just everything, why did I go, who sent me, and what organizations did I belong to, how much money did I have, how much did my car cost, who was paying me to do this and so forth.

She added that the FBI had also asked her if she belonged to any Communist organization.

The Reverend Ralph Ruiz, who ministers to a *barrio* in San Antonio, appeared in a TV documentary alleging widespread hunger and malnutrition in San Antonio. He said the House Agriculture Committee's Appropriations Subcommittee sent FBI agents to interview him and his parishioners: to "prove that what we claim is not true. I can handle these guys myself, they don't frighten me and they don't intimidate me. But then when they go and bother people who are no match for them, I think this is a crime."

Superficial investigations have also met the complaints of Mexican-Americans. After an incident in Uvalde, Texas, for example, the Civil Rights Commission complained to Washington about the obvious inadequacy of an FBI investigation. Justice Department attorneys reinvestigated and a Texas Highway Patrolman was charged with a violation of federal law.

One persistent problem in Texas was the repeated allegation that the FBI did little to discourage improper actions by the Texas Highway Patrol. The Texas Highway Patrol is a textbook example of how the power structure in a given area may use its law-enforcement agencies to repress poor and minority groups. To ensure a plentiful supply of cheap farm labor, growers employed both migrant workers and "commuter" labor—Mexican citizens with special permits to cross the border temporarily. In Texas, as late as 1971, farm workers were not covered by workmen's compensation, unemployment or disability insurance. Texas law allowed growers to pay farm workers 20 cents per hour less than the federal minimum, and to ignore minimum wage laws altogether when employing other members of a worker's family living with him in housing owned by the grower. Housing and education standards were poor, and workers' health suffered because many hospitals refused to treat them unless they paid a deposit of $50 to $75.

Laws existed to hinder any efforts to organize farm workers, such as a "mass picketing" statute requiring pickets to remain 50 feet apart. The Texas Advisory Committee to the U. S. Commission on Civil Rights also found massive deployment of officers, including Texas Rangers, at the behest of the growers, and "strong evidence . . . that the conduct of law officers in strike situations in South Texas is not neutral, but rather supportive of the farm operators' position and intimidating to laborers and labor organizers."

In other words, thousands of workers were systematically locked into a cycle of poverty and exploitation. These conditions prompted the Reverend Theodore Hesburgh, President of Notre Dame University and Chairman of the U. S. Commission on Civil Rights, to observe that "this is about as close as you can come to slavery . . . or a complete deprival of normal civil and human rights . . . and it ought to be made a Federal case."

Far from making such activity a "Federal case," the U. S. Government contributed to the situation by tolerating the most minimal use of federal food programs for the thousands of needy families in the area. When FBI agents began interviewing hungry people with the implication that their efforts to reach a mere subsistence standard of living were somehow subversive, Mexican-American leaders like Rev. Ruiz commented bitterly:

> . . . Characters like the FBI agents come around asking these kind of questions, you know, about how much money you get,

does your husband work, what do you eat, are you telling the truth.

To these people, such actions made the FBI seem no more than an extension of the Texas Rangers, sympathizing with their brutalizers rather than seeing to it that justice was administered impartially.

Without question, an increase in minority group employment would have helped the FBI meet civil rights problems in the Southwest. A survey of five states (Texas, New Mexico, California, Arizona and Colorado) revealed that at the end of 1967, only 2.7 per cent of 1,811 GS (General Schedule) FBI employees were Mexican-American. This included only 3 of 772 employees in the executive and supervisory grades of GS12–18, and 3 of 365 from GS9–11.

A review of complaints of police brutality involving Mexican-Americans in the Southwest led the U. S. Commission on Civil Rights to observe that "more aggressive initial investigation [by the FBI] and more frequent reinvestigation by Department of Justice attorneys could potentially have produced" evidence to prosecute many cases which instead were "closed." Frequently, investigations appeared to be incomplete, halfhearted or even biased.

A young Mexican-American from Uvalde, Texas, complained of being beaten by a deputy sheriff, and later being called a "damn liar" by the FBI investigating agent. After a Mexican-American who had been a leader in the fight against drugs in his community complained of being beaten by police in Blythe, California, he reported that FBI agents clearly indicated they did not believe his story and had asked whether he might have been under the influence of drugs. When the car in which Natividad Fuentes and his wife were driving home skidded out of control on an icy highway near Uvalde, Texas, in January, 1968, two highway patrolmen came upon the accident. Finding the shaken couple still sitting in the car, one patrolman yanked open the door, jerked Fuentes out, accused him of being drunk, hit him repeatedly over the head with a blackjack and jailed him on a charge of drunken driving. Two months later an FBI agent investigating the case reportedly spent only five minutes interviewing the victim, asked him nothing pertinent to the beating, but inquired instead whether Fuentes had any previous arrests and whether he was actively supporting two local Mexican-American political candidates. When this investigation brought no action from the Department of Justice, a Civil Rights Division attorney reinvestigated, and a charge of assault was filed against one of the patrolmen.

Police claims that a victim was injured because he stumbled or fell "were so frequent . . . as to be suspect," said the commission report. Numerous complaints against the same officer apparently had no influence on a decision whether to prosecute him. Events like the ones capsuled above were apparently frequent enough to prompt the Texas Advisory Committee of the Civil Rights Commission to recommend that ". . . an agency other than the Federal Bureau of Investigation have the primary responsibility for investigating all cases of alleged police brutality that might be a violation of Federal law."

The parallels are obvious between the treatment of Mexican-Americans by law-enforcement authorities in Texas and, say, black sharecroppers by law-enforcement authorities in the Deep South and between the 1970's stirrings among Puerto Ricans and Mexican-Americans and the 1950's stirrings in the South. The FBI needed to demonstrate sensitivity to the unique problems and racial overtones inherent in both situations. As has already been seen, there were unfortunate failures to meet this need with regard to blacks. Similar failure with regard to Puerto Ricans and Mexican-Americans is reflected in a statement by Hoover, as reported in the December 14, 1970, *Time* magazine: "You never have to bother about a President being shot by Puerto Ricans or Mexicans. They don't shoot straight. But if they come at you with a knife, beware."

Another perspective on the question of Hoover's and the Bureau's attitude toward minority groups was offered at the Princeton conference by Charles Morgan, Jr., then Southern Regional Director of the American Civil Liberties Union, and a board member of the Southern Christian Leadership Conference. Morgan noted that there was "an equation in the Bureau's mind" between groups like the Klan and groups like SCLC. Yet the Klan was dedicated to violence while Dr. King was dedicated to non-violence.

"One thing I know about this country," said Morgan, "is that a man has a constitutional right to hate and he has a constitutional right to talk about it. But he *doesn't* have a constitutional right to kill folks and he doesn't have a constitutional right to deprive other people of their rights. Yet the Klan was under surveillance and so were we. I think it's extremely important that law-enforcement agencies bear in mind the distinction that must be made between political thought and the commission of violent crimes. They are not the same things even though they can merge. The FBI eavesdropped and infiltrated groups there was no business infiltrating."

Many civil rights advocates contended there were racial undertones in the FBI's decision to infiltrate and eavesdrop on non-violent groups. They also believed that as black militancy in the late 1960s spawned groups like the Black Panthers, Hoover exaggerated their importance because of his own racial attitudes combined with faulty information. Hoover stated in his 1968 year-end summary that "the growing number of black extremist organizations . . . represent a potential threat to the internal security of the nation, and their growth has definitely added to the FBI's work in the racial intelligence field." In 1970 Hoover's report discussed the Black Panthers as the very first order of business, calling them "the most dangerous and violence prone of all extremist groups," and in 1971 the Panthers again received featured attention.

Two leading black civil rights figures at the Princeton conference told why blacks felt Hoover's estimation of the Panthers was grossly exaggerated. The Reverend Andrew Young said the FBI's "totally irrational pursuit of the Panthers" added to its attacks on Dr. King, had ruined the Bureau's credibility among blacks. "I don't think anybody takes them seriously except as a strong police effort to . . . keep blacks down," he said. The Panthers had almost no support in black communities, said Young, "until they became the victims of the persecution campaign of the FBI and of the Chicago police." Young said this mistaken emphasis occurred because the FBI "didn't learn to distinguish verbal violence and frustration from hard-core revolutionary activity. Their intelligence into the black community was so farfetched they really couldn't understand the information they were getting. They didn't understand minorities. The FBI must be far more integrated . . . and it's got to be open to learn from its minority staff members rather than try to put them into the emotional and political bind of its Director." Roger Wilkins, former Director of the Justice Department's Community Relations Service, seconded Young.

Civil rights advocates contended that exaggerated suspicions about blacks resulted in the type of activity revealed in the Media documents, namely, instructions to infiltrate every black student group in the nation. Moreover, the racial implications of such instructions added considerable new fuel to the already heated debate over the propriety, legality and limits of employing infiltrators and informers at all.

It was beyond dispute, however, that the FBI solved some of the most heinous civil rights crimes of the middle 1960s only through the use of informers. One major case thus broken was the 1965 murder of Mrs. Viola Liuzzo, the white housewife shot to death while ferrying marchers back and forth on the highway between Selma and Montgomery. It turned out that one of the four Klansmen riding in the murder car was an FBI informant named Gary Thomas Rowe. While Rowe's revelations solved the case, the value of informers in that particular situation was brought somewhat into doubt since Rowe did not act to save Mrs. Liuzzo's life—perhaps by bumping against the triggerman as he took aim.

But there were no questions about the value of informers in solving one of the most infamous cases of all: the murder of James Chaney, Andrew Goodman and Michael Schwerner by Klansmen and police near Philadelphia, Mississippi, where their bodies lay hidden for months, buried in an earthen dam. The case would never have been solved had the FBI not acquired informers. Such a striking success gave impetus and general support to the FBI's publicized tactic of infiltrating every Klan klavern in Mississippi.

The tactic understandably had the strong support of John Doar, who led the successful prosecution of many of the killers before Mississippi juries. As Doar recounted it to the Princeton conference:

> The Bureau did a real job. Now they did a lot of things. They did a lot of surveilling. They took down a lot of license plates. They penetrated some secret and some private organizations. They used informants. They paid large sums of money to get information. But as they did this, and they did it in a situation where there was really no local law enforcement, conditions improved. The violence subsided. The bombings were reduced.

This conspiratorial midnight group of killers was controlled—
and brought to courts for trial, prosecution and conviction.

While everything John Doar said was true, another Mississippi event revealed just how tangled the efficacy of such
tactics can be. On the night of June 30, 1968—as the result
of arrangements made between the FBI, Meridian police,
the Anti-Defamation League of B'nai B'rith and leaders of the
Jewish community in Meridian—two young Klan terrorists were
lured into a bombing attempt by two informers who were paid
$38,500 for the job. One of the would-be bombers, Thomas
Tarrants III, 21, was wounded, captured and sentenced to
thirty years in prison. His companion, Mrs. Kathy Ainsworth,
twenty-six, was shot to death by the police.

"Policemen who sprang the trap say they expected a gun
battle and never thought either Klan member would be
taken alive," wrote Jack Nelson, who broke the story in the
Los Angeles *Times*. Thus, while pursuing the very worthy
purpose of stopping a wave of bombings that had terrorized
Jewish and Negro residents of Meridian and Jackson, the FBI
and police acted as judge, jury and executioner of a young
woman of whom the authorities knew nothing until after they
had killed her.

Because the victims of that particular case of entrapment
were both members of the White Knights of the Ku Klux Klan,
a group most people regarded as undesirable, there was virtually no public furor, even though Mrs. Ainsworth, a popular
Jackson teacher, was known to have committed no crime other
than the one into which the police had lured her.

But if the FBI and police could use informers to lure
"undesirables" into the commission of crimes—who might the
police next consider undesirable enough to punish without
benefit of trial? Might it be Black Panthers? Or student radicals?

IV: Control of Informers and Infiltration

Some of those doubts were answered, and the doubts over *agents provocateurs* fully ignited, in the ensuing years. Police did indeed start shooting down Black Panthers, often under highly doubtful circumstances, and there was evidence that undercover agents, not student radicals, were provoking violence on many campuses North and South, from coast to coast.

The President's Commission on Campus Unrest noted that it was frequently difficult to draw the line between a legitimate informer and an *agent provocateur*. The commission stated:

> The credibility and therefore the continued effectiveness of an informer or undercover agent may well depend on his willingness to participate in unlawful activity. It is a matter of no great moment if he merely becomes a passive participant in a sit-in. But it becomes deeply troubling when he begins hurling rocks, and it is plainly intolerable when he urges others to engage in violent conduct.

Such considerations sparked sharp debate during the Princeton conference. Some called for total prohibition of informers on the ground that they were used mainly for the illegal purpose of political surveillance. They argued that the FBI must be strictly limited to the investigation of crimes actually committed, and not be allowed, in effect, to engineer crimes through entrapment or other manipulation by informers. If a political group—whether Klan or Weatherman—throws a bomb, that is a crime, not a political act, and should by all means be investigated by the Bureau. If not, there are absolutely no grounds for surveillance.

On the opposite side were those arguing for extensive, virtually unchecked use of infiltration and informers on the ground that many of today's politically motivated crimes, especially bombing, leave no evidence and can only be detected through surveillance.

In the middle were those like Professor Thomas Emerson of Yale who agreed there is a place for informers but that their use must be strictly controlled by such judicial safeguards as a warrant. "No one is going to say that with respect to a terrorist organization there can be no use of an informer," said Emerson, calling for strict separation of law enforcement from the collection of political intelligence. Or, to put it another way, it might be proper to infiltrate the Klan, with its long record of lawlessness, but not the John Birch Society— which operated solely in the realm of ideology. Every safeguard must be taken, however, to ensure that informers do not stimulate further violent activity. Their warrants to operate should be of limited duration, and their activities constantly monitored by an outside agency.

V: *Past Failure, Future Possibilities*

The FBI's civil rights performance in the South of the 1960s—when it was dealing with what may have been the greatest non-violent revolution the world has ever seen—cannot be evaluated without also considering the leadership provided by the Department of Justice. Observers have said, for example, that the department did not establish effective enough coordination of civil rights activities among other agencies of the government. They have noted that the department tended to view civil rights issues too often in terms of litigation alone, ignoring administrative enforcement possibilities. And in the litigative area itself, they have contended that the department could have made far broader use of injunctions, which would have eliminated the vagueness over jurisdiction, federal protection and on-the-spot arrests. At the same time, there is no question that the department's Civil Rights Division was woefully understaffed, and that its lawyers certainly would have been more effective had Congress earlier provided sharper statutory tools with which to work.

For all that, the fact is inescapable that the FBI's civil rights performance was at best vacillating. Its work in Mississippi in 1964—where one day it said it lacked jurisdiction and the next day suddenly found it—belied the limitations it claimed. Such vacillation underlined the fact that no future Director should be as independent of his superiors as Hoover.

No one can know how much suffering and violence would have been averted had the FBI—and the other government agencies—moved sooner in the South. How tragic, looking back now, that the segregationist tactic of massive resistance was tolerated, given time to work its way to a frenzy of false fears stirred for the benefit of demagogues.

Several suggestions for strengthening the FBI's ability to enforce civil rights laws were made repeatedly as the result of experience in the South.

First and foremost was integration—the need for the FBI to make a substantial increase in the number of agents from minority groups. No lily-white agency, however well-intentioned, can fully appreciate the subtle but potent problems stemming from race.

Another persistent suggestion called for a separate team of agents to make civil rights arrests, while others perform normal investigative work. This could help solve the problem of relations with local police, making possible better handling of cases of police brutality against minorities. Another recommendation called for legislation making employers of police financially liable for damages in cases of police brutality, on the ground that communities would be less likely to tolerate such misconduct if they had to pay for it.

The very presence of the FBI has nearly always curtailed

violence. Many people felt that essentially lawless regions, like parts of the Deep South in the 1960s, could be controlled by the conspicuous daily presence of authorities who made it unmistakably clear they would not tolerate violence. The same could be true in any future emergency, whether it be a wave of police shootings of blacks, or a pattern of brutality against Mexican-Americans.

Of vital over-all importance is the image the Bureau projects in the eyes of minorities and local authorities alike. The need is for a Director with a clearly enunciated understanding of civil rights and liberties. The Reverend C. T. Vivian put it another way in 1965:

> All we're concerned about Mr. Hoover is that he does his job. Less than a week after his "liar" charge at Dr. King, a week when he had time to see the worldwide impact, he came out again in a speech declaring himself for states' rights and against minority groups trampling on the rights of others. Now everybody knows what a statement like that translates into down here, and we resent it. Negroes are the ones who have had their rights trampled on for decades. And if Mr. Hoover doesn't know that by now, it's time he learned.

VI: Conference Discussion

MR. SCHLESINGER: I think if the recommendations that have been made at this conference by, for example, Mr. Emerson or Mr. Donner had been operative in the South in the 1960s, the Bureau could not have done the job it did in Mississippi. The job described required the use of methods of surveillance that, I take it, Mr. Emerson and Mr. Donner would deny the Bureau. If this is so, I'd be interested in Mr. Emerson's and Mr. Donner's reaction.

MR. EMERSON: My suggestion was to divorce the actual enforcement of federal law, on the one hand, from the collection of political intelligence on the other. I said that I thought one example of this difference would be that the Bureau could properly keep track of the Klan, but should not attempt to infiltrate the John Birch Society.

The situation in the South seems to have involved overwhelming violation of federal law. There was, of course, a political ideology in the background. But the immediate problem was not with the ideology; the immediate problem was the use of violence and methods of terror.

It is the FBI's job to deal with that kind of situation. This is totally different from, for instance, the Bureau's memorandum in the Media papers to infiltrate and maintain surveillance over all black student groups.

MR. COUNTRYMAN: The trouble I have is that many people around this table can't get too alarmed about getting informants and surveillants into the Klan. So we tell the law-enforcement agency it's all right. But the law-enforcement agency can't see any difference between the Klan and the Communist party. They've been told time and again by courts and others that the Communist party advocates forcible overthrow of the government. If it's justified in one place, it's justified in the other.

Then, from the law-enforcement agency's point of view, there's no real difference between the Communist party and what they regard as fellow traveler groups sympathetic to the party.

It seems to me that when we open the door in one place for all practical purposes we've opened it across the board. Law-enforcement agencies will not make these nice distinctions.

MR. MARSHALL: Mr. Countryman's right. I think that these matters involve questions of judgment and degree.

The South entered a period where there was extreme violence. But even before that, we had many letterhead memoranda with facts about meetings and so forth of, in addition

to the Klan, White Citizens Councils and other extreme segregationist groups.

I think we needed that information. The Bureau would not
have been as prepared in 1964 to move so effectively against
the organization of a new Klan group if this prior work had
not been done.

The problems are inescapable. We're kidding ourselves if
we think we can say that one rule applies to the Klan and
a different rule applies to leftist groups. But the problem does
exist. I'm sure Mr. Emerson wasn't suggesting the contrary.

MR. EMERSON: Yes, this is the point I raised yesterday
and asked for enlightenment on. It is a difficult point.

But I disagree with Mr. Countryman and Mr. Marshall. One
mustn't throw up one's hands. If one can't tell the difference
between the problems posed by the Ku Klux Klan and the
investigation and surveillance of black student organizations,
one might as well give up.

But there is an obvious difference. Applying it is more difficult. Essentially it's the difference between an organization
engaged in criminal action and an organization engaged in
ideology or political expression.

And the line must be drawn, however difficult. I think that
what Mr. Countryman says is true—the police organization
will always tend to move further and further from the line.
That's the way a bureaucracy works. But that doesn't mean
nothing can be done about it.

We must give outside groups access to what the police are
doing and power to supervise them. We must also develop
some kind of judicial safeguard before an informer is placed
in an organization or sent to a meeting. There are other ways
of handling this and I think they can be worked out if we
give it our time and attention. The line must be drawn and
I think it can be drawn.

MR. NEIER: Yesterday John Doar seemed to imply approval

of the notion that the FBI could infiltrate the Klan and render some of the Klan organizations non-violent. Today he said that the FBI could infiltrate the Klan, get Klan organizations warring against each other and take advantage of or exacerbate internal divisiveness. There's no way in which I can relate that kind of political manipulation to the detection of criminal activity.

I may trust John Doar to do good things, but I don't trust everybody to do good things. And I don't know how to create legal distinctions between my trust in John Doar and my nervousness when William Rehnquist talks about executive self-restraint.

Therefore, if you believe detection activity of this sort is proper, and if you then try to impose the safeguards Frank Donner suggests with Fourth Amendment warrant standards, you still have to stop short of engaging in political manipulation, even of a group like the Klan.

If you engage in anything beyond investigation of specific crimes, you get the absurd consequences Mr. Elliff indicated. Under that reasoning, if a Klansman becomes a member of the YMCA—it's permissible to exercise political surveillance of the YMCA because you have to protect the YMCA against contamination by the Ku Klux Klan. You will never stop the process of political surveillance and that's why it must always be restricted to the detection of crime.

MR. DOAR: That isn't quite the way I see the problem. It wasn't a case of detection of violent crime. This was a matter of control of violent crime. The Bureau knew who were committing these acts of violence. The violence had occurred. And more deaths could have occurred; it was reasonably predictable that they would. The problem then is how do we control the future activity of this violence-prone group?

CHAPTER EIGHT

APPRAISAL BY FORMER JUSTICE DEPARTMENT OFFICIALS

(CONFERENCE DISCUSSION BY PANEL OF FORMER OFFICIALS OF THE UNITED STATES DEPARTMENT OF JUSTICE)

MR. MARSHALL: I would like to begin by asking Bill Hundley, Bill Bittman, Bob Owen and Roger Wilkins to talk about how the Bureau looked to them in their day-to-day relations with it.

Bill Hundley started with the department in 1951, and a great deal of his work was in organized crime cases.

Bill Bittman was an assistant U.S. attorney in Chicago. He tried an extraordinarily complicated case against officials of the Teamsters, including Jimmy Hoffa, and then he tried a case against Bobby Baker.

Bob Owen has tried many civil rights cases in the South, some civil and some criminal. And he put together and presented to the grand jury the case against the people in Neshoba County who killed the three young civil rights workers.

Roger Wilkins had a responsibility which was sort of thrust upon the Department of Justice, for conciliation and mediation service. He was involved in affairs in which the Bureau was exercising some sort of a surveillance and law-enforcement function. Bill?

MR. HUNDLEY: I joined the Department of Justice in 1951. When I first came down, I was a young attorney in the Internal Security Division. At that time, as some of you remember, we were prosecuting Smith Act cases.

Without getting into the merits of that policy, the relationship that the prosecutors of those cases had with the FBI agents, both on a personal and a policy level, was excellent. There was an agent assigned to every defendant. If you were thinking out loud and thought it might be a good idea to have somebody interviewed in Canada, an FBI agent immediately did it. There was no talk about red tape. Anything you wanted done was done. Whatever the constitutional merits of the statute involved, I state categorically that nobody was framed. The cases were well prepared. The agents in the field acted with great tact and integrity. I had a very high opinion of the agents and the Bureau hierarchy.

When I was transferred by Bill Rogers to head the organized crime section, the official change in attitude that I encountered on the part of the FBI was just unbelievable. Whereas in the Smith Act prosecutions you could get anything legitimate done that you wanted, in organized crime there was no program. It was like pulling teeth to get anything done in that field at all. When the Apalachin meeting was discovered, there was some activity in the FBI, as Bill Turner indicated. They started a top hoodlum program, which did not amount to an awful lot.

When Attorney General Kennedy came in, the FBI gradually entered the area. As we developed an organized crime program under Kennedy, the relationship with the agents became excellent. But Bureau policy in the field of organized crime was, at least in the beginning, very difficult. The top agents were still in the internal security field.

We always favored a task force approach to organized crime. But the Bureau, in my day down there, just would not play that game. My understanding is that they still will not. They will contribute to the organized crime program but they're going to do it in their own way. One of the difficulties we always had was in the dissemination of information. We considered that very important if we were going to have an effective organized crime program. We were constantly told by other federal investigative agencies and local investigative agencies that the Bureau's policy was a one-way street. They would take, but were very reluctant to give.

My personal view of the Bureau is that, on balance, it is still one of the most effective law-enforcement agencies we have. I subscribe to some of the criticisms that have been voiced here. But if there are problems with the Federal Bureau of Investigation, I think they are problems that are not solely the making of the FBI. Their policy of going alone, their policy of not disseminating information, these are areas in which Attorneys General and Congress have acquiesced.

The really valid criticism of the Bureau is, as Mr. Shaw indicated, that they feel so strongly about any type of criticism. As Mr. Broderick put it, they do need an infusion of new ideas. I don't think the Catholic Church was bad before Pope John came along, but I think the FBI needs a Pope John today. With corrections of that nature, we can again bring the FBI up to the excellence it had fifteen or twenty years ago.

MR. BITTMAN: For many years I was one of the many government lawyers out in the field trying cases. I tried many cases for the federal government; I worked with perhaps all of its various investigative agencies: Secret Service, Post Office, Internal Revenue Service, Federal Bureau of Narcotics, all of them, including many, many cases with the FBI.

Number one, I would like to state, unequivocally, that I think there is a definite need today for an agency such as the FBI, particularly in the more complicated crime areas. Crime is now very mobile. It's not centralized like it used to be fifty years ago. Local law-enforcement agencies mean well, and some are excellent, but many are not. A further difficulty is that they do not have jurisdiction out of their communities or state. They don't have the really experienced, well-trained manpower. They don't have the subpoena power. They don't have the money to conduct an in-depth, exhaustive investigation. And local law-enforcement agencies are sometimes, and I emphasize sometimes, subject to local pressures when they're investigating controversial cases or influential people.

The FBI, I believe, is beyond this. They have the resources, they have the jurisdiction, they have the well-trained manpower, they have the know-how, they have the facilities. It has always been a pleasure to work on complicated cases with the FBI, because of what they can do.

I'm sure everyone knows how efficiently the FBI conducts its investigations. If I'm trying a case in Chicago, Illinois, and I want a witness interviewed in Los Angeles, California, I can get the results of that interview the same evening by telephone and have a report on my desk the next morning. No other agency, generally speaking, can do this and do it in the competent way that the FBI does.

Now, the FBI's stated position for years is that it is only an investigative agency, a fact-finding agency. It does not make recommendations or draw conclusions. It will not evaluate a witness's testimony; it will only state what that witness told them. Obviously, when you develop a close relationship with most field agents, if you ask them what they think of the veracity or integrity of a particular witness, they will tell you informally. But the reports are only interview reports. They're not based just on observation or the investigator's feeling about the case. I have found almost without exception that you can rely on an FBI report. When they tell you that an individual stated something, that individual will have stated it. They're accurate, they're reliable and they're precise.

There's been a lot of discussion here about statistics and the minor cases the FBI gets involved in. I think a lot of this criticism is justified; I think some of it is unwarranted. If Congress doesn't want the FBI to investigate stolen cars or the Migratory Bird Act, why doesn't it give the jurisdiction to some other agency? This has always been the FBI's answer, and though I don't accept it 100 per cent, it certainly is a reasonable response. We may ask: why don't you limit stolen car investigations to the large commercial stolen car rings? Their answer is the law doesn't contain that limitation. And it doesn't. This is one of the problems. They read these statutes literally; they know what their authority is. If you ask them to conduct an investigation, and they don't have clear-cut authority, they will probably refuse to do it.

The Bureau has some internal rules that I disagreed with. They have a reason for them and it's not up to me to question them. The FBI will refuse to interview an individual in the presence of his attorney. I think that's wrong. Another rule involves Bureau cars. In some cases, I worked until one or two o'clock in the morning with agents. They had a Bureau car and they'd have to drive twenty miles to return it, then drive home. There's a very hard and fast Bureau rule against taking cars home. I think that's wrong.

The reason agents have a reluctance to serve on task forces is that the Director believes that he loses effective control over his agents that way. He wants the agents directly responsible to the Bureau, and to him. He doesn't want them under Department of Justice task force lawyers. There's no doubt in my mind that he would lose such control. But I think there's no problem there. By and large, experienced task force attorneys are very good and could well assume that type of control over the agent.

One of the major disputes I've had with the Bureau concerns its refusal to get into an investigation when another government agency is involved, even a local law-enforcement agency. You ask them to investigate a certain crime. If there is a local police department conducting even a *pro forma* investigation of that crime, the FBI generally will refuse to conduct that investigation on the ground that it is being adequately investigated by the local police department. They always add that if any facts come to your attention to indicate that it is not being adequately investigated, contact them again and they'll reevaluate their decision. In the middle of a trial, if you need a certain investigator, and it's an IRS or Bureau of Narcotics case, the FBI will not do the investigation on the grounds that it's not their case.

Now, of course, the reason I frequently ask the FBI to conduct the investigation is my respect for the Bureau. I think they are better equipped and better qualified. And they can do it; they have the manpower. They can do it expeditiously and when they want to do something, they can do a fantastic job.

On informants, it's a myth that the government obtains successful prosecutions solely on the basis of informant testimony. The standard is proof beyond a reasonable doubt. I have not seen an informant yet whose credibility, motive, bias or interest cannot be attacked. In all these cases, you have to corroborate the informant by independent, credible evidence, or you're not going to win it.

MR. MARSHALL: Bob Owen, the charge has been made, over and over again, that the Bureau is slow in civil rights cases. Could you say something about how they functioned in preparing cases, how they worked with you, whether they gave you enough resources, whether that changed over time, whether it was different if you were trying a criminal or a civil case?

MR. OWEN: I came to the department in 1958, into the Civil Rights Division shortly after it was set up. There's just no question that the early cases in the Department of Justice, particularly the voting discrimination cases, simply were not prepared by the Bureau. They were prepared by Department of Justice attorneys.

In one case in Forrest County, Mississippi, we had, as of 1961, been unsuccessful in getting a court to give us copies of the Forrest County voting records. An election was coming up. The question was: how were we going to prove universal white suffrage and no black registration? We had asked the Bureau to interview witnesses. We indicated we needed white as well as black witnesses to show the discrimination. None of the reports we received were of interviews with white witnesses. The Bureau didn't have the voting records either and they didn't know how to go about finding good white witnesses. The Bureau didn't have the voting records either and County, and got college yearbooks of people who would now be of voting age, and went over the newspapers for the high school graduating classes, and then ran the names through telephone books. The Bureau did, in fact, send fifteen agents to Hattiesburg to interview these people, but only after we had located the names.

After 1964, particularly in Mississippi and the southern part of Louisiana, the FBI did a superb job. It was principally the people who were there. The agents, whom I got to know, did well.

In the police misconduct area, the performance and the co-operation with Civil Rights Division lawyers was not as good as it was in Mississippi. Partly, this was because they didn't know us. We hadn't educated them about the way we work. They were suspicious of us and I suppose to some extent we were suspicious of them.

One of the police misconduct cases grew out of the Chicago convention. It was a case in which a young man who had been in the demonstrations in front of the Hilton Hotel had, because of the bus strike, tried to hitchhike home. He was picked up by a police officer who had been on duty at the convention, but not at the demonstration.

When the officer learned that the young man had been at the demonstration, he flipped. He struck the kid. The kid jumped out of the car. The cop jumped out of the car, drew a gun on him, got the kid back in the car, crushed his glasses, and the kid jumped out of the car again and jumped on a garbage truck. The truck had an Italian name on it. That's all the kid could remember. The garbage truck driver viewed some of the conduct of the police officer. We asked the FBI to look into this matter and to locate and interview the garbage truck driver.

The response to that request was that the Bureau couldn't determine the name. There was no name similar to the name that the young man remembered in any of the phone books in Chicago.

So what we then had to do was sit outside at the time the young man had been there. I sat out one night and nothing happened. It was about three o'clock in the morning when the young man had jumped on the garbage truck. One of the attorneys who was with me sat out the next night. And sure enough, here comes the garbage truck. He jumped on the running board and asked the garbage truck driver, "Do you remember a couple of weeks ago when a kid jumped on your truck running board right about here?" And the garbage truck driver's response was, "Yeah, did the cop kill the kid?"

MR. MARSHALL: Roger Wilkins was in a high policy position, particularly during 1967 and 1968, when there were lots of problems with civil disorders.

MR. WILKINS: When you asked us to talk about our day-to-day relationship with the Bureau, I guess the first thing that I'd have to say was that in the three years that I was in the department, I saw my other colleagues who held similar positions, even ones in unrelated fields like tax and anti-trust, three times a week. In my three years in the department, I saw Mr. Hoover twice—once at a judicial reception at the White House, and once on an elevator when we happened to be going home at the same time. I think that's instructive about the relationship of the Bureau to the rest of the department.

The small agency that I headed had responsibility for trying to deal with organizations in black ghettos, during the years when the ghettos were volatile. The Bureau was also involved in that. The criticisms of the Bureau that I'm about to voice are not solely the fault of the Bureau. It's another one of those cases of a President, an Attorney General, needing a service. They turned to the Bureau for that service without making a very careful judgment about the Bureau's capacity to deliver.

Bill Turner told us that as of now the Bureau has one half of 1 per cent black agents. In 1966 I suppose the proportion was smaller. What was going on in the ghettos in those days was a kind of giant catharsis among poor blacks, psychic release from internal repression, a new discovery that you could stand up and say what you really felt about white people though you had repressed it for years. The Bureau was really in no position to collect that information. And it was in a much worse position effectively to analyze it.

As Andy Young said at lunch today, a bunch of black guys sitting around drinking in the middle of the night, yelling about how mean white folks are and what they'd like to do to them, is part of the catharsis. But the Bureau was not equipped to deal with black hyperbole. So, if some black guy said, "I'm going to kill that so-and-so," the Bureau took it fairly literally. But it didn't recognize its limitations. It collected that information and passed it around to high policy officials in the government who were unsettled themselves and frightened about what was going on in the ghettos. They took the Bureau's information seriously. The silliest story I can recall occurred one night in 1967 when I was about to sit down to dinner and I got an urgent call from the Vice-President's office. The caller said, "You've got to go down to Birmingham right away." I said, "But I'm about to eat dinner." And he said, "You've got to go. The Vice-President is about to go there and he wants you to go down there. There's a big problem."

So I went. I was met by a man on the Vice-President's staff and by a Secret Service man. They told me that they had learned through Bureau sources that disgruntled blacks in the Birmingham community planned to put a ring around the Birmingham airport the next day and prevent the Vice-President from leaving the airport when he arrived.

That information was patently absurd on its face. I knew the black people in Birmingham. Even if they had wanted to do that, they couldn't muster enough people to ring that airport. Besides, it sounded like something that didn't make any sense. I called about three people in Birmingham; they all said it was untrue. They all gave me their plans, which was to have a few people show signs, demonstrate and disperse.

This is exactly what happened. As a matter of fact, they were there when the Vice-President came. He went over, shook hands with them, talked to them, then left and went about his business.

You might say it didn't cost very much. It cost the taxpayers a round-trip ticket to Birmingham.

VOICE: And your dinner.

MR. WILKINS: And my dinner. And my hotel bill. But it emotionalized the Birmingham police. Once the Bureau tells them it may happen, they continue to think that things like that will happen.

This kind of occurrence took place over and over again during my years in the department. I think that the exaggerated view of the Panthers is due to an inability to deal with this kind of information. I think the idiocy of infiltrating black student groups, in Bill Turner's phrase, promiscuously, is a product of that incapacity to understand. I'd say that in those areas where I dealt with it the Bureau had a very limited capacity to do what it was assigned to do. The information it provided did not illuminate the stream; it polluted it.

MR. CHARLES MORGAN:* I'm interested in the political cases. Of course, there are different kinds of political cases. I'm particularly interested, Mr. Hundley, in the Smith Act prosecutions involving the Communists. Did you find any FBI reluctance there?

MR. HUNDLEY: There wasn't any at all. The Bureau is ideological. Mr. Hoover investigated the Smith Act cases with real enthusiasm. He genuinely believes that domestic Communism is probably the No. 1 threat to America.

The enthusiasm for the organized crime program came from individual agents, Turner and others. They all wanted to get into that. I can't speak with any knowledge of civil rights. I am sure that he did investigate the Klan and did a good job. But, from my own experience, I just don't think he has the same enthusiasm for that as he had for the Smith Act prosecutions. That is one of the prices you pay when, as Burke Marshall indicated, the Attorney General and the Congress accede to a monolithic organization. The agents have to reflect the feelings of a strong, centralist Director.

MR. ELLIFF: I'd like to ask whether in the area of intelligence, since it's very important to have people who are sophisticated in their understanding of these problems, whether it would be better to have some kind of separate organization, either inside or outside the Bureau, that is essentially concerned with security problems, like the British special branch.

Secondly, I'd like to know whether, in dealing with police misconduct problems, there should be a permanent force within the Bureau with responsibility in this area, rather than use field offices which have continuing relationships with the

* Director, ACLU Southern Regional Office, Atlanta, Georgia, at time of conference; now Director, ACLU Washington, D.C., office.

local police under investigation. The intelligence question is for Mr. Wilkins and the police question for Mr. Owen.

Mr. WILKINS: I would go along with an intelligence entity but I would prefer, for a variety of reasons, to see it developed within the Bureau rather than set up a new organization.

Mr. OWEN: In civil rights cases, I don't believe, from a prosecutor's point of view, you're better off with a separate group. You couldn't build a bureaucracy large enough to cover all the police misconduct complaints in the country unless you duplicated the Bureau. But you need better performance from the Bureau.

Mr. MARSHALL: That suggestion, as I'm sure you know, has been made periodically for a number of years. Bill Bittman wants to make a general comment.

Mr. BITTMAN: I think something that just occurred to me should be mentioned. That is how the FBI actually conducts its investigations. I'm not going to go through a long dissertation. But if the FBI believes that there's sufficient probable cause to obtain a search warrant, some people might get the idea that the FBI collars a magistrate at twelve o'clock at night, and obtains a search warrant or an arrest warrant.

That's not the way it's done. In all instances when agents believe they have sufficient probable cause to obtain a search warrant or an arrest warrant, they seek permission from the United States attorney's office. The facts of that case are reviewed with the U.S. attorney's office and permission is given or not given. The U.S. attorney's office may then draft the necessary warrant plus the affidavit.

The same thing is true with prosecutions.

The FBI will come to the United States attorney's office with the facts of the case. I'm speaking of a very routine case, now, but I think it's important to get this across. The prosecutor will state that there are not sufficient facts to warrant prosecution, and decline prosecution, and will fill out the necessary forms.

Or he will state that there might be a case but that additional investigation is required. Then, normally, they will have a discussion of the evidence to find out exactly in what areas additional investigations should be conducted.

I don't want to give anyone the idea that agents run around on their own. I'm sure everyone in the Criminal Division of the Justice Department and assistant U.S. attorneys have received, as I have, many phone calls at one, two, three o'clock in the morning by agents, for example, at the scene of a hijacking. They have a truck located and stolen television sets are being unloaded. Do they have sufficient probable cause to make an arrest? They will not make that arrest unless they secure permission from the United States attorney's office. So there are a lot of built-in checks and balances within the system.

DISSEMINATION OF DEROGATORY INFORMATION: A WEAPON AGAINST CRIME OR PART OF THE PROBLEM?

BY ARYEH NEIER

On December 10, 1970, Attorney General John Mitchell authorized the FBI to proceed with the development of a computerized system for the gathering and dissemination of identification data. This new system is known as the National Crime Information Center.

The presumptive purpose of these FBI operations is to enable the nation's law-enforcement agencies better to control and reduce crime. Certainly, this appears to have been the intention of Congress when it enacted the legislation that provides the basic authority for these operations. But my belief is that the manner in which the FBI has gathered and disseminated data has exceeded the authority which Congress intended to confer. Moreover, the manner in which the FBI has strayed beyond the intentions of Congress *may* have undercut the purpose of Congress—to control and reduce crime. At the very least, millions of people have been injured by data dissemination functions assumed by the FBI which go beyond the Bureau's legislative authority.

I: Dissemination Not Limited to Law Enforcement

Since its organization in 1924, the FBI's Identification Division has accumulated the fingerprints of some 200 million persons. The process of adding to these records is taking place at a rapid pace. In 1970 the division was receiving some 29,000 sets of fingerprints on an average working day, or more than 7 million sets of prints during the year. Thirty-three hundred employees are required to gather, maintain and disseminate the records of the Identification Division. The computerized system was authorized because the Attorney General was apparently not satisfied that the Identification Division, which receives and disseminates information through the mails, is adequate to the task.

The legislative authority for the identification operations of the FBI is provided by 28 U.S.C. § 534. That section states that the Attorney General shall "acquire, collect, classify, and preserve identification, criminal identification, crime and other records," and that he shall "exchange these records with, and for the official use of, authorized officials of the Federal government, the States, cities and penal and other institutions."

The statute also says that "the exchange of records authorized . . . is subject to cancellation if dissemination is made outside the receiving departments or related departments or related agencies."

It finally empowers the Attorney General to "appoint officials to perform the functions authorized by this section."

The forerunner of this section was enacted in 1930. The discussion in Congress leading to its adoption makes clear that Congress intended to limit this authority to criminal law-enforcement purposes. As Federal District Judge Gerhard Gesell stated in his decision in *Menard* v. *Mitchell*, the statute "is obviously designed only to facilitate coordinated law en-

forcement activities between the federal and local governments, that is, to assist arresting agencies, courts, and correc-
tional institutions in the apprehension, conviction and proper
disposition of criminal offenders."

But the FBI's Identification Division has not been limited to
law-enforcement activities. The larger scope of FBI operations
has proceeded under a series of rulings from the Attorney
General which are codified in 28 C.F.R. § 0.85 (b). These
regulations provide that the FBI's identification services are
available not just to law-enforcement agencies but to banks,
insurance companies and "other governmental agencies." The
"other governmental agencies" include such federal agencies as
the Internal Revenue Service, the Armed Forces, the Immigration and Naturalization Service and a host of local agencies
across the country.

During 1970 between seven thousand and eight thousand
state and local government agencies received information
from the FBI files based on fingerprint checks. About half
were not law-enforcement agencies.

A few examples of the uses such local agencies make of the
information from the FBI will illustrate how far the operations
of the Identification Division have strayed from serving the
law-enforcement purposes intended by Congress.

—According to a 1962 letter from the Willard, Ohio, Police
Department, an ordinance requires that all civilian applicants
for city jobs be fingerprinted. This letter was regarded as
authority for the FBI to perform fingerprint checks and disseminate data.

—According to Ordinance Number 31-58 of the city of
Owensboro, Kentucky, transient salesmen "shall register with
the City Clerk at City Hall immediately upon their arrival in
Owensboro and shall have their pictures taken and their
fingerprints made at Owensboro Police Headquarters and shall
allow sufficient time to process said registration." This ordi-

nance is on file with the FBI and was regarded as authority for
the FBI to perform fingerprint checks and disseminate data.

—According to a letter from the Provincetown, Massachusetts police on file with the FBI, a town ordinance requires that
all non-residents seeking employment must submit to photographing and fingerprinting. This letter was regarded as authority for the FBI to perform fingerprint checks and disseminate
data.

Of the 29,000 sets of fingerprints that the FBI received on an
average working day in 1970, only 13,000 came from law-
enforcement agencies. The remaining 16,000 sets a day, or
about 4 million a year, were from banks, insurance companies,
government agencies engaged in employing or licensing people, or from other sources not directly connected with law enforcement. The standard procedure followed by the FBI on
receiving these prints was to report to the submitting agency
the material in the FBI files on the subject of the fingerprints.

Judge Gesell in his decision in the *Menard* case stated that:

> . . . it is abundantly clear that Congress never intended nor
> in fact did authorize dissemination of arrest records to any
> state or local agency for purposes of employment licensing
> checks . . . neither the statute nor the debates so much as
> mention employment, and it is beyond reason to assume that
> Congress intended that this confidential quasi-investigative
> data should be handed to anyone who under authority of local
> ordinance or statute was authorized to take a fingerprint from
> an applicant for a position in public or private employment.

II: Proliferation of Dissemination

In *Menard* an effort was made to determine whether the
FBI at least took pains to see that the recipients of information
disseminated by the FBI did not, in turn, disseminate it to
anyone else. The issue is of some moment. There is a considerable industry in the United States in the sale of data

about individuals to creditors, landlords and employers. In a report undertaken for the ACLU, Ralph Nader noted that:

> The "dossier industry" is a huge and growing business. There are 105 million files kept by the Association of Credit Bureaus of America (ACBA). Retail Credit Company of Atlanta, Georgia, the giant of the industry, has forty-five million files and makes thirty-five million reports each year. Credit Data Corporation, the second largest firm, has twenty-seven million files and adds seven million new dossiers each year.
>
> These economic interests have almost total control over the information they collect and sell. They are not accountable to anyone except those who seek to purchase information. Further, for reasons of profit, these companies place a premium on the derogatory information they assemble.

In their search for derogatory information, the credit bureaus are extremely anxious to obtain information from law-enforcement agencies. In fact, according to New York County District Attorney Frank Hogan, credit bureaus may resort to bribery of law-enforcement officials. Mr. Hogan's office is prosecuting New York City policemen who are alleged to have sold confidential arrest information.

In the absence of strenuous efforts by the FBI to limit the further dissemination of derogatory information, it would be foolish to assume that the information once given out by the FBI would go no further. With several thousand public agencies privileged to receive FBI data, and with such private agencies as banks, insurance companies and hospitals also receiving this data, only diligently enforced precautions could hope to keep FBI data from entering into the business operations of the nation's credit bureaus.

The pre-trial examination in *Menard* of Beverly Ponder, special agent of the FBI and chief of the Technical Section of the Identification Division, produced the following colloquy:

QUESTION: Is there any procedure whereby the FBI or any division of the FBI inquires into the uses to which the arrest information is put by contributing agencies?

MR. PONDER: No.

QUESTION: Are any restrictions imposed by the FBI on the use to which that information is put?

MR. PONDER: Yes. Official business only.

QUESTION: Are there memoranda or orders indicating that there is a restriction?

MR. PONDER: It is right on the record itself.

QUESTION: Are there any form letters that are sent to contributing agencies explaining what "official business only" means?

MR. PONDER: Well, in years gone by we have brought this to the attention of contributors that this information is disseminated strictly for official use only.

Special agent Ponder was asked to supply copies of all instructions and suggestions containing restrictions on further dissemination by the FBI of arrest information. The most recent notice he was able to supply was a memorandum by J. Edgar Hoover of October 18, 1965. Apparently, no additional notices had been sent out between then and the examination of Mr. Ponder on December 17, 1970.

The only penalty mentioned in the 1965 Hoover memorandum if records were used for something other than "official uses" was that "this service is subject to cancellation." Special agent Ponder was asked to provide a list of recipients of FBI arrest data currently barred from receiving data, and a list of those barred at some time during the past ten years.

The current list consisted of Police Department, Cabazon, California; Sheriff's Office, Northumberland County, Sunbury, Pennsylvania.

The following agencies were on the list at some point during the past ten years for periods of between one month and thirteen months: Police Department, Brook Park, Ohio; Police Department, Westport, Washington; Police Department, Hobbs, New Mexico; Sheriff's Office, Bernalillo County, Albuquerque, New Mexico.

No governmental agency other than a law-enforcement agency appeared on the lists. The absence of any private agencies on the lists is a circumstance possibly attributable to the difficulty in determining what is meant by "official use only" in the context of, say, a bank. Special agent Ponder testified that no special instructions are sent to banks which might help to clarify for them the meaning of "official use only."

Special agent Ponder did cite one example of what would alarm the FBI with regard to record dissemination. He said, "If we get a complaint that an FBI identification record has been used by a local politician or something like this and this would be a clear violation of the confidentiality of the records, we do institute inquiries promptly to resolve this matter. These have been rather infrequent."

It does not seem to be easy to get the FBI to investigate the further dissemination of the records it disseminates. Here is another exchange from the examination:

QUESTION: Sir, in 1968 it was brought out that the D.C. Police Department maintained a list of 50 companies to which arrest record information was dispersed by the D.C. Police Department. Did the FBI ever investigate whether that list included dissemination by the D.C. Police Department of FBI arrest records?

MR. PONDER: We didn't make an investigation but we know as a matter of course that it did not include FBI records.

The response asks us to assume that, even without an investigation, the FBI was confident that the D.C. police engaged in the rather unusual practice of segregating arrest information received from the FBI and arrest information accumulated in other ways.

III: *Efforts to Override* Menard

On June 15, 1971, Judge Gesell decided the *Menard* case and ordered the FBI to stop disclosing arrest records to private agencies or to state and local public agencies which are not law-enforcement agencies. In addition, Judge Gesell ordered that the distribution to state and local enforcement agencies could only be used for law-enforcement purposes.

The thrust of Judge Gesell's decision was to bar the FBI from activities not permitted by the congressional legislation enacted in 1930.

Two bills have recently been introduced in Congress to give the FBI power to disseminate data to the kinds of institutions that were its recipients prior to Judge Gesell's decision.

S. 2545 was introduced by Senators Bible and Cannon of Nevada. It provides that eligible recipients of FBI arrest data shall include "any non-law enforcement official or agency of any state or city if the laws (including regulations) of such state or city authorize or require such official or agency to acquire criminal record information in the performance of his or its official duties or functions."

Commenting on their bill, Senators Bible and Cannon have emphasized the importance to the state of Nevada of access to the FBI's files for control over persons seeking licensing or employment in that state's gambling industry.

Moreover, according to Senator Bible:

In other areas, Nevada's statutes or regulations required criminal record checks on applicants for licensure as lawyers, doctors of medicine, real estate brokers, private investigators, for employment in the business of dispensing alcoholic beverages, and in connection with other professions, businesses and occupations. And Nevada is certainly not unique. I daresay most, if not all, of the states and localities throughout the nation have similar statutory or regulatory requirements in connection with employment in sensitive public service occupations.

Mr. President, this sudden termination of an investigative service that has been available to state and regulatory agencies for many, many years is completely unacceptable. The FBI is the only agency in the nation in a position to provide centralized criminal records services. Its authority to render this service in non-law-enforcement cases must be restored—and promptly.

S. 2546 was introduced by Senator Hruska of Nebraska at the request of Attorney General John Mitchell. At first glance, it appears more restrictive than the Bible-Cannon bill. It states that "access to criminal justice information systems shall be available only to law enforcement agencies. Criminal justice information may be used only for law enforcement purposes."

It is in defining law enforcement that S. 2546 shows its hand. According to the bill: "(5) 'law enforcement' means any activity pertaining to crime prevention, control, or reduction or the enforcement of the criminal law, including, but not limited to police efforts to prevent, control, or reduce crime or to apprehend criminals, activities of corrections, probation, or parole authorities."

Barring persons with arrest records from employment or licenses has previously been construed by the FBI as an effort at "crime prevention, control, or reduction." So the Attorney General's bill would probably put the FBI back in the business of disseminating data which would be eventually used in the same manner—and probably by the same groups—as private credit bureau data. Moreover, the Attorney General's bill contains an exception to make FBI data available "for such additional lawful purposes necessary to the proper enforcement or administration of other provisions of law as the Attorney General may prescribe by regulations."

IV: The Presumption of Innocence

A person is innocent until proven guilty. So, at least, goes
the theory. If this theory were put into practice, an arrest—by
itself—would be considered meaningless.

Unfortunately, there is a large gap between the theory and
the practice. As the U. S. Court of Appeals for the District of
Columbia Circuit stated in *Menard:*

> Information denominated a record of arrest, if it becomes
> known, may subject an individual to serious difficulties. Even
> if no direct economic loss is involved, the injury to an in-
> dividual's reputation may be substantial. Economic losses
> themselves may be both direct and serious. Opportunities for
> schooling, employment, or professional licenses may be re-
> stricted or non-existent as a consequence of the mere fact of an
> arrest, even if followed by acquittal or complete exoneration of
> the charges involved.

The court cited a survey which showed that 75 per cent of
New York area employment agencies would not accept for
referral an applicant with an arrest record, and another survey
of seventy-five employers which indicated that sixty-six of
them would not consider employing a man who had been arrested for assault and acquitted.

The FBI has been, at best, careless in making distinctions
between "arrests" and "crimes." A Bureau publication refers to
the persons whose fingerprints appear in its files as "a criminal
army of six million individuals who have been arrested and
fingerprinted." The FBI's new computerized system for disseminating *arrest* records is called the National Crime Information Center. Under the Attorney General's bill (introduced by
Senator Hruska), arrest records are grouped under the general
heading of "criminal offender record information."

During the pre-trial examination of special agent Ponder in the *Menard* case, counsel tried to determine what efforts the FBI made to determine whether arrests had been followed by convictions and to include that information in disseminated data:

QUESTION: Does the FBI make any effort to obtain final dispositions where requests are received for arrest records? Before disseminating those arrest records?

MR. PONDER: We urge the contributors to submit to us final dispositions, but we don't go out and try to pick them up.

Mr. Ponder testified that he had no knowledge of percentage of final dispositions; that there is no statistic available within the FBI indicating the percentage of final dispositions and that he knew of no way to make an intelligent estimate based on his experience.

Civil service application forms were changed a few years ago, in an apparent effort to assure that arrests without convictions would not exclude applicants from federal employment. Here is the examination of special agent Ponder on that issue:

QUESTION: Is the FBI aware that recently, federal job application forms were changed, and the question which asked if the applicant was arrested, now asks if he has been convicted?

MR. PONDER: Yes, I am aware of that.

QUESTION: Do federal agencies, in particular Civil Service Commissions, receive at present all information about arrests, or only arrests with convictions, when they apply to the FBI?

MR. PONDER: They receive all the material that appears on the identification records.

QUESTION: And that includes conviction and non-conviction arrests?

MR. PONDER: That is correct.

There are laws in many states which establish the confidentiality of arrest and disposition records of juveniles. The purpose is to ensure that youthful missteps, or allegations of youthful missteps, are not lifelong barriers to opportunities for employment and other societal benefits.

By and large, safeguards for the confidentiality of juvenile records are entrusted to family and juvenile courts for administration. However, when juveniles are arrested by the police, they are frequently fingerprinted and the prints sent to the FBI.

The FBI's treatment of juvenile records was considered in the examination of special agent Ponder:

QUESTION: Does the FBI make any distinction in its records between juvenile and adult arrest records?

MR. PONDER: There is no distinction made in FBI identification records.

QUESTION: Are there any differences in dissemination practices with respect to juveniles and adults, of arrest records?

MR. PONDER: No.

QUESTION: Has there ever been an effort to estimate a percentage of the arrest record files of the FBI which are juvenile arrests?

MR. PONDER: No, sir.

On January 22, 1971, a memorandum from J. Edgar Hoover went "to all Fingerprint Contributors." It noted "the FBI has no provisions for keeping certain fingerprints, such as might be submitted on a juvenile, in a separate or confidential file." All data on juveniles, as on adults, were disseminated to recipients of FBI data. In practice, therefore, the elaborate schemes in state laws for protecting the confidentiality of juvenile records have been nullified through the administrative practices of the FBI.

The FBI's disregard of state laws protecting the confidentiality of juvenile records contrasts with its practice of honoring any state or local law which purports to confer authority upon a local agency to receive data from the FBI.

V: Social Consequences

A recent decision by Federal District Judge Irving J. Hill of California ordered Litton Industries to stop using arrests which did not result in convictions as a disqualification for employment. Among the findings by Judge Hill which led to the decision were:

> Negroes are arrested substantially more frequently than whites in proportion to their numbers. The evidence on this question was overwhelming and utterly convincing. For example, Negroes nationally comprise some 11% of the population and account for 27% of reported arrests and 45% of arrests reported as "suspicion arrests." Thus, any holding that disqualifies prospective employees because of having been arrested once, or more than once, discriminates in fact against Negro applicants. This discrimination exists even though such a policy is objectively and fairly applied as between applicants of various races . . .
>
> If Litton is permitted to continue obtaining information concerning the prior arrests of applicants for employment which did not result in conviction, the possible use of such information as an illegally discriminatory basis for rejection is so great and so likely, that in order to effectuate the policies of the Civil Rights Act, Litton should be restrained from obtaining such information . . .

Judge Hill noted that "arrest information, which is not a matter of public record, can apparently be obtained cheaply and easily from sources other than the [job] applicant . . ." He might have added that the reason it can be obtained so cheaply and easily is that the FBI has seen to it that this information is readily available.

Hess and Le Poole have explained why information about arrest records is so devastating: "The fact of an arrest indicates some possibility that the individual concerned engaged in the criminal activity with which he was charged. Investigation may disclose whether he has or not. Yet so long as there exists an employable pool of persons who have not been arrested, employers will find it cheaper to make an arrest an automatic disqualification for employment."

Jobs are the most important but by no means the only societal benefits which people lose because arrest records are available "cheaply and easily." The availability of credit, bank loans, mortgages, apartments, licenses, admissions to schools can all hinge on whether a person has any kind of criminal history or arrest record.

To people caught up in the workings of the criminal law, the lifelong sentence which closes off their ability to obtain societal benefits may be punishment that is worse by far than any sentence they might serve if convicted on a criminal charge. The situation of the person who has been convicted of crime was described recently by an ex-convict: "Once you have a 'jacket'—a dossier with all the past details of your life, all the detrimental ones they can put together, that is . . . you are a *criminal*. The jacket does not disappear; it grows fat and follows you around wherever you go. Someday this sentence you are serving will chronologically run out, but Society does not forgive; it keeps tabs . . ."

But it is not just the ex-convict who has such a "jacket." The juvenile or the adult with an arrest and no conviction also has a "jacket" and the FBI's records will not forgive—even if there is nothing to forgive, even if no crime was ever committed.

According to the FBI, law-enforcement agencies make some 7.5 million arrests during a year for all criminal acts, excluding traffic offenses. Of those arrested, more than 1.3 million are never prosecuted. Nevertheless, they have arrest records. Approximately another 2.2 million are acquitted or have the charges against them dismissed. Nevertheless, they have arrest records.

The fingerprints of a large proportion of these 3.5 million persons each year who are never prosecuted, are acquitted or have the charges against them dismissed find their way into the FBI files. From there, they have been finding their way to public and private employers, creditors, landlords and licensers. But because the FBI has been careless about assuring that records of dispositions accompany the arrest records it so efficiently disseminates, the recipients do not know if the result was a conviction or something short of it.

The rationale for the FBI's entire system for the distribution of data is to enable the nation's law-enforcement agencies better to control and reduce crime. Is crime being controlled or reduced by the dissemination of this data? It is a dubious proposition. It would be more reasonable to say that the FBI's data dissemination policies have served to increase crime. Once people have been denied jobs, licenses, homes, admissions to schools and credit, the likelihood that they will commit crimes would seem to rise rather than fall.

The FBI's Crime Reports tell a grim story of rising crime rates and of staggering rates of recidivism. Could it be that the rising crime rates and the recidivism have something to do with the rising efficiency with which records are distributed? Are people forced into crime by their inability to escape a "record-prison" of things they have done and things they never did but are alleged to have done? These are important questions to which answers are difficult to find. They are questions, however, which should at least act as a brake to the FBI's rush further to improve the efficiency of its data dissemination programs through the computerized systems of its National Crime Information Center.

VI: Controls

It is, of course, possible to propose controls designed to mitigate, if not eliminate, the abuses of FBI practices. However, it is important to note that any controls are necessarily fragile.

The first problem is that no controls are ever better than the persons who administer them. Whatever is meant by the FBI's policy of limiting the dissemination of data to "official use only," it certainly doesn't mean that the data can be used for purposes of settling a personal score. And yet, that is precisely what was done by J. Edgar Hoover in a recent notorious incident.

A TWA pilot was publicly critical of the FBI for what he thought was the reckless endangerment of the lives of passengers in a plane hijacking incident. Subsequently, the Chairman of TWA, Charles Tillinghast, received a letter from J. Edgar Hoover attacking the pilot and drawing from the FBI files on the pilot's military record to buttress the attack.

Another problem with controls is that the ground rules can always be changed through legislative action. One of the state systems linked to the FBI's National Crime Information Center is the New York State Identification and Intelligence System (NYSIIS). The Director of this system, Dr. Robert Gallati, is noted as one of the professionals in the identification industry most sensitive to the right to privacy. When the New York State system was established in 1964, Dr. Gallati was emphatic in his insistence that the system was to be concerned exclusively with improving the efficiency of law enforcement and would certainly not be available for private employment checks.

Nevertheless, in 1969, the New York State legislature passed a law requiring the fingerprinting of all employees in the securities industry, one of the state's largest. Under the law, the fingerprints were checked against the files of NYSIIS and information in the files was forwarded to the state attorney general who, in turn, made it available to the employers in the securities industry. In his first report on the operations of this law, the state attorney general announced that several hundred employees had been found to have "criminal records" and many were dismissed from employment. Approximately half of those fired had no record of convictions, but only of arrests.

Once the information is on file, it is extremely tempting for an administrator to make use of it, or for a legislature to direct the use of it. Therefore, the first aim of controls must be to limit the information gathered and kept on file. There seems to be no basis to collect information on persons neither convicted of crime nor fugitives from some law-enforcement agency. The information collected should be available only to law-enforcement agencies for crime detection and prosecution, and to agencies which need the data for sentencing, probation or parole.

The FBI has no procedure to allow an individual to consult or challenge his own record. Such procedures are contemplated in Attorney General Mitchell's bill. But they should be expanded to require a log of all official consultations with a file and notice to a person when his record has been consulted or disseminated. There is also a vague reference to purging outdated information. This needs to be spelled out.

The main reason the FBI has been able to depart from the policies Congress enacted is that the secrecy of its operations has kept this departure hidden. Much of the foregoing information about Bureau policies became available for the first time when the U. S. Courts in the District of Columbia forced the FBI to make it available in the *Menard* case.

Now that the FBI's data dissemination policies have had some public scrutiny, they cannot be allowed to disappear again from view. The FBI's promiscuous data dissemination practices have injured millions of people. They may also have been part of the cause of crime rather than part of what Congress intended to be a weapon against crime. If the situation is to get better rather than worse, the Bureau's data dissemination policies will have to remain under close public scrutiny.*

* Mr. Neier's paper was presented at the conference with Mr. Elliff's paper. The ensuing discussion follows Mr. Elliff's paper, at p. 291.

PART III
CONTROVERSIAL
METHODS AND
PROCEDURES

CHAPTER TEN

THE FBI AS A POLITICAL POLICE

BY THOMAS I. EMERSON

I: Subjects of Investigation

The proportion of Bureau resources devoted to national security matters is not precisely known. It has been estimated that the Bureau has two thousand agents investigating political activities. A breakdown of the Media documents, as released by the Citizens Commission to Investigate the FBI, shows that of more than eight hundred files taken, 40 per cent involved political surveillance. The evidence is by no means conclusive. There can be small doubt, however, that a substantial proportion of the Bureau's enormous energies and manpower is devoted to watching over or influencing the political activities of American citizens.

What are the criteria by which the Federal Bureau of Investigation, as "guardian of the national security," determines when to collect information about a particular individual, organization or group? The precise answer is not known since no standards have ever been made public by the Bureau. It is possible, however, to draw some conclusions from the facts that have come to light.

Some subjects of Bureau inquiry are persons or organizations suspected of being in violation of federal statutes under the Bureau's jurisdiction. These laws cover a wide area where political activity is taking place. They include laws against espionage, some forms of sabotage, and sedition, primarily the Smith Act. They also include the Internal Security Act of 1950, which provides for a listing of Communist-action, Communist-front and Communist-infiltrated organizations, and the members of a Communist-action organization; laws calling for deportation of aliens on certain political grounds; recently passed laws prohibiting the crossing of state lines with the intent to blow up buildings, participate in or encourage a riot or engage in similar activities; and the federal loyalty-security programs. Under the main loyalty-security program no person may obtain or hold a federal job unless his employment is "clearly consistent with the interests of national security." The program also involves maintenance by the Attorney General of a list of organizations that are "totalitarian, Fascist, Communist, or subversive." Other programs, such as the industrial security one, cover millions of persons outside the government. All these provisions furnish the Bureau with a broad mandate to launch inquiries into areas of political conduct.

From these foundations the Bureau investigations take off and proliferate. Investigation of an individual leads to investigations of his friends and associates, then to the organizations of which he is a member and from there to the leadership of the organizations. The duty to check on Communist party members carries the Bureau on to checks of fellow travelers, "pseudo-liberals," "dupes" and the associates of any of these. A "non-subversive" organization may be deemed to need investigation in order to determine whether it has "subversive" members, or whether "extremists" come to its meetings. As Hoover describes the process, "We, of course, do not investigate labor unions . . . We have, however, investigated innumerable instances of Communist infiltration into labor unions." The chain of inquiry which starts with searching out "loyalty" and "subversive activities" is an endless one.

The Bureau also conceives its function to include the collection of general political intelligence and preventive data on matters relating to national security. Under this view, there are even fewer limits on the kinds of individuals or organizations that become subject to Bureau scrutiny.

Full implications of the Bureau's theory of its investigative function are revealed whenever its internal operations are exposed to public view. Thus the Coplon reports showed that the Bureau compiled a dossier on the actor Fredric March and his wife, Florence Eldridge, because they were reported to have participated in the activities of various organizations associated with the Henry Wallace movement. A music student was investigated because he visited the New Jersey headquarters of the Communist party and talked with his mother there. Another person came under surveillance because he "was connected with some pro-Israel organization which was sending representatives to various parts of the world." A committee of the National Lawyers Guild, after a detailed study of the Coplon reports, summarized its findings in the following terms:

> It is, then, perfectly plain that, by and large, the FBI investigations described in the Coplon reports were attempting to determine not what crimes the subject had committed, but what kind of a person he was with reference to his social, political and economic views, his personal associations, and his organizational affiliations. The Coplon investigations demonstrate that the FBI investigates persons in order to determine whether they have radical views and associations.

The Media documents demonstrate how in recent years the FBI has cast its net even more widely. One document is a lifetime profile of an anti-war activist who had committed no offense beyond a breach of the peace for which he was fined $5 in 1954. Another revealed an investigation being made of a student at the University of Maryland who had been "a constant source of agitation at the University for the past few years" and a leader in a demonstration which resulted in some arrests. Hoover himself ordered the "discreet, preliminary inquiries . . . into all BSUs (Black Student Unions) and similar organizations . . ." A watch was kept on other black organizations, including CORE, SCLC, the Black Coalition, the National Black Economic Conference and a settlement house. Indeed, the Bureau was under general instructions that it was "essential" to develop "racial informants" in ghetto areas. Also included in the Media documents was a memorandum directing surveillance of the Conference of War Resisters, a pacifist group meeting at Haverford College, in order to determine whether "it will generate any anti-U.S. propaganda," and a report on a peaceful demonstration in Philadelphia on chemical warfare.

The scope of the Bureau's political surveillance appears also from other sources. Thus, in the hearings on the Bureau's 1960 budget Hoover testified: "We now have 155 known, or suspected, Communist-front and Communist-infiltrated organizations under investigation." By the hearings on the 1962 budget the number had increased to "some 200."

In April, 1971, Senator Edmund S. Muskie revealed that the Bureau had conducted a "widespread surveillance" of anti-pollution rallies held on Earth Day in 1970, including one at which the senator himself was a speaker. Attorney General Mitchell defended the surveillance on the ground that the Bureau had advance information (the source not disclosed) that persons with records of violence were planning to attend. Finally, we have seen how the Bureau's inquiries into political affairs carry even into such sensitive areas as the campus.

It is fair to conclude that the FBI's interest and attention extends to virtually all politically active persons who do not operate within the confines of the two major parties, to all organizations who take a militant or strong dissenting position, to all groups which are considered by the Bureau potentially disruptive and to all persons associated with these.

II: Kinds of Information Collected

The information collected by the FBI includes data on most aspects of public life and many aspects of private life. It deals with virtually every feature of organizational existence. One is hard put to discern any criteria of relevancy. Of course, any investigation by its very nature probes into outlying areas, the investigators not knowing in advance what may turn up. And any investigating agency is likely to acquire or be furnished with large amounts of raw material which prove to be of no use to it. But the Bureau's investigations—no doubt in part due to the use of informers, wiretapping and bugging, and in part because the inquiry delves into beliefs, attitudes and opinions—seem to extend far beyond normal limits.

The Coplon documents abound in examples of the type of data the Federal Bureau of Investigation considers relevant, or at least puts into its reports. The first six items on a longer list compiled by the National Lawyers Guild Committee were:

Being affiliated with the Progressive Party [Henry Wallace Party].

Admiring the military feats of the Russian Army during World War II.

Acting (in 1945) in a skit about the battles of Leningrad and Stalingrad.

Opposing the Committee on Un-American Activities.

Writing a master's thesis on the New Deal in New Zealand.

Attending a rally against the Mundt bill.

The Media papers contain other illustrations. The investigation of an anti-war activist included the following information:

Statements from unnamed informants who worked with him at the Bellevue Medical Center in New York City in 1957, in which he was "described as 'queer fish,' 'screwball,' 'smarty pants.'"

A report that he volunteered for risky research experiments and was described by the psychiatrist who did the work as "altruistic, sincere, believer in God, but not in conventional religion."

Reports from police intelligence in Haverford, Pa., of the distribution of anti-war leaflets in 1968.

A report of his presence at a rally at which the war in Vietnam was called "unconstitutional" and "illegal."

References to newspaper clippings on letterheads of anti-war organizations stationery that indicate connections with anti-war and anti-draft groups.

An investigation of a philosophy professor at Swarthmore records that he invited controversial speakers to the campus without permission, was visited by "hippie types" and had printing equipment in his garage. We also learn from the Media documents the names of all identifiable persons at meetings of a black church group, that a lay brother at Villanova Monastery reported that a Villanova University priest had borrowed a monastery car, and that a student under surveillance had majored in Greek.

Materials from other sources confirm that these samples of data collected by the FBI are not atypical of its operations. Once the eye of the Bureau fastens on a particular individual or organization there is virtually no limit to where the inquiry may carry. The process is by nature Orwellian.

III: Methods

The FBI utilizes the full panoply of detection techniques. Its agents make inquiries of friends, acquaintances, neighbors, employers, landlords, bankers, schools and any other person or institution likely to have information about the subject. The time span of the investigation often reaches into family background and early childhood history. Information is obtained not only through interrogation of potentially knowledgeable persons but through photographing, tailing, wiretapping, bugging, placing informers and infiltrators, searching premises, observing mail, inspecting trash cans, clipping newspapers and many other techniques. Quantities of raw data are stored in dossiers and reports are prepared summarizing the material deemed most relevant.

All this is not necessarily different from the methods used by other police forces or private detective agencies. But we are concerned here with investigations into political conduct. In that context, two considerations take on special significance.

First, FBI practices, like those of any other police force, can easily slip into patently unconstitutional conduct. Despite a comparatively good record on this since reorganization of the Bureau in 1924, the Coplon reports do disclose that in the post-World War II period, the Bureau engaged not only in extensive wiretapping (then illegal) but on occasion intercepted and opened mail and, at least in three cases, entered private homes and searched personal effects without a warrant. The very existence of an elaborate investigatory apparatus makes such practices quite possible, though they can rarely be documented.

Second, the Bureau's investigations cannot be viewed as the mere gathering and storage of data. The investigatory process itself affects attitudes, careers and lives in crucial ways. The Swarthmore philosophy professor, mentioned in the Media documents, was being checked in connection with the case of two women alleged to have participated in a bank robbery and murder engineered by a radical political group. The Bureau's agents made contact with the college security officer, a neighbor, the switchboard operator, the local chief of police who lived two doors away and the postmaster, all of whom gave information and promised to keep the professor, his telephone calls, his mail and his other doings under close surveillance. None of this is necessarily illegitimate, but it illustrates that the side effects of a Bureau investigation have to be reckoned with.

IV: Activities Beyond the Collection of Data

The FBI constantly asserts that its sole function is to collect information and pass it on to other government officials, who draw all conclusions from the raw data and make all decisions regarding further action. Plainly, the Bureau underestimates its role even as a gatherer of information; obviously, it must determine what to collect, evaluate what it receives and pass on what it considers relevant. Beyond that, the Bureau, as an integral part of its operations, engages in various activities which have far-reaching effects upon American political life.

1. *Public Relations:* We have seen how wide in scope the FBI's public relations system has been and how it focused on building a good image of the Director. Creating a national hero out of the head of the security police raises troublesome questions about American democracy. But other features of the publicity are even more troublesome.

The FBI, primarily through its Director, has vigorously spread its simplistic ideology through the mass media, as we have seen. And it has employed more direct methods of propagandizing. The Media documents reveal that all agents were sent copies of an article from *Barrons* entitled "Campus or Battleground," subtitled "Columbia Is a Warning to All American Universities," and urged to furnish the reprints "to educators and administrators who are established sources." The covering memorandum went on: "It may be mailed anonymously to college educators who have shown reluctance to take decisive action against the 'New Left.' Positive results or comments by recipients should be furnished to the Bureau." How much of this sort of thing the Bureau has undertaken is of course not known.

Much of the Bureau's publicity seems intended to arouse fears and anxieties about national security. Events have not borne out the dire predictions, and skeptics have suggested that the major purpose has been to assure an increase in appropriations. Whether or not this has been the design, the result has been that a rational approach to security questions has been made difficult and public attention turned away from the real problems.

2. *Disclosures and Leakage:* The FBI claims that the materials in its files are never revealed to any person other than a government official in connection with law enforcement or similar duties. There is abundant and convincing evidence, however, that substantial amounts of data from the Bureau's files ultimately become public through disclosure or leakage, and that the possibility of such exposure is ever present. Without attempting an exhaustive survey of the matter, it is sufficient to note the following:

First, Hoover himself quoted previously unpublished material from Bureau files in his book *Masters of Deceit.* In 1954, Attorney General Brownell read material from the Bureau files in making an attack on the previous Democratic administration for continuing Harry Dexter White in government employment. President Truman followed a general policy of refusing to disclose Bureau files but in some cases allowed individual congressmen to see them at the White House. President Eisenhower adhered to the general policy of non-disclosure but conceded that summaries and factual information from Bureau files had been turned over to congressional committees. Vice-President Nixon, in October, 1954, disclosed extensive material from Bureau files in an attack upon Representative Robert L. Condon of California.

Second, over the years a steady volume of information has found its way from FBI files to various congressional committees investigating "subversive activities." Senator Joseph

McCarthy's Permanent Subcommittee on Investigations obtained substantial amounts of material from Bureau sources, apparently by way of military intelligence. On one occasion Robert Morris, counsel to the Senate Subcommittee on Internal Security, read into the record extracts from the loyalty files of Solomon Adler, a former Treasury official. Likewise, in the Senate debate over the confirmation of Charles E. Bohlen to be Ambassador to Russia, Senator Gillette described several items of information which had come from the Bureau by way of Secretary of State Dulles. There is substantial evidence, also, that the House Committee on Un-American Activities continually received material originating in Bureau files.

Third, vast quantities of information are transmitted by the FBI to various government agencies under the loyalty-security programs or simply by way of informing the agencies of public opposition to programs or practices. The official policy is to keep such reports confidential but in the ordinary course of business numerous persons read them or have access to them. Leaks from this source are inevitable.

Fourth, state legislative committees investigating "subversion" also seem to have obtained information which originated in FBI files.

Fifth, it has recently been disclosed that a private collection of files on 125,000 alleged "subversive" persons and organizations, maintained by former Major General Ralph H. Van Deman (onetime head of Army Intelligence) and his wife, contained massive materials from FBI files. The New York *Times* reported: "The heart of the Van Deman files, according to military sources who have seen them, comprises confidential intelligence reports that General Van Deman obtained regularly from Army and Navy intelligence and from the Federal Bureau of Investigation."

Sixth, there were leaks of material on Martin Luther King, Jr., and an admission by the Department of Justice that damaging material from the Bureau files on Mayor Alioto had been given to *Look* magazine.

Thus, whether through internal decision, outside pressure or bureaucratic looseness, substantial disclosures and leaks of confidential material from FBI files do and always will occur.

3. *Harassment:* The dynamics of any police force move toward a mode of operation that goes beyond legitimate police activity and ends in harassment. Given the Federal Bureau of Investigation ideology, one might expect that institution to exhibit these tendencies especially in its work in national security. Conceiving its mission to be that of carrying on a holy war against a diabolical foe, the Bureau, or the more zealous parts of it, might easily be tempted to carry the struggle beyond the collection of data to more affirmative action. There is no doubt that this has occurred.

On occasion Director Hoover himself led his forces in this kind of warfare. Thus, recently, before any indictment had been returned, he accused the Berrigan brothers of participating in a plot to kidnap a government official and blow up underground electrical conduits and steam pipes in Washington. Earlier he had launched the personal attack on Dr. King.

There are other examples. At one time a federal judge severely rebuked Hoover for issuing statements highly prejudicial to a Smith Act defendant on the eve of his trial. More recently, as has been pointed out, Senator McGovern presented evidence that Hoover had attempted to get a TWA pilot, who had criticized the Bureau for its handling of a hijacking episode, discharged by informing his employer that the pilot had "experienced some personal difficulty in the Air Force prior to his employment by TWA."

At lower levels, harassment has taken the form of photographing persons participating in peaceful demonstrations, obvious presence of agents at, or outside, meetings, open shadowing, recording of license plates of cars, unnecessary interviews and other forms of ostentatious surveillance. Excessive or ill-conceived use of informers or infiltration has had the same effect.

4. *Political Influence:* A predisposition to wield political influence inheres in all security police forces. The basic attitudes and ideology of the FBI place it in a position of fighting a political movement on political levels. Moreover, an underlying distrust of the political reliability of the American people —the fear that they are easily misled by radical political propaganda—makes it difficult for the guardians of the national security to remain aloof from the political scene. The Bureau officially takes the position, of course, that it does not engage in any kind of political activity, and the myth of J. Edgar Hoover was that he was "above politics." So far as narrow partisan politics are concerned, this is largely true. But in a broader sense the Bureau is an intensely political organization.

A large part of its political influence emanates from its public relations activities. But the Bureau can have a much more specific kind of political impact. For example, Hoover publicly defended Senator Joseph McCarthy against his critics and gave him a personal blessing: "I've come to know him well, officially and personally. I view him as a friend and believe he so views me." When George McGovern was running for the Senate against Senator Karl Mundt in South Dakota, Hoover made public a letter praising Mundt's anti-Communist activities. Later, when Senator Eugene McCarthy was campaigning for President and said Hoover had become too independent and should be replaced, Hoover wrote in the Federal Bureau of Investigation Bulletin: "All Americans should view with serious concern the announced intentions and threats by a political candidate, if elected, to take over and revamp the FBI to suit his own personal whims and desires."

Many Washington observers believe that a major source of Bureau political power lies in the fact that the Bureau files contain information about members of Congress which would be embarrassing (or worse) if disclosed. Other government officials are subject to the same pressures. As the New York *Times* reported recently: "Sophisticated lawyers in government and on its fringe contend that many office-holders believe that the Bureau has files with material on personal peccadilloes of people in the government and were—justifiably or not—afraid of being blackmailed." Though the Bureau vehemently denies that investigations of congressmen, "as such," are made, or that special dossiers on government officials are kept, the truth of the situation is not known. In any event, many legislators and executive officials are sufficiently concerned by the possible existence of Bureau dossiers on them that their political conduct is affected.

There can be no doubt but that the political influence of the FBI is enormous. It is equally clear that the potential power of such an organization is even greater.

5. *Cooperation with State and Local Police Authorities:* The FBI has established close relations with state and local police authorities, as we have seen. Indeed, as Frank Donner has pointed out, "local and national intelligence agencies are beginning to coalesce into an 'intelligence community.'" And there is evidence that the Bureau has undertaken the task of developing counterinsurgency politics and plans on a nation-wide scale.

In this network of police forces, the FBI occupies the dominant position. Its leadership, in both theory and practice, is generally followed. It sets the general tone of police work at all levels. Thus, the influence of the Bureau extends far beyond the sphere of federal law enforcement. It plays a role in the operation of virtually every police force in the nation.

V: *Concentration of Power*

The FBI is highly centralized and highly disciplined. It is run from the top and dissent is not tolerated. At Hoover's death it seems to have been in the grip of a "cult of the Director." And as we have seen, the Bureau is a virtually autonomous institution. It is highly sensitive to criticism and reacts savagely to crush the critic. Sometimes the blows come directly from the Bureau; on other occasions from its allies. Plainly the FBI is striving to achieve the status of untouchability.

In the meantime, its unbridled power has been used in violation of the most fundamental American rights. Moreover, there is grave danger of an expansion and intensification of its unconstitutional activities. The potential is frightening enough that to speak of the possibility of a police state is not inappropriate. It is in this context that its most controversial methods—electronic surveillance and the use of informers—and its prime weapon of intimidation—the collection of data about individual citizens—need the closest possible scrutiny.

VI: *Conference Discussion*

MR. PINCUS: Both Mr. Hoover and the Bureau are political forces unto themselves. And the fact that they've become that is attributable in part to Mr. Hoover. He has done extraordinary things with the assets he's had. Some of these, people would approve of. Some of them people would not. And a great many things he's done, only a few people know of.

But another reason Hoover, with the agency, has risen to his present position of power is that Presidents have left him alone. Attorneys General have left him alone. Congress has left him alone. And, I should add, the press, in most cases, has

left him alone—except when he helped them achieve some notoriety.

I think these overseer groups, particularly the government
in Washington, have permitted Hoover to reach his unique
position—and the Bureau with him—out of both myth and
practical political fear.

I don't think you can judge his power or his lack of power
without feeling the impact the Bureau itself has through threat
of action. Politicians have drawn back from attacking the
Bureau for years. It is very much like the telephone tapping
business; everybody seems to be fearful of what Mr. Hoover
may know. And what Mr. Hoover may know is not an abstract fear. Mr. Hoover, on occasion, does pass around information—personal information, damaging information—about
his enemies. He does it when he feels it would do him the
most good.

I think the record will show that he is doing it more often
these days because he's under greater pressure. He's a man
who reacts to pressure. He has passed information of a private
nature to Presidents, both liberal and conservative, when it
suited his purpose. He also has this kind of relationship with
key members on the Hill, and enough of it is known around
the Hill to keep other people from attacking him.

So I think, in discussing the FBI's role as a political police
force, you're dealing with a unique organization, one that's
risen to preeminence not solely on Mr. Hoover's capabilities
but also with the assistance of other elements of government
and through failures in our democratic society. If you want
to assess the future, what you've got to do to prevent a
political police force is appoint Attorneys General who will
take control. I think people have to realize that for an Attorney
General or an assistant attorney general to move on the Bureau it is not enough simply to cite authority they may have
under an executive order. The Bureau is a good bureaucracy

and Washington is a highly competitive place. Infighting can take the form of a release of devastating information far away from the Bureau, information that can't be traced back to the Bureau.

I think you can go back and find Presidents who, you might like to think, would have done differently, but who, nevertheless, reappointed Mr. Hoover. John Kennedy did so very early, although, I think, in private, it was something he wasn't particularly proud of and would have liked to have undone at a later date. Everybody wants to do it *at a later date*. But nobody's faced up to it. The press, in many ways, is equally responsible for permitting Hoover to go unchallenged.

As a result, Hoover has built a powerful bureaucracy. There are eleven assistant directors. The most newly appointed of them has already served twenty-three years in the Bureau. None has served any less. And they've all served under Hoover. There isn't a bit of outside air at the top of that organization. Nobody is floating in and out, as they are in every other agency in government.

The future ought to be devoted to discovering how, from the President down, we can bring a little fresh air to the FBI, how we can make it responsive and make sure it performs its very important job.

CHAPTER ELEVEN

THE SCOPE AND BASIS OF FBI DATA COLLECTION

BY JOHN T. ELLIFF

Within weeks after more than a thousand documents were stolen from the FBI's resident office in Media, Pennsylvania, on March 8, 1971, newspapers began receiving copies of selected memos disclosing normally secret details of Bureau operations. In the midst of these revelations, Senator Edmund Muskie made public an FBI report, prepared in 1970, on Earth Day activities in Washington, D.C. From these and other sources emerged a vague picture of FBI domestic intelligence activities; but the image was far from complete.

Fragmentary news stories, secondhand accounts, papers taken out of context and unverified charges brought more confusion than enlightenment. This occurred largely because very little has been done to bring available historical and contemporary materials together into a coherent analysis of the scope and basis of FBI intelligence. Few other institutions of comparable importance in the American political system have been so completely ignored by scholars and students of government. Consequently, major changes in the Bureau's mission have not been readily perceived and disclosures like the Media documents and the Earth Day report are distorted because they enter an analytical vacuum.

Bureau executive themselves appear concerned that their current assignments are widely misunderstood. During the

1960s the federal government confronted new kinds of problems, difficult to define in a way that would secure general acceptance for the FBI's response. New Left and racial extremism, civil disorders and mass demonstrations became the most important subjects of FBI intelligence collection. The Bureau was concerned that increasing doubts about its legitimacy might result in less public cooperation, to the detriment of its operations. After publication of the stolen documents, Attorney General Mitchell acknowledged a need for better public understanding of the nature of domestic intelligence, "of the standard that is used and why it is used," so that the American people would not feel they were "being disturbed by government activities." Without a clearer definition of the scope of FBI intelligence, these misgivings might continue to grow.

Bureau officials see another, perhaps more fundamental, issue emerging. The FBI is an intelligence arm of the President. The primary foundation for the Bureau's domestic intelligence role is inherent executive power. Only recently have Congress and the courts begun to explore the ramifications of that power and to require the Justice Department to articulate a constitutional rationale.

For Congress, the main question is the proper separation of powers between the two branches. In the courts, it is the constitutional authority for certain governmental intelligence policies weighed against competing civil liberties claims. Justice Department testimony on civil disorders intelligence before the Senate Subcommittee on Constitutional Rights, plus its briefs in litigation over electronic surveillance, have cited inherent executive power doctrines to justify FBI operations. Disregarded for decades, the over-all question may now seriously be considered. Should the President direct an agency to secure domestic intelligence without formal legislative authorization?

Analysis of the FBI might profitably begin, therefore, with two themes. First, how does the Bureau interpret the scope of its domestic intelligence mission? Second, what do the FBI and the Justice Department see as the basis for their authority to carry out their intelligence assignments? Both issues were raised in April, 1971, when Senators Muskie and Nelson, among others, proposed inquiries into intelligence policies. In disclosing the Earth Day report, Muskie called for a review board to conduct a detailed survey so that Congress could "legislate precise limits over the scope of domestic surveillance and over the use of collected information." At the same time, Senator Nelson introduced legislation that would set up a congressional commission "mandated to investigate the entire range of domestic surveillance and intelligence activities." It would determine "the legal authority upon which these activities are based" and "the range of people and organizations who are subject to any aspect of surveillance." No private study, however comprehensive or scholarly, can substitute for one or another of these public inquiries. Only with the sanction of the people's elected representatives could an investigation obtain sufficient access to relevant confidential materials. Without that authority it would be difficult to win the confidence of the public or Washington officialdom. Nevertheless, since preliminary efforts may be necessary to prepare the way for official scrutiny, this brief study presents a tentative analysis of the scope and basis of FBI domestic intelligence.

I: Surveillance and the Intelligence Function

At the outset it is important to get our language straight. We need to know how the Bureau defines some of the terminology used in describing its activities.

There is a difference between "intelligence gathering" and

"surveillance." "Surveillance" refers to the observation of a subject through physical or electronic means. If the Bureau targets an individual for surveillance, persons who have contacts with him will come to the attention of the investigator. Neither they nor the event at which the contact occurs are necessarily the objects of surveillance. The Bureau has "gathered intelligence" about them, but it has not engaged in "surveillance" of them.

At the 1970 Earth Day rally, for instance, Senator Muskie was not under surveillance—Rennie Davis who appeared on the platform with him apparently was—but surveillance of Davis did result in the FBI gathering intelligence about Muskie and others which could be used, along with data from other sources, in preparing an intelligence report on "National Environmental Actions, April 22, 1970." As the Bureau sees it, surveillance is an investigative technique, not a broad function.

Bureau terms like "mission" or "coverage" refer to the general aims and objectives of the Bureau's intelligence efforts. For example, why did the Bureau prepare an LHM (Letterhead Memorandum) on "National Environmental Actions" in Washington, D.C.? The memo was written, like all LHMs, for limited release outside the Bureau. But when field offices prepare an LHM, they also draft an internal administrative memo (which in this case we do not have) stating the reason for the LHM, the specific sources used and suggestions for further investigation, if any. The Bureau's mission would be substantially clarified if we could know all the purposes for which it writes LHMs.

The Earth Day LHM gives us a few leads. It begins by summarizing the application of the local representative of the Sierra Club for a demonstration permit on behalf of the Washington Area Environmental Coalition. It then quotes a newspaper article describing the Earth Day movement, gives a description of a press conference held by the Washington Coalition, summarizes press releases and publications issued by associated environmental groups and supplies background data linking two local environmental activists with the Communist party and SDS. Another short passage describes agent observation of picketing by environmental groups outside a Washington hotel where highway lobbyists were going to hear Transportation Secretary Volpe. Finally, a full page is devoted to the Earth Day rally, also observed by FBI agents. In view of its contents, then, what purpose did the LHM fulfill?

The answer provides a key to comprehending the multiple facets of FBI intelligence coverage. One primary user was undoubtedly the Justice Department's Interdivisional Intelligence Unit (now known as the Analysis and Evaluation Unit of the Internal Security Division), which keeps track of every organization that might participate in protest demonstrations, especially in Washington, D.C. A second function might have been to assist the Internal Security Division's continuing review of organizations associated in one way or another with subversive or extremist groups. The participation of persons linked to the Communist party and SDS might have brought the environmental action movement within the purview of the Federal Employee Security Program. It is conceivable, finally, that the LHM would also inform the White House or other executive agencies involved in making federal environmental policy of the possible role of subversives in this area.

The Bureau does not have a file on each person coming to its attention. But the absence of a separate file does not impede the FBI's ability to retrieve information on a person. All names are indexed either at the field office level or at headquarters, so appropriate memoranda can be recovered even if an individual does not have his own file.

For instance, one of the Media documents, dated February,

1970, refers to a person under investigation in connection with a possible attempt to recruit him as a foreign intelligence double agent. In its investigation, the Bureau was able to learn that the subject's deceased brother appeared in a 1941 memo entitled "National Negro Congress, Internal Security-R." This memo indicated that the brother had attended a meeting held in Communist party headquarters following a youth conference in New Orleans in 1940. From another file, labeled "Maritime Industry, IS-R," the Bureau retrieved a copy of the official ballot of the National Maritime Union which listed the brother as a candidate and described him as being a Communist or Communist sympathizer. Since these references were obtained through a check of Washington field office files only, further requests to "check indices" and "review indices" were sent to Bureau headquarters and to the New Orleans field office. These overlapping indices ensure that a comprehensive field search can retrieve all the data about an individual that appears in any FBI file, either at headquarters or at one or more field offices. The Bureau has not, to this writer's knowledge, made public the number of names included in all such indices. This total would provide a measure of the maximum scope of intelligence data retrieval capacity. But it would not represent the scope of surveillance.

II: *The Legal Basis*

In order to understand the legal foundations for the Bureau's intelligence mission, intelligence coverage must be compared with closed-end investigations. Ordinary criminal investigations and federal employee background investigations, for example, have a beginning and an end. But the Bureau's intelligence assignment is an ongoing process of "developing" information about events, persons, groups and even the attitudes of large segments of the public.

The FBI's own statement of objectives, prepared annually for appropriations purposes, describes domestic intelligence as follows:

> The FBI's responsibilities in the domestic intelligence field are authorized under legislative enactments, Presidential directives, and instructions of the Attorney General. They include investigative jurisdiction over matters relating to espionage, counterespionage, sabotage, treason, sedition, subversion, and related internal security functions. Various laws of the United States bring within the investigative jurisdiction of the FBI the activities of the Communist Party—USA, its members and sympathizers; communist front groups; totalitarian organizations; as well as any other subversive individuals or groups which are alleged to either seek the overthrow of the Government of the United States by force or violence or to conspire against the rights of citizens. The FBI has primary responsibility for investigating matters of these types in the United States, Puerto Rico and the Virgin Islands.

Neither the Bureau's basic statutory authorization nor its own statement of responsibilities makes a clear distinction between traditional closed-end investigations and continuing intelligence coverage, with the possible exception of intelligence for protecting the President. Congress gave the FBI specific authority to "assist" the Secret Service following the assassination of President Kennedy.

It is the position of the Justice Department that these domestic intelligence functions are within the inherent powers of the President and "are not dependent upon any grant of legislative authority from Congress, but derive from the Constitution itself." The Department cites the Supreme Court's decision in *Totten* v. *United States* as recognizing "the power of the President to employ agents to gather intelligence information, and . . . the fact that the nature of the Presidential responsibilities being exercised may require that the type of investigative technique employed, or even the fact that any such technique is being employed, not be made a matter of public record."

This precedent is rather remote; it arose out of the Civil War and held that the President may employ secret agents to enter the enemy's lines and obtain information on its strength, resources and movements. More significant is the Justice Department's reliance on another nineteenth-century decision interpreting the President's duty under Article II, Section 3 of the Constitution to "take Care that the Laws be faithfully executed." The court's opinion in *In re Neagle* construed the word "Laws" to encompass not only statutes enacted by Congress, but also "the rights, duties and obligations growing out of the Constitution itself, our international relations, and all the protection implied by the nature of government under the Constitution." Department executives have asserted that the government may collect any information which is "legitimately related to the statutory or constitutional authority of the Executive branch to enforce the laws." In effect, this view gives the President the constitutional power to authorize intelligence coverage of any subject upon which he needs information for carrying out his governmental responsibilities.

The department has admitted that the President "has no power to authorize electronic surveillance of an organization simply because it has expressed disagreement with the policies of the United States Government." But under the department's theory of executive power, may it use less drastic methods of intelligence gathering for this purpose? The way the department explains one aspect of its intelligence role, the answer is yes. President Nixon has assigned to the Attorney General responsibility for coordinating "all federal civilian activities in connection with mass demonstrations." In performing this function Attorney General John Mitchell adopted the following policy regarding intelligence:

> Accurate and complete information is essential for the planning necessary to achieve peaceful demonstrations and for dealing with disorders. It is not only important to know how many are coming at a particular time, but who they might be and why they are coming. This kind of relevant information is freely available to anyone; it is only necessary to collect it in one place and, having collected it, to evaluate it in order to make value judgments and to formulate a plan of action. To provide the concerned departments and agencies with reliable information there has been established within the Department of Justice an Interdivisional Information Unit (IDIU) and an Intelligence Evaluation Committee. Whenever the information indicates a large demonstration may occur, all intelligence concerning that potential demonstration is reviewed by the Intelligence Evaluation Committee . . . [which] weighs all of the available information and reports its conclusions regarding the potential for disorder to the Attorney General.

As a result of this policy, intelligence is gathered about organizations simply because they are expressing—by means of a demonstration—their disagreement with government policies. The IDIU, originally created in 1967 to monitor the potential for urban riots and provide riot control intelligence, is now part of the Internal Security Division.

Another constitutional ground cited by the Nixon administration for gathering intelligence about both protest demonstrations and the climate of ghetto unrest is Article IV, Section 4 of the Constitution, which requires the United States to "guarantee every State in this Union a Republican Form of Government and [to] protect each of them against Invasion [and] . . . domestic Violence." Until recently, this provision has been understood to authorize dispatch of federal troops in certain cases. But the Justice Department believes it is "another basis of the information gathering authority of the Executive Branch," therefore justifying "investigative activities . . . directed to determine the possibility of domestic violence *occurring at a particular* place or at a particular time."

It is unlikely that the FBI has ever fully exercised the broad domestic intelligence authority now claimed for the executive branch. Over the years, however, succeeding Presidents and Attorneys General have placed increasingly greater responsibility on the Bureau to obtain information they think they need. The growth of FBI intelligence duties has taken place in three stages. The initial period, beginning in the mid-1930s, saw development of the Bureau's security operations, covering foreign agents and domestic Communist and Fascist movements whose revolutionary ideologies and potential allegiance to powerful foreign governments made them appear threats to national security. A second stage, starting in the 1940s and more clearly recognized after the Supreme Court's ruling in the 1954 school desegregation cases, established the FBI's racial intelligence assignment. This focused at first on groups committed to preventing persons from exercising their civil rights. Both missions underwent gradual evolution until the third period in the 1960s when urban riots, black militancy, civil unrest and new forms of violent protest brought major changes in both security and racial intelligence coverage.

III: Security Intelligence Today

The basic pattern of FBI internal security intelligence coverage was set during World War II and the Cold War era. Until 1943 Bureau intelligence reports were reviewed by the Justice Department's Special War Policies Unit, which prepared so-called "danger cards" on suspect individuals and lengthy analyses of dangerous organizations. Attorney General Francis Biddle abolished the Special Unit before the war ended. However, as Cold War tensions increased in 1947, Attorney General Tom C. Clark assigned the Internal Security Section of the department's Criminal Division to set up a similar intelligence analysis program. In 1954 Attorney General Herbert Brownell created a separate Internal Security Division.

FBI intelligence data served, after 1947, as the basis for placing organizations on the "Attorney General's list"—part of the Federal Employee Security Program. Under the Internal Security Act of 1950, "Communist-front" groups were required to register. The Internal Security Division's Subversive Organizations Section prepared "guidelines of investigation . . . for the Federal Bureau of Investigation to cover its work in connection with infiltrated organizations." These functions remain today. Although the Attorney General's list was not revised after 1959, a congressional report implies that the list does not represent or limit the scope of the Attorney General's "discretion with respect to what [confidential] advice he shall give the President respecting subversive organizations."

Several Media documents show continuity in the Bureau's security assignment over the years. One document, for example, indicates that a confidential FBI source furnished a list of names taken from Addressograph plates at the New York headquarters of the Fair Play for Cuba Committee in 1961.

Another explicit example of intelligence regarding Communist fronts is a 1965 memo headed "Communist Infiltration of the Women's International League for Peace and Freedom (WILPF)/IS-C," copies of which were "furnished to all offices having branches of WILPF for information." This included thirty-seven cities besides the office of origin, Philadelphia. Two sources of information were cited—a confidential informant who advised when and where WILPF's annual meeting would be held and an issue of the group's publication announcing that Martin Luther King, Jr., would address the annual banquet and containing names and biographical data of nominees for the national board.

A third illustration is the Bureau's August, 1969, instruction to its Philadelphia field office to inquire "through established sources only" about a conference to be held by War Resisters International at Haverford College. The Bureau desired "to determine its scope and whether or not there are any indications it will generate any anti-US propaganda." The special agent in charge (SAC) of the Philadelphia field office noted that the Bureau wanted the inquiry "in view of current international situation and the Paris Peace Talks."

In recent years the FBI has distinguished between Old Left and New Left intelligence. An informal description of the two as perceived by the Philadelphia office appeared in a September, 1970, memo:

> During the recent inspection this office was instructed to separate security matter supervision to create a "New Left" and an "Old Left" desk.
>
> Squad #3 was designated to be the "Old Left" desk. While retaining espionage and foreign intelligence matters, it will handle the investigations of all organizations and individuals who fall in the "Old Left" category. Generally, "Old Left" means the Communist Party and the various splinter and Trotskyite groups which have been in existence for many years. The youth groups and satellites of the Communist Party and these splinter groups are also to be handled in the "Old Left" category and on Squad #3.
>
> Squad #4 was designated to handle "New Left" matters which includes both organizations and individuals. This is a relatively broad term insofar as newly formed organizations with leftist or anarchistic connotations. Among other things, desk #4 will be responsible for such matters as SDS, STAG,

underground newspapers, commune investigations, the Resistance.

It is not contemplated that such organizations as the Women's International League for Peace and Freedom, SANE, AFSC, etc., which have long been in existence and are now attempting to polarize themselves toward revolting youth will be considered within the investigative purview of "New Left." To include such organizations would defeat the purpose of setting up a flexible activist group designed to deal with violent and terroristic minded young anarchists.

A New Left Events Calendar will be maintained by Squad ⚡4 secretary. When from reviewing underground newspapers, calls from outsiders, complaints or informants we know of a demonstration gathering, educational, or similar event planned by a New Left group, it should be given to SA Davenport who will coordinate this calendar. He will log it with ⚡4 secretary. This will enable us to project ahead what manpower needs we will have and enable us to answer all kinds of queries about the date we know a particular event is scheduled. It will correlate the knowledge of all.

Because the New Left lacks structured organization, the FBI's coverage is less clearly focused than for other subjects. One Media document reports an informant's visit to a commune to attend a particular meeting, which upon arrival he discovered was postponed. Undaunted, the informant related what was available. "He was invited to sit and talk awhile with those present." He noted their names and college affiliation. "All individuals were sitting around discussing the coming Black Panther Party Conference and smoking marijuana . . . A meeting of the Women's Liberation group was being held in another room."

It is perhaps indicative of the range of New Left intelligence coverage that in 1970, William C. Sullivan, then assistant director in charge of the Domestic Intelligence Division, said that the New Left was "made up of over 200 committees, organizations and groups consisting of 15,000 to 20,000 activists, plus over 300,000 general supporters."

But not all domestic revolutionary groups are found on the left. In the 1960s the FBI maintained intensive coverage of the Minutemen to locate its units and discover "the identities and backgrounds of the officers of each unit as well as the principal active members of each unit."

Coverage of another right-wing group, the Jewish Defense League, was disclosed by one Media document. Headed "IS-Nationalistic Tendency-JDL," an October, 1970, memo instructed agents "to immediately conduct credit, criminal and public sources [checks] for additional identifying data on JDL members." In addition, the memo cited information from a source of information (SOI), an Anti-Defamation League member whose identity was to be protected. This source had advised that a high school teacher, an attorney and another individual had been "active in JDL affairs." "New cases" were to be opened on two of these persons "in order to obtain details of background and activities for evaluation as to need for interview and/or inclusion on S.I." S.I. apparently refers to the Security Index.

The Security Index is mentioned in another document, recounting the investigation of a Berkeley student who had attended a meeting of the Venceremos Brigade and had applied to travel to Cuba with the fourth contingent of the Brigade. One FBI informant described her as "known to be an inveterate Marxist revolutionist, and a type of person that should be watched as she will probably be very active in revolutionary activities." However, another informant, who spoke with her at a meeting of the Brigade (during which "there was no discussion of violence or revolution"), had "received no indication that she was anything other than the average liberal-minded student that is common in the Berkeley area."

The report concludes: "Due to lack of information and activities of Subject, San Francisco is not submitting a summary report at this time. Subject is not being recommended for inclusion in the Security Index as it is felt additional investigation is acquired [sic] before this evaluation can be reached." The original informant was to be recontacted and apparently asked to be more precise about why he thinks the student "far out."

Until the recent repeal of the Emergency Detention Act of 1950, the Security Index was based in part on the need to prepare for wartime apprehension of persons likely to engage in sabotage. However, the list continues to serve other purposes. Its primary one now is to identify individuals who might present a threat to the safety of the President. For instance, an informal memo among the Media papers tied the Security Index directly to Secret Service functions: "In disseminating reports recommending for the SI it is preferable to designate and disseminate to Secret Service immediately. . . ."

FBI testimony before the Warren Commission in 1964 revealed that the Bureau broadened its criteria for submitting data to the Secret Service after the Kennedy assassination. The new standards covered ". . . subversives, ultrarightists, racists, and fascists"

(a) possessing emotional instability or irrational behavior,

(b) who have made threats of bodily harm against officials or employees of Federal, State or local government or officials of a foreign government,

(c) who express or have expressed strong or violent anti-U.S. sentiments and who have been involved in bombing or bomb-making or whose past conduct indicates tendencies toward violence, and

(d) whose prior acts or statements depict propensity for violence and hatred against organized government.

The Security Index can function equally well whether under the Bureau's authority to assist in protecting the President or under the Emergency Detention Act. According to Alan H. Belmont, then assistant to the Director, the FBI was "furnishing names of people who have expressed beliefs, who have belonged to or do belong to organizations which believe in violent revolution or taking things into their own hands." In 1964 the FBI estimated that about nine thousand names went over to the Secret Service, which relied on the Bureau for further investigation. As J. Edgar Hoover explained, "Frankly, I don't see how they can go out and recheck those names. We keep the records up to date; if additional information comes in on these names we furnish it to the Secret Service."

Since 1964 the Bureau's Domestic Intelligence Division has developed certain rules of thumb to give coherence to the Security Index. FBI field offices do not view each suspected individual in isolation, outside the context of his organization activities. Instead, persons are generally considered either as leaders of extremist groups, as key activists who have engaged in violent activity, as persons who are members of such groups or as individuals who share the group's extremist views. Thus, in his 1971 appropriations testimony, the Director said the FBI had "identified over 1,544 individuals who adhere to the extremist strategy of the Weathermen." He also emphasized the danger posed by the Venceremos Brigade, whose members were encouraged "to become active revolutionaries upon their return to the United States." Some 1,550 persons had either visited Cuba as Brigade members or were "undergoing indoctrination" in anticipation of a future trip. The Director mentioned two other groups composed of "local communes of New Left terrorists who are capable of committing revolutionary violence. The White Panther Party has an estimated national membership of 400 individuals and the Yippies has no formal membership but has 20 individuals identified with its leadership." As described by the Bureau, members of these groups would be likely candidates for the Security Index. Not all are on the left. In 1964 Hoover told the Warren Commission, "There are groups, organizations, and individuals on the extreme right who make these very violent statements, allegations that General Eisenhower was a Communist, disparaging references to the Chief Justice . . . Now I have felt, and I have said publicly in speeches, that they are just as much a danger, at either end of the spectrum."

Alan Belmont stated in 1964 that in compiling the Security Index the Bureau considered other front groups besides those on the Attorney General's list. He added that "each case would have to be considered on its own individual merits as to what is the extent of the activity and the purpose and intent of the activity." When asked whether FBI agents exerted "some selection before they would send these names over to the Secret Service," Belmont replied, "Our agents use judgment in the pursuance of this work, and they would continue to use judgment in the selection of people who meet this criterion. Otherwise if you carried this to the extreme you would get out of hand completely. So there is judgment applied here and our agents are capable of applying the judgment."

Several Media documents show how the FBI relies on local police for intelligence on protest demonstrations. The Civil Disobedience Unit of the Philadelphia Police Department reported on a May, 1968, demonstration. Although information about the protest had been "previously reported to the Bureau in LHM," copies of the police report were obtained a month later "for dissemination to individual files." After giving the location and the names of eighteen policemen and two policewomen assigned to the event, the police report form read:

DEMONSTRATORS:
  a. Name of organization: "S.D.S."
  b. Reason for demonstration: Protesting research for weapons
     being used in Vietnam
  c. Demonstration leader: A [coordinator]
  d. There were (100) demonstrators and no spectators at the
     highest count taken
  e. Identification of demonstrators: [9 persons' names, with
     affiliations]
SIGNS:
  "Science Is For Helping People Not Removing Them In
  Vietnam Or West Philadelphia"
INCIDENTS:
  a. There were no incidents during the course of the demon-
     stration
  b. F.B.I. notified, and also Police radio
  c. The handling of this detail was under direct super-
     vision of Lieutenant X, Civil Disobedience Unit
PRESS-TV-RADIO COVERAGE
  a. WCAU-TV-Ron Miller
  . . . .
FUTURE PLANS ASCERTAINED
  a. On Thursday . . . S.D.S. will have a meeting at . . .
     Time unknown at this time.

Another Justice Department function has been to provide
"an analysis of incidents of student disorder on American
university and college campuses." Attorney General Mitchell
told a House subcommittee in 1969 that the FBI "is obtaining,
and we are evaluating, information about campus disorders
and those who cause them . . . Through our investigative
activities we hope to develop a full picture of the problem."
However, in dealing with college campuses the FBI has been
extremely sensitive to the risk of obtrusive agent contacts that
might appear to infringe academic freedom. Hence, when the
Bureau's jurisdiction over campus bombing incidents was
widened in 1970, the Director asked that "restrictive guide-

lines" be established, requiring Justice Department clearance before any investigation takes place and delimiting jurisdiction with the Treasury Department.

Even in foreign counterintelligence work the FBI requires clearance with headquarters before a field office interviews a "student, professor or scientist who visited the USSR for at least one month . . ." Such interviews are conducted to "discreetly ascertain if any attempts have been made by the Soviet Intelligence Services to recruit the individual for intelligence purposes either in the USSR or after his return to the United States." The instructions stress, "Utmost care must be exercised to prevent any embarrassment to the Bureau and possibly jeopardize the Bureau's program in countering Soviet Intelligence Services' recruitment of students. The motives of the Bureau in investigating American students, professors, and scientists must not be construed as infringements of the American educational system and the pursuit of intellectual freedom." We can only speculate about how much more difficult the FBI's foreign counterintelligence assignment must be when the Bureau's image on campus is affected by its more controversial duties.

The FBI's domestic security intelligence mission today imposes tremendous responsibilities on the Bureau for monitoring not only subversives and extremists, but also the entire range of groups who express their dissatisfaction through protest demonstrations. This impressionistic review of security intelligence since the 1930s shows its evolving character. New problems have resulted in new conceptions of the intelligence function. From fifth columnists to the New Left, from front organizations to radical communes and the Jewish Defense League, the FBI has provided federal executives with a flow of information about certain forms of domestic political activity.

At the same time, the Bureau has either compiled itself or

aided the Justice Department in putting together various analytical tools—wartime "danger cards," the Attorney General's list, the Security Index and Internal Security Division computer printouts. Some have been abandoned, some revised, others maintained. The bureaucratic momentum behind these intelligence policies is hard to check. Departmental analysis programs have served to justify FBI data collection, just as Bureau reports have made analysis appear necessary. Yet there is always a danger in intelligence work that information overload may create so much "noise" that truly vital data is not perceived.

IV: Racial Intelligence

Racial intelligence constitutes the other half of the FBI's domestic intelligence mission. As early as 1947 designations for the Attorney General's list included organizations advocating denial of constitutional rights. This criterion may have had its source in several proposals made during the 1940s for exposure of anti-civil libertarian groups. The Institute of Living Law, a non-profit association influential in drafting amendments to the Foreign Agents Registration Act, urged extension of the disclosure principle to all "anti-democratic propaganda." Its research consultants, Felix S. Cohen and James E. Curry, wrote in 1943: "The hate campaigns which are designed to break apart our society into a maze of conflicting racial and religious groups are probably in the long run a much greater threat to our democracy than the activities of all foreign agents, subversive organizations, and aliens put together."

Four years later the President's Committee on Civil Rights endorsed "the principle of disclosure . . . to deal with those who would subvert our democracy by revolution or by encouraging disunity and destroying the civil rights of some groups." (These recommendations helped create the climate for use of a similar standard in the Federal Employee Loyalty

Program.) So it was that the first Attorney General's list included various anti-Semitic and Ku Klux Klan groups.

FBI annual reports did not mention racial intelligence until 1960, when the Bureau included among the nation's internal enemies "explosive legions of hatemongers." During the 1950s, however, the FBI had begun devoting resources to collecting data about organized opposition to civil rights. Some of this information appeared in J. Edgar Hoover's briefing for the Cabinet in 1956 on "Racial Tensions and Civil Rights."

To the FBI's "certain knowledge," said Hoover, 127 organizations designed to maintain segregation had come into being since the Supreme Court's 1954 decision. Special attention was given to the Citizens Councils, whose members included "bankers, lawyers, doctors, state legislators and industrialists." Senators Eastland and Thurmond and Governor Griffin of Georgia had "given oral support to these organizations," as well as to another new group, the Federation for Constitutional Government. The Director described the Federation's efforts to coordinate pro-segregation activity at a December, 1955, meeting in Memphis. In his conclusion Hoover warned of the danger posed by "the extremists who stand adamant against change and who adhere to the doctrine of white supremacy."

After a decade of increasing attention to racist activity, culminating in a drive against the Klan in Mississippi, the FBI's 1965 annual report stated that intelligence work extended to "Klan and hate-type organizations when they advocate, condone or incite the use of force or violence to deny others their constitutional rights." The Bureau penetrated such groups "with highly qualified sources consisting of not only rank-and-file members but also individuals who are in a position to have access to plans and policies." At the same time, the FBI disclosed coverage of "a number of Negro nationalist groups which are antiwhite and actively promote racial hatred."

During the first ghetto disorders in the summer of 1964,

President Johnson instructed the FBI to investigate their origins and extent. Possibly because Republican candidate Barry Goldwater was making political capital out of the breakdown of law and order, the President made portions of the FBI report public in late September. The Bureau surveyed nine cities where riots had occurred and concluded that the causes of the disorders were "demoralizing" social and economic conditions in the ghettos; the "breakdown of respect for law and order among young people"; and the reporters and television cameras which "provided an opportunity for self-seeking individuals to publicize wild charges." At the President's direction the FBI had drawn conclusions from the data it collected —conclusions which turned out to negate charges that the riots were part of a conspiracy.

As civil disorders intensified after 1964, FBI intelligence data continued to flow into the Internal Security Division, the Civil Rights Division and the Criminal Division, which started a summer project in 1966 to monitor urban unrest. The summer project relied not only on the FBI, but also on assistant U.S. attorneys in major cities who telephoned reports directly to Washington. Bureau channels were apparently considered not flexible or rapid enough to provide immediate estimates of fast-moving events.

Following the Detroit and Newark riots in 1967, Justice Department officials undertook a review of intelligence policy, leading to creation of an Interdivisional Intelligence Unit. Attorney General Ramsey Clark advised the FBI in September, 1967, of the importance of using "the maximum available resources, investigative and intelligence, to collect and report all facts bearing upon the question as to whether there has been or is a scheme or conspiracy by any group of whatever size, effectiveness or affiliation, to plan, promote or aggravate riot activity." The Attorney General emphasized "that this is a relatively new area of investigation and intelligence reporting for the FBI and the Department of Justice." He believed the activities of persons "who make the urban ghetto their base of operations . . . may not have been regularly monitored by existing intelligence sources."

The FBI was already gathering data for these purposes. One Media document, for example, is an intelligence report obtained by the Bureau from Pennsylvania State Police in October, 1967. A college administrator was interviewed regarding "a Black Power movement" on campus. He informed the State Police that approximately eighty to ninety students attended meetings of the Black Student Congress; and he identified two of its leaders, one of whom was the brother of "a Negro extremist and member of the RAM organization who was arrested in Philadelphia recently." According to the administrator, "most of the meetings held by the students related to the new Civil Rights Laws of interest to the students." There were "no indications of violence or civil disturbance proposed by the students." The administrator said he would "be in contact with the members of the Black Student Congress and their activities which will be supplied to the [State Police] in the event of any violence on or off campus." Cooperation with state and local police intelligence undoubtedly provided many similar reports for the FBI.

A significant change in racial intelligence coverage took place in early 1968 when the FBI inaugurated a "racial informant (ghetto)" program. The Philadelphia field office saw its assignment in the following terms:

It is a major part of our responsibility to learn in advance, if this is humanly possible, if a riot is planned or is expected to occur. In this way it may be possible to actually forestall a riot or at least to be better prepared if it does happen. Whether or not a riot does occur, the Bureau holds us responsible to keep the Bureau, the Department and the White House advised in advance of each demonstration. The Bureau

expects this coverage to come through informant sources
primarily. In addition, we must advise the Bureau at least
every two weeks of existing tensions and conditions which
may trigger a riot. This type of information can only come
from a widespread grass-roots network of sources coupled
with active informant coverage by individuals who are members of subversive and revolutionary organizations.

Suggested sources of ghetto informants included existing and
former criminal informants, "men honorably discharged from
the armed forces, members of veterans organizations . . . employees and owners of businesses in ghetto areas . . . persons
who frequent ghetto areas on a regular basis such as taxi
drivers, salesmen and distributors of newspapers, food and
beverages. Installment collectors might also be considered in
this regard." Agents were instructed that ghetto informants
were to be contacted at least every two weeks and all information "recorded by memo . . . with copies for the files on any
individuals or organizations mentioned." There was a special
file for "information pertinent to the general racial situation."
A brief memo to resident offices stated, "The purpose of these
informants is to be aware of the potential for violence in each
ghetto area." One unstated side benefit of the program was to
improve FBI agents' familiarity with an understanding of
ghetto conditions.

Several months later the Domestic Intelligence Division of
the Bureau instructed all field offices that they "must now
give serious and penetrative thought to methods for obtaining
maximum productivity from the ghetto informants developed
by each individual office." These instructions "set forth a number of assignments which the Bureau feels should be given to
each informant in order to insure productivity." Omitting
references to specific locations in Philadelphia, the following
nine points outlined the mission:

1. Attend and report on open meetings of known or suspected black extremist organizations . . .

2. Identify criminal individuals and gangs operating in the ghetto areas and analyze the effect they have on creating or aggravating situations of violence.

3. Determine if efforts are being made by black extremists to take over such criminal activities as narcotics traffic and the operation of numbers rackets . . .

4. Visit Afro-American type bookstores for the purpose of determining if militant extremist literature is available therein and, if so, to identify the owners, operators, and clientele of such stores . . .

5. Furnish copies of black militant literature being circulated in the ghetto area.

6. Travel to and furnish running telephone reports on areas where situations of violence are rumored.

7. Identify black extremist militants who attempt to influence the Negro community and report on the effect of such efforts.

8. Report on changes in the attitude of the Negro community towards the white community which may lead to racial violence.

9. Report on all indications of efforts by foreign powers to take over the Negro militant movement. In those cases where you have an exceptionally intelligent and knowledgeable informant, such an informant may be given the assignment of reporting on the general mood of the Negro community concerning susceptibility to foreign influence whether this be from African nations in the form of Pan-Africanism, from the Soviet or Chinese Communist bloc nations, or from other nations.

Finally, field offices were directed to "ascertain among all Negro informants, including ghetto informants, which informants are planning to enter college this fall and would be in a position to infiltrate black power groups on campuses."

Among the Media papers are several memoranda of racial informant coverage of black organizations presumably considered extremist. The first is an FD-209 form, which agents submit at the end of each month to record informant contacts. According to the contacting agent's summary, his informant, a woman, reported on several individuals and a black organization. She advised that the organization "is not going to buy a type setting machine. They are buying an electric typewriter and are supposed to have the use of a type setter the location of which she does not yet know. She said the members are fighting and drinking more than ever." One named person had left the group and another was "no longer around." A third was "becoming very discouraged," was "fed up," seemed to be "blowing his stack" and was "even talking about getting a job." Four members stayed at the headquarters, while a fifth was there "from 9 a.m. until closing time but no longer sleeps there." The informant thought the group "was on the verge of breaking up." Besides furnishing identifying data on other individuals in separate cases, the informant suggested that the wife of a Black Panther party leader "be contacted" because she was "very angry" at her husband and "may be receptive."

Additional memos based on informant coverage deal with the Black Economic Development Conference in Philadelphia. One lists the persons attending an evening meeting and calls attention to the name of the group's secretary for indexing purposes. Another report describes a meeting where the group's leader met with several other persons for the purpose of forming "a new stronger organization which will bring in other black groups in the city of Philadelphia." The proposed structure of the organization is then described in some detail. A list of persons "being considered for Chairmen of the various committees" of the organization follows, with a notation that when they are named and accept the position, "a memo will be submitted to the individuals' files." This organization was also the subject of reports on its checking account records at a local bank and on its leader's unlisted phone number obtained from Bell Telephone Company records.

The Black Panther party is the subject of memos that suggest the scope of intensive FBI intelligence coverage. Prior to the Panthers' Revolutionary People's Constitutional Convention in 1970, the Domestic Intelligence Division "issued instructions that all offices must report the following information on a weekly basis":

1. various organizations planning to participate
2. mode of travel and identities of persons planning to attend
3. identities of organizers and persons who are to lead workshops
4. identities of the leading speakers at the convention
5. agenda of the convention
6. plans for violence or disruptive demonstrations
7. plans to carry weapons or explosive devices
8. convention security precautions to be observed
9. literature regarding the convention
10. details concerning available housing

The Bureau advised "that about 15,000 are expected to attend; this group will comprise of white as well as black extremists."

The Media documents provide further insight into the scope of racial intelligence on black student groups after 1968. For example, a police chief gave the FBI a memo recounting a meeting he had with two college administrators. They informed him "that the college had been served a set of demands by a group of students known as the . . . Afro Students Society. They number approximately twenty although this figure seems to fluctuate somewhat." The chief and the administrators discussed procedures for calling in state police in case of student violence. "Their only request at this time," the chief reported, "was for the Police not to be involved until asked as they wanted an opportunity to play their hand. They felt the college could handle this problem as long as outsiders did not appear on the scene." Later the chief checked with a state police officer who had "two men . . . here daily observing and obtaining all printed literature from college available."

Also among the Media papers was an otherwise unidentified "list of current Black students" at the same college, dated several months later and apparently obtained from a college source.

FBI intelligence covered national black student groups as well as campus activities. In mid-1970 the Domestic Intelligence Division called attention to the National Association of Black Students (NABS) which "was formed in August, 1969, when Black Students split from the National Student Association." The group's national coordinator was "on the AI" (Agitator Index). Each field office was requested to "canvass logical informants to locate NABS chapters and representatives." The Bureau was "also desirous of having informants, in a logical position to do so, attend the convention" planned by NABS at Wayne State University.

The FBI stepped up its collection of intelligence about "black student groups on college campuses" in November, 1970. The following instructions went out from the Domestic Intelligence Division:

Increased campus disorders involving black students pose a definite threat to the Nation's stability and security and indicate need for increase in both quality and quantity of intelligence information on Black Student Unions (BSU) and similar groups which are targets for influence and control by violence-prone Black Panther Party (BPP) and other extremists. The distribution of the BPP newspaper on college campuses and speakers of the BPP and other extremist groups on campuses clearly indicate that campuses are targets of extremists . . .

Effective immediately, all BSUs and similar organizations organized to project the demands of black students, which are not presently under investigation, are to be subjects of discreet, preliminary inquiries, limited to established sources and carefully conducted to avoid criticism, to determine the size, aims, purposes, activities, leadership, key activists, and extremist interest or influence in these groups . . .

. . . This program will include junior colleges and two year colleges as well as four year colleges. In connection with this program, there is a need for increased source coverage and we must develop a network of discreet quality sources in a position to furnish required information . . .

. . . I cannot overemphasize the importance of expeditious, thorough, and discreet handling of these cases. The violence, destruction, confrontations, and disruptions on campuses make it mandatory that we utilize to its capacity our intelligence-gathering capabilities.

The Philadelphia field office's response to this directive provides a detailed picture of routine intelligence procedures. The office first contacted "established sources" at colleges in the area. As a result of these inquiries, the office opened or reopened limited investigations of thirteen black student groups. Six of these had already been and two currently were the subject of investigations.

Detailed reports on one of the other five reveal the nature of Bureau objectives toward an apparently innocuous black student organization. Two memos were prepared on the basis of the same data—one an internal administrative memo, the other an LHM. The internal memo read:

Enclosed herewith for the Bureau are eight copies of an LHM on captioned student group.

In view of the information developed concerning this group, specifically, that the group has not been involved in advocating or sponsoring black militant activity, it is a legitimate student activity and does not appear to be linked with any black militant groups on or off campus, Philadelphia is suggesting that no further action be taken on this organization. The activities of this organization will be followed through

regular contacts with our sources in the racial field . . . , and
should any information come to our attention to indicate the
organization is engaged in any militant activity, the Bureau
will be promptly advised.

Philadelphia will, however, open cases on the two individuals listed as leaders of the BSU and information will be
developed on these individuals so that this office is aware of
their identity and background.

[The first source listed is a security officer at a college;
the second source is a "Ghetto Racial Source"; and the third
source is a sergeant in the Pennsylvania State Police, Community Relations Office.]

Indices of the Philadelphia Office contain no information
identifiable with [the two leaders].

In addition to the file already opened on the group, individual file numbers were assigned to each leader so that copies of
any Bureau reports on other subjects which produced references to them could be placed in their files and thus, if derogatory, trigger reopening of the investigation.

The LHM, which could have outside distribution, states:

A confidential source, who has furnished reliable information
in the past and is in a position to know of activities among
students at [the college], advised during November and December, 1970, the following information:

During October, 1970, a Black Festival Week was held at
[the college]. This was organized by about ten of the 35 Negro
students who are currently enrolled . . .

The purpose of the festival was to invite persons to view the
works of art and products developed out of neighborhood
arts and crafts programs which were displayed at the
school . . .

This source stated that out of this activity, and as a result
of the planning that went into the activity, there was formed
on campus, a Black Student Union (BSU).

The BSU, at the outset, reportedly comprised all of the
black students at [the college] who had stated that the pur-

pose of this organization was to enkindle a "spirit of black awareness" among the whole student body, and encourage a larger number of black high school students to seek enrollment . . .

This source stated that BSU . . . is a legitimate organization in that it is recognized by the school administration as a proper school activity . . . Also, there has been no indication that the BSU is influenced or controlled by any black militant individuals or organizations outside the campus . . .

On February 24, 1971, this same source advised that he had learned that the BSU does not have designated officers or leaders with specific titles as do so many of the other campus student groups. He noted, however, that the leaders of the BSU and: [A and B . . .]

Note that the LHM does not identify the sources, nor does it disclose the FBI's decision regarding further investigative action. A recipient of the LHM may not know why the data was originally collected or whether investigation is continuing. It might appear, for instance, that the FBI had conducted surveillance of Black Festival Week at the college instead of the group it produced.

Association with black extremist groups like the Black Panthers was one reason for FBI interest in two students elsewhere. The Portland field office initiated a check on a girl because of her association with the Revolutionary People's Constitutional Convention. The check involved questioning a security officer at her college and obtaining "background data" from her high school. The FBI also interviewed a university chancellor about another student involved in "black nationalist" activities. The chancellor advised that the student (X) was

an exceptionally bright young man who comes from a well-to-do family. X has been a source of agitation at the University for the past few years and in April, 1970, was one of the

leaders in a student demonstration on campus which resulted
in one hundred eighty-one arrests by . . . State Police for
trespassing and disorderly conduct. X is the President of the
Student Government Association at the University and has
constantly attempted to raise issues with the University Administrator with no success.

Copies of this memo were sent to Bureau headquarters and to
field offices in Philadelphia, Denver, New York and Alexandria
(Virginia).

The final example of racial intelligence in the Media papers
is a written report from an informant in a Klan chapter. The informant's typewritten statement read:

> People whom I know: A, B, C, D, E, F.
> A arrived at B's farm at approximately 10:00 p.m. B told
> A there would be a klavern meeting of Klavern ⚹— on
> Thursday . . . B told A he would show the new klan movie
> he bought in New York City for $300 in which it shows
> a "nigger with KKK carved in his chest and another nigger
> who was castrated by the klan" . . .
> Also present at B's farm was a young woman called F
> (LNU) [Last Name Unknown] whose husband is called H
> (LNU) and is a new member of the klan. F was operating
> a . . . Pontiac convertible approximately 1964 with . . .
> Registration . . . F is a member of the women's unit . . .

The informant never mentions his own activities or conversations in this or previous reports. This document also shows that
the FBI still relies on written statements from some informants, besides agent summaries of oral reports.

From an over-all perspective, FBI racial intelligence has
three sides—one concerning groups with racist and anti-civil
rights beliefs, another relating to militant extremists who may
resort to violence, and the third involving the climate of
racial tension in specific cities. The latter two elements took on
greater importance during the 1960s, so that racial intelligence

coverage came to rival the security mission in the demands placed on FBI resources.

In the years since 1968 the number of major civil disorders has steadily declined while minor disorders have increased. Small-scale "microviolence" has become so commonplace that it is not widely reported. Local authorities are now much better prepared to cope with such violence. Yet, as long as outbreaks continue, federal executives will probably want the FBI to monitor the trouble in the cities.

V: *Conclusions*

By far the FBI's most controversial function is gathering intelligence. Information is also an extremely valuable resource for the exercise of political power. One of J. Edgar Hoover's greatest achievements was his establishment of a highly objective and politically neutral system for efficiently processing, filing and retrieving data gathered by the Bureau. Nevertheless, the FBI now has new leadership. As former Attorney General Francis Biddle observed, the Director has been given "immense authority." Although Biddle believed this delegation of power to Hoover was "justified by the record," he raised a disturbing question about "the future use of this great machine of detection, with its ten million personal files, its reputation grown sacrosanct . . . its obvious possibilities of misusing the power it has won. When Hoover resigns or retires or dies, what will happen—can the same freedom be given to another man, the virtual freedom from control? I do not believe it can." With the departure of Hoover, there may be a very real danger of the organization becoming an instrument for partisan political advantage. Despite the high degree of professionalism among subordinate Bureau executives, the risk of possible abuse of power under future Directors makes new controls all the more imperative.

The main problem with the Bureau is that it has gone fifty

years without a public accounting. As a result, it has generated pent-up fears, hatreds and jealousy. A little fresh air is needed. When an agency operates in such a politically charged atmosphere as this one does, the very nature of our political democracy demands at least that it undergo periodic public scrutiny. Such an inquiry would not seek to discover illegality, but rather to evaluate for the first time the Bureau's over-all mandate against the norms of the Constitution. If fault is to be found, it would not be sought in the Bureau and its former or current Director, but in the long line of Attorneys General, Presidents and Congresses who have given power and responsibility to the FBI, but have failed to give it direction, guidance and control. Such an investigation would not be beyond the capability of a select Senate committee composed of members above question in terms of integrity, conscience and judgment.

The current Administration takes the position "that self-discipline on the part of the Executive branch will provide an answer to virtually all the legitimate complaints against excesses of information gathering." It vigorously opposes "unnecessary and unmanageable judicial supervision of such activities." Nevertheless, the Justice Department is willing to consider "legislation which is carefully drawn to meet demonstrated evils in a reasonable way, without impairing the efficiency of vital federal investigative agencies." Appropriate legislation or administrative reforms can be drafted and adopted only after thorough scrutiny of FBI functions. However, a few specific observations may help clarify the issues at this stage.

First, a firm constitutional foundation should be established for domestic intelligence. Reliance on assertions of inherent executive power, no matter how candid, undermines the legitimacy of the Bureau at a time when distrust of government is increasing. A legislative framework, perhaps, implementing the guarantee clause like the statutes providing for use of federal troops to suppress domestic violence, might adequately authorize the most vital functions.

Second, serious consideration should be given to separating the FBI's domestic intelligence operations from its criminal investigative activities. Special qualities are needed for countering foreign intelligence probes and coping with extremists who would use violence to enhance their political power or violate civil rights. A compact intelligence service, subject to review by men of independent mind and stature, might focus Bureau efforts more precisely and avoid charges of "political surveillance."

Third, careful review should be made of the Domestic Intelligence Division's standards for the preparation and distribution of letterhead memoranda, currently and in the past. Their various functions should be specified, not by statute, but by administrative order of the Attorney General. Such an order would serve as a regular reference point for supervision and oversight, replacing the diverse standards that apply to reports for the Secret Service or the Federal Employee Security Program, for example. There should be regular audits of data retrieval and dissemination practices.

Fourth, a permanent domestic intelligence advisory council, similar to the existing foreign intelligence advisory board, should be established. The latter is a part-time group of outside consultants, assisted by a three-man staff; its reports to the President are not made public. Composed of respected jurists and law-enforcement experts, the advisory council should be empowered by the President to review all aspects of domestic intelligence operations.

Fifth, the domestic intelligence analysis units in the Justice Department's Internal Security Division should be closely scrutinized for their functional utility and effectiveness. To the extent that they merely duplicate tasks adequately performed by the FBI and other law-enforcement agencies, they should be abolished. World War II experience suggests that the built-in momentum of such analysis units can be curtailed only by decisive action.

Sixth, the FBI should accept and acknowledge formal authority to make recommendations and draw conclusions on the basis of its intelligence data and its agents' experience. It already has done so in several instances at presidential request and in certain day-to-day operations. Full accountability would encourage responsible exercise of influence.

Seventh, the principles of strict discipline, thorough regular inspections and by-the-book procedures should continue to govern the Bureau's intelligence work. However, the FBI would benefit at all levels, but especially at headquarters, from more frequent contact with interested scholars and community leaders who may contribute insights from different perspectives.

Eighth, certain crucial questions about the scope of domestic intelligence should be explored. Does federal employee security require continuing intelligence about subversive or extremist groups, beyond individual background investigations? Do the President, the White House staff or other executive agencies need to know whether outside pressures for or against government policy are inspired or influenced by subversives or extremists? Does federal intelligence significantly improve the capability of state and local law enforcement to prepare for demonstrations, to control civil disorders or to prevent political violence? These and similar questions are not easy to answer objectively from the outside.

In the ideal America there would be no place for a Security Index, an employee security program, civil disorders and demonstration intelligence and all the rest. Indeed, we probably do not need a good deal of the intelligence apparatus we have now. But as long as violence, however noble or evil its motives, interferes with the functioning of the political process because men and women believe their ends justify any means, we will need some form of domestic intelligence. For years we have assumed that a federal agency, by virtue of its national outlook, was better equipped than state and local governments to do the job. Perhaps that assumption should be reconsidered. No agency should be immune from criticism; and no critic should avoid the duty of proposing reforms. It is hoped that the material and analysis presented here will contribute to both responsible criticism and constructive reform.

VI: Conference Discussion*

MR. BITTMAN: It sounds ominous that the FBI disseminates information to banks. But it is my understanding that national banks are required by federal statute not to hire anyone with a criminal record. Isn't it on the basis of this statutory authority that the FBI disseminates such information to them?

MR. NEIER: The FBI is no longer disseminating that information because as of last June they were ordered not to by Judge Gesell. Judge Gesell found that they were not permitted to disseminate this information under the law. What banks do to check employment records in satisfaction of federal statute should not be facilitated by a law-enforcement agency with power to disseminate information to police agencies for law-enforcement purposes only. If we have a giant, national credit bureau, which is what the FBI was becoming, we're going to end up with the large numbers of disabled people I described in my paper.

MR. EMERSON: I'd like to say a word about the inherent power of the President to collect general political intelligence.

I think we would all agree that the inherent powers of the President do not extend beyond constitutional limits. That is, the President is bound by the First Amendment and the Fourth

---

* At the FBI conference, the papers by Aryeh Neier and John Elliff were presented seriatim. The following discussion responds to both presentations.

Amendment and other constitutional limitations to the same extent as the legislature. So if there are constitutional objections, they carry against any inherent power in the President. And a valid inherent power would have not only to be constitutional, but also one which had not been denied to the President by Congress. This is true whether the President seeks to exercise the power himself or delegate it to the FBI.

I think, furthermore, when Congress gives the FBI certain powers in very specific statutes, but does not extend them, you cannot imply congressional acquiescence in the extension of such investigatory powers beyond those expressly given. On the contrary, one would be inclined to imply a congressional intention not to give powers beyond those expressly mentioned.

I would also add that I see constitutional overtones in Attorney General Stone's statement that the FBI should not have powers beyond those necessary for criminal law enforcement. He didn't put it expressly on constitutional grounds, but what he said certainly implied a constitutional basis for what he was doing.

MR. NORMAN DORSEN:† May I supplement the point about inherent power? Actually, the parallel of the steel seizure case is even closer, I think, than has been suggested. In the steel seizure case, Congress did give the President authority to deal with emergency strikes in certain ways. And one of the reasons Justices Jackson and Frankfurter and Clark were unprepared to uphold the power of the President was his failure to use the particular method for acquiring the property or settling the strike.

The situation is the same here. There are ways in which Congress allows the President to deal with some of these problems. But it hasn't gone as far as the President and the Attorney General now claim. The failure of Congress to provide

† Professor of Law, NYU Law School, one of the conference chairmen, and Chairman of the Committee for Public Justice.

the specific authority desired by the government suggests, to me at least, that the power is lacking—as the steel case held. The parallel is even more striking when one realizes that, in the steel case, the Korean War was on and the President and the Attorney General claimed that the nation's very survival would be harmed if the steel mills were shut down and munitions weren't delivered to soldiers fighting in the field. Despite that suggestion, the court, by a six to three vote, declined to acknowledge the inherent power claim. The situation here is nowhere as compelling or strong for the President as it was in the steel seizure case.

MR. ELLIFF: According to Whitehead, J. Edgar Hoover says FDR called Hoover in and said he'd like to find out about Communists and Fascists in relation to the political and social life of the country. Roosevelt was a man who was confident of his inherent powers and his prerogatives. He assigned a trusted agency of government to find out this information and bring it to him. I wonder if Professor Schlesinger would care to comment on this.

MR. SCHLESINGER: The source for this, of course, is Whitehead, relating what Hoover said to Whitehead. However, there's nothing in this that is inconsistent with the way Roosevelt operated. I'm not quite clear, and I therefore appeal to Mr. Emerson and Mr. Dorsen, the constitutional lawyers, whether it is their contention that a President of the United States, concerned, say, about activities of Fascist groups in the United States, has no authority to ask the FBI to look into that absent an authorizing statute?

MR. EMERSON: It would depend on the degree of investigation undertaken. What I understand FDR did, if he did it, was simply to call in J. Edgar Hoover and ask for a report on what was going on in this particular field. FDR was not a constitutional lawyer. Very often he did things that constitutional lawyers objected to. I don't think he was considering the constitutional question. But I also don't think he intended the authority the FBI has inferred from that brief conversation. Certainly he could ask for information. But to set up a whole system of political surveillance, on the basis of alleged inherent presidential power, is a totally different thing. Of course he can get a certain amount of information. But we are far beyond that. We have institutional arrangements involving millions and millions of dollars and the time of thousands of federal agents, affecting the whole system of freedom of expression in the United States. That sort of arrangement was certainly never contemplated by President Roosevelt.

MR. SCHLESINGER: May I pursue this question, because I think it's interesting.

At what point does the constitutional question arise? It's OK for the President to say, "I want a report on what Fritz Kuhn in the Bund is doing," but at what point does he require more specific authority? Is it when they send an agent to penetrate the Bund to report on what it's doing?

I'm unclear on where the border, the frontier, is, when does a government's need to protect itself against Fascists or Nazis or Communists require specific legislation to authorize this protection?

MR. EMERSON: The courts have never worked that out on a case-by-case basis. It's never been dealt with expressly. So it's impossible to answer that question exactly. It's relatively easy to conclude that certain government activities are on one side of the line or another, but exactly where you draw the line is a legal question that you can't answer in the absence of a rather long legal development.

MR. MARSHALL: On this point, I wanted to reiterate a point some people, including me, have made before. If we're talking about improper activities, we're talking about improper activities that are not the Bureau's fault alone. It certainly stems expressly from the President and the Attorney General and is at least acquiesced in by Congress through the appropriation system.

It's certainly true, as Mr. Pincus and Professor Elliff said, that Congress doesn't probe deeply into these things. It may be that Bureau activities are unconstitutional and go beyond what a system of freedom can tolerate under our Constitution. But I think that we should recognize that the Bureau is not acting through a usurpation of authority. It is acting with the acquiescence of a government that has been democratically elected.

MR. JOHN STRANGE:‡ I would like the former agents to comment on Mr. Neier's comments. Also, earlier today, we were talking about the dissemination of information to Congress and other groups. I wonder if they would have any comment on that.

MR. WALL: The Internal Security Squad of the Bureau's Washington field office regularly disseminates letterhead memoranda to the House Un-American Activities Committee, now the House Internal Security Committee, when it asks for it. These reports are the basis for their investigations of so-called radicals. Recently the committee tried to put out a list of radicals who speak on campuses. There was some to-do about it in court and they were enjoined, but the names were finally published anyway. The names on that list were supplied by us based on reports collected from around the country.

MR. SHAW: The agents working in the field would not have express knowledge of the dissemination of information from identification records. That would be handled by central controls in Washington, from a separate building. The actual agents working in the field have very little knowledge about the release of criminal records.

The second part of the question, about the distribution of

‡ Associate Professor and Chairman of Political Science Department, Livingston College, Rutgers University.

letterhead memoranda, relates to various internal security laws. One outcome of the Oswald investigation, or the Warren Report itself, was that the Bureau had to increase dissemination of information to other federal agencies, including the Secret Service. I think there was an issue whether the Bureau had in fact failed effectively to disseminate certain information regarding Lee Harvey Oswald.

So it is probably the chief responsibility of the Internal Security Section of the FBI to disseminate information to other agencies. Most of the internal security cases do not lead to prosecution. There are many investigations that are conducted for intelligence purposes only. Consequently, the whole purpose of the investigation is preparation of the letterhead memorandum and a wide dissemination of it.

CHAPTER TWELVE

ELECTRONIC SURVEILLANCE

BY VICTOR NAVASKY AND NATHAN LEWIN

I: The Omnibus Crime Act

It is ironic that Ramsey Clark, the first Attorney General in more than thirty years who did not ask Congress to legalize wiretapping, was presented with the Omnibus Crime Control and Safe Streets Act of 1968, which legalized both wiretaps and bugs. The argument of his predecessor Attorneys General was, in part, that since the FBI already engaged in wiretapping at the margins of the law (especially in the national security area), it would be better if such tapping were brought under explicit statutory control. So Title III of the 1968 act, with few exceptions, authorizes wiretaps and eavesdrops only on judicial warrant and with specified inventory and reporting conditions.

Attorney General Clark, who opposed electronic surveillance on principle and also believed it an inefficient law-enforcement instrument, declined to act under the provisions of the new law, but his successor, John Mitchell, enthusiastically moved to implement the new tapping and bugging authority.

One year's experience under the act is analyzed below. Here it is sufficient to note that despite the so-called legalization of tapping and bugging, the Nixon administration's actions are as dangerous and disingenuous as those of any preceding administration in this dark corner of law enforcement.

In April, 1971, President Nixon told the annual convention

of the American Society of Newspaper Editors: "Now in the two years that we have been in office—now get this number— the total number of taps for national security purposes by the FBI, and I know because I look not at the information but at the decisions that are made—the total number of taps is less, has been less, than 50 a year."

But one month earlier, Assistant Attorney General Mardian wrote the Chairman of the Administrative Practices Subcommittee of the U. S. Senate that a total of ninety-seven warrantless telephone taps were operated in 1970—almost double the President's figure and almost triple the figure the Solicitor General mentioned in a brief filed with the U. S. Supreme Court in September, 1970, when he said only thirty-six warrantless telephone surveillances were operated in 1970.

Moreover, as Senator Edward Kennedy has observed, "the repeated references by Government officials to the limited number of warrantless devices ignore the far more significant question of the duration and total usage of these devices. I am extremely concerned by the fact that in 1970 there were from 3.4 to 9.6 times as many days of federal listening on warrantless devices as there were devices installed under judicial authorization."

As the Chairman concluded in a letter to the members of the Administrative Practices Subcommittee, contrary to recurring claims by "informed sources" that federal electronic surveillance is shrinking, a study of correspondence with the U. S. Department of Justice and related public materials suggest that:

1. The number of federal wiretapping and bugging devices installed without court authorization is substantially greater than the executive branch has led the public to believe.

2. The average duration of such devices is many times longer than the average duration of court-approved devices.

3. As a result, the total amount of federal electronic eaves-

dropping without court permission far exceeds the eavesdropping with judicial approval.

4. There is strong reason to doubt the validity of the repeated public assurances by the Justice Department that it fully complies with the 1968 congressional standards before installing any tap or bug without a court order.

5. Despite the department's assertions to the contrary, there is an absence of well-defined procedures which would promote compliance with the statutory standards and permit meaningful congressional scrutiny of this extraordinary executive activity.

When J. Edgar Hoover appeared before Congressman Rooney's subcommittee in 1970 and 1971, he also testified to the number and type of electronic surveillances then maintained by the FBI. He had been doing the same thing for many years, but these were the first two years that the activity was supposed to be regulated by a specific federal law. Examination of his testimony also suggests that the safeguards of the new law are not enough.

Hoover's testimony implied that the total number of wiretaps and bugs was small and carefully limited—thirty-six and thirty-three in the national security field at the time of each respective appearance, and four and fourteen in the organized crime field. (Mr. Hoover was accused of turning off taps the day before he testified—and denied the accusation. But it would be consistent with the FBI's fetish for statistics for him to have chosen the date of his testimony with an eye to reduced tap figures.) Beyond that, there are three reasons why it is difficult to take Hoover's testimony (and other official estimates) at face value.

For one thing, the figures do not reflect the FBI's access to non-federal wiretaps and bugs. But as one recently retired Justice Department official told us, not only do agents have access to state and local electronic eavesdropping, but:

"When I was there agents routinely inspired bugs and taps by
others. They'd go to state and local police agencies and say,
look, do us a favor. The local guys would get the information
and there'd be nothing in the FBI files to indicate where it
came from. It's a loophole, like the tax laws. They'd use the
loophole."

In 1970, in addition to the national security surveillance referred to in Hoover's testimony, the federal government got
court warrants for 180 electronic surveillances and state and
non-federal officials got warrants for 403.

Second, Mr. Hoover's testimony itself is incomplete even for
the internal security area he purports to cover.

Since his 1968 testimony before Rooney's subcommittee (in
support of the 1968 budget), Mr. Hoover framed his reports
in terms of the number of wiretaps "in Bureau cases." This
leaves open the possibility (indeed informed sources within
the department indicate it is a fact) that although he has
neglected to mention it to Congress, Mr. Hoover is not referring to all of the taps in which the Bureau is involved. (1) He
may be omitting the long-term embassy taps which were put
on in the first place—some as long ago as during World War
II—not at the instigation of the FBI, but of other agencies,
such as the State Department, but which the FBI services. (2)
He is omitting all of the taps requested by foreign intelligence
agencies such as the CIA, which are not permitted to tap
domestically yet have domestic intelligence needs. The FBI
handles those taps and passes on the information (which it
also absorbs). (3) He is omitting the interception of teletype
messages.

Third, there is the issue of unauthorized taps and bugs.
Former agent William Turner is quite insistent that the "suicide tap"—wherein an agent, knowing that if he is caught he
will be dismissed, nevertheless, under the pressure to produce,
conducts illegal, unauthorized surveillance on an ad hoc basis.

Most authorities on the FBI find stories of hit-and-run taps difficult to credit, since "Mr. Hoover runs a tight ship," and "Why should an agent risk it?" Nevertheless, Turner, who attended the FBI's sound school in Washington, D.C., and monitored Bureau taps for a year and a half in the Bay area, points out, "All I know is that I did it and the term 'suicide tap' is a common term. You hear it whenever agents gather."

Turner adds, "My impression was that at least in the internal security area they had a pretty cavalier attitude. The idea was that our job was to protect the security of this country; that the Federal Communications Act was really meant for telephone companies anyway. They told you never to take your credentials when you do a *black bag job* [surreptitious entry]. They taught lock-picking at sound school. There was a procedure whereby a fellow agent would go over to the local police and hang around in case a burglary were reported in the house you were breaking into. Then he would tell the police what was happening and they would leave you alone."

It is, of course, impossible to tell how extensive such unauthorized tapping and bugging is. But once information from them gets into the FBI files, it is attributed to anonymous confidential informants and nobody is any the wiser.

Yet another problem in assessing the real quantity of electronic surveillance to which the FBI has access was pointed up by Ramsey Clark. He told a federal judge in Harrisburg, in connection with the Berrigan case, that false reports by FBI agents on their electronic surveillance activities caused the Justice Department "deep embarrassment" many times while he was Attorney General. "Often we would go into court and say there had been no electronic surveillance and then we would find we had been wrong."

Clark said that the government's response to the Berrigan defense motion for disclosure of all evidence by eavesdropping —that there was no evidence of surveillance except the overhearing of Sister Elizabeth McAlister—"is equivocal and amounts to a refusal to search their records."

"I served in the Department of Justice for a good many years. Often you could not find out what was going on . . . frequently agents lost the facts," Clark said. One can argue that things have changed since then. Clark himself instituted elaborate reporting forms, and then there are the reporting requirements of the 1968 law. But there is really no way of knowing the effect of either.

A further problem in detecting the amount of electronic surveillance—authorized or otherwise—is that the issue never arises until a defendant in a particular case raises it, or until the government moves toward prosecution. One U.S. attorney recalls: "We were going to indict a lawyer in Florida in a fraud case. It was around August, 1967, and the SAC in charge came down to see me and asked could I hold up the indictment. He showed me a wire he got from the Bureau telling him that the lawyer's office had been bugged around 1963 in connection with Las Vegas skimming. Then I asked them to let me know what it showed. It turned out that this lawyer had had conversations with Hoffa, Bobby Baker, you name it. I finally thought they did this to make it as difficult as possible for me to indict because they didn't want the bug discovered. And they *did* scare me. I didn't bring the case. They had overheard about twenty top figures. We found out from an agent that the bug was installed by illegal trespass. It was *totally* unrelated to our case but we didn't want to go through all of that publicity and crap. I just didn't want to be in the position of justifying what the Bureau had done, and you always wonder, were they really telling you everything?"

Finally, there is the problem of translating what the public is told into what is really going on. As Professor Herman Schwartz of the law faculty at the State University of New York at Buffalo has shown, when the public is told that there were only 302 court-ordered electronic surveillances in 1969, it is not told this means 31,436 people were overheard in 173,711 conversations, not counting all those overheard without a court order.

The wiretapping provisions of the Omnibus Crime Act of 1968 require judges and prosecutors to file reports with the Administrative Office of the U.S. courts on each court-ordered wiretap or eavesdrop. Section 2519 of Title 18 specifies that the judge's report must cite the suspected offense, the kind of eavesdrop, its duration and the identity of the government official making the application. The prosecutor's report must specify, in addition, "the frequency of incriminating communications intercepted," and the frequency of "other communications intercepted," the approximate number of persons overheard, the cost of the interceptions and the number of arrests, trials and convictions arising out of the interceptions.

The report for the 1970 calendar year issued by the Administrative Office of the U.S. courts covers all orders—federal and local—issued under the 1968 act. Its federal section, however, contains some interesting statistics.

1. A total of 183 federal eavesdrops were authorized by court order, and 180 were installed (three were abandoned after a court order was obtained). Every one was applied for by the assistant attorney general in charge of the Criminal Division.

2. Approximately two thirds of the 183 surveillances were for gambling and bookmaking charges, and drugs and "extortionate credit transactions"—not traditional "extortion" but what is known as "loan-sharking"—covered all but five of the remainder (these were broken down to two "robbery," two "stolen property" and one "forgery and counterfeiting").

What these figures plainly demonstrate is that the FBI, with the acquiescence and consent of the Justice Department, has seized all the benefits it can from the 1968 act without assum-

ing any of its burdens. Having claimed for almost thirty years
that it needed authority to tap telephones for espionage, sabotage, extortion and kidnapping cases, it has not found the need
to take a single case of that kind before a federal judge for a
wiretap order. Instead, it has channeled all cases coming
within the jurisdiction of the Internal Security Division and
Assistant Attorney General Mardian into the "national security" category which it said the act excepted from requiring a
warrant, and has continued its pre-act practice of tapping and
bugging in these situations without a warrant.

This is inconsistent with the representations made by the
Department of Justice to the Supreme Court in the case testing
the legality of warrantless electronic surveillances in national
security investigations. In his brief, the solicitor general argued
that to permit national security wiretaps without prior judicial
approval would not open the door to "sweeping electronic
surveillance . . . as a general law enforcement technique." He
explicitly disavowed "a broad definition of national security
that could cover many or most criminal investigations."

A more realistic appraisal is that the FBI and the Department of Justice were expanding the national security rubric
(lately to include surveillance of domestic groups, such as the
Panthers, which the previous administration refused authorization to tap) and in addition were loath to bring under the
court-order procedure any of the kinds of wiretaps or eavesdrops in which they engaged before the act was passed. The
only change had been that narcotics and gambling surveillances, which were probably conducted unlawfully before
1968 even under a national security standard, were now
brought to a judge for a court order.

The real point is that to get a warrant you need probable
cause to believe you can acquire information about a specific
crime that has been committed. Probably, one former Justice
Department official speculated, "they are not asking for war-

rants in national security cases because they are not seeking factual information on a crime and therefore they couldn't comply with the statute."

On June 19, 1972, a unanimous Supreme Court rejected the government's domestic national security exception to the Fourth Amendment. At least in certain cases, said the court, "prior judicial approval is required for . . . domestic security surveillance." The case leaves many troubling questions unanswered, but the answer it does give clearly rejects the legal theory six administrations have relied on to conduct warrantless electronic surveillance.

The 1970 wiretap report, like Sherlock Holmes' hound, is also interesting for what it does *not* show. Although the act requires a report whenever an application for surveillance is denied, the report shows no denials whatever.

Other interesting facts emerge from the year-end report of experience under the act:

1. The breakdown between wiretaps and bugs gives some clue to the FBI's methods in the past. Only three of the 180 surveillances were bugs, and five were combination bugs and taps. The other 172 were wiretaps alone. Only one of the bug installations resulted in arrests, and that was a follow-up to a surveillance order issued in 1969.

2. The average cost for 1970 was $12,106 per surveillance, which compares, for example, with the New Jersey state attorney general's average cost of a little over $2,000 per wiretap (on a total of eighty-two taps). It cost the federal government, for example, over $84,000 to tap an apartment telephone in California for 20 days and overhear 18 people engage in 266 conversations (of which 34 are listed as "incriminating," although there were no arrests). Or, to take the most successful case listed, it cost the Bureau $146,300 to listen for eighteen days in September and October, 1970, to a residence telephone

in California. Forty-six persons were then arrested and twenty-one convicted, on narcotics charges.

3. Wiretaps are, of course, "general searches" in that they are totally indiscriminate and pick up innocuous private conversations of innocent people along with incriminating conversations of law violators. It was nothing less than remarkable, therefore, to read of Attorney General Mitchell's recent statement to a national meeting of police officials that "more than two out of every three messages intercepted by Federal investigators [under the 1968 act's wiretapping provisions] were incriminating . . ." The law requires prosecutors to report the number of "incriminating communications intercepted," and an analysis of the 1970 statistics shows how he got his figures.

The statistics show, for example, a tap kept for thirteen days in the latter part of 1970 on a "business-residence" in Michigan where "gambling" was suspected. Eight persons are said to have been overheard engaging in 3,655 conversations. Of these, 3,525 are listed as "incriminating intercepts." Yet under "number of persons arrested," the report lists "none." Another tap, also in Michigan, overheard only one person (is that possible?) engaged in 1,350 conversations, of which 1,300 were "incriminating." Again no arrests.

In fact, the statistical tables show an extraordinary number of gambling taps, each with a phenomenal number of "incriminating intercepts" (presumably calls placing bets or giving information) and a minuscule number of arrests in these cases. Such reports are not limited to gambling cases, or even to wiretaps. Consider, for example, the eighteen-day bug in a Michigan apartment where "extortionate credit transactions" were suspected. Twenty-two people were heard, forty-four conversations are reported to have been intercepted and twenty-four of these are listed as "incriminating." No arrests.

Indeed, the ratio of success is so phenomenal that it raises some questions about the integrity of the FBI's reporting. In only 6 of the 180 surveillances installed in 1970 were no incriminating conversations overheard. With a society as paranoid as ours on the subject of wiretapping, and with an organized crime network allegedly so sophisticated that it can outsmart ordinary crime-detection techniques, is it within the realm of possibility that so many people are talking freely about their criminal activity into the telephone or on "bugged" premises?

II: Paranoia, Confusion and Ambivalence

Hundreds of thousands of Americans—perhaps millions—are convinced that the FBI is listening in on them personally. True, there is more such surveillance going on than Hoover admitted—but not that much. Yet no matter that there are too few agents, that it takes too many to install and monitor a tap or bug, that the FBI has too many other things to do (most unrelated to electronic surveillance) or that it, as much as any other organization in the country, is aware of the inefficiencies of tapping and bugging. Nothing can dissuade a man who wants to believe that the FBI Director personally has on a set of earphones and is monitoring his every call.

The public paranoia is not exclusively—and probably not primarily—the public's fault. When Burnett Britton, who served with the internal security section of the FBI's San Francisco office for ten years, was asked why the Bureau, with its public relations consciousness, did not do something to dispel the impression, he replied: "It's very nice to know that the people you're chasing are afraid to use telephones. In fact that's one reason why in chasing the Communist Party we didn't have to use many taps. They were scared to use telephones!"

In addition to the FBI's own reasons for promoting the no-

tion that Big Brother may be watching you (undoubtedly offset now by the public relations reasons for denying it), a number of other variables add to and account for public confusion
and misinformation.

Part of it has to do with the inherent nature of the activity—
secret surveillance in an open society. Superimposed is the
FBI's own cloak of secrecy and its unique freedom from the
normal controls exercised over government agencies. Even
the Director's boss, the Attorney General, has been, until
relatively recent years, ignorant of the particulars of the FBI's
electronic surveillance practices and content to permit the Bureau to conduct its own operations under the general guidelines so long as it didn't get him into any trouble. And this
hands-off attitude from the nation's chief legal officers was
surely encouraged, in part, by the extraordinary circumstance
that the Director, with the exception of a brief three-year
period under the Kennedys, had direct access to the White
House and was able, more or less when the spirit moved him,
to bypass the chain of command.

The FBI's independence kept not only the various Attorneys
General ignorant; it obscured the facts for line government
lawyers who might have flushed the issue earlier. This was because of the FBI's organizational determination not to reveal
the identity of its informants, a policy which found expression
in the reports and memoranda seen and used within the Justice
Department. Language such as "NKT-1, a usually reliable informant, says John Smith will be arriving in New York at 10
P.M. at La Guardia airport on American Airline flight 303"
might mean that Smith's travel plans had been overheard on a
tapped conversation. But it did not occur to Justice Department attorneys (many of whom are young lawyers who leave
after a few years on the job), until the matter became the subject of a minor scandal, that NKT-1 could as easily be an
electronic informant as a live one.

One U.S. attorney recalls a meeting with an FBI agent and an assistant U.S. attorney. The assistant was pushing the agent to get more information than his report revealed, but the agent didn't have any more information. The assistant said, "But if your informant was close enough to hear what was being said, surely he can give us a description of these men?" In exasperation, the agent blurted, "The informant is blind." Retrospectively, the U.S. attorney said, "I caught it—but my assistant didn't know what the hell he was talking about."

An additional source of continuing confusion is the distinction between tapping, which is interception of a telephone conversation through a direct link-up to a telephone line, and bugging, which is microphone surveillance of a room. That distinction is critical in evaluating the legal and policy justifications for FBI practices for a number of reasons: First, under the constitutional theory which was the law of the land between 1928 and 1967, a telephone tap could almost never be unconstitutional, while microphone surveillances, which often required a "trespass" on private premises, might well be violations of the Fourth Amendment. Second, until 1968 there was no federal legislation specifically prohibiting bugging, but Section 605 of the Communications Act made interception and divulgence of telephone conversations criminal acts. Third, the FBI publicly announced that it sought the Attorney General's authorization for each and every tap it installed. But departmental procedures—until Nicholas deB. Katzenbach became Attorney General—did not involve either authorizing or notifying the Attorney General on the installation of bugs on a bug-by-bug basis.

Part of the misunderstanding today is undoubtedly a cultural lag from the days when federal law differed from state law and tapping law differed from bugging law. At one point, wiretap evidence, barred in federal courts, could be used in the courts of twenty-nine states, with the Supreme Court ruling that the Federal Communications Act made it inadmissible only in federal courts. And evidence obtained in violation of the Fourth Amendment—where a microphone was installed by trespass—could still be used in a state court.

To complicate matters further, electronic surveillance has been a principal tool of the FBI's war against those who would conduct espionage and sabotage against the country—a tool which the FBI has been encouraged to use by Franklin Delano Roosevelt and all his successors to date. It has seemed unpatriotic to question its use for national security purposes; so, again, electronic surveillance has been insulated from effective scrutiny.

In addition to all this, the public itself has been ambivalent —shocked when a congressman like Hale Boggs charges that his phone has been tapped, titillated when treated to thousands of pages of illegally overheard organized-crime telephone conversations. Such ambivalence on the part of the public and officeholders has marked the history of FBI use of electronic surveillance.

This public ambivalence has been reflected in the attitude of its representatives. Francis Biddle, in his memoir *In Brief Authority*, relates the following characteristic story of a President's responses to the discovery that the FBI was engaged in dubious electronic surveillance:

> . . . the Judiciary Committee met to hear objections from a few opposing witnesses connected with the Citizens Committee for Harry Bridges, who testified that they had watched FBI agents through binoculars from a neighboring building tap Bridges' telephone wire in New York City. There was no doubt that an FBI agent had applied the tap. Suddenly realizing that he was being watched, he made such a hasty exit that he left a letterhead identifying him with the Bureau, which was captured by the Bridges group . . . When all this came out in the newspapers I could not resist suggesting to Hoover

that he tell the story of the tap directly to the President. We went over to the White House together. FDR was delighted; and with one of his great grins, intent on every word, slapped Hoover on the back when he had finished. "By God, Edgar, that's the first time you've been caught with your pants down!" The two men liked and understood each other.

III: The Lessons of the Past

In many areas the FBI has commendably been ahead of the rest of the country's law-enforcement establishment in respecting the rights of American citizens. The now much-criticized *Miranda* decision, for example, requires local officials to give the same warnings to arrested suspects that the FBI had been giving voluntarily for years—namely that all accused have the right to remain silent, that statements voluntarily made may be used against them and that they have a right to consult a lawyer. By and large FBI security over its files has been good, leakage has been the exception, rather than the rule. (The Bureau does, however, tend to make some files public indiscriminately, as Aryeh Neier pointed out with regard to arrest records.)

But the experience with FBI electronic surveillance over the past three decades gives little ground for confidence that discretion left to it—with or without the supervision of the Attorney General—will in the future be exercised in the interests of good government.

The problem was not necessarily a personal one with J. Edgar Hoover. If Hoover in his later years had a permissive attitude toward wiretapping and electronic surveillance, he may, on the basis of the record, be taken at his word that it was a technique he preferred not to use. In his earliest statement on the subject (in 1931) he said, "While it may not be illegal, I think it is unethical, and it is not permitted under the regulations by the Attorney General." He wrote to the *Har-*

vard Law Review in February, 1939, that wiretapping was an "archaic and inefficient" practice which "has proved a definite handicap or barrier in the development of ethical, scientific and sound investigative techniques." His February, 1949, letter to the *Yale Law Journal* quoted his earlier expressions "opposed to uncontrolled and unrestrained wiretapping by law enforcement officers."

But the best of intentions and the finest-sounding general instructions and guidelines are insufficient guarantees that the executive—even at the level of the Director, the Attorney General, the President—can be relied upon, operating in secret, to respect this or that individual's right to privacy when it conflicts with some immediate concern and apparent national priority. Whether these dangers are alleviated by *ex parte* court review is uncertain, but the history demonstrates that more control, or abolition of the practice altogether, is necessary.

A. *1920—40*

Ambivalence and uncertainty began almost as soon as the art of electronic surveillance was born. After Hoover became Director in 1924, Attorney General Stone issued an order prohibiting wiretapping by the Bureau. That instruction was reaffirmed by Attorney General Sargent in 1928.

The Bureau of Prohibition was not subject to these restraints, and it broke a bootleg "conspiracy of amazing magnitude"—to use Chief Justice Taft's description—by extensive wiretaps in Seattle in 1927, and thereby gave rise to the *Olmstead* case. By a 5-to-4 majority (over now-famous dissents by Justices Brandeis and Holmes and less-well-known opinions by Justices Butler and former Attorney General Stone), the court ruled that evidence "secured by use of the sense of hearing and that only" was not unconstitutionally obtained because it was not a "search" or "seizure" as those terms are used in the Fourth Amendment.

In the meantime, in 1930, the Bureau of Prohibition was transferred to the Department of Justice, and Attorney General William D. Mitchell directed on January 19, 1931, that the bar on FBI wiretaps be withdrawn and the following department-wide language substituted:

> No tapping of wires should be permitted to any agent of the Department without the personal direction of the Chief of the Bureau involved, after consultation with the Assistant Attorney General in charge of the case.

Bills to prohibit wiretaps were introduced in the Seventy-first and Seventy-second Congresses, and hearings were held at which Attorney General Mitchell and Prohibition Director Woodcock testified. The Attorney General maintained that he had issued instructions permitting the installation of a wiretap only on "the personal direction of the Chief of the Bureau involved, after consultation with the Assistant Attorney General in charge of the case." The justification given for wiretapping by the Attorney General named Mitchell in 1931 was not much different from what his namesake said later.

The flurry of congressional debate finally culminated in a rider to the 1933 Department of Justice Appropriation Act which forbade "wiretapping to procure evidence of violations of the National Prohibition Act . . ." And with the demise of Prohibition, interest in specific legislative restraint on wiretapping waned.

But in 1934 Congress enacted the Federal Communications Act, and Section 605 of that principally regulatory law forbade the interception and disclosure of interstate telephone messages. In 1937, in *Nardone* v. *United States*, a prosecution for conspiracy to smuggle into the United States almost 10,000 gallons of alcohol, it developed at trial that federal agents had tapped the conspirators' phones and overheard approximately five hundred calls. Of these, seventy-two were incriminatory enough to be used directly as evidence at trial. Nine years after *Olmstead*, seven members of the Supreme Court held that the "plain words" of Section 605 forbade testimony in federal court which would divulge an intercepted telephone message. The majority opinion was written by Justice Owen Roberts.

Without explicitly overruling *Olmstead*, the court majority rejected its narrow view of privacy, observing that Section 605 may have been passed by Congress for "the same considerations . . . as evoked the guaranty against practices and procedures violative of privacy, embodied in the Fourth and Fifth Amendments of the Constitution." That rejection was confirmed two years later by the Court's second *Nardone* decision. It held that Section 605 prohibited not merely divulgence of "the exact words heard through forbidden interceptions" but also "derivative use" of such proscribed evidence. The court's understanding of *Nardone I* was that it was "not the product of a merely meticulous reading of technical language," but "the translation into practicality of broad considerations of morality and public well-being."

Arthur Krock reported in the New York *Times* (April 4, 1940) that Mr. Hoover had, after the Supreme Court decision, "asked his superiors for a ruling and was informed that wiretapping to obtain leads on criminality was not banned by the decision." This was consistent with Hoover's own statement— made after embarrassing tapping disclosures and congressional concern the following year—on FBI policy:

> The Federal Bureau of Investigation has utilized wiretapping as a method of securing information *of investigative value only* in extraordinary situations and *in an entirely legal manner,* where either a human life was at stake or where the activities of persons under investigation were of such an

aggravated criminal nature as to justify the use of extraordinary means to detect their activities and cause their apprehension. [Emphasis added.]

Whatever Mr. Hoover's personal views may have been (and various statements showed him still cautious about electronic surveillance) the practice authorized by the Justice Department in the late 1930s raises serious legal and constitutional questions. Formal and informal statements and reports of the FBI's practices and Mr. Hoover's standards in the late 1930s tend to show that the lines on what kinds of cases warranted tapping were flabby and indistinct. Combating highly organized crime syndicates was mentioned, as were kidnapping, extortion, and *"flagrant white slavery."* (One is tempted to wonder why any "flagrant" violations require secret electronic surveillance.)

Obviously, then, the Justice Department's and FBI's view of what warranted tapping went beyond cases where "human life was at stake." How broadly Mr. Hoover exercised the discretion given him by the 1931 wiretap order has never been—and probably never will be—fully or even substantially known. Nor do we know how many individuals were sent off to jail in that period on evidence which was the fruit of wiretaps.

There was similar lack of public scrutiny of the use of bugs. The record in the *Goldman* case, which the Supreme Court decided in 1942, shows that in 1937—in an ordinary bankruptcy fraud investigation—Bureau agents were planting microphones in private rooms and listening to conversations without the agreement of any of the parties or the occupant of the premises. Apparently the limitations on wiretaps (under Section 605) to certain kinds of cases did not apply to microphone surveillances (controlled by the Fourth Amendment). Nor, indeed, was there even a requirement that a microphone surveillance be approved by the Director—possibly leaving the final decision on its installation to a SAC. Apparently, the only restriction was on disclosure, although the Fourth Amendment—unlike Section 605—has no "non-divulgence" provision.

So the FBI came to the threshold of World War II with apparent authority to tap wires on the signature of the Director and similar authority to bug in the field. Both were highly dubious—the first possibly criminal (under the Federal Communications Act) and both possibly unconstitutional. It was in this context that, in September, 1939, the FBI was given supervisory authority over investigations relating to espionage, sabotage and violations of the neutrality regulations. Its electronic surveillance activities swung into their next stage.

B. *1940–47*

Robert Jackson was nominated to be Attorney General on January 4, 1940. In February, 1940, the FBI admitted wiretapping in a celebrated case, and a public outcry ensued. The Director thereupon issued the public release previously quoted. Two days later, a press release was issued out of Robert Jackson's office stating that upon the "recommendation" of Hoover, the Attorney General was repealing the 1931 authorization given by Attorney General Mitchell and superseding it with the pre-1931 language which imposed an absolute ban on "unethical tactics," including wiretapping.

The new policy did not last even a hundred days. Whether President Roosevelt was personally concerned with the effect of the no-tapping rule on espionage investigations or whether a suggestion was made by Mr. Hoover or someone else is not yet known, but on May 21, 1940, Roosevelt sent Jackson a confidential memorandum which said:

> I have agreed with the broad purpose of the Supreme Court decision relating to wiretapping in investigations. The Court is undoubtedly sound in regard to the use of evidence secured

over tapped wires in the prosecution of citizens in criminal cases and is also right in its opinion that under ordinary and normal circumstances wiretapping by Government agents should not be carried on for the excellent reason that it is almost bound to lead to abuse of civil rights.

However, I am convinced that the Supreme Court never intended any dictum in the particular case which it decided to apply to grave matters involving the defense of the nation.

It is, of course, well known that certain other nations have been engaged in the organization of propaganda of so-called "fifth columns" in other countries and in preparation for sabotage as well as actual sabotage.

It is too late to do anything about it after sabotage, assassination and "fifth column" activities are completed.

You are, therefore, authorized and directed in such cases as you may approve, after investigation of the need in each case, to authorize the necessary investigating agents that they are at liberty to secure information by listening devices directed to the conversation or other communications of persons suspected of subversive activities against the Government of the United States, including suspected spies. You are requested furthermore to limit these investigations so conducted to a minimum and to limit them insofar as possible to aliens.

This document and its results tell much about the perils of delegating unwarranted electronic surveillance authority to the Director-Attorney General-President axis on national security grounds—just about the most important problem today in the area of electronic surveillance.

First and most important, the authorizing paragraph of the memorandum is rife with ambiguous and troublesome terms and phrases. Some of those which, with hindsight, appear most flagrant are:

1. "in such cases as you may approve"—Was the President intending to permit the Attorney General to define classes of cases other than the "sabotage, assassination and 'fifth column' activities" which were described in the preceding paragraph?

2. "after investigation of the need in each case"—Does this require Attorney General approval of each installation of a tap or bug or does it permit blanket surveillance authority to cover an entire investigation?

3. "to secure information"—Was this intended to limit the authority to "intelligence" activities as contrasted with investigation for prosecution?

4. "listening devices"—Were bugs, as well as taps, to be covered?

5. "directed to the conversation or other communications"—Was this intended to limit the wiretap authority to particular conversations rather than to authorize a continuing tap (particularly in light of the exhortation that it be kept "to a minimum")?

6. "persons suspected of subversive activities against . . . the United States"—Was this group to include the kind of "domestic security" cases in which the present Administration is bugging and tapping without a warrant?

Second, the difficulties growing out of its ambiguous language are compounded by the history of the memorandum. As Francis Biddle noted some years later, "The memorandum was evidently prepared in a hurry by the President personally, without consultation, probably after he had talked to Bob [Jackson]. It opened the door pretty wide to wiretapping of *anyone suspected of subversive activities*. Bob didn't like it, and not liking it, turned it over to Edgar Hoover without himself passing on each case . . ." [emphasis added].

Third, the memorandum appears singularly unconcerned with legal and constitutional problems, and treats the firm holding in the *Nardone* cases as simply "dictum."

Fourth, Jackson, being a skilled enough lawyer to know that the memorandum rested on no acceptable legal rationale, worked out a justification for the departmental practice. In March, 1941, he announced that the "only offense under [Sec-

tion 605 of the Communications Act] is to intercept any communication and divulge or publish . . . Any person, with no
risk of penalty, may tap telephone wires . . . and act upon
what he hears or make any use of it that does not involve divulging or publication." This reasoning was very thin. It
appeared to conflict with the decision in the second *Nardone*
case (where evidence obtained through intragovernmental disclosure of wiretap leads was barred). And it was ultimately
condemned by the organized bar.

Fifth, again seeking to shore up the legal authority for what
the President had done, the Administration supported wiretap
authority legislation—which it had not two years earlier. In his
1940 Attorney General's Report, Jackson urged the enactment
of such a law to avoid abuse of wiretapping powers. He sent
Alexander Holtzoff, as his representative, to testify in support
of legislation with safeguards, although the specific bill which
was first introduced by Congressman Hobbs (H.R. 2266) was
thought too broad.

Sixth, in response to a request to comment on the Hobbs
proposal, the President wrote Congressman Tom Eliot a letter
which appeared to extend the authority of his May, 1940,
memorandum to the kinds of cases which Mr. Hoover had
cited in the 1930s—kidnapping and extortion.

Interestingly enough, the copy of the Eliot letter shows signs
of last-minute alterations to include extortion along with kidnapping. One can fairly assume that this was done to prevent
the added authority from being virtually useless. For while
"extortion" may be a term that could include much of "racketeering" activity, "kidnapping" had a very definite and limited
meaning. Congressman Hobbs subsequently introduced an Ad-
ministration-approved measure permitting the FBI to tap
phones when specially authorized by the Attorney General,
and making the taps admissible in evidence. The bill was re-

ported out of the House committee, but was defeated on the floor.

A final point about the FDR memorandum to Jackson is perhaps crucial. What authority did the President have to "direct and authorize" conduct which might be a criminal act under a federal statute or—in the case of a trespassory "listening device"—might violate the Constitution? Whatever fine legal distinction the Department of Justice's lawyers were relying upon to separate impermissible divulgence from permitted tapping and bugging apparently did not enter into FDR's reckoning. Nothing in his memorandum to Jackson relates to whether the overheard conversations are or are not disclosed. Nor does it appear in the letter to Congressman Eliot.

The Roosevelt memorandum has been relied upon to this day in national security wiretaps. But no adequate answer has been given to Judge Sylvester Ryan's subsequent dismissal of the "authorization" claim in the Coplon case: "It is stated that these taps were installed 'pursuant to written authorization in each instance received from the Attorney General of the United States.' Such authorization did not clothe with legality the unlawful activities of the wiretappers nor detract at all from the interdiction of the Supreme Court on evidence secured by this type of investigation."

The FDR memorandum—with all its holes gaping—nevertheless became the authority for wartime electronic surveillance. The uncertainty about the meaning of "listening devices" was apparently resolved within the Justice Department to include only wiretaps. This meant that no Attorney General approval was required to install a bug—even when done after "trespass." So until 1965, when the whole issue got into the newspapers, whenever Hoover wanted to install a wiretap he filed an application with and secured the authorization of the Attorney General. But when he wanted to install a bug, he did so without checking with anybody. That was true even though the Supreme Court had said in the *Goldman* case that the installation by federal officers of a listening apparatus *by trespass or unlawful entry* would violate the Fourth Amendment.

C. *1947–54*

A new phase began with the end of World War II and the Attorney Generalship of Tom C. Clark, President Truman's appointee. Clark, like Jackson and Biddle before him, tried to get legislative authorization for wiretaps. Before doing so, however, he sought support from Truman in a confidential memorandum in which he quoted part of one paragraph from FDR's 1940 memorandum to Robert Jackson, and added:

> It seems to me that in the present troubled period in international affairs, accompanied as it is by an increase in subversive activity here at home, it is as necessary as it was in 1940 to take the investigative measures referred to in President Roosevelt's memorandum. At the same time, the country is threatened by a very substantial increase in crime. While I am reluctant to suggest any use whatever of these special investigative measures in domestic cases, it seems to me imperative to use them in cases vitally affecting the domestic security, or where human life is in jeopardy.
>
> As so modified, I believe the outstanding directive should be continued in force. If you concur in this policy, I should appreciate it if you would so indicate at the foot of this letter.

President Truman marked "I concur" on the memorandum on July 17, 1947, and returned it to Clark. Thus the FDR memorandum was extended well beyond its intended scope. Professor Athan Theoharis of Marquette University has pointed out how this was accomplished:

> While implying that this new directive would be a simple extension of Roosevelt's policy, and thereby reducing any sus-

picions that Truman might have held about wiretapping and
the relationship of this policy to that of his predecessor,
Clark had significantly distorted the Roosevelt directive. In
his quote from the operative paragraph of Roosevelt's directive, Clark had deleted its last qualifying sentence—"You are
requested furthermore to limit these investigations so conducted to a minimum and to limit them insofar as possible to
aliens." Moreover, Clark's letter did not convey the essence
of the Roosevelt memorandum, whether Roosevelt's concern
about the abuse of this authority or his restriction of wiretapping to foreign activities involving sabotage. In addition, Clark's
intent went significantly beyond Roosevelt's, in that he proposed that wiretapping be used to investigate domestic crime
or "subversive" activities. In the absence of good staff work
that would have apprised him of the specific nature of Roosevelt's policy, and accepting the assurances of his Attorney
General, Truman signed the letter. By so doing, he provided
the basis for a significant change in executive wiretapping
policy.

Soon thereafter came the Judith Coplon case with its large
bag of disclosures on FBI wiretapping. During her first trial,
her attorneys demanded that full texts of FBI reports she
was charged with stealing be introduced, and they showed
that in fifteen of the twenty-eight, wiretap information was included. A demand that FBI agents be questioned whether
Miss Coplon's phone was tapped was denied.

But in her second trial, such questioning was allowed. It
revealed that forty FBI agents had tapped telephones in her
Washington apartment, her office and her family's home in
Brooklyn. The tapping occurred for some time before and for
two months after her arrest.

The Coplon case and the public furor over it persuaded
Attorney General Clark to withdraw the request for legislation
authorizing wiretapping—after the Americans for Democratic
Action demanded an investigation of the Justice Department's

tapping practices. And at the same time—without disclosing the 1947 memorandum to Truman and the President's concurrence—Mr. Clark announced publicly: "There has been no new policy or procedure since the initial policy was stated by President Roosevelt, and this has continued to be the department's policy whenever the security of the nation is involved."

J. Howard McGrath, who followed Clark as Attorney General (serving from 1949 to 1952), announced in 1950 there would be no change in the FBI's wiretapping policy and that standards for "limited" use of wiretapping had been fixed by President Roosevelt and former Attorneys General. He also resolved bugging problems by advising the FBI in a 1952 memorandum—which has never appeared publicly—that (1) the Bureau could not install any microphones involving trespass; (2) whenever evidence in any case was referred from the Bureau to the department where a telephone tap or microphone surveillance was used, the Bureau should inform department attorneys of that fact. But the disclosures in the Fred B. Black case, and its successors, in 1966 indicate that these instructions were simply not followed.

D. *1954–66*

Attorneys General are transient but Hoover was not. So the FBI bided its time until a new Attorney General came in. Then, according to recollections of former Justice Department attorneys, immediately after the Eisenhower administration took office, the Bureau commenced negotiations with the department to erode the McGrath positions. A series of meetings took place in 1953. They apparently culminated after the Supreme Court decided the *Irvine* case, and the Bureau solicited an opinion from Attorney General Herbert Brownell to give the FBI blanket authority to install microphones by trespass.

It was this memorandum, apparently, on which the Solicitor

General relied twelve years later, in the *Black* case, when he told the Supreme Court:

> Under Departmental practice in effect for a period of years prior to 1963, and continuing into 1965, the Director of the Federal Bureau of Investigation was given authority to approve the installation of devices such as that in question for intelligence (and not evidentiary) purposes when required in the interest of internal security or national safety, including organized crime, kidnappings and matters wherein human life might be at stake.

The "authority" referred to so definitively has yet to be specifically identified by the Justice Department. Yet it was the basis of every FBI eavesdrop from 1954 until bugging was legalized under the Omnibus Crime Control Act of 1968. No document other than the Brownell memorandum of May 20, 1954, has surfaced. The full text of the memorandum, reprinted from *Kennedy Justice,* by Victor S. Navasky, follows:

May 20, 1954 "CONFIDENTIAL"

To: Director
From: The Attorney General
Subj: Microphone Surveillance

The recent decision of the Supreme Court entitled *Irvine* v. *Calif.* 347 US 128, denouncing the use of microphone surveillances by city police in a gambling case makes appropriate a reappraisal of the use which may be made in the future by the Federal Bureau of Investigation of microphone surveillance in connection with matters relating to the internal security of the country.

It is clear that in some instances the use of microphone surveillance is the only possible way of uncovering the activities of espionage agents, possible saboteurs, and subversive persons. In such instances I am of the opinion that the national interest requires [that] microphone surveillance be utilized by the Federal Bureau of Investigation. This use need not be limited to the development of evidence for prosecution. The FBI has an intelligence function in connection with internal security matters equally as important as the duty of developing evidence for presentation to the courts and the national security requires that the FBI be able to use microphone surveillance for the proper discharge of both of such functions. The Department of Justic approves the use of microphone surveillance by the FBI under these circumstances and for these purposes. I do not consider that the decision of the Supreme Court in *Irvine* v. *California* requires a different course. That case is really distinguishable on its facts. The language of the Court, however, indicates certain uses of microphones which it would be well to avoid, if possible, even in internal security investigations. It is quite clear that in the Irvine case the Justices of the Supreme Court were outraged by what they regarded as the indecency of installing a microphone in a bedroom. They denounced the utilization of such methods of investigation in a gambling case as shocking. The Court's action is a clear indication of the need for discretion and intelligent restraint in the use of microphones by the FBI in all cases, including internal security matters. Obviously, the installation of a microphone in a bedroom or in some comparably intimate location should be avoided wherever possible. It may appear, however, that if important intelligence or evidence relating to matters connected with the national security can only be obtained by the installation of [a microphone in such a location and under such] circumstances the installation is proper and is not prohibited by the Supreme Court's decision in the Irvine case.

Previous interpretations which have been furnished to you as to what may constitute a trespass in the installation of microphones, suggest that the views expressed have been tentative in nature and have attempted to predict the course which courts would follow rather than reflect the present state of the law. It is realized that not infrequently the question of trespass arises in connection with the installation of a microphone. The question of whether a trespass is actually involved and the second question of the effect of such a trespass upon the admissibility in Court of the evidence thus obtained, must necessarily be resolved according to the circumstances of each case. The Department in resolving the problems which may arise in connection with the use of microphone surveillance will review the circumstances of each case in the light of the practical necessities of investigation and of the national interest which must be protected. It is my opinion that the Department should adopt that interpretation which will permit microphone coverage by the FBI in a manner most conducive to our national interest. I recognize that for the FBI to fulfill its important intelligence function, considerations of internal security and the national safety are paramount, and therefore, may compel the unrestricted use of the technique in the national interest.

The major references in the Brownell memorandum which might remotely be interpreted as going beyond national security are its concluding two sentences. But they are qualified by all the preceding language. And while the earlier reference to "internal security matters" is preceded by the word "including," the context of that reference indicates that it *restricts* the Bureau's use of microphones rather than expands it. By noting that the *Irvine* decision shows the need for discretion and restraint in all "use of microphones by the FBI"—"including internal security matters"—the Attorney General could hardly have been authorizing microphone installations in *other* situations.

It would, of course, be inconceivable for any closely watched organization—continually exposed to public scrutiny (as the FBI is not)—to leap on phrases like "national interest" or "national safety" in a secret document, wrench them out of context and then use them as an excuse to eavesdrop on a bookie joint in Miami. And it is difficult to accept the FBI's reliance on a memorandum that explicitly condemns the trespassory installation of a microphone in a gambler's bedroom as authority for trespassory installation of a microphone in the bedroom of a Las Vegas casino manager.

The most elementary question, however, is how the FBI could rely on a memorandum stating that the department would "review the circumstances of each case in the light of the practical necessities of the investigation and of the national interest" if Hoover did not submit bugs to the Attorney General for authorization on a case-by-case basis. Yet he did not.

In 1964 the scene shifted to the Congress and the courts. Congressional interest had been revived with the internal security frenzy of the 1950s, and again with the Kennedy administration's efforts to fight organized crime in the early 1960s. But no substantive congressional action resulted in either instance.

Meanwhile Attorney General Robert Kennedy (1961–64) listened to tapes of what he thought were local police bugs (permitted under local law) in Chicago and New York, and after great pressure, prodding, insistence and a sort of bureaucratic blackmail (described in *Kennedy Justice*) he authorized the tapping of Dr. Martin Luther King's telephone under the "national security" theory of the Jackson memo. After Robert Kennedy's death it was explained that it was not Dr. King who was the security risk, but alleged Communist party members in his entourage. And Dr. King was tapped "to protect him"—for in the absence of such a tap, which could prove Dr. King's innocence, the Bureau might disseminate derogatory charges against King that southern members of the United States Senate would use to undermine the strong civil rights bill of late 1963, which the Kennedys considered an imperative.

Hoover had earlier informed Kennedy of tapping procedures in the FBI, but not about bugs, and Kennedy did not ask about them. Both oversights reflect the etiquette which had developed over the years in the electronic surveillance business.

Kennedy's successor, Nicholas deB. Katzenbach, upon discovering that the FBI had indulged in bugging after trespass, had a meeting with Hoover. Hoover informed him that if the bugs were removed forthwith it would spell the end of the Justice Department's organized crime program. They compromised on a phase-out program for the bugs, and Katzenbach instituted a procedure whereby he was notified of existing bugs on the same basis that he authorized taps.

On June 30, 1965, President Johnson issued a directive prohibiting the use of listening devices by agencies other than the Department of Justice, and authorized the latter to use such devices only where necessary to collect "intelligence affecting the national security."

E. *1966–68*

Eavesdropping again came to public attention on May 24, 1966, when Solicitor General Thurgood Marshall filed a "Memorandum for the United States" in the Supreme Court in the criminal tax evasion case of Fred B. Black, an associate of Bobby Baker's. The memorandum told the court that FBI agents had bugged Black's hotel suite early in 1963, at approximately the time when the tax-evasion evidence was presented to a federal grand jury in Missouri. The Solicitor General took the position that the proof was not tainted by the overhearing, although conversations between Black and the lawyer representing him in the tax case were overheard.

On June 13 the court asked details on the kind of listening apparatus used, the authority under which it was installed (including "the person or persons who authorized its installation"), whether recordings existed and the time when government lawyers first learned of this information. The response was drafted in the Solicitor General's office with many personal consultations with Attorney General Katzenbach.

It admitted that there was "no specific statute or executive order . . . relied upon in the installation of the listening device in question." It stated that since 1940, wiretaps—"limited to matters involving national security or danger to human life"—have required "the specific authorization of the Attorney General in each instance." But, it said, there was no similar procedure until 1965 governing eavesdropping—notwithstanding "records of oral and written communications" which reflected concern by Attorneys General and the FBI Director that use of such devices should be severely limited. It then cited the previously quoted "departmental practice" of authorizing the Director to install such devices.

The court on November 7, 1966, vacated the conviction and ordered a new trial (385 U.S. 26). And a month later it did the same with another bugging case in which the Solicitor General had admitted that evidence at trial may have been tainted by trespassory eavesdropping. Many other such cases followed in the Supreme Court and in lower courts, and procedural issues were still being sorted out in late 1971.

Recognizing that the problem was becoming unmanageable, Acting Attorney General Ramsey Clark issued an instruction to the United States attorneys on November 3, 1966, in which he directed that no prosecution "go forward" until all illegally obtained evidence and its fruits were "purged."

And on June 16, 1967, he issued a detailed policy statement on tapping and bugging. In it, he reiterated that tapping "is prohibited by Presidential directive . . . whether or not the information which may be acquired through interception is intended to be used in any way or to be subsequently divulged outside the agency involved." While noting that nontrespassory eavesdropping had still not been held unconstitutional, Clark observed that there was "support for the view" that any eavesdropping on conversations in a private area was forbidden by the Fourth Amendment. Accordingly, he directed that no such surveillance be conducted without "advance written approval" from the Attorney General. National security investigations were mentioned separately as matters "to be taken up directly with the Attorney General."

Any remaining doubts about the vitality of *Olmstead* and the constitutionality of the non-trespassory eavesdropping approved in *Goldman* were laid to rest by *Katz* v. *United States,* 389 U.S. 347, decided in December, 1967. Both *Olmstead* and *Goldman* were squarely overruled, the court holding that the government's "activities in electronically listening to and recording the petitioner's words violated the privacy upon which he justifiably relied . . . and thus constituted a 'search and seizure' within the meaning of the Fourth Amendment." And after *Katz* and *Berger* v. *New York,* 388 U.S. 41 (1967), which enumerated the necessary constitutional conditions for court-ordered wiretapping, came Title III of the Omnibus Crime Control and Safe Streets Act of 1968.

F. *Lessons*

The history of electronic surveillance, then, is a history of deception, confusion, ambivalence and after-the-fact rationalization, ranging from FDR's May, 1940, memorandum and February, 1941, letter to Jackson's 1941 strained interpretation of the words "intercept and divulge" to Tom Clark's overbroad 1947 note to Harry Truman to Hoover's failure to alert Robert Kennedy to the FBI's microphone surveillance procedures to Katzenbach's pragmatic decision on outstanding FBI bugs . . . The practice has been degrading to the President, the Attorney General, the Director, the FBI, the Justice Department, the men who have had to partake in it, the victims of it and ultimately the polity.

This is true regardless of the law-enforcement arguments in favor of wiretapping as a way of catching criminals. What it shows is that general standards, no matter how phrased, cannot restrain excesses if there is no outside agency to scrutinize what is being done. No matter how well-intentioned an Attorney General, no matter how distasteful wiretapping seemed to a younger Mr. Hoover, they found themselves drawn further into practices of dubious legality and constitutionality.

The men involved are not to be condemned personally. The system—the relationship between the Bureau and the department, the permanent Director and the transient Attorneys General—made it possible, probable, perhaps inevitable that without external (court-warranted) supervision, there would be vast abuses in the government's electronic surveillance. Whether or not a well-conceived warrant procedure can cure this problem, it is apparent that in its absence, the executive branch acting on its own has been irresponsible. The short experience of unilateral executive self-restraint under the 1968 Crime Act proves as much.

IV: Questions

In view of that failure and in hope of better control, these are questions for which Congress and the public ought to demand answers:

What is the extent of electronic surveillance carried on today? How much control do the President and the Attorney General exercise over the FBI's electronic surveillance practices? Is there more or less than before? Has the new law made a difference? What can be learned from the past? Should the Attorney General, the President and the Director of the FBI ever be trusted—without court supervision—to authorize electronic surveillance in the national security area?

How much tainted evidence finds its way into court without anyone being any the wiser—as a result of inter-agency cooperation in the exchange of information without divulging the manner in which the information was procured? What more has to be known before recommendations can be made along these lines?

The practice before the Supreme Court rejected a domestic national security exception to the Fourth Amendment is still important for what it tells us about the government's assumptions about its role and power in the area and because national security may again be used to justify warrantless surveillance. Did all "internal security" electronic surveillance requests automatically bypass the warrant procedure, or was a separate determination made on each case by the Attorney General? To what extent did the Nixon administration extend the national security or internal security umbrella to cover domestic organizations with an international dimension? By what standards did an agent decide to apply for a national security tap? Did Hoover ever turn him down and what standards did *he* use? How was it decided whether to go to court for a warrant?

Finally, are the provisions of the law requiring service of a notice upon an individual under surveillance and filing of an inventory being complied with? Is *any* weight given to the countervailing values of privacy protection in this area?

V: *Conference Discussion*

MR. ELLIFF: Among the Media documents is a summary of a wiretap on the Black Panther headquarters in Philadelphia. It raises some interesting questions about the merits of wiretapping for preventive intelligence purposes and I wonder if you'd comment on this. I'll describe it briefly.

Three or four pages of conversations are summarized. Much of this is extraneous to any preventive or general intelligence needs of the government. But the last conversation reads as follows:

"A called B who advised the neighborhood was saturated

with pigs and was asked by B if the machinery was all set up for such things. A said the machinery was ready and that they had everything going for them."

It seems to me, though the wiretap here reported all kinds of irrelevant data, it did produce an immediate warning of a possible violent confrontation with the police. I was wondering how we weigh the value of that kind of warning, which, if properly used, could help a community relations officer defuse a situation that might be building up into a gunfight.

Balance the need for that sort of information against the clear risks required to obtain it, risks of public paranoia and of damage to principles of constitutional doctrine. How do we balance that?

MR. NAVASKY: That, you know, is the critical question. By what standards do you tap? How do you make that judgment?

When Ramsey Clark was Attorney General, he asked a young attorney in the department to take twelve random bugs—they were all in the organized crime area as it happened—and analyze them for their utility and effectiveness and whether other investigative techniques could have developed the same information.

The attorney came to the conclusion that they weren't worth it. But, then, everybody who considered the evidence reached the same conclusion they already had before looking at it. Most people who didn't believe in wiretapping concluded it wasn't useful. And those who did believe in it concluded it was.

So it's a very difficult problem. But one solution is to set standards and require law enforcers to go to an outside agency like a court and prove they meet the standards.

MR. LEWIN: All I want to add to that is that we have not in this paper, or I think generally, come to any firm conclusion that wiretapping under all circumstances and all conditions is unjustified. In fact, federal law authorizes it.

Certainly, at one extreme, one supposes that if a wiretap were installed on every telephone in the United States, and there were enough agents to listen in on every telephone, random wiretaps would turn up information that might be useful to law-enforcement authorities. But obviously that's an impermissible infringement on constitutional rights. So the only mechanism that has been devised thus far, and which we're constitutionally committed to, is examination by an impartial magistrate of the facts used to justify a tap. Our view is that even in national security cases, that is a mechanism that could and should be used.

I think anybody who's had anything to do with the search warrant system, however, in both federal and state courts, will tell you that the examination by an impartial magistrate is not always what the Supreme Court may think it to be. There are magistrates and judges who just rubber-stamp what's put before them. In fact, as we said, although the act requires that every eavesdropping warrant that's turned down be reported to the administrative office in the U.S. courts, there's not a single report of a warrant being turned down this year.

MR. MARSHALL: As I understand, you've been talking about taps and bugs that were authorized by someone, maybe wrongly authorized, but authorized by the Attorney General or the Director.

I think people have the impression that Bureau agents are sometimes forced, through the incentives and the pressures on them, to get the job done, to use these devices in ways that are not authorized even within the rules of the Bureau. For example, in cooperation with local authorities. Does your paper evaluate that aspect of it?

MR. NAVASKY: Yes, to some degree, but we found conflicting evidence. As our paper states, Bill Turner will tell you when he was an agent he installed unauthorized electronic surveillance. But other people deny that it goes on and will say it's not within the psychology of the FBI, it's not the way it's run. It's

a very tightly run organization. But Bill Turner calls these unauthorized taps suicide taps and says every agent knows what
a suicide tap is.

Now it seems to me that a more interesting question is how
much the Bureau inspires other agencies to do things they're
not supposed to do. If you look at the reports filed with the U.S.
courts, there may be 180 federal wiretaps. But there are also
320 state and local wiretaps. The Bureau has access to these
because they have contact with local law-enforcement agencies.

How many illegal taps does the FBI inspire? In 1965 it was
revealed by a former member of Army intelligence that he had
tapped Mrs. Roosevelt's hotel room during World War II. The
newspaper report indicated that he did it at the invitation of
the FBI. They asked: Can you help us?

But a lot of times this is not done. They don't say: Go tap
someone's telephone. They say, to the local police agency in
Georgia, for example: can you tell us when Dr. King will be
arriving in New York? And the local police agency in Georgia
calls back a week later and says: Dr. King is coming to New
York on the four-thirty plane from Atlanta on American Air-
lines. The Bureau's piece of paper will say, "T 3, a reliable informant, says Dr. King is arriving in New York on the four-
thirty plane from Atlanta." Well, the Bureau may have silently
inspired the local agency to listen in on Dr. King's travel plans.
and yet the Bureau has done nothing illegal under the arrangement.

MR. BITTMAN: Mr. Navasky stated that one of the major
problems with wiretapping and electronic eavesdropping is the
fact that these have often resulted from unilateral decisions by
the executive branch. There was no external auditing body
governing the actions of the executive branch. In 1968, as I'm
sure almost everyone in this room knows, Congress gave specific statutory authority for wiretapping and bugging. It has

set up certain procedures governing this activity. You must get judicial approval. There are certain built-in safeguards.

Now, I have a few questions. Are you unalterably opposed to all bugging and wiretapping, whether done in national security cases or in organized crime cases? Do you believe the statute is unconstitutional? Do you believe that the requirement of judicial authority is nothing but a rubber stamp? And if you do not believe there are sufficient safeguards, what additional safeguards would you suggest?

MR. NAVASKY: Number one. We distinguished in our paper between bugging and tapping before and after the 1968 act.

Now as of the 1968 act, which does provide procedures, I don't know whether the procedures for national security taps, as interpreted by the Attorney General and, presumably, the President, are going to hold up in court. The law has language which says, in effect, go to court and get warrants even in espionage, sabotage, treason and riot cases, among others. But then a second part of the law says the President can tap and bug without a warrant if national security is involved.

And so it's under the second part of the law that the Attorney General has found authority to allow Mr. Hoover to tap telephones in the so-called national security area, without going to court.

I would contend, number one, that as a matter of legislative intent that was not what was intended. This interpretation of the law should be struck down.

Number two, if there is a national security exception, that exception still cannot constitutionally apply to domestic groups, like the Panthers.

Number three, you asked if I believe in wiretapping and bugging under any circumstances. We were talking at lunch about that. I told Mr. Lewin that I used to think that the government ought to be able to listen in on hard-core international espionage matters. It ought to be able to listen in on "the enemy." The more I look into it, however, and the more I see how ingenious the executive branch is at going beyond the little words that lawyers and congressmen draft, the less confident I become that even this ought to be allowed.

MR. LEWIN: I think in answer to Bill Bittman's question, if I can supplement what Vic said, our concern is that the act has really made no substantial difference in restricting what the FBI does. It's expanded it instead. First, the act has given the Bureau a procedure under which it can lawfully wiretap and bug in gambling cases, narcotics cases and the entire range of cases that, before 1968, could not be justified at all. Second, in the so-called national security area, the Bureau and the Attorney General are still not going to court for judicial warrants, even where there is really no need for confidentiality. This is because the national security exception is broadly construed, thereby allowing them to keep many cases from judicial scrutiny.

So in answer to one of your questions, I'm in favor of meaningful judicial oversight of wiretapping and electronic surveillance—in other words, based on a warrant for a limited period of time. But I'm afraid that as the act is construed by the present Administration, far too many cases are excluded from its reach by the national security exception.

The talebearer shall defile his own soul,
and be hated by all
Ecclesiasticus, XXI, 31.

CHAPTER THIRTEEN

POLITICAL INFORMERS

BY FRANK DONNER

I: The Uses of Informers

While the law-enforcement justification for the use of informers is, in reality, quite limited, the FBI relies on it, along with "national security," as a sort of "cover" to justify surveillance where there is no plausible reason for it. The key significance of the informer is political. Of approximately ten thousand political undercover agents, only a small number report on violence-prone groups in order to forestall bombings and the like. The rest are used as informers against left, liberal, anti-war, racial and ghetto groups and individuals.

The "mission" of American political intelligence is to keep alive and renew the contemporary version of the "Red menace" of the 1920s, the myth that the country is under a permanent threat of internal subversion which presents enormous dangers to our government and its institutions. We have seen how Hoover projected this myth endlessly—in congressional testimony, magazine articles and speeches.

But what authenticated his testimony and his tirades was the fact that he was an insider. Acting through his informer proxies, he pursued the subversive monster to his lair and outwitted him. Every great spy master in history has exploited within government the feeling of awe aroused by his penetration of secret plots and knowledge of hidden mysteries. But in a wholly new way, Hoover also exploited mass dependence and fear to free himself and his agency from official control. When he testified that there were precisely 22,263 Reds in the country—not one more or less—he conjured up in the minds of his followers a patient midnight review and evaluation of untold numbers of informers' reports.

Hoover's power flowed from a dual strategy of alarm and containment. His legislative and mass constituency was stirred by anxiety about the undiminished perils of subversion. Here his intelligence role was invaluable. But it would hardly have done to create such deep fear as to have cast doubt on the ability of the Director to cope with the situation. He regularly issued assurances that his vigilance had frustrated the subversives, and his surveillance network of informers stood behind the assertion. But the escape was always a narrow one. He was not able to cope with the danger by himself—everyone had to join in fighting the menace.

Hoover and various functionaries of the Department of Justice tried to explain and justify the use of informers in a variety of ways. Yet neither the Attorney General nor the President nor Congress was ever known to seek, either on an ad hoc or systematic basis, a review of the Director's informer policies. And private citizens—scholars, writers, journalists—were discouraged from prying because it might have endangered the national security.

In an article in the *Elks Magazine* for August, 1956, Hoover denounced those who "indulge in sabotage by semantics—they stigmatize patriotic Americans with the obnoxious term 'informer,' when such citizens fulfill their obligations of citizenship by reporting known facts of the evil conspiracy to properly constituted authorities. It would require very little time for these critics to pick up a dictionary. Webster's unabridged volume specifically states that an 'informant' is one who gives information of whatever sort; an 'informer' is one who informs against another by way of accusation or complaint. Informer is often, informant never, a term of opprobrium."

This Kafkaesque passage seems to mean that since FBI spies are "patriotic Americans," it is duplicitous and subversive to describe them with a "term of opprobrium." The import of Hoover's tirade is that good citizens discover facts about the "evil conspiracy" (which are already known anyway) and, discharging their civic duty, report them to their authorities. This is, of course, a crude forgery of the FBI informer's relationship and role. If there was "sabotage by semantics"—the Director loved alliteration—Hoover was the guilty party.

In a speech to the International Association of Police Chiefs on October 3, 1955 (also reprinted in a pamphlet, "Our Common Task"), Hoover devoted himself to a brief defense of informers and a protracted attack on their critics. Informers, he insisted, are "used as a means of establishing truth"; they are "as old as man." But they are victims of a "determined . . . campaign of vituperation" which is "part and parcel of a Communist strategy," devised "for the most part" by Communist lawyers, "skilled in concealing foul and despicable acts behind the Fifth Amendment." These lawyers employ "unscrupulous" tactics shunned even by the underworld mouthpiece. It is the "technique of the smear."

The Communists are godless, pliant tools of their masters, who "will lie, cheat, steal or do anything for the Communist cause." Confidential informants alone can uncover their dark conspiratorial deeds and "much of the future security of the United States" depends on them because they have "firsthand knowledge of the secret, diabolical purposes of the Communist Party." Behind this vituperative campaign against informants is the false claim "that the Communist menace is a myth."

This is a sterling example of Hoover-speak, which hardly needs exposition. This same address also uses another deceptive ploy: "We cannot minimize the hate of the underworld whether it be the underworld of hoodlums or the underworld of subversive traitors and its urgent desire also to identify and discredit the confidential informant. There needs to be a greater effort to protect those who risk their lives for the protection of society." This is a masterly formulation, for not only does it assimilate the political to the criminal informer, but it lumps the criminal underworld with the political victims of informers.

Whatever may be said of the use of informers for conventional law enforcement (and there are many authorities who insist that even here, their use must be narrowly confined), the fact is that it involves situations different in many respects from the use of political informers. Most important, it does not involve doing deliberate injury to freedoms protected by the First Amendment.

II: *The Informer*

The informer is a universal object of loathing because he undermines mutual trust, an indispensable precondition of social relations. There is no way for him to avoid betrayal. In order to overcome suspicion he must become friendly with the target, share his social life. His wife and children must be used to further the deception. In America, both the FBI agents and their informants usually ignore these dilemmas or glorify the objectives of the surveillance to justify informing. But the reality cannot be exorcised by patriotic rhetoric.

The ugliness of the reality breaks through in this short passage from an interview with an ex-agent:

I had an informant in the Nation of Islam, a Black Muslim group. He was sick for quite a while and sent in reports that were completely useless; but we continued to pay him. Finally he had to be hospitalized. While he was in the hospital, he was visited by some of the Brothers. They left him a get well card which they all signed. He sent me the card and asked me to accept it as a substitute for a regular report and pay him his monthly reimbursement for services because he needed the money very badly.

Nor can we blind ourselves to the fact that informers have always been a means of curbing minorities and maintaining despotic rule. They have been used against the Jews and Christians in Roman times, non-Catholics under the medieval Inquisition, Catholics in seventeenth-century England, the colonists in eighteenth-century America, slaves seeking emancipation in the nineteenth century, British reformers in the England of Pitt and Castlereagh, the British Chartists and the trade union movement of the nineteenth century, the continental socialists and Communists of the same era, the struggle for Irish independence, the labor movement in America from its very beginning and all American radical movements from the First World War until the present.

Contributions of informers to our security turn out, on examination, to be highly dubious. Informers produce a tainted product. Inevitably, they find what they are expected to find, what supports their role.

Informers are not only highly inaccurate in reporting facts, but even more so in drawing inferences. If the target's words when transmitted literally are innocuous, they are interpreted figuratively. If they were intended figuratively, then they receive a literal interpretation. Similarly, political utterances which are not intended to be acted on, the fantasies of the oppressed and the powerless, are transmitted as though they were firm proof of a sinister conspiracy.

The unreliability of informers' reports is rooted in the motivations which lead them to work for the Bureau, and in the drives and compulsions which arise out of relationship with the target. It would be a psychological miracle if a reasonably normal individual entered upon such a course of deception without suffering profound guilt feelings. He is thus forced into compensatory justifications for his betrayal by distorting and fantasizing the target's conduct.

Many who become informers are not "reasonably normal." The most frequent reason for informing is extreme patriotism aroused by conviction that a sinister conspiracy of subversives has sunk its fangs in the nation's throat. Such a person's observations and inferences tend to be divorced from political reality. In addition, he works in expectation of grateful admiration for his courage and resourcefulness.

The FBI's financial support becomes in a large number of cases the *raison d'être* of the relationship. But such financial dependence inevitably leads the informer to slant his reports in order to give the Bureau what it expects. When an informer transmits reports which exculpate the target, thus jeopardizing his future, his agent frequently argues with him that he is in error, that he has been duped, etc.

As a judge put it long ago: "The experience of the ages sustains the conclusion that where the truth is made to depend upon the pecuniary interest of a witness . . . his utterances wear a cloak of suspicion, and they should not be accepted unless the taint is removed by the testimony of credible witnesses or by circumstances that cannot be denied."

Another group of informers, a small one, is really apolitical and not primarily after money. Many of them are compulsively driven to do injury to the targets. Thrill seekers, weavers of fantasy and correspondence-school hawkshaws, they are frequently psychotically alienated. Some are dominated by a need to exercise power over others. Many have records of deviance in other areas.

Another equally unreliable group lives under the shadow of

some prior cloud: fear of being charged as an accomplice, of deportation, of perjury charges. The number of such informers who have good reason to fear the law or to ingratiate themselves with law-enforcement authorities is disturbingly large. The defector who turns informer is a special case. The records of court cases in the 1950s are full of the bias and bitterness of this kind. I was told by an agent that the Bureau expects within three years a stream of defectors from the young radical movement today. "Just wait till the screws begin to tighten."

"Why," asks Professor Richard Donnelly, "does an apostate turn against his former comrades? Psychiatric studies are wanting. Conceivably, he is moved by hate, fear, revenge, or perhaps a pathetic desire to regain status and respectability. If he has meanwhile embraced a new dogmatism, his retaliation may be a form of expiation or atonement—his denunciation a rite of absolution."

Just as the informer lies in order to bend reality to conform to his political prejudices, so he is led to act under the same compulsion. We are witnessing in our time a renewal of the classic formula of the political *provocateur* who "corrects fortune" by committing the crimes which his political stereotypes impute to his targets.

One of the Media documents seems intended to warn FBI agents against *provocateurs:* "There have been a few instances of when security informants on the New Left got carried away during a demonstration, assaulted police, etc." The document advises the FBI's supervisory agents to exert "control" over such informants.

The assessment of only a "few instances" is, I believe, grossly inaccurate. But more serious is the implication that informers are subject to "control," that they are cool operatives, and, if they become *provocateurs*, have only been carried away for a moment. The "control" notion ignores the strange drives and hostile passions that cause people to act as spies in the first place as well as how the atmosphere of risk in which they work is likely to intensify such feelings. As the informer becomes more involved, new and terrible energies may be released in him. The need to preserve his "cover" gives him a pretext to act out hatred and rage, washing away the cautions prescribed by his "controllers" or "handlers." Thus, an informant may directly involve himself in the commission of a crime either as part of a planned intelligence strategy or simply because he cannot help himself.

The undercover man may also induce others to commit a crime. Here the spy may be instructed or authorized not only to plan the crime but to buy guns or explosives and make all the appropriate arrangements to set up a subject for apprehension and arrest.

The FBI consciously uses informers to demoralize a target or handicap political activity—counterintelligence. The idea is to divide a group and sow suspicion among its members. One familiar means is planting forged papers compromising a leader. Another is using an informer to promote a quarrel—as was done in the late 1960s between black militants and antiwar forces and today between Panther factions. Another is having a spy circulate charges that one of the organization's members is an undercover agent.

Four basic varieties of political informers are in the service of the FBI: the plant who is recruited for the express purpose of infiltrating a target group; the informer who is already "in place," i.e., a bona fide member of a group who is induced to spy on it; the lapsed member who is persuaded to rejoin; and the defector or renegade who plays no surveillance role but who "cooperates with the FBI." This phrase belongs to a sizable body of euphemisms used as cosmetics for surveillance practices.

Members of an organization are most highly prized as spies because they have no need of "cover" or to dissemble their loyalties. But in recent years, they have become extremely difficult to recruit, forcing increased reliance on plants. According to a former agent, "Your best bet . . . was to get somebody who was completely unconnected with the organization, preferably somebody on the college campus, some kid who was young enough to fit in the group, had time to spare and was willing to cooperate and put him in the group cold . . . It was rare you got an informant who was already established in an organization because first of all you couldn't talk to him without getting the door slammed in your face . . . So you usually tried to recruit somebody fresh and new."

III: Functions of Informers

The informer is the classic instrument of political intelligence and remains indispensable despite growing resort to electronic surveillance. In fact, the Warren court's limitations on wiretapping and bugging have themselves led to a heavier reliance on informing. Moreover, these limitations encourage the use of informers because they can supply "probable cause" of a crime and so justify a wiretap order.

Even when limitations on electronic surveillance are ignored or circumvented—as in the case of Attorney General John Mitchell's "national security" claims—informers are a superior vehicle for political espionage. They are better suited to the slow pace, ambiguity, confusion and factionalism of dissenting political activities.

Nor are informers displaced by cameras or tape recorders. As photography has increased in importance as a surveillance tool, the recruitment of informer-photographers has intensified. They are paid a bonus if they are in a position to furnish photos otherwise unattainable by the agent. For example, Louis Salzberg, a New York photographer, received about $10,000 in the two years he served as an FBI informer. He used this money to finance a studio which sold pictures for left publications, the negatives of which were turned over to the FBI. He surfaced at the Chicago conspiracy trial and subsequently testified before the House Internal Security Committee. He supplied the committee with negatives as well as the documents and correspondence he had taken from the files of the Veterans for Peace and the Fifth Avenue Peace Parade Committee.

Similarly, informers attending meetings where speeches are amplified or recorded are instructed to add a microphone to those surrounding the speaker. In some cases the Bureau furnishes the equipment.

Even on the level of law enforcement, the role of the political informer is a part of repression, for the political crimes which he investigates are typically victimless, consensual offenses.

Informers play a particularly important role in conspiracy cases. The vague character of the conspiracy charge and the atmosphere of plotting and hidden guilt which accompanies it make a perfect foil for the undercover agent who surfaces on the witness stand. Besides, group crimes like conspiracy offer the maximum punitive return for the smallest commitment of intelligence resources. Under conspiracy law, evidence of acts and statements of one conspirator to bring about the purposes of the conspiracy are admissible against all the co-conspirators. The informer's tale in this way becomes binding on all of the alleged co-conspirators, including individuals he has never seen or met.

The informer plays a significant part in the functioning of the congressional anti-subversive committees. When an informer has surfaced as a witness, is exposed or ends his informer status voluntarily, the FBI turns him over to the House Internal Security Committee (which has also developed informers of its own) or the Senate Internal Security Subcommittee. The surfaced informer is then debriefed by committee staff members, and his FBI reports become a scenario made public from the witness stand and subsequently printed and widely circulated.

Informers are also useful as witnesses in hearings of committees considering anti-subversive legislation. They have testified as experts in a number of such legislative hearings, most notably those leading to the passage of the Taft-Hartley Act of 1947, the Internal Security Act of 1950 and the McCarran-Walter Immigration Act of 1952.

Another function which absorbs much of the informer's activity is the internal development of the intelligence system itself. The end product of intelligence is files, dossiers and literature of various kinds, indices and photographs sorted and arranged biographically, geographically, organizationally and by subject matter. Informers are encouraged to report names, "especially of the leadership and then, from there, report names of individuals who are a moving force in the organization, who are the committee chairmen, who are organizers."

Here is how an agent describes the file system and its relationship to informers' reports:

In D.C. we have an individual file and an organizational file . . . We start out by investigating an organization; then when we had compiled a big file on the organization itself, we'd start investigating all of the officers in the organization on an individual basis and then prominent members of the organization, also on an individual basis. Each one of these people would have a separate file on them and into that file would go, first of all, all the background information we could dig up on a guy—from whatever source we could get it from. Then we'd go into all of the informant's statements that identified him at a given meeting or at a given demonstration or rally. Then we also would go into the reports from other agencies that this guy had done such and such.

Files are the lifeblood of the intelligence system. Their mere existence, no matter how limited their access, powerfully strengthens the system. The secret political files were also a key source of Hoover's power. Let trouble stir and the Director knew in a trace the names and numbers of the agitators who caused it. Thus, Hoover could testify on the causes of social and student protest before the National Commission on the Cause and Prevention of Violence that "Communists are in the forefront of civil rights, anti-war and student demonstrations, many of which ultimately become disorderly and erupt into violence." He named one "leading organizer" of the Berkeley Free Speech movement as a member of the Communist National Committee, and cited a statement by Gus Hall, CP general secretary, that Communists were on most major college campuses and involved in student protests. (Such charges of Communist control of protest groups have been disproved by a number of investigating commissions.)

Surveillance is an especially attractive weapon in a democracy with explicit constitutional limitations on invasions of free expression, because its sanctions are submerged. It is "only" an investigation of the "facts," we are told; it neither enjoins nor punishes political expression and activities. Yet it can hardly be denied that the self-censorship which it stimulates is far more damaging than many express statutory or administrative restraints. It yields a maximum return of repression for a minimum investment of official power.

Law enforcement is, for the most part, a pretext for the wholesale recruitment and subsidization of informers. And it cannot be plausibly argued that the informer's reports are needed to prevent the violent overthrow of the government. The recruitment of informers is *intended* as a restraint on free expression, as a curb on movements for change. This is why informers are kept in organizations for years, turning in worthless, tedious and repetitious reports and why, within the same infiltrated organization, more than one informer is paid for similar reports.

In the overwhelming majority of cases, it is not the information furnished by the spy which makes him a Bureau asset but the fact that he is there—an intruder who intimidates and demoralizes his targets. This coercive aim explains the curious dualism in American infiltration practice: while the identity of the individual informer is concealed, the fact that there is a widespread network of informers in the American left is widely publicized.

IV: Target Groups

Concentration of informers on the left originated in reactions to the Bolshevik Revolution. In the intelligence mind, the term "national security" distills and summarizes a series of paranoid stereotypes: the very existence of the nation is now threatened by a conspiracy of identifiable individuals. These conspirators are prepared to use indescribable ruthlessness and cunning to achieve their objectives. Demands for social and political change are frequently disguised machinations of the conspiracy. In view of the seriousness of the threat, to take risks is folly. Vigilant surveillance is therefore indispensable in order to identify the conspirators, unmask their schemes and prepare for the showdown.

The tenacity of these assumptions, their resistance to reality, is dramatically conveyed in the enforced retirement in the fall of 1971 of William C. Sullivan, a fifty-nine-year-old key official of the FBI who was regarded as a possible successor to the Director. Conflict with Hoover erupted in the fall of 1970 when Sullivan, a veteran of thirty years' service, said in a convention speech that the Communist party "is not in any way causing or directing or controlling the unrest we suffer today in the racial field or in the academic community." This was not

Sullivan's first heresy. Early in the 1960s he expounded the view that the Ku Klux Klan is a greater threat to the country than Communism. Hoover forced him out, a step which gave great satisfaction to his anti-subversive following and to his collaborators in the legislative intelligence community, particularly the staff of the Senate Internal Security Subcommittee.

Intelligence insists that it is equally concerned with threats from the right. Violence-prone organizations, such as the Klan and the Minutemen, are in fact infiltrated by FBI informers. But the main body of the American right wing—the entire constellation of patriotic-nationalist groups, for example—is not only immune to surveillance, it is a part of the intelligence establishment and shares its files, a form of collaboration that originated in World War I days. An analysis of the Media documents by the Citizens' Commission to Investigate the FBI claims that 40 per cent of the files dealing with substantive matters involve political surveillance and related investigations of political activity. Of this number, two cases concern right-wing groups, ten involve immigration problems and more than two hundred deal with left or liberal groups.

The Communist party has had top priority for surveillance and penetration by informers—with no question but that this is necessary. A growing number of organizations, ranging from the Students for a Democratic Society to the Black Panthers, have come to be similarly regarded. Informers in such groups are discouraged from reporting on the views or "line." They are instructed to confine themselves to such matters as names of members, sources of funds, foreign influence and planned activities. (The "Moscow gold" thesis and topical variations of it have always dominated the intelligence mind. Today the FBI looks for subversions by Chinese, African and Russian governments and, among domestic sources, churches and foundations.)

The FBI infiltrates a wide spectrum of non-Communist

groups for the asserted purpose of determining the extent of
Communist influence or control. Hoover testified in Appropriations Committee hearings on the number of such groups. In
1960 it was said to be 160; in 1961, 200; in 1962, 185; and
1964, 150. Since that date he did not publicly report the
number of organizations. But information from other sources,
including the Media documents, indicates it is still substantial.
The recent revival by executive fiat of the Attorney General's
list of proscribed organizations supplies an additional justification for infiltration by the FBI.

The ferreting out of subversion among such groups rein-
forces the importance of "names" in American intelligence. An
individual considered subversive is—politically speaking—in-
curable and contagious. His presence in any organization or
involvement in any form of political activity taints the entire
enterprise. The highest priority of intelligence is to determine
who "they" are and what "they" are up to. This explains the
key role of files and is the reason the primary assignment of
every informer is to feed his agent names.

There is no way of determining whether an organization
should be placed under heavy surveillance and deeply penetrated by informers without first "investigating" it. Even if a
preliminary probe produces negative results, the informer is
told to continue his undercover activity. The preliminary probe
usually turns out to be permanent.

The objectives and concerns of some organizations automatically attract suspicion. Anti-war organizations of all stripes
are heavily infiltrated. The same is true of groups designated
by the Bureau as "black extremist" or "black militant." Beginning in the early 1960s, student groups became targets of
intensive surveillance. The justification for the penetration of
anti-war groups is that they may constitute a direct threat to
the nation's vital interests. Infiltration of the other two areas of
activity is justified as a safeguard against violence.

Some relatively innocuous organizations are systematically infiltrated in order to provide informers with cover for penetration of more inaccessible groups. The plant's supermilitance gives him credibility for acceptance by more radical groups. I have also encountered the reverse of this process: FBI informers planted in the Communist party who are urged by their controlling agents to infiltrate non-Communist organizations in order to help establish that these groups are Communist-dominated and influenced.

The fact that an organization is already infiltrated does not inhibit further infiltration. There is no optimal number of spies. Of thirty-two participants at a meeting of the Washington Peace Mobilization in winter, 1969, nine were undercover agents of the FBI. Washington's Black Liberation Front of about thirty members was blanketed in 1970 by fourteen informers.

Whether the justification is the prevention of revolution or some more immediate evil—such as violence—the scope of surveillance and infiltration completely outruns the Bureau's stated intelligence goals. For the various reasons I have discussed, activities ranging from Earth Day to a church convention, and organizations from the NAACP to the Women's International League for Peace and Freedom, are penetrated by FBI informers. Even when a group is not under surveillance, informers may turn up at its meetings and rallies because of the presence or participation of a particular individual considered subversive.

V: *Modus Operandi*

The Bureau places the highest priority on recruitment of informers and offers extremely generous financial terms for their services as, say, "security informants," "racial informants" and, a new category since 1967, "racial informants—ghetto."

The paid informant is first used to obtain specific items of information. At this stage he is known as a PSI (potential security informant) or PRI (potential racial informant). After he is "developed" by the agent and proves his worth, he becomes an SI or RI and is referred to as a "reliable informant" or "an informant of known reliability"—embellishments derived from legal requirements.

The informer then acquires a file, a code symbol and a name or initials. A method and place of reporting is agreed upon and supplementary channels of communication are established.

Here, according to former FBI Special Agent Robert Wall, is how the system operated in the District of Columbia in 1970:

> Originally—when you first opened a case on a guy—before you did anything in the racial field you had $400 that you could use to bring him in, so to speak. In other words, you had $400 that you could get right in the office without going across the street for permission. When you exhausted that $400 on an individual, then you had to write a letter to the Bureau . . .
>
> This is in the racial field; the only difference between this and the security field is that the top limit you could pay him off without contacting the Bureau was $200 in the security unit.
>
> That eventually changed so that both of them were $400. The idea was you'd pay him off with this $400, which you could pay him for doing services. Then when your money was going to be exhausted and when you saw that the guy was going to keep on going and you were paying him $20 per meeting or $15 per meeting or whatever you were paying him—then you would sit down and write a letter to the Bureau. You would say who the guy was, what his background was, his education, the whole background on him, as much as you could get without, you know, doing an open investigation to blow the guy out, to blow his cover. Then you would tell the Bureau all the interesting facts about how much information he's given you, how he's working and how valuable the information was

and then make a request for an amount of money for this guy to be set aside every month—it might be $100 per month.

And after a given period of time—like say you handled a guy and you've been paying him $100 a month, or usually you vary the amount, you give him $95 this month or $110 the next month until you had him for a certain length of time—then you write another letter to the Bureau saying this guy has performed so well for so long that we are removing the "P" from him and now he's a full-fledged informant and we want to give him a symbol number (and each office controlled the symbol numbers) and also we've decided to give him a code name, and then probably in the same letter you would ask for an increase in the amount of money you could pay him each month.

Heavy pressure to recruit informers is reflected in open solicitation of young people. ("Will you work for us?" an agent asked student volunteers as they entered the elevators on the way to the office of a committee coordinating a Washington peace mobilization in the fall of 1969.) Stepped-up recruitment has increased the risk of hoaxes, recanters and counter-intelligence penetration by radicals. A twenty-year-old high school dropout was recently charged with reporting to the FBI in late 1969 an imaginary plot to bomb a federal building in Chicago. He selected the names and addresses of the plotters at random from a telephone book and gave agents a letter, written as a joke by his girl friend, detailing the plans to dynamite the building. He convinced the bureau to send him on expense-paid trips to Philadelphia and Chicago to meet with the fictional plotters.

The *modus operandi* of the FBI's political espionage by informers is illuminated by the Media files. An initial series of documents singles out black organizations and especially student groups for infiltration. Thus, a Washington directive of June 17, 1970, calls attention to a projected convention of an organization called the National Association of Black Students. It requests the local recruitment of informants both to pinpoint the NABS chapters and representatives and to infiltrate the convention. The only reason given for this is that the national coordinator of the convention "is on the AI." (The AI is the "agitator index," a file on radicals and activists. Individuals considered more dangerous are on the "security index," originally compiled to implement the now repealed concentration camp provisions of the Internal Security Act of 1950.)

The second group of Media documents deals extensively with the Bureau's campaign in 1968 to recruit "racial informants—ghetto." The Bureau has the responsibility, a memo points out, to warn of demonstrations. "This type of information can only come from a widespread grass-roots network of sources coupled with active informant coverage by individuals who are members of subversive and revolutionary organizations." Each agent in the squad with jurisdiction over the subject matter is required to obtain at least one "ghetto informant."

The agents are exhorted to scour all possible sources of the desired class of informers—including friends and relatives of Bureau employees, tavern keepers, janitors, barbers, salesmen, newsboys and installment collectors. In addition, existing criminal and security informants are to be converted to ghetto informants.

Six months later another memo instructed agents to utilize methods of obtaining "maximum productivity" from ghetto informants. Among other things, this would include urging them to report "on open meetings of known or suspected black extremist organizations," to determine if militant literature is available in "Afro-American-type bookstores and if so to identify the owners, operators and clientele of such stores," to report on attempts of foreign powers (African, Chinese, Russian) to take over "the Negro militant Movement" and, in the case of an exceptionally intelligent spy, to assess the susceptibility of the Negro community to foreign influence. As final assignment, agents are instructed to find out which "Negro informants, including ghetto informants," would soon enter college and be in a position "to infiltrate black power groups on campus."

Another of the first set of Media documents, one from Hoover, seeks to develop informer coverage of all campus groups which "are targets for influence and control by violence prone . . . extremists." Such campus groups as the Black Student Union "and similar organizations organized to project the demands of black students" are "immediately to be placed under surveillance and individual files are to be opened on" officers and key activists. Informants along with other "discreet quality sources" must be activated "to develop continuing information."

The widely quoted "New Left Notes—Philadelphia" of September 16, 1970, reports on an FBI conference which produced the consensus that more intensive contact with "these subjects and hangers-on" is desirable. "It will enhance the paranoia endemic in these circles and will further serve to get the point across that there is an FBI agent behind every mailbox." Moreover, such contacts might induce the subject "to volunteer to tell all—perhaps on a continuing basis." Agents are urged to take advantage of the Director's approval for the first time of recruitment of PSIs and SIs between eighteen and twenty-one.

In accordance with earlier directives, the Philadelphia office reported to the Director on December 2, 1970, that "sources" had been established in four-year, two-year and junior colleges in the Philadelphia area for the surveillance of groups such as the Black Student Union. As a result, investigative files had been started on black student groups at thirteen Philadelphia-area campuses to determine their size, purpose, activities, leadership and "extremist interest or influence." After preliminary inquiries, results would be submitted in a form appropriate for Bureau-wide dissemination along with recommendations for further investigations. It would be reasonable to assume that similar surveillance was set up on college campuses throughout the country.

VI: *Informers on the Academic Community*

The campus has been a high-priority surveillance target since the early 1960s. The private character of the university bars FBI agents from direct and unfettered access. So they have deployed a nationwide corps of planted informers ("FBI scholarship boys," they are often called) to penetrate faculty and student political activities.

The FBI recruiter is frequently indignantly rebuffed. Most students regard informing as a betrayal and the invitation to engage in it as an insult. Committed rightists are another matter. A combination of ideological, financial and draft inducements sharpens their eagerness. The risks of exposure are minimal: the student community is extraordinarily open, and the plant has a perfect cover.

Although a few students refuse to accept money for informing, money is an important inducement. During the 1950s a student informer at the University of North Carolina ultimately received $450 a month and expenses as his services became more valuable to the FBI. A beginner, also at North Carolina, earned $100 a month and expenses, plus a draft deferment. At the 1963 trial of the Advance Youth Organization to compel registration under the Subversive Activities Control Act, eleven young informers testified that they had received more than $45,000 for brief periods of undercover work. One had a total take of $6,371.65, reflecting his value as an officer of the organization (which had an estimated membership of between one and two hundred).

The prime recruiting prospect is the questioning and idealistic student who is not deeply committed to activism. For him there is a special pitch: to "save" you from the "mistakes you may regret later on." This warning also reflects a sort of political neo-Freudianism in intelligence thinking: that political attitudes are irrevocably fixed before the age of twenty and, unless the subject defects or informs, he will bear watching for the rest of his life.

Students are induced to inform when they impulsively join an organization and, in the cold gray dawn, are stricken with misgivings. A visit from the FBI at the opportune moment or a telephone call by the student to the local FBI office results in a promise of "cooperation."

Reluctance is overcome by a promise that the informer's identity will be kept secret, by patriotic appeals ("Don't you want to help your country?"), by the assurance that "all the kids are doing it," by hints that the agent already is in possession of compromising information, by the expression of sympathy for the humanitarian impulses which led the subject into a political lapse and by a prediction that "You'll get over it."

Agents do not scorn cruder methods—such as accosting a stubborn subject outside his place of employment and, if resistance continues, reporting a refusal to cooperate to his employer. Often effective is a threat to report a law student to the bar association's character committee which must approve all admissions. A related form of blackmail is used on teacher candidates. If all else fails, agents may appeal to the prospect's parents, warning them that an offspring is associating with the "wrong people" on campus.

Another likely recruit is the defector who, for ideological

reasons, leaves an organization or movement after a long period of time. The FBI quickly learns of the defection and invites him to return. A 1967 letter from a student at the University of Wisconsin is illustrative:

There is one case of a student who had been a member of the Socialist Club a number of years ago and who left the Club and did so by making a denunciation in the *Cardinal* [student newspaper]. A year ago he returned to Madison to do graduate work and informed me that the FBI had approached him in Boston—somehow they knew he was returning to Madison—and asked him to work as a spy in the Club. He refused.

One who did not refuse was Tommy Taft, a Duke junior and assistant housemaster in charge of thirty freshmen. During an interview by Doug Adams for membership in Duke's delegation to the model United Nations, Taft blurted out that he and others had secretly made written and oral reports to the FBI about the anti-war activities of politically suspect students, including Adams. He admitted this apparently out of the guilty realization that Adams was really a good guy. Taft published, on March 2, 1967, a guarded version of his original confession in the student newspaper, the *Duke Chronicle*, including this account of his recruitment by the FBI:

During my freshman year (1964–65) I had noted a good deal of antiwar literature on campus that described such things as American advisors torturing Vietnamese women, etc. According to the manner in which I was brought up, these flyers and handouts seemed less than patriotic and so I gathered several and mailed them to FBI Headquarters in Washington.

Shortly thereafter—in early Spring of 1965—a special agent who lived in Durham, Rufus Powell, contacted me and questioned me concerning why I sent the material, where it had been posted, etc. I gave him what information I had.

Taft's published statement omitted the fact that he had continued to give reports to Powell in 1966, after Powell had resigned from the FBI and become, first, assistant law school dean and, later, secretary of the university. Powell had denied he had any ties with the Bureau after resigning. Taft explained to Adams that "he hoped to go to work for the State Department and could not afford to come in conflict with the FBI by involving other of their personnel."

Taft conceded that he had given "misinformation" to the FBI not only about Adams but about others as well. According to another student, Barb Wilmot, Taft "reported that one fellow was a 'hard core Marxist.' This student was not being investigated for any security clearance but for some unknown future purpose. What is worse is that Tommy admitted to us that he did not even know personally the student . . . but . . . had relied on second and third hand information."

One night in the spring of 1968, Robert Harris, a conservative engineering student and president of his dormitory association at the University of Illinois, was working in the university's computer lab alongside another student, P. Michael Young. Harris was shocked when Young, a neo-Nazi and supporter of the Klan, showed him a gun. Harris notified the university police, who suggested that he keep an eye on Young. Harris began to devote all his spare time to infiltrating Young's group. After about a month, he agreed to continue the infiltration for the FBI. His surveillance resulted in Young's arrest on criminal charges.

In October, 1968, at the request of the local FBI agent, Harris agreed to infiltrate the local SDS chapter. "I was glad to cooperate with the FBI. Though the FBI offered to pick up my expenses, money was not a motive. It was just my loyalty to my country. And I figured that the university had been good to me and I didn't want anyone to wreck it or burn it down."

Harris was disappointed in the SDS. "The group was disorganized and anarchic, all talk and no action." But he was curious about the values of the group and asked a lot of questions. "And in the process of educating me about radical politics, they accepted me."

A "straight" student from the farm country of downstate Illniois, Harris mastered a strange "hip" lingo and also, to improve his cover, increased his activity. As he became more involved, he was won over. He not only made friends with his targets, but came completely to share their views about racism and the draft. Yet he continued to file reports and was pressed to supply names and confirm identification of the organization's leaders on campus.

Early in 1969 Harris reported to the FBI about an impending visit to the campus of some members of the Black Panther party and information about where they would be staying. The visit resulted in the arrest of the Black Panther members in a confrontation with the university police. Harris thought the police had been unnecessarily rough and felt guilty about his role.

The arrests resulted in a broadening campus conflict. Harris found himself sincerely advocating sit-in support for a black student group on campus, yet reporting the proposed sit-in at the same time. Shortly after that, Harris took on the job of housing for visiting delegates to an SDS conference to be held in March, 1969. He turned over a list of local SDS sympathizers who made their homes available.

But he became increasingly tormented by his disloyalty to his friends. Just prior to the SDS conference, the chief FBI agent in Urbana requested personal details about SDSers: "He wanted to know where they banked, where they got their money, and whether they had girl friends they slept with," Harris said. A week later he confessed his informer role to his

SDS friends. "Whereupon we dropped our teeth," one of them commented.

Harris wrote a letter of resignation from the FBI, but was asked to stay on and attend SDS conferences, all expenses paid. Harris decided to make public his break with the Bureau (despite cloudy threats of reprisal), convinced that this was the best way to live with himself. "My political views have changed, of course, but the friendships I've made are the most important reason why I'm no longer cooperating with the FBI," he wrote.

On February 23, 1967, a hushed group of faculty members of the New York State University at Brockport Chapter of the American Association of University Professors was stunned by the story of the Reverend John Messerschmitt, ecumenical chaplain to the college, representing the Rochester Board for Campus Ministry. Reverend Messerschmitt disclosed that two weeks earlier a college staff member requested him to tell about a campus organization to which he and Dr. Ernest A. Wiener, of the college's sociology department, were faculty advisers. Rev. Messerschmitt was asked if he "knew" about Dr. Wiener and especially his involvement with civil rights and peace groups which, it was darkly hinted, were subversive. When Chaplain Messerschmitt protested that the accusation was irresponsible, the following exchange took place (as the chaplain wrote it down shortly thereafter when recollection of it was still vivid):

"John, I know I can trust you with this information. I'm in regular contact with the FBI. There are four or five of us on the campus: two with the FBI and three with the CIA. We've been asked to watch Wiener very closely. Believe me when I tell you, he has quite a background. Be careful."

At this point, shocked at the disclosure, I lost a bit of my poise. I said I could hardly believe he was doing this kind of thing, that in my opinion it was in contradiction to what the university stood for and extremely dangerous to the civil liberties of all the individuals he was keeping under surveillance. We debated for perhaps a half hour, he making such remarks as, "Wouldn't you do this FBI work if your country requested it of you?" "How can you attack the FBI when it's only trying to protect you?" "This surveillance work is occurring on every campus in the country." "Those who are being watched shouldn't have anything to hide if what they are doing and saying is aboveboard." "Don't think I get paid for this, I don't. I was asked to do this and I agreed as a service to my country."

He indicated to me that those who did this were often recruited as a follow-up to FBI or CIA investigations, such as those that followed a recent "Teach-In on Vietnam." Faculty who were cooperative with the investigator and in positions to know what was going on were asked to "kind of keep an eye on things on a permanent basis."

Not long afterward Hoover, in a letter to Chancellor Samuel Gould, the administrative head of the New York State University system, wrote: "I would never permit the FBI to shirk its responsibilities. I feel certain that you, as a responsible educator and citizen, would never condone this Bureau's failure to handle its obligations in the internal security field, or that you would have us ignore specific allegations of subversive activity in any segment of our society, including college campuses."

Professor Wiener did, indeed, have "quite a background"—but one of citizenship, not subversion. He promptly announced, "I have never made an effort to hide my opinions or beliefs." He told the press that he had participated in the 1965 Selma-Montgomery march, was concerned with local problems of school integration, was an active opponent of our Vietnam policy and a member of the Fellowship for Social Justice of the Unitarian-Universalist Church.

On April 20, 1967, Professor Wiener committed suicide. In a letter found after his death he had written:

It is too painful to continue living in a world in which freedom is steadily being constricted in the name of freedom and in which peace means war, in which every one of our institutions, our schools, our churches, our newspapers, our industries are being steadily engulfed in a sea of hypocrisy.

Thoughtful Americans must begin to ask themselves whether "national security"—if we can ever scrape off the shibboleths which encrust it—really requires that we corrupt and bribe our youth, blacks, professors, students and others to betray friends and associates, whether there is no other way to defend ourselves as a people from the violent overthrow of our government than to institutionalize the surveillance of non-violent protest activity. We ought to think hard about the Nation of Islam "informant" and his get-well card. We must learn before it's too late that suborning betrayal on a whole-sale scale only mocks the challenge of our time and, if unchecked, will transform us into the kind of Judas society made familiar by police states.

VII: Conference Discussion

MR. WRIGHT: Mr. Donner, you have a loose and interchangeable usage of the word "political." For instance, in your paper you say that the key significance of the FBI informer is political.

I want to know exactly what you mean by that. It seems to me that you could be using the word "political" interchangeably with what I call political rights, rights which are established under the Constitution.

But whenever you use the word "political," it seems that you would make the point that the FBI should not have any concern with political groups, particularly using informers in political groups. But isn't it true that crimes can be committed with political motivation, that political groups can be criminal groups? Take the most horrid example of our recent history, assassinations of Presidents and senators. That can be a political act. Isn't that true?

MR. DONNER: When I use the term "political" in the context in which you read it, I mean that the FBI uses its intelligence information to influence opinion formation about politics. And I think it is reprehensible. Let me give you a startling example of what I regard as a political use of intelligence: the testimony of J. Edgar Hoover before the Senate Appropriations Committee on November 27, 1970, in which he named the Berrigan brothers as participants in "an incipient plot." And he spelled this out before this charge had been considered by a grand jury, before the evidence had been weighed, before anything had happened. Now, to me, this was grossly improper. This was an attempt by Mr. Hoover to build his own power and to affect opinion in this country in a wholly illegitimate way and in conflict with the rights of the Harrisburg defendants.

MR. WRIGHT: Could I ask him to answer my question?

MR. DONNER: Well, I thought I did. Now, of course, there can be political crimes. But as I said to you before, I don't think that what I have been talking about has anything to do with political crimes or law enforcement in any way.

MR. ELLIFF: This last point raises a fundamental question that I think is posed by your analysis of the problem of the use of informers by the FBI.

You've suggested very strongly that the FBI is fundamentally independent and autonomous in its operation. But is it not true that the FBI's basic intelligence assignments that require informers are not instigated by the FBI? Haven't these all had their origin in policy decisions by Attorneys General and by Presidents who have desired certain missions to be undertaken by the FBI? While it's true that J. Edgar Hoover has contributed to arousing fears, aren't there independent forces, independent events that take place in the society, and political pressures on the executive branch, that might have really served as the basis for the development of the FBI's mission over the years?

While we may look at particular operational details, the broad outlines of what the FBI is supposed to do have not been the product of J. Edgar Hoover, but the product of the succeeding Presidents and Attorneys General who have been in a position to define the Bureau's mission.

MR. DONNER: It's rather hard for me to trace the surveillance of specific targets to any policy decision. What policy decision justifies infiltrating Earth Day demonstrations?

MR. FRANK CARRINGTON:* Within ten days of the bombing of the buses in Pontiac, Michigan, the FBI had that case solved because of an informant in the Ku Klux Klan in that area, which I don't think had been particularly active until the bombing. They had him in for some years. I think this is a good example of what good effects so-called political surveillance can have.

Now when you talk about the FBI's failure to solve bombings, you must consider that these bombings are by nature secret, terroristic types of crimes. I think that infiltration, the political surveillance that you're condemning, is the only way that bombings are going to be solved. It's going to be a long process to get people deeply enough into the bombers' confidence so you can start to solve the criminal act. It took a long time, as I read the papers, to get this informant into the high councils of the KKK in Pontiac.

MR. COUNTRYMAN: My judgment would be that if the only way to detect that bombing is to have the FBI infiltrate political organizations, I would rather the bombing go undetected.

MR. CARRINGTON: No matter whether somebody was killed?

MR. COUNTRYMAN: Yes. Yes. There are worse things than

* Executive Director, Americans for Effective Law Enforcement.

having people killed. When you get an entire population intimidated, that may be worse. We put some limits on law enforcement in the interests of preserving the free and open society, or at least we try to. And every time we do that, through safeguards like the privilege against self-incrimination or the Fourth Amendment, everytime we do that, it involves a judgment that even though some crimes will go on undetected, it is better in the long run to have a society where there's protection from police surveillance.

MR. CARRINGTON: I'm not sure that the family of the man who was blown up in Wisconsin, or the family of the kids killed in the Birmingham church bombing, would agree with you.

MR. COUNTRYMAN: I'm sure that the families of victims would not agree in any of the instances I've mentioned. But I don't believe that we should say that for that reason we should repeal the Fourth and Fifth Amendments, for instance.

MR. ELLIFF: It seems to me that even if we are talking about straight criminal activity, whether it has a political context or not, there are problems with informers, problems with infiltration, in criminal cases, which are similar to those encountered in political situations. If anybody is going to be concerned with devising protections against some of the abuses which take place, the protections have to be devised also with the completely non-political uses of informers and undercover agents.

Entrapment is just as much a possibility in a straight criminal case as it is in a political case. The problem of an informer, who wants to account for a great deal, who wants to maintain himself on the payroll of the institution that is keeping him in this kind of work, is just as great in straight criminal activity as it is in political activity. So let's not give away too much on the side of saying that anything is fair as long as it's non-political.

CHAPTER FOURTEEN

WHY I GOT OUT OF IT

BY ROBERT WALL

"How did you feel when you were following someone around? I mean, what did you think about? How could you do something like that?"

These questions were put to me by an acquaintance recently when he learned that I had been a special agent of the FBI for five years and had worked in the field of internal security during the last three. The tone of the questions was not angry, but there was a note of disbelief.

I could well understand this, because toward the end of my short career as an agent, I had begun to loathe myself for doing what I was doing. I had become sorely disillusioned by my work. I could no longer accept the platitudes and rationalizations offered by the FBI directives and policy pronouncements. My own investigations and surveillances coupled with intensive reading and study of reports received from other areas of the country had convinced me that the threat to the security of the country was not the anti-war or civil rights movements, but the government itself, which refused to respond to the voices of those dissenting, and the police agencies employed to suppress those voices.

But to answer my acquaintance's questions fairly required that I trace back through the various investigations and surveillances of which I had been a part and recall my thoughts at those times.

In May of 1965, after serving as a naval officer for several years, I arrived in Washington, D.C., to begin my training for the position of special agent with the Federal Bureau of Investigation. I was both naïve and apolitical. I thought of myself as an intense idealist and was convinced that the FBI was an organization in which personal integrity was highly valued. To me the organization was above all a protector of the innocent public and only secondarily the relentless pursuer of wrongdoers. In short, I was an ideal candidate for the job. I would not question; I would simply learn to do as I was told, content to believe that the FBI would never direct me wrong.

This belief managed to survive my first two years in the Bureau, during which I worked on criminal investigations and government job applications. It was when I was assigned to work in internal security in Washington, D.C., that I began to have my first serious doubts about the integrity of the organization, its motives and its goals.

The Washington Field Office is the operating arm of the FBI in Washington, D.C. Like other field offices, we reported to the Bureau's Washington headquarters, but our office was one of the largest. Assigned to the office were between five and six hundred agents, broken up into squads of from a handful to fifty or sixty. Two squads worked only on applications for government jobs and five or six handled criminal investigations. In addition, there were nine squads assigned to do "security" work. One of those nine was charged with investigating all of the various individuals and organizations that allegedly threatened the national security or that advocated the overthrow of the United States Government by force or violence. It was to this squad that I was assigned in May, 1967, shortly before my second anniversary as an agent.

In the beginning, after sitting around the office for a few days reading the parts of the manual of instructions dealing with security investigations, I jumped at a chance to get out and cover a demonstration to take place that afternoon. I knew little or nothing about what our squad actually did, so was surprised to see that five or six agents, including one specially trained and equipped for photography, were to take part. I tried to imagine what sort of activity would necessitate the watchful eyes of six armed FBI men.

Soon I was briefed on the dire threat to the internal security of the nation which occasioned this show of force. It seems that two busloads of steelworkers from Bethlehem Steel's Sparrows Point Plant (near Baltimore) were planning to picket the Department of Labor in support of their charges of racial discrimination by Bethlehem in hiring and promotion and their demand that the department step in to protect the rights of the workers discriminated against. I remember asking at the time, "Why are we covering this demonstration?" The answer was something to the effect that the FBI is responsible for reporting on situations from which possible racial violence could arise. I accepted it unquestioningly. The riot in Watts was still a fresh memory. The Congress of Racial Equality (CORE) was sponsoring the demonstration. I knew of a case in the office titled "Cominfil CORE" (shorthand for Communist infiltration of CORE). And I reasoned that we wouldn't have such a case unless there was good reason to believe that the Communists were, indeed, trying to take over the civil rights movement. So, logically, we would cover the demonstration to ferret out the secret Communist conspirators.

By 1967 the Communist party in Washington, D.C., had only three members remaining. The main function of the squad then was to verify the residence and employment of the persons who once had been subjects of FBI investigation and who were still considered dangerous enough to keep track of, even though they were no longer active with the party or any other subversive group, for that matter. Every three, six, nine or twelve months the files on these persons would be reopened and assigned to an agent on the squad who would make certain that the individual still lived at the same address and worked at the same job.

To accomplish this task, the agent could use several methods. He could personally observe the subject at his home and follow him to work. Or he could request the agents handling one of the three remaining informants familiar with former party members to ask the informants about the man in question. The latter method was usually chosen since it would eliminate any real work for the agent. After the informant had reported, the case could then be closed again. In closing the case, the agent could either certify that the subject was still worthy of the Bureau's attention or try to give him a lower priority, thereby lengthening the interval before the file had to be reopened. It was simpler and required much less paper work to certify that the subject still needed watching. Thus, the investigations of hundreds of perfectly harmless people continued on through the years.

By 1967 the anti-war movement was growing from its lean beginnings to a movement of national significance. The response of the Bureau was consistent with its history. It determined that the movement was a part of the larger Communist conspiracy to overthrow the United States Government. Having decided this, the Bureau set about to investigate the movement to show the existence of the conspiracy.

Proof sufficient to satisfy the Bureau was readily available. For example, it was noted that among the thirty-five to forty thousand persons who took part in the march on the Pentagon in October, 1967, approximately twenty persons who had once been named as members, suspected members or sympathizers of the Communist party were reported to be in the crowd. A few among them had actually assisted in organizing the march. Although the Bureau always insists that it neither draws conclusions nor makes recommendations from the facts that it gathers, the FBI report on the march on the Pentagon was leaked to the press and its impact was obvious: the thousands who marched to protest the war in Southeast Asia were publicly labeled as mere pawns in a Communist master plan to spread dissent throughout the nation. They had been duped into giving aid and comfort to the enemy and demoralizing our fighting men.

Had the Bureau believed its own propaganda, it would have investigated only the "Communist agitators" in the anti-war movement. Instead we were directed to investigate all the leaders in all the local peace groups and to determine among other things the source of any money used to finance the movement. From there it was a simple step to the investigation of anyone connected to the peace movement in any way. The number of investigations was limited only by the time available and the problem of distinguishing the organizers and leaders of mass rallies from the passive followers.

We determined quite early that the anti-war movement was not organized, directed or financed by Moscow. But Hoover insisted on using the claim of Communist conspiracy to justify violating the rights of countless people. Frequently, when I returned to the office after interviewing a subject whom we were investigating because of his participation in or support for an anti-war rally, I was reluctant to put the results down on paper. I knew by then how dossiers were collected on individuals and how they could be used to intimidate.

As the anti-war effort increased and more people of intellect and perception joined in, it became difficult for even the most conservative agent not to question these investigations. After all, why spend hours investigating the leader of a local anti-war group who spoke out at some rally against the war when United States senators were doing the same thing on the floor of Congress?

But then the rationale changed. When the demonstrators began using civil disobedience, Hoover labeled them violence-prone activists who were giving aid and comfort to America's enemies. Now, the "violence of the militant anti-war groups" became the justification for expanded investigations by the FBI.

To deal with the peace movement the FBI followed its usual practice of planting informants. It was easy to recruit young people to infiltrate the anti-war organizations and other groups in the so-called New Left since large numbers of volunteers were needed to hand out leaflets, run mimeo machines, answer phones, stuff envelopes, and for similar chores connected with political organizing. All one of our FBI informants needed to do was walk into the office and state briefly that he was opposed to the war and wished to volunteer his services. He would seldom be challenged to prove his allegiance to the movement. Then, with little additional effort, he had access to mailing lists, names of contributors, copies of leaflets and handbills, and was able to report in detail on any organizational meetings that might take place.

Since an organization gave an informant a convenient base from which to operate, the Bureau tried to place informants in all the organizations likely to participate in any mass march or demonstration. Then if a coalition of groups was formed to plan a large rally, at least one informant would, we hoped, be among those selected to represent a group when the coalition met to plan its activities. Frequently this was the case.

The informants were always directed to look especially for any indication that violence was being planned by any group or individual within a group. But during my three years working on radical groups I never found any evidence that would lead to a conviction for criminal violence.

The Bureau also had an active counterintelligence program which was titled "Cointelpro—New Left." This program was designed to develop means to thwart and undermine the activities of any organization that fell into the category of New Left. A frequent tactic was to leak stories to the press and television shortly before any mass march or rally. This was easy enough to do. Agents in our offices would write often fanciful press releases warning that violence was expected on the day of the rally, or that the organizers of the march were in contact with Hanoi, or that some known Communists were active in organizing the march. Our superiors in the Internal Security Division at FBI headquarters would then pass on the information to conservative newspapers, which published it immediately. The purpose of such stories was not only to influence the general public but to scare away those whose commitment was weak and thereby reduce the number of persons who might otherwise attend.

Another purpose of the program was to create dissent among the various groups involved in the New Left to prevent them from working together. In one case we addressed a letter to the leaders of the National Mobilization Committee (NMC) which said that the blacks of Washington, D.C., would not support the upcoming rally of the NMC unless a $20,000 "security bond" was paid to a black organization in Washington. At the same time we instructed some informants we had placed in the black organization to suggest the idea of a security bond informally to leaders of the organization. The letter we composed was approved by the Bureau's counterintelligence desk and was signed with the forged signature of a leader of the black group. Later, through informants in the NMC, we learned that the letter had caused a great deal of confusion and had a significant effect on the planning for the march.

I should stress that such "counterintelligence" activities were carried on frequently, although some were quite absurd. For example, some of the agents in our office tried to confuse peace demonstrations by such collegiate tactics as handing out leaflets giving misleading information about the time and place when the marchers were supposed to meet.

The FBI claims to be a non-political organization and asserts that it is not a national police force. But in its intelligence and counterintelligence work on the New Left it was engaging in activity that clearly was political. Moreover, in trying to suppress and discourage a broad-based national political movement, it acted as a national political police.

While we were investigating anti-war groups and student activists, the squad also handled what were called "Racial Matters." This category was an absurdly and frighteningly broad one. Investigations on almost anything done by or for black people could be opened simply by labeling it a Racial Matter. The surveillance of the Bethlehem workers is one example. Here are other "cases" we investigated:

—A group of teen-agers from the ghetto areas of Washington, D.C., who marched to the city council chambers and demanded restoration of funds for summer jobs for ghetto youth.

—A group of high school students who staged a protest in their school cafeteria complaining that the food was not fit for human consumption.

—Two members of the Student Nonviolent Coordinating Committee (SNCC) who opened a bookstore on Fourteenth Street in northwest Washington. The FBI quickly responded with an investigation titled "Drum and Spear Bookstore, Racial Matter."

When the Poor People's March was organized to dramatize the plight of the poor in our nation and a camp was set up near the Washington Monument, this was a Racial Matter. More logically perhaps, investigations of the Ku Klux Klan, the American Nazi party and similar groups were also Racial Matters.

Clearly the Bureau had no rational criterion for opening these investigations. The only consistent pattern that I found was that if an individual or group is black and does something to gain attention it is likely to be investigated.

Our guide to Racial Matters at the field office was the early edition of the Washington *Post*. A typical news item would read: "Police arrested six persons early this morning when a crowd gathered as detectives of the Metropolitan Police Department were attempting to arrest a suspected narcotics peddler at the corner of 14th and U Streets, N.W. Some rocks and bottles were allegedly thrown at police," etc. Inevitably, when such a story appeared, we would receive a call from the supervisor of the Racial Desk in Bureau headquarters asking what we knew about the incident. It was his firm conviction that incidents of this type were a manifestation of the conspiracy by blacks to take over their community by driving out the police.

So that we would not be embarrassed when the supervisor called, it became standard practice for one of the early arrivers in the office to scan the paper for articles like the one above. He would clip the item, call the precinct to verify the names of the persons arrested, and then paraphrase the news item in a teletype message to Bureau headquarters, advising them that we were following the incident and would report any further developments. A month or two later, the agent to whom the case had been assigned would close it with a letter stating that the incident was apparently spontaneous and not part of a conspiracy, and giving an estimate of the damages, the names of those arrested and the background of those who already had records in FBI files.

Often the supervisor on the Racial Desk at the Bureau would request specific information about a case under investigation by the field office. The agent to whom the Drum and Spear Bookstore case was assigned received such a request. For months he had been investigating the bookstore, watching its operations, checking out its owners, looking into its bank records, trying to ascertain the source of its funds. He had found nothing connected with crime, conspiracy or evil doings. Now he was instructed to go to the bookstore and purchase a copy of the "little red book" containing the quotations of Chairman Mao Tse-tung. It was pointless to ask what purpose the purchase of this particular book would serve. It was obvious to us that the supervisor felt that the bookstore, by selling this book, was somehow implicated in the oriental branch of the Communist conspiracy.

The agent dutifully made his way to the Drum and Spear, where he learned that they had sold their last copy of the book. Rather than order a copy to be mailed to the supervisor, a cheeky solution which he admitted considering, he returned downtown, bought a copy at Brentano's and duly passed it on to the Bureau supervisor, just as if it had come from the Drum and Spear. Thereafter, the written description of the Drum and Spear contained the note that radical literature including the "little red book" of Mao Tse-tung was obtainable there.

As I worked on Racial Matters in Washington (a city whose black population comprises more than 70 per cent of the total), the appalling racism of the FBI on every level became glaringly apparent to me. It seemed that every politically dissident black man was a candidate for investigation. Perhaps this racism was no worse than in other branches of government, but it was extremely discouraging to find it so firmly entrenched in an organization of supposedly educated, professional men charged with responsibility for investigating violations of the civil rights laws.

Only the fact that the organizations to be investigated were black could explain the horrendous abuse of logic that the Bureau used to justify its invasion of campuses throughout the country. J. Edgar Hoover had publicly announced that the small and largely ineffectual Black Panther party was the greatest single threat to the security of the country. Having itself created the threat, the Bureau set out to neutralize it. Even if Hoover could have seriously documented his charges against the Panthers, which he never did, it was absurd to investigate hundreds of people whose only connection with the Black Panther party was that the party was trying to influence them. Hoover might similarly have justified an FBI investigation of every member of a "working class" union because the Communist party directed its propaganda and organizing effort at workers, or an investigation of every college student organization because the SDS sought to influence and control students.

Nor was this assault on the black student unions an isolated incident. I could cite many similar ones, for example the FBI's interest in the Smithsonian Institution when it opened an annex in the largely black Anacostia section of Washington, D.C. One of the annex's first events was a program for Black History Week centered on the life and contributions of Frederick Douglass. The FBI actually paid informants to attend the program and report the contents of the speeches given during it.

In the case of Stokely Carmichael the FBI was particularly determined and vicious. When he moved to Washington, D.C., in December, 1967, our squad kept him under surveillance twenty-four hours a day, following him about the city from lookouts and cars, and on foot. The investigation became even more intense a few days after Martin Luther King was assassinated. When blacks in Washington, D.C., as well as in many other cities, outraged by the murder, rioted for a day and a half, in the Washington Field Office a fifty-man special squad was assembled to get Carmichael for inciting to riot. We were directed to gather evidence showing that Carmichael had plotted, planned and directed the rioting, burning and pillage that took place in Washington, D.C. Fifty agents spent their full time for over a month on this one case.

One man, who later admitted that he had "been mistaken

and perhaps exaggerated a bit," claimed that Carmichael had a pistol which he fired into the air and then told the crowd to go home and get guns. A great many others stated firmly that Carmichael had urged the crowd not to dishonor Dr. King's memory by rioting and had politely asked shop owners to close their shops in his memory. Lacking any substantial evidence on which to base a charge, the Bureau nevertheless submitted voluminous reports on the minute-by-minute activities of Carmichael that were heavily weighted to imply that he had actually incited the mobs. Had Carmichael not decided to leave this country and go to Africa, the FBI, I am confident, would eventually have found something with which to bring an indictment against him.

Quite by accident I learned that the Internal Revenue Service (IRS) was aiding in the hunt for something with which to pin a charge on so-called "black militants." In early 1969 I was checking the background of a former member of SNCC, a man I had been investigating for almost two years. On three occasions I tried to close the case because I could find no indication that the subject was doing anything that would warrant an FBI investigation. Each time permission was refused, his status as a former member of SNCC being sufficient justification for going on with the investigation. I learned that the IRS had requested his arrest record from the Identification Division of the FBI. When I went to the IRS I found it had secretly set up a special squad of men to investigate the tax records of a list of "known militants and activists," and that the FBI was supplying the names of the persons for the IRS to include in this list. After talking to several IRS officials I was sent to a locked soundproofed room in the basement of the IRS headquarters in Washington where I found a file on my subject, among hundreds of others piled on a long table.

The Bureau's broad investigations of civil rights leaders and groups followed a logic like the one used to justify investigations of peace groups.

Our training emphasized that the FBI did not investigate "legitimate" civil rights organizations. Yet every major civil rights group was and probably still is being actively investigated. Here again, the titles of the cases all had that magic word "Cominfil." The Bureau line went something like this: We do not investigate legitimate civil rights groups. We do, however, keep track of their activities to determine whether there is or may be an attempt by the Communist party to infiltrate them and take over control and direction.

This very fine distinction on paper was a gaping chasm in reality. We were never troubled that our intensive "preliminary" investigations failed to uncover the Red menace lurking in the black movement. We could still continue our efforts to identify the leaders, catalogue the membership, follow and report on their activities, recruit informants and place them in these groups or in short, investigate civil rights organizations.

Later, when Stokely Carmichael dared utter the phrase "black power" while marching through Mississippi, the fine distinction dissolved. "Cominfil" was dropped and the "violent tendencies of the militant black extremists" became the official justification. Nothing changed but the title of the case.

There are hardly any limits on the Bureau's activities in compiling political information, particularly about the New Left. A case in point is the Institute for Policy Studies, an organization set up by dissenting officials in Kennedy's administration to carry out independent studies in international and domestic questions. The Institute caught my attention shortly after I began investigating the New Left. Reports from FBI informants showed that many of the leaders and spokesmen of anti-war and civil rights organizations called at the Institute when they visited Washington.

I reasoned that if there were a conspiracy that linked all

these groups the Institute was the logical place to look for it. I drafted a memo to that effect and requested that a case on the Institute be opened and assigned to me. My supervisor quickly agreed; he was then trying to increase the case load of the squad to justify a request for an increase in manpower.

Most of the information about the Institute's work is easily available and I was soon able to accumulate a vast dossier on it including biographical sketches of its founders, sources of its financial support, a general idea of its day-to-day operation and a pile of scholarly studies published by it. After analyzing this data I concluded that the Institute was not the secret mastermind of any conspiracy to overthrow the government but simply what I described in my report as a "thinktank of the Left," where a wide variety of current and former government officials, lawyers, journalists, radicals and others were holding seminars, doing research, writing reports, etc. I closed the investigation. To do otherwise, incidentally, would have meant a mound of paper work that would have occupied me full time for months.

About a year later another agent newly assigned to the squad came to see me with the closed file of the Institute and asked whether I thought the case ought to be reopened. This agent, like so many others, had strong right-wing views and could not believe that the Institute was merely sponsoring seminars and doing the other work I had described. It seemed necessary to him to think that a grand New Left conspiracy existed. In spite of my opposition, he had the case reopened and began a full-scale investigation of the Institute. He began monitoring the checking account of the Institute to determine where its money was going. He asked for telephone company records and compiled a list of the Institute's long-distance telephone calls. He attempted to place informants in the Institute as student interns and gathered every available paper published by it. Individual investigations were then opened on the people who worked for or received money from the Institute.

When I left the Bureau in April, 1970, the case on the Institute was still being investigated with gusto, and a huge collection of papers and reports on it had accumulated. So far as I have been able to determine, the FBI has found no evidence whatever of any illegal activity by the IPS, but the Institute continues to be investigated.

There are lighter moments even in security investigations. In October, 1967, the Washington Field Office was preparing to cover the march on the Pentagon sponsored by a coalition of anti-war groups. Everything was in order. Agents had their assignments, two-way radios were allocated, photographic surveillance teams were briefed and stenographers and agents stood by to report in triplicate every step of the march. Then a report was forwarded from a New York informant. He told of a group of undetermined number that had left New York City to join the march. The rest was not too clear, but the gist seemed to be that this group practiced some oriental religion and that their purpose in Washington would be to circle the Pentagon with a living chain of bodies and, by chanting the sacred word "om," levitate the building, thereby freeing it from the evil spirits of war and hatred dwelling within. They had also predicted that the Potomac River would run red.

I remember sitting in the office reading the teletype containing this "hot info," laughing quietly and wondering how much the informant had been paid. Almost immediately, a Bureau supervisor, who had also received a copy of the teletype, phoned to be briefed on what special steps the Washington Field Office was taking to handle this new threat. I was dumbfounded. How could anyone, much less a supervisor, take the report seriously?

But orders are orders, and so the agent teams at the Pentagon were instructed to be alert for any attempt to form a human chain, and report it promptly. Then, I supposed, we would alert the National Guard or the U.S. marshals to check carefully before exiting any of the Pentagon's doors. To counter the red river threat, some agents who owned powerboats volunteered their crafts to patrol the Potomac during the duration of the march.

The Pentagon escaped levitation, but in midafternoon we received a report that an individual on the Key Bridge was throwing something into the river. A boat was quickly dispatched, and three packages of red Air Force marker dye were fished from the river. The Potomac had been saved by the FBI in action.

Printed boldly in Bureau propaganda literature is the statement that the defense of innocence is as important as the proof of guilt. It heads the list of cardinal virtues of the Bureau and is tacked up for all to see in FBI offices throughout the country. Yet the very basis of the so-called security investigations is that the subject is a conspirator who is wittingly or unwittingly setting out to subvert the nation. He is prejudged guilty.

These things ran through my mind as I went on my daily routine. I rationalized in various ways at different times. For a while I pleaded ignorance: perhaps there really was some conspiracy behind the upheaval in America and I just didn't have the big picture yet. Or I would say that I was just a guy doing a job and if I didn't do it, someone else would. Or, if I do my job and keep my nose clean, eventually I may be in a position to change the policy of the Bureau. I was finally unable to accept these as valid excuses for harassing innocent people because of their political beliefs.

The Bureau's action after the 1968 Democratic convention in Chicago had a strong influence on my eventual decision to leave. Following the disturbances of convention week, there were charges and countercharges by police and demonstrators, newsmen and politicians, and public outcries for an investigation of the whole affair. True to form, the FBI set out to do its impartial investigation. We received a case with a usual dual title. It included both Police Brutality and violation of the Interstate Riot Law.

Offices, such as Washington Field, were instructed to contact and interview persons who had gone to Chicago to take part in the convention or the protest demonstrations. (It was no coincidence that we already knew the names and locations of most of the demonstrators. For a number of months before the convention we worked to compile a bookful of biographical information, descriptions and photographs of every "agitator" likely to go to the demonstrations.)

A short time later the Police Brutality caption was dropped from the investigation, and the Bureau concentrated on possible violations of the Interstate Riot Law. The result was the travesty of justice called the trial of the Chicago Seven. Nothing was heard again of the statements taken from those who were injured or beaten in the demonstrations and cooperated with the Bureau voluntarily, believing they were aiding an investigation of police brutality.

When I attend anti-war demonstrations now, I look for my former co-workers and watch them making notes and taking photographs, and I wonder what they are thinking.

I got an answer on May 5, 1971, when I was in downtown Buffalo, New York, observing an anti-war rally. About thirty or forty demonstrators sat down blocking a street. Without warning, a phalanx of six or seven motorcycle police drove their cycles into the group from behind.

I spotted an agent from the Buffalo office nearby jotting down notes and approached him. I asked him simply, "What do you think about this?"

"You know," he said. "We're not paid to think."

PART IV
A QUESTION
OF BALANCE:
PROTECTION OF SOCIETY,
PROTECTION OF INDIVIDUAL RIGHTS

CHAPTER FIFTEEN

THE BRITISH ANALOGY

BY C. H. ROLPH

I suppose that a dominant consideration at this conference should be the politically significant fact that it is possible to hold it at all. There are countries where the mildest criticism of anything like the FBI is enough to qualify a man for inclusion in a special register of suspects, and I am not altogether sure that the United States is not one of them. There are countries where the kind of thing I am proposing to say today would be followed by my prolonged disappearance from the social scene and official harassment of my wife and family. And I *am* quite certain that the United States is not one of those.

I wish therefore to acknowledge that the freedom we are openly concerned about includes the freedom to be openly concerned about it. And what we are discussing, secure in the knowledge that no one can stop us, is the various ways in which that freedom is currently being whittled away. It may be that the whittling away will continue so long as we are reasonably content to do no more than discuss it at conferences and seminars. But in Great Britain, where we have no national institution quite like the FBI, the discussion is gathering momentum as it is over here. And it is the kind of discussion, conducted at the kind of level, that sometimes enforces change without appearing to be the agent of it.

I: *The Right to Privacy*

I consider the turning point in Anglo-American legal thinking on the right to privacy to be the famous 1890 article in the *Harvard Law Review* by Samuel D. Warren and Louis D. Brandeis. Their article, "The Right to Privacy," advocated a statutory remedy for unwarranted and unnecessary press intrusions into private life. They urged that the half-and-half remedies, then relied upon in America and still relied upon in Great Britain, were inadequate. This includes such theories as violation of property, trespass, breach of confidence or copyright and so forth. Brandeis and Warren introduced the legal notion of "inviolate personality" as something which, in itself, the law should vigorously protect. In the half century that followed they saw their notion embodied in more than thirty-five state legislative enactments.

In England, on the other hand, the legal notion of privacy has not so far established itself. To a good many of us in England it was an occasion for some astonishment that our 1948 Committee on the Law of Defamation expressly disapproved, in its report, any extension of the law of libel and slander so as to cover invasions of privacy. Only a few weeks ago the Society of Conservative Lawyers submitted to a Home Office Committee on Privacy a memorandum of evidence which "saw no necessity to establish any statutory right of privacy." The Conservative Lawyers said they were not satisfied that invasions of privacy have assumed the proportions of an "evil of sufficiently general importance" and this in spite of their own finding that "the Common Law" of England "affords no protection against unauthorised invasion of privacy." The explanation or excuse they gave was that the reasons for prying into the affairs of others may sometimes be good reasons, as indeed they may.

There may be something in the suspicion, and the Society of Conservative Lawyers has helped to deepen it, that lawyers in general do not like straightforward statutory remedies, preferring to dredge around in the morass of case law for wisdom that has the appearance of being hard to come by. I do not myself believe that statutory prescription is always or necessarily the best way, but I do believe that "privacy" could and should be defined by statute, whether breaches of it be made civilly or criminally actionable.

II: *The Right to Intrude*

If that were done, so that every good citizen was by law an "inviolate personality," there would have to be exceptions to take account of the bad citizens. Many forms of anti-social behavior would have to be recognized as diminishing or for the time being destroying the inviolability of the personality normally protected by the law, and this is perhaps the moment to glance at them and consider how the law of England, in effect, penalizes good and bad alike by so often withholding any redress. We can consider at the same time how the police, the magistrates and the judges sometimes connive at breaches of such inadequate laws as there are, or, if they don't actually connive, "pass by on the other side"—all in the public interest. And in the process we shall be able to see whether the Englishman is justified in his belief, I mean his certainty, that he does not live in a "police state."

First, we have to recognize that a policeman is said to need rather greater powers than other citizens, greater protection against the consequences of genuine mistake or even of stupidity and overzealousness. A policeman in England, as in America, can obtain from a magistrate, by making a sworn statement, a warrant of arrest for someone he genuinely believes to have committed a crime. Suppose he then arrests the man and the whole thing turns out to have been a mistake. The policeman is protected by the law: he cannot be sued for wrongful imprisonment or unlawful arrest (though sometimes the magistrate can). Most arrests are made *without* going to a magistrate for a warrant. The policeman can arrest on his own authority and so, in a great many cases, can any ordinary citizen. Suppose, again, the arrest is a genuine mistake. Then, again, the policeman is protected and the citizen is not.

The policeman is in a special position in this one sense, that the law will often assume him to have been in a certain state of mind which affords him full protection even if it happens to have been a mistaken state of mind. This makes the policeman's state of mind a highly important part of the structure of a civilized society, and establishes the thinking processes of a large number of not very imaginative men as a source of immense coercive power over the citizen.

The policeman's power to arrest "on suspicion" has developed considerably in the course of the past hundred years or so. Suspicion of what used to be called felony (a narrower term than in most American jurisdictions), or treason, or of having inflicted a dangerous wound, is enough to justify police arrest. It is a power that extends to drugs and firearms offenses, to homicide of course, to rape and robbery and to theft of almost every description. It also extends to suspicion on the part of anyone, and not merely a policeman, that a known and loitering thief is *thinking* of committing a crime, and (in certain parts of England and Wales) it extends to suspicion on the part of a policeman that someone is carrying stolen property.

In London, for example, you can be asked by a policeman to display to him the contents of your briefcase or even of your pockets. If you refuse he can take you to the police station for the night, although what you were concealing from him may be no more sinister than a pair of your pajamas, a half-eaten meal or a copy of *Playboy*. Unless his suspicion that you were conveying stolen property or prohibited drugs was so unreasonable as to be quite ludicrous, not in your eyes but in the eyes of a judge, you will have no chance of redress against him. And nothing has done more than this particular law, which, as I have said, is capriciously local in its application, to befoul the relationships in England between police and public.

There are countries in the British Commonwealth, and the traditionally liberal-minded New Zealand is one, where the police are empowered by statute to go into a private house, without any warrant from a magistrate, and search it from top to bottom for evidence of drugs offenses. That is not yet the position in England, though in fact the police do seem to search private dwellings without authority—and hitherto the criminal courts have taken absolutely no notice. There are indications, rising from a recent criminal prosecution which I will mention in a moment, that the English courts may shortly find themselves obliged to give the matter more attention.

But on this question of local differences in police powers and practice, in America you have made more progress than we have in eliminating them, and it seems to us that you have done so in the face of greater difficulties.

III: "Long Usage"

I mentioned just now that there were reasons why the privacy of the individual must sometimes be invaded for the protection of society. If there is good ground for supposing that a man is plotting some bombing outrage, or the destruction of the democratic system by way of revolutionary violence, or even a large-scale robbery which is going to affect the lives of a large number of people, I *want* that man's privacy invaded.

If his house is searched, it is searched with my approval; and I speak as somebody who, as a police officer, has taken part in the search of a man's private house—so that I know the misery and embarrassment and bitter resentment that a police search can involve for the occupants of a private dwelling. No one who has not seen such a thing at first hand can truly envisage the distress it causes.

Similarly, if I know or strongly suspect that a man is using the telephone or the mails in the course of a crime of sufficient magnitude or gravity, I want that man's telephone tapped and his mail intercepted. These interferences with his privacy are done with my full approval, and I would think little of a police system that was unable to do them.

The police system in England is able to do them. If the police can satisfy a magistrate that there are good grounds for searching a house, which means grounds for believing it contains evidence of a crime, he will give them a signed warrant authorizing them to search it and take possession of anything relating to that particular crime. Sometimes in the search they will take possession of other things too, which seem to them to furnish evidence of other crimes or even to implicate other people. And in England the judges will support them in doing so—or will at least fail to condemn what they have done.

Sometimes the police in England search the house of a man they have arrested, and do so without obtaining a magistrate's warrant: this they do because the time taken up in getting the warrant might be utilized by accomplices of the man arrested to dispose of valuable evidence from the house. And this, too, the courts will tacitly condone without actually giving it their approval.

A great deal of what the police do, like a great deal of what the judges do, has no other authority than the fact that it has been done for a long time without being effectively or vigorously challenged. But this does not make it lawful.

Equally unlawful is telephone tapping, which is much rarer in England than a lot of Englishmen suppose. Until the year 1937 it was not unduly difficult for the police to get the cooperation of the telephone service in tapping a phone, though they had to show that some serious crime or treason was in contemplation or preparation and that this was the only way of getting vital information about it. In 1937, for the first time, the practice was reviewed by the Home Secretary and it was decided that in future there must be no telephone tapping without a warrant signed in person by the Home Secretary.

Thousands of people in Great Britain sincerely believe today that their telephones are being tapped by the police or the security services. It is a form of paranoia. I know something of the difficulty of getting a Home Secretary to sign a warrant for this purpose, and I would be extremely surprised if there were ever more than twenty or thirty such warrants in force at any one time. Even so, they mostly relate to plans for political violence, terrorist outrage or large-scale organized crime likely itself to involve violence.

In 1957, in consequence of a case in which the transcripts of a tapped telephone conversation had been unwisely disclosed to someone other than a court of justice, the Prime Minister set up a Committee of Privy Councillors to inquire into the whole process of intercepting private communications. There had been similar inquiries before—there was one in 1844, when telephones were unknown. And as before, the 1957 committee found that interception had no basis in law, whether common law, acts of Parliament or what is called royal prerogative: the only basis the committee could discover was "long usage." This is another way of saying that it is unlawful but no one cares to stop it. And "long usage," though not so long as you might suppose, is the basis of a very high proportion of the powers exercised by the police. As a matter of interest, the police in England were regulating road traffic for very many years before they were given the legal power to do it by the Motor Car Act of 1903. And they are still doing many things for which they have no legal power whatsoever, many of them entirely beneficent.

It should be noted that there are "private detective" firms which certainly use bugging devices, and probably tap telephones, with permission from no one, and there is nothing to prevent the results from being communicated to the police, probably on a reciprocal basis. It may well be this private activity, more than anything, that will eventually lead to a salutary control of this kind of snooping, which has obvious and frightening possibilities.

IV: *The British "Secret Police"*

It is when political and criminal police activities are combined in one organization that liberal uneasiness is always most aroused; and there is no doubt that this is the combination at the root of the criticisms currently leveled at the FBI. In England we tend to believe, I think a little complacently, that this is something we have skillfully avoided, and there are even those who see this supposed avoidance as an important example of British political skill and sophistication.

There are several organizations in Britain which together make up our equivalent to the FBI. These are the Security Service, particularly the branches still sometimes referred to as M.I.5 and M.I.6 and other branches, e.g., M.I.12, which deals with Northern Ireland; the Special Branch of the Criminal Investigation Department of the London Metropolitan Police, which in some matters concerns itself with the whole country, and the smaller Special Branch units in provincial police Criminal Investigation Departments.

Great Britain, as you well know, has no national police force, though there seems to be a growing weight of opinion that it should have. I do not know what degree of uniformity the FBI has managed to induce among the eight thousand local police forces in the U.S.A. which provide the material for the famous "Uniform Crime Reports," but I can imagine the diversity which eight thousand different police forces would be *likely* to have produced when the FBI first persuaded them to do it. I have been a member of the Parole Board of Great Britain, where we now have less than fifty police forces; and the diversity among the crime reports produced for the Parole Board's information even by these fifty closely related police forces is something that would have to be seen to be believed.

Inefficiencies of this kind, slowing down procedure interminably, are tolerated because no one makes enough fuss about them and every local police force behaves as though it were a law unto itself. It is *not* a law unto itself, and the Home Office, which is our nearest approach to a Department of Justice, will occasionally—but very rarely—demonstrate that it is not by threatening to withhold from the local authority the 50 per cent government grant toward running its police force. But the local identity is considered so precious that it tenaciously survives.

All these local police forces maintain Criminal Investigation Departments (CID) which we are told we must not describe as "secret police," though it's a little difficult to see what else they are. For men who are not behaving secretly, they keep themselves very quiet. Where they differ from the secret police of non-democratic countries is in the methods they can use, the methods that are to some effect imposed upon them by the vigilance of bodies like the Committee for Public Justice and (in England) the National Council for Civil Liberties.

The methods denied to the police of democratic countries are the use of families as hostages, the threat of lifelong detention without trial or even accusation, the systematic use of torture to extract statements or to enforce the signing of documents and so on in an ever-worsening progression of ends justifying means, and with an uninformed public opinion easily satisfied by the publicized attainment of the ends.

But even if the CID in each of these local police forces is not a "secret police," what about the Special Branch? This *corps d'élite* of a few hundred specially selected policemen, in various parts of Britain (but mostly at Scotland Yard), is as close as Britain gets to having an FBI. It came into being as a branch of the CID at Scotland Yard in 1883 and at first it was called "The Special Irish Branch," because its purpose was to combat the Irish-American dynamite campaign through which Home Rule for Ireland was to be achieved by blowing up England.

By the time a number of public buildings in London had been dynamited, it was decided to bring some members of the Royal Irish Constabulary to London for the protection of public buildings and ministers who were members of the Cabinet. (It is said that competition among ministers, at that time, for appointment to the Cabinet was keener than ever before or since.)

These Irish policemen, when they appeared on sentry duty with their rifles and their green uniforms in Whitehall and the neighborhood, were the focus of much resentment among the London CID. Why were the CID not considered able to cope with Irish terrorists? There was so much trouble that it was decided to form at Scotland Yard a staff specially assigned to Irish or Irish-American crime. They were assisted by experienced detectives, and by some men transferred from the uniform branch—mostly Irishmen. These included a Sergeant Quinn, who years later as Sir Patrick Quinn was the superintendent in charge of the Special Branch.

The Royal Irish Constabulary men went back to their own

troubled country, and the Branch was fully launched—this was in 1896—as a special unit concerned with terrorists, anarchists and visitors to Britain who were politically unwelcome. In 1894 an anarchist attempting to blow up the Royal Observatory at Greenwich blew himself up instead, and his story is the theme of Joseph Conrad's book *The Secret Agent.* As the years went by the Special Branch was kept busy by the suffragettes, Communists and Fascists and foreign propagandists of numerous kinds.

In both world wars it worked closely with the naval and military authorities in counterespionage. And in what are rather dubiously known as "times of peace" it is still in constant cooperation with the Security Service—that is to say with M.I.5, which is a defensive organization mainly against subversion, espionage and counterespionage, and with M.I.6, which is responsible for British spying abroad. M.I.5 is answerable to the Home Secretary and M.I.6 to the Foreign Office. These initials of course mean "Military Intelligence," but their members no longer use that phrase, probably because the scope of both departments has spread far beyond the kind of thing that military gentlemen, however intelligent, would be expected to know about.

The Special Branch is specially recruited from among men of the uniformed police, one of the qualifications being a knowledge of languages: but there is no pretense that the Special Branch in this sense is a rival to the FBI, which I understand originally admitted no recruit unless he was a qualified lawyer or accountant and still maintains an educational standard considerably higher than has been found possible in England.

Special Branch men are on duty at all the British airports and most of the busier seaports. As you go up to the immigration officer's desk when you next come to England, the quiet-suited man standing next to him will be a Special

Branch man, peeping at your passport as the immigration officer flicks the pages through and sometimes taking it into his
own hands to have a better look. He can recognize a visa
stamp, and even the country it relates to, from quite a distance, and there are certain visas that will arouse in him a
special interest in your name and destination, your lady
friend, your onward bookings by air and the duration of your
visit to Great Britain.

In its early days the Special Branch was unofficially called
the "Political Branch," and although that name was quickly
disowned and suppressed as something utterly indecent in a
country professing to have neither "secret police" nor "political police," a political branch it really was and really remains.
Its members, if they are to be of any use, *must* be politically
aware and informed. If a foreign head of state is visiting
Great Britain, he must be protected against insult or assassination by extremists or lunatics. A Special Branch man also needs
to know, as he considers the country from which the VIP is
coming, not only which *other* countries there are whose citizens might like to do him injury, but which dissident minorities there may be in his own country that might feel similarly
disposed. If a Special Branch man is not a political policeman,
he's the nearest approach to it that England is likely to produce. And when it is said that he is not acting in support of
any political ideology, the answer must be that he is usually
acting in support of the political ideology that is dominant in
Parliament at the relevant time.

Inevitably, the Special Branch gets involved in ordinary,
or non-political, crime as well, when that has political conno-
tations. The burning of a synagogue might be the work of a
Fascist organization or a fanatical pro-Arab movement and the
local police would need the help of the Special Branch in the
listing of likely suspects. A terrorist explosion is at once a
criminal offense, involving the local police and CID, and a

political gesture involving the Special Branch. The same is true of the discovery of an illegal store or consignment of firearms or drugs.

But a specially important fact about the Special Branch is that, since its members have no more power than that of an ordinary constable, they tend to resort even more than he does to extra-statutory ploys. Notable among these is the search of houses without a magistrate's warrant, but there are numerous other ways in which a strict observance of the law would truly "defeat the ends of justice." The Commissioner of the London Metropolitan Police could at any time say to the Home Secretary (who is his titular boss), "If you disapprove of something the Special Branch has done in producing a result that you nevertheless welcome, you must provide it with the statutory authority to do it the way you would prefer." This would mean, in other words, "My men will *not* go on breaking the law in the public interest unless you leave us alone. If you want the results you are getting now, but you want them to be immaculately obtained so that you can defend our methods in the House of Commons, then it's up to Parliament to make that possible."

V: "Quis Custodiet?"

I have said enough, perhaps, about the Special Branch to show that it is rather unlike the FBI in that it rarely involves itself in non-political crime. But its function, like that of the FBI, is the protection of the state, and in a democratic country that is the protection of what the majority of its citizens are supposed to want. It works and makes its inquiries with *extreme* discretion. A Special Branch man who went in for any bullying would soon be "out." Being interviewed by a Special Branch officer is quite a pleasant experience, the pleasure often lasting until he has gone away and you are trying to remember the conversation. The Branch does not want a bullying image, and has perhaps acquired, in the process of avoiding it, a cloak-and-dagger image that is not quite right either.

I think you may be surprised to learn, and I'm sure my compatriots in England would be surprised to know, that in protecting the state the Special Branch often comes *to the rescue* of an individual. It may be an individual who is being penalized in some McCarthyite situation that has involved him in "guilt by association." A good many such men have cause to thank the Special Branch for the detailed inquiries that have led to their vindication, ending perhaps in a visit by a Special Branch officer to the man's employer with the assurance: "Look, you can stop worrying about this chap—he's about as subversive as Queen Victoria."

But as a police officer said to me once: "If a man's a Communist, why *shouldn't* everyone know? If he's a Fascist, why *shouldn't* everyone know? And if he's a Communist, it's government policy that access to certain information shall be denied to him. He knows this. And if he conceals his political adherence, it can only be with one object. So why *shouldn't* we resort to every possible means to find out?"

One answer of course is that a man might conceal his Communist sympathies not only because he could thus more effectively do his political work, but because they would make him unpopular with his neighbors, or his workmates, or his girl friend or his wife's mother.

But it's only when he seeks a job in which he might have access to "classified" information that the Special Branch may become involved in investigating his background and allegiances. So far as I'm concerned, I hope they will go on doing it. I hope, even more fervently, that the civil liberty watchdogs will go on watching them and raise hell when they go too far.

So the Special Branch has no special methods. It has police

methods. They do include, on rare occasions, the authorized tapping of telephones, the cooperation of the postal authorities in intercepting letters and the "surveillance" of known extremists. They also include, as do police methods all over the world, the use of unlawful methods in the sense that what is done has no legal sanction, written or unwritten. (Police methods also include the use of computers. But in Great Britain the computers available to the police are all in the hands of the local authorities—the County Councils. And so far they are used only for the computation of police pay and allowances, accident statistics and other administrative calculations. They *could* be fed with any kind of data, and the time will come, I suppose, when they will play a big part in the prevention and detection of crime. But in England that time has not yet arrived.)

VI: *The End of Privacy*

I want to turn now to the growing problem of retired police officers and FBI men acting as "security agents" and "private eyes." I do not believe, myself, that there is yet a full public realization of what this can mean to the privacy of the law-abiding citizen. As in most industries and professions, speed and efficiency depend to an enormous extent on the right kind of human contact, on knowing the right man to call up at the right moment. We call it the "Old Boy Network." It is vitally important in police and Special Branch work.

And when a man leaves the police or the FBI and takes a job in industry as a security man, or sets up as a private detective, he does not at the same time leave the Old Boy Network. It becomes, overnight, more important to him than it has ever seemed before. There are probably fifty thousand such men pursuing their inquiries in Great Britain today, and some hundreds of them are former Special Branch men.

In America, which one regards as the home of the private eye, there must be many more than that. And one reads in *The Naked Society* that there are in the U.S.A. "thousands of firms offering their services as investigators [and] a large number of management consultant firms that derive most of their income from screening, assessing, or observing employees . . . Many of these enterprises with a vested interest in anxiety among business managers work strenuously to keep reminding the nation's industrialists of the untrustworthiness or undependability of a good many employees."

This is part of the problem of privacy. I offer the simple view that our privacy is doomed because we are too many. The sanctity of privacy declines with the growth of *anonymity*. The more we don't know each other, the more we want to keep secrets from each other. In the small town and village community, such as would be found in Europe and America two hundred years ago, there were family secrets and other matters shared only with servants and friends and neighbors, but there was no anonymity.

Anonymity and the lock on the front door are twin products of centralized methods of government, of civilized and urban living and perhaps, above all, of the need to defend oneself against mass communication methods and the universal hunger for "news." What I am saying is that the democratic way of running a country is absolutely dependent on the continual debate of all matters of public interest, and that today, accordingly, in one way or another "everything concerns everybody." That is an atmosphere in which privacy would be unlikely to flourish, even if one looked no further into its condition.

But one *must* look further. Forces have drawn together into a huge social machinery most of the engines of economic and political power, so that the state and the big corporations between them would make it impossible for you and me, even if we wanted to do so, to opt out and live the life of a recluse.

It ought to seem strange, but it is in fact obvious, that the size of these states and corporations makes them vulnerable. They are giants who cannot see their own knees or the ground at their feet. They are struggling in a hardening climate to maintain their positions against each other, to enlarge their share of the market, to devise more and more ingenious methods of competition. Accordingly, their rivals and their own employees are a source of potential danger to a gigantic form of privacy, against which the pygmy privacy of individuals like ourselves seems to them of little consequence. In the general atmosphere of apprehension and suspicion thus engendered, possibly half the population of a modern civilized country are "security risks."

VII: Possible Safeguards

I want to offer you a final glance at possible legal remedies in England, bearing in mind that "civil liberty" is at the receiving end of a legal system which is based so largely on "long usage," and that long usage *may* mean some malpractice about which no one has had the courage to complain or a big enough voice to be heard. It is also relevant that the *state of mind* of a policeman or an FBI man, no less than that of a judge or a Supreme Court of judges, can be a highly important part of the structure of a civilized society, since the law seems to conform so often to what someone allows himself to think it is, and the suspicions he forms are so often the reason for putting it into practice.

There is in England no general law of criminal trespass. There are special statutes and regulations treating a trespass as criminal—on railway premises and in prohibited areas occupied by the armed forces and the Atomic Energy Commission. Otherwise the countless notice boards you can see on farmland and private parks announcing that "Trespassers Will Be Prosecuted" are sheer bluff; a famous judge once said that every such notice was "a wooden falsehood." There can be no criminal prosecution for individual acts of trespass to private land and buildings. There can, of course, be a civil action for damages and there is no need to prove that the trespasser did any damage to property, though it would hardly be worth while to sue if he did none.

But if trespass itself is not a criminal offense, what about the law of conspiracy? It is a crime to conspire to do any unlawful act, criminal or not, and trespass is certainly unlawful. No one much likes the law of conspiracy, which has a ghastly history going back to the days of the Star Chamber and religious persecution. But no one in recent years had thought of a prosecution for "conspiracy to trespass" until two brothers, Ian and Stuart Withers, who had planted bugging devices in bedrooms to get evidence for a divorce action, were convicted at the Central Criminal Court in London on June 16, 1971, of conspiring to commit trespass in two private houses when, after trying to get in under various pretexts, they knocked on the door at midnight, and after it was opened, burst into the house and rushed upstairs to a woman's bedroom. No doubt to their disappointment, she was in bed alone.

Mr. Justice Roskill said this was "a serious breach of a citizen's right to privacy," but the conviction for conspiracy to trespass passed relatively unnoticed in the newspaper reports because they were all preoccupied with the more sophisticated story about the bugging devices. There could be no appeal against conviction—the two men had pleaded guilty.

But it would not be the first time that a decision by a single judge had set the pattern for a long-sought method of dealing with a growing menace to private rights. A charge of conspiracy requires two or more offenders acting in concert, but it is seldom that these intrusions are the work of a solitary individual. It will be interesting to see whether it is to be the once infamous law of conspiracy that comes to the rescue, where lawyers in England have for so long been saying that the criminal law offers no protection against invasion of the Englishman's castle.

I should like to end, I hope you may think appropriately in view of our surroundings today, with one of the many memorable utterances of President Woodrow Wilson. "Liberty," he said, "has never come from the government. Liberty has always come from the subjects of it. The history of liberty is a history of resistance."

VIII: Conference Discussion

MR. EMERSON: I wonder if Mr. Rolph could elaborate somewhat more on the distinction between political crime and other types of crime.

MR. ROLPH: I think it is not possible to differentiate even theoretically. I always find line drawing terribly difficult anyway, but it might be that any crime, which on the surface seemed entirely criminal, could in fact have political motives or political consequences. That could include a kidnapping or a shooting episode or even a smuggling offense. For example, a smuggling offense might be a gunrunning operation in connection with the trouble going on at the moment in Northern Ireland.

I think a blurring of the line between what is criminal and what is political is reflected in our Extradition Act. You know the difficulty in getting extradition orders against purely political offenders. Many and long have been the arguments in court, on a writ of habeas corpus, to establish or refute the suggestion that this is a political crime. It is usually a question of fact, with the lawyers pretending as hard as they possibly can, as they always do, that it's a question of law.

MR. EMERSON: But the M.I.5 and Scotland Yard must have some general guidelines where their jurisdictions lie.

MR. ROLPH: There isn't a guide that exists, outside the corpus of the criminal law. We don't have a criminal code; we have a hodgepodge of statutes and common law decisions. M.I.5 doesn't need to know much about those. And I wouldn't think, in any event, that they would be the first persons to recognize that a crime was a political crime. It would be brought to their notice by the police, who would have reported it to their own special branch, who, in turn, would say no, this is an M.I.5 thing, and it would go to them.

There might or might not be a prosecution. There was no prosecution recently in the case of a Soviet defector who was arrested on a charge of drunken driving and, possibly to save his skin, gave the information to M.I.5 that resulted in the expulsion of 120 Soviet agents. That began as an ordinary criminal offense and grew until diplomatic privilege was involved, the relationships between embassies and so forth. It was accordingly taken away from the ordinary police area. When the case came up, in the normal routine of prosecution, the Crown offered no evidence. The case was dropped.

MR. DORSEN: There is a question from one of our observers that I might put to Mr. Rolph. To protect the political system in England, are dossiers collected on millions of people? Are political groups and social groups infiltrated?

MR. ROLPH: Well, number one, there is a small, and I think somebody here said genteel, system of compiling dossiers about people whose potentialities are important from a state security point of view. It's very often no more than the private locker of a zealous police officer or Special Branch man. It's only when that man has found, shall we say, a series of letters by the same person in the *Morning Star,* our Communist newspaper, or a series of attendances by the same person at certain kinds of meetings, for example, that such a person begins to acquire a special sort of significance.

I make no complaint about this because I've had this kind of significance myself. I tried for a long time to find out whether I myself was a subject of a file. I wasn't, as it turned out. No doubt, quite a lot of respectable citizens are. But there is nothing, in proportion to the population of Great Britain, that would compare with the millions of dossiers one hears about in this country. There's no law against the compilation of such information, and I don't think myself that there should be. I think people who are likely to be a source of danger to the state, or to me, or to any other individual, ought to be known about. And I don't mind how much the police know about them.

With regard to infiltration, the Special Branch infiltrates, and so in fact does every law-enforcement agency. There are criminal investigation departments belonging to every police force.

I've infiltrated clubs in circumstances where information was required. And after I left the police service, which is longer ago than I propose to reveal, I was asked by the Board of Deputies of British Jews to become a member of the British Union of Fascists. That was the leading polarity of the day, Fascists versus Jews. Would I become a Fascist as an undercover man, for a sum which I will not name, and report to the Board of Deputies of British Jews? I declined.

MR. VORENBERG: As I listen to Mr. Rolph, and think about what I know of the British police, it strikes me there really isn't any reason built into the structure of the politics in the two countries why we should have ended up with the kind of agency the FBI has turned out to be. It really is more a question of bad luck, of having had somebody who has survived so many administrations and drawn so much power to himself. In a way, you might have expected that more from a system with a permanent civil service. But ours does not normally have that kind of stability at the top level.

If that's so, maybe there is some hope that a different kind of a chief, a chief that sees a different model for the FBI, could at least make very drastic changes. In other words, I don't think that one has to assume that this is the only kind of FBI that one can live with. I get a little bit of hope from what Mr. Rolph says.

MR. LOCKARD: My question is brief. I have heard it reported that if a British subject wants to know whether a dossier is being kept on him, he has the right to find out. Is that true?

MR. ROLPH: No sir, I know of no such right. And if the right existed, I don't know how you would enforce it. I don't think you could ever find out whether a dossier existed with your name and circumstances on it. Everybody knows that he has a national health insurance number, that under the national health system any doctor can get the details of his medical past life, including, to many people's distress and horror, whether he's had mental trouble or not. That's the nearest I can imagine to a right to know what is on your private dossier. But in a series of bills which have been promoted lately, and one of which I think is bound, sooner or later, to come into force, there has been provision for the right to know.

MR. MORGAN: In light of what Mr. Rolph said about compiling dossiers, I want to point out that even though in England no one has ever suggested that this activity's against the law, one of the great differences between our country and yours, Mr. Rolph, is that we fought against writs of necessity and have a Fourth Amendment. The legal structure is quite different in this country with respect to infiltrators, preparation and usage of dossiers, and wiretapping and bugging.

MR. ROLPH: Yes. I think the difference is inherent, and looks to me like being endemic.

I find it difficult to accept the idea that the possession of an FBI is due to bad luck. I think it might be nearer the truth to say that it's due to a mixture of inherent romanticism and boredom in a vast developing country.

CHAPTER SIXTEEN

THE FBI AND THE
BILL OF RIGHTS

BY THOMAS I. EMERSON

The inescapable message of much of the material we have covered is that the FBI jeopardizes the whole system of freedom of expression which is the cornerstone of an open society. The philosophy and much of the activity of the Bureau is in direct conflict with the fundamental principles underlying that system.

The Bureau's concept of its function, as dedicated guardian of the national security, to collect general political intelligence, to engage in preventive surveillance, to carry on warfare against potentially disruptive or dissenting groups is wholly inconsistent with a system that stipulates that the government may not discourage political dissent or efforts to achieve social change so long as the conduct does not involve the use of force, violence or similar illegal action. An ideology which single-mindedly rejects new ways of thought, is skeptical of the capacity of the American people to think for themselves, fears to leave any looseness in the structure of law and order and views criticism of the Bureau as *lèse majesté* is in total opposition to a system that seeks to promote diversity of opinion, a clash of ideas and indeed a limited degree of conflict within the society.

The magnitude of the Bureau's operation, particularly in the national security field, makes its influence pervasive and creates the danger of an uncontrolled center of despotic power. The vast range of persons and organizations subject to the Bureau's scrutiny and the unconfined scope of its inquiries create a chilling effect quite opposed to our "profound national commitment to the principle that debate on public issues should be uninhibited, robust and wide-open." And the very process of investigation itself may have effects that are as intrusive and repressive as those of totalitarian police.

It is not only in the performance of its investigating function, however, that the FBI poses a serious threat to our political freedoms. The Bureau has become much more than a data-collection agency. In its official statements and other publications it has had an important influence on public attitudes and opinions. Disclosure of materials in the Bureau files and leakage from those files have had a devastating effect upon some citizens, and the possibility of disclosure hangs heavy over all citizens. The Bureau has it within its power, should its Director or some subordinate so desire, to make the life of any citizen highly uncomfortable, or even unlivable. At times it has done so.

As an important center of power in Washington, the Bureau is in a position to influence political events in situations where a police force, like the military, should keep its hands off. The building of the Bureau into a smugly independent, highly centralized, professional organization raises critical issues of the ability of the administration or of Congress to keep it under control.

The present position of the FBI in the American political scene thus threatens, at best, grave injury to our democratic institutions. At worst it raises the specter of a police state. The search for ways in which these dangers can be met is a matter of urgency for all Americans.

Two main sets of problems confront a democratic society in controlling the operations of its police. One relates to specific police methods and procedure. Protection of the citizen against arbitrary arrest, illegal detention, official brutality, improper interrogation and similar unjust or inhuman treatment is essential to a civilized community. The Bill of Rights has been invoked most often in this context.

The other set of problems raises broader issues and relates more to the substantive rights of the people than to the procedures of law enforcement. These questions concern the extent to which the operations of a police force tend to limit and confine the openness of the society, particularly as they inhibit its system of free expression. Of course, enforcement of the laws inevitably restricts, in some ways, the freedom of the individual. The problem is to draw the line between order and vitality. That is the problem with which this chapter deals.

I: Dangers to the Bill of Rights

Much of the threat to our freedoms originates in operations of the FBI in the area of national security. A look at these operations provides something of a summary of other papers presented at the Princeton conference.

The FBI view of the dangers to national security—dangers which it believes the government must combat at all costs—includes not only espionage, sabotage and the use of force or violence to effect political change. The FBI's interests and activities extend also to the sphere of "loyalty," an area that encompasses the attitudes, beliefs, opinions and associations of individuals. While the Bureau's concern with loyalty is legally grounded in the federal employee loyalty program, its operations tend to cover the loyalty of all citizens. It also is concerned with "subversive activities." This area, vague in the extreme, extends far beyond acts of force or violence to militantly expressed opinions, organizational activities of radical groups and any signs of potential dissidence or disruption.

The concepts of loyalty and subversive activities, as developed by the Bureau, carry it very far in the direction of viewing all militant or radical dissent as a threat to the national security. The result is that, in essence, the FBI conceives of itself as an instrument to prevent radical social change in America. This view, when implemented in practice, leads to three significant features of the Bureau's operation.

First, throughout most of its history the FBI has taken on the task not only of investigating specific violations of federal laws, but gathering general intelligence in the national security field.

Second, when the Bureau addresses itself to the enforcement of specific federal laws, it collects information which is relevant not only to a violation that has already occurred or is about to occur, but to violations which might occur in the future.

Third, the Bureau's view of its function leads it beyond data collection and into political warfare. The pronouncements of Hoover, presumably based upon material collected by Bureau agents and made in his capacity as an expert on subversive activities, were intended to arouse government and public hostility against political groups disfavored by the Bureau. At another level of action, investigation turns into harassment.

Ultimately, the FBI's concept of its role comes down to the proposition that the Bureau should not merely assist the prosecuting authorities in enforcement of the law but should take direct measures of its own.

The basic ideology of the FBI—its concept of the dangers to national security and the way in which they must be combated—has remained largely unchanged over the years. Many observers have commented upon these fundamentally political assumptions:

1. The Bureau tends to equate national security with preservation of the traditional American way of life, as understood by the most conservative Americans, in its most pristine form. Any serious disagreement with the principles underlying this way of life is likely to be viewed as "disloyalty," and any conduct which seeks substantial alteration of its institutions is viewed as "subversive."

2. The main danger to the American way of life (and hence to national security) comes from alien ideologies, primarily as espoused by the Communist party, which is a powerful and diabolical force in the United states. Americans, if left to themselves, are liable to be seduced or deceived by these purveyors of false ideas, and those who propose or work toward serious change in the established order are giving aid and comfort to the enemy.

3. National security can be assured only by total vigilance. There is little room for play in the joints of the American system. To take another metaphor, every radical spark must be rubbed out ruthlessly, lest it start a conflagration. Hence, the interest in national security normally takes precedence over the risks of conflict inherent in the toleration of strong dissent.

4. National security will be achieved primarily through application of official coercion against those who threaten disruption. Hence, emphasis is placed upon enforcement of law and order rather than upon methods of relieving social discontent.

5. The appropriate limits on political opposition are determined by the nature of the ideas advanced and the moderation with which they are put forward. Freedom of expression does not include "license."

6. An individual who for any purpose associates with another individual or a group working against the American system is likely to have adopted, or is prepared to adopt, all

the beliefs and actions of the other person or group. Hence association with subversives is itself subversive. Furthermore, any organization is susceptible to influence and control by its most extreme members.

7. The policies and practices necessary for protection of the national security are not matters to be left to the ordinary "civilian" but require a professional organization of experts. That agency must be tightly organized, rigidly disciplined and ready to give unquestioned obedience to the commands of its chief. Criticism or dissent within the organization is not to be tolerated. The organization must operate in complete secrecy and must have absolute independence in the conduct of its investigations and other activities.

8. Outside criticism of the agency charged with protection of the national security is likely to be motivated by anti-American beliefs and to be subversive. If the criticism is worthy of answer at all, it deserves utter condemnation.

This listing is not meant to imply that the Bureau's actions are always rigidly controlled by these principles, and that no other ideas or values find a place in the conduct of its affairs. The specific formulations, likewise, may be exaggerated. Nevertheless, one cannot come away from a study of the material on the Bureau without a clear feeling that these formulations give a reasonably accurate impression of the world in which the Federal Bureau of Investigation lives.

The operations of the FBI, as described at this conference, pose evident dangers to the system of individual rights embodied in our Constitution. These dangers are not confined to the way in which the Bureau currently performs its functions. They are inherent in the very existence of a police force. But the current operations of the Bureau serve to focus attention upon some of the specific problems which must be met if a free and open society is to survive.

II: Protective Measures: Judicial

In considering protective measures against the threats to our Bill of Rights posed by the Federal Bureau of Investigation, or by any similar security police force, it is natural to turn first to our laws and legal institutions. But it is well to keep in mind as we do so that other avenues of approach are equally crucial.

A. LIMITING THE STATUTORY AUTHORITY OF THE FEDERAL BUREAU OF INVESTIGATION STRICTLY TO LAW ENFORCEMENT

The most important single step which should be taken to safeguard the Bill of Rights is to limit the statutory authority of the FBI to the narrow function of assisting directly in the enforcement of those federal laws over which it is given jurisdiction. The significance of such a limitation was clearly understood by members of Congress at the time the Bureau was created and this restriction was expressly imposed upon the Bureau when Attorney General Stone reorganized it in 1924.

Under such an arrangement, the FBI would be confined to investigations where there were reasonable grounds to believe that a violation of law had or was about to occur. The Bureau might also perform other duties, such as investigation of an individual under consideration for appointment to federal office, but such an investigation would be strictly limited to that subject. The Bureau would have no authority to collect general political intelligence, to prepare for possible future events by infiltrating a political group or to maintain dossiers except on persons specifically investigated under its limited authority. Its mission to carry on general political warfare would be eliminated.

Cutting back the operations of the FBI to their 1924 scope

could be achieved through action of the President or the Attorney General. Or it could be specifically prescribed in legislation enacted by Congress. Or it very likely could be achieved through court proceedings.

The FBI has no inherent power to exist, no more than any executive agency. The Bureau must derive its authority from a statute passed by the legislature or, in limited instances, from a constitutional power of the chief executive. Existing legislation does not contemplate or sanction the Bureau's excursions beyond the area of strict law enforcement. It undertook such an expansion by seizing upon statements of the President, by stretching its statutory authority beyond recognition and by sheer usurpation.

Indeed, supporters of the Bureau's present mode of operation rest their argument not on the existence of any statutory authority, but upon the inherent powers of the President. This claim, however, seems clearly insufficient. The President does have some implied powers to collect information and keep himself abreast of events and trends in the country. That he possesses any inherent power to establish a national security police force, which keeps dossiers on millions of citizens, conducts surveillance of dissenting political groups and maintains the whole apparatus of a secret police, would appear constitutionally inconceivable. The decision of the Supreme Court in the *Youngstown Sheet & Tube* case, invalidating President Truman's seizure of the steel mills, makes plain that no such presidential assumption of power is contemplated by our Constitution.

Nor can it be persuasively argued that Congress by appropriation of funds for the Bureau has *sub silentio* given consent to the exercise of Bureau powers. In the first place, the full sweep of the Bureau's activities has never been revealed to Congress, but rather concealed from it. More importantly, in an area which touches so deeply the right to freedom of expression, freedom from unreasonable searches and other individual rights protected by the Constitution, an inference of this sort would not be lightly drawn. All in all, it seems most unlikely that the Supreme Court would uphold an implied presidential power to maintain a secret police.

It should be noted that the Bureau itself has always understood the basic distinction between the exercise of law-enforcement powers and of intelligence-gathering and political-warfare powers. Indeed, the Bureau, until recently, has consistently confined itself to the law-enforcement function in the field of civil rights. Speaking of the Bureau's operation in this area, Hoover observed, "Our agents cannot be used as instruments for social reform. They are law-enforcement agents. Their job is to gather facts when there is an indication that a Federal law has been violated." Criticism has, of course, centered on lack of alacrity in civil rights law enforcement. But there is no reason why this policy should not be un-hypocritically applied to the field of national security.

Any effort to establish the Bureau's existing legal authority in court might run into the question whether a private citizen or organization has standing to challenge the Bureau's scope of operation. But the courts have been expanding rights of standing in recent years and this problem could probably be overcome. If so, there seems no reason why a court should not then enjoin the Bureau from operating beyond the scope of its statutory authority and confine it to strictly law-enforcement functions.

B. CONSTITUTIONAL LIMITS ON POLITICAL SURVEILLANCE

In addition to statutory limits upon the scope of FBI activity, important constitutional restrictions exist. These are applicable, of course, whether the Bureau is assumed to be operating under legislative authority or under inherent presidential authority. The main constitutional limits on the general powers of the Bureau to engage in political surveillance derive from the First Amendment and the right of privacy. These issues may be considered together.

There can be little doubt that the operations of the FBI, in their present form, infringe upon rights guaranteed by the First Amendment. The general impact of the Bureau's activities upon the system of freedom of expression has already been described. Knowledge that the government is watching and recording one's political thoughts and moves is, for most people, a shattering experience. Only the most resolute remain uninhibited. The same sort of chilling effects flow from other activities of the Bureau.

The decisions of the Supreme Court leave no room to question that government conduct which produces such an impact impairs freedom of expression. The court has held that the First Amendment is violated by the mere requirement that a citizen file a request with the government in order to receive "foreign Communist propaganda" in the mail; by a law compelling the disclosure of the names of authors or distributors of a political leaflet; and by exposure of the membership lists of an organization like the NAACP. In another series of cases the court has ruled that government measures which go beyond the point strictly necessary to accomplish a legitimate purpose and thereby infringe First Amendment rights are invalid as overbroad; "less drastic means" must be used to accomplish the government's objective. Both lines of cases point clearly to the conclusion that much of the Bureau's operation would be prohibited by the First Amendment.

On the other hand, the FBI performs some legitimate functions in a legitimate manner. It can be given the basic power to investigate violations of valid federal laws. And the nature of the investigatory process is such that the Bureau may not always find it easy to foretell at the initial stages what information may be relevant and what not. Furthermore, a police force, through patrolling, deploying or by other means, may seek to prevent as well as punish the commission of crime. Likewise it may, in some degree, develop general information which will enable it to carry out its functions more effectively. These activities may, in a certain sense, have a retarding or inhibiting effect upon lawful political conduct. A citizen may curtail his political activity in the presence of a police officer because he does not know exactly how far he can go, or fears that a police mistake will be made, or simply decides to stay on the safe side of the law. The problem for the court, therefore, is to draw the distinction between legitimate investigative activity and unlawful invasion of First Amendment rights.

The place at which the court will establish this line depends to some extent upon what legal doctrine it employs in deciding First Amendment issues. If the court adopts the balancing test—a doctrine frequently invoked in comparable situations—it will undertake to weigh the government interest in law enforcement against the individual and social interest in freedom of expression. As an alternative test it has been proposed that the government must show a sufficient nexus or connection between the particular investigatory activity and the needs of law enforcement. A third theory, designed to give full protection to First Amendment rights, would seek to determine whether the predominate effect of the agency's conduct was to secure law enforcement or to inhibit freedom of expression.

The Supreme Court decisions to date leave unclear which of these doctrines, if any, it would apply in this situation. One cannot, therefore, predict with any assurance what the outcome of a lawsuit would be. Nevertheless it seems reasonable to assume that at some point the Bureau's mode of operation would be ruled in violation of the First Amendment.

The constitutional right of privacy also establishes a boundary to political surveillance by the FBI. In *Griswold* v. *Connecticut*, in which the right of privacy was first given recognition as part of the Bill of Rights, the Supreme Court held the Connecticut birth control statute unconstitutional on the ground that it would permit police snooping into the privacies of the marital relation.

The scope of the constitutional right of privacy has not yet been fully developed by the courts. Nevertheless, the doctrine would be applicable to some of the operations of the Bureau. Probing into personal affairs, shadowing, compiling dossiers and similar practices, where unrelated to specific law-enforcement needs, are plainly intrusions into privacy. Very likely the courts would apply a balancing test, in which the governmental interest involved is weighed against the individual and social interest in privacy.

Until more decisions are forthcoming the right to privacy boundaries will remain obscure. And in any event, they do not seem as confining for the Bureau as those imposed by the First Amendment since most political conduct is carried on in the public arena. Nevertheless, the privacy doctrine would not only support the First Amendment position at important points but would in its own right operate as a significant limiting factor.

Taking the First Amendment and privacy doctrines together, it can be persuasively argued that the constitutional guarantees in the Bill of Rights preclude the Federal Bureau of Investigation from engaging in the following kinds of activity:

1. Photographing peaceful demonstrators, recording license numbers of persons attending a meeting, ostentatious surveillance of a public gathering or similar blanket collection of data on persons not engaging in criminal activities.

2. Compiling dossiers of political intelligence upon persons who are not charged with or reasonably suspected of a specific violation of federal law, or who are not applicants for federal office.

3. Making investigations or maintaining political surveillance of organizations or groups in the absence of a charge of, or reason to suspect, a violation of federal law, or carrying such investigation beyond that necessary to dispose of the violation issue.

4. Disclosing material from any dossier or other place except for specific law-enforcement purposes.

5. Conducting investigations or other activities in such a way that they constitute political harassment of the subject.

6. Engaging in political action or expression not directly related to the strict performance of law-enforcement functions.

These undoubtedly do not cover all operations of the FBI that go beyond the bounds of the constitutional limitations. In essence, what is proscribed is all activity of the Bureau which attempts to deal with national security *through preventive measures that infringe upon rights protected by the First Amendment*. It is a fundamental principal of the First Amendment that the government may not curtail freedom of expression as a means of achieving social controls. This is what the Bureau has, more and more, attempted to do. No agency of the government should wield such powers, least of all the security police. Real prevention of danger to national security requires affirmative measures to solve the underlying problems, not suppression.

It is readily admitted that the drawing of a constitutional line between legitimate and illegitimate Bureau conduct will sometimes pose hard questions. Probably the only current answer is that the law must develop, as it customarily does, on a case-by-case basis. The principle is clear, though, and its statutory or judicial application would immediately result in drastic alteration in the Bureau's operations. More precise formulations of the rule would follow later.

One crucial point should, however, be emphasized. Under the best of circumstances, judicial restraint upon FBI practices will only be partially effective so long as federal legislation exists that imposes sanctions upon political conduct which takes the form of expression. This legislation includes federal anti-sedition laws, such as the Smith Act and the Internal Security Act; the federal Anti-Riot Act, which penalizes the crossing of state lines with intent to "encourage" a riot; and the federal loyalty programs. To the extent that the federal government can penalize expression, the Bureau can investigate expression. Only by confining federal controls to conduct that amounts to action, and allowing expression to be free, will we be able to end serious encroachment by the Bureau upon the Bill of Rights.

In any event, the difficulties in rolling the Bureau back to its constitutional boundaries through litigation should not be underestimated. The courts, like all other parts of the government, are reluctant to inject themselves into Bureau affairs. Technical problems, such as the standing of private parties to raise the constitutional issues, will have to be met. More important, the problems of proof will be serious. The usual legal rules for disclosure will result in some information on Bureau operations. But the very sensitive issues involved in forcing the security police to provide data about their operations are not easily solved.

If the courts reach a decision upholding the constitutional rights of citizens against the FBI, troublesome questions remain with regard to enforcement of the court rulings. How can a decree be formed so that it will protect the individual without impairing the legitimate functions of the Bureau? Equally important, how will the parties, the court or the public know whether the Bureau has complied with the court's order? If the court requires that certain Bureau records be destroyed, or sequestered, how can anyone be assured that microfilm copies will not be retained? Can the court appoint a receiver or trustee to supervise the enforcement of its orders?

Plainly, vigorous and innovative action on the part of the judiciary, such as some courts have applied in the enforcement of civil rights orders, will be necessary.

Lawsuits raising these and other problems, most of them aimed at police forces other than the FBI, are being brought with increasing frequency. This is a promising development. It is important that the facts be brought into the open and that the evolution of necessary legal doctrines begin. Thus far, encouraging successes have been achieved, but the major questions remain to be resolved.

C. CONSTITUTIONAL LIMITATIONS ON THE USE OF INFORMERS

What judicial controls might be available to restrain the activities of the Bureau in the use of informers? The main constitutional limitations flow from the First Amendment, the right of privacy and the Fourth Amendment. There are also potential limitations derived from the law of entrapment.

1. The First Amendment

It is apparent that the Bureau's widespread employment of informers in its national security operations, and its heavy reliance upon their product, seriously impair free and open expression. The effects are the same as those caused by political surveillance generally, but with much more serious damage to freedom of association. The prevalence of informers in a political organization is highly disruptive, alters the character of the organization and often leads to its disintegration. An impact of this sort infringes upon the rights which the First Amendment seeks to protect.

The question then becomes whether, under the applicable legal doctrine, such an infringement violates the constitutional mandate. The Supreme Court has never passed upon this issue. It has never had a case involving a full factual presentation of

FBI informer practices and their impact upon freedom of expression, in which the First Amendment issues were fully developed. Nor has the law been expounded in the decisions of other courts.

The Supreme Court has held that "the use of secret informers is not *per se* unconstitutional." By the same token some uses are unconstitutional. It would seem reasonable to conclude that the same basic dividing line should be drawn here as in the case of political surveillance generally. This would mean that the Bureau may use informers only for direct law-enforcement activities, and not for the collection of general intelligence data or for information relevant only to the prevention of events that have not yet taken place.

Even if the courts refuse to accept this general doctrine, they ought to take special account of the impact on the right of association of certain types of informers. An informer who is placed by the police within an organization, or has such a relation with the police as to be in effect a government agent, surely ought not be permitted to function except in a narrow, crime-investigation capacity.

Efforts to apply these constitutional principles through a series of lawsuits would present the same practical hazards noted above. There would, indeed, be some extra difficulties. Since informers operate under cover, problems of proof would be even more burdensome. The task of separating crime investigation from political surveillance would be more exacting. Nevertheless, it would be important to begin ascertaining constitutional limits. Only time can give the answer.

2. The Right of Privacy

The constitutional right of privacy interposes a limitation upon the use of informers the same as upon other investigative operations of the FBI. If the relationship of the informer to those upon whom he is informing remains entirely impersonal, or organizational, presumably no issue of the right to privacy would arise. But where an informer establishes a personal relation with another person, representing himself to be a private citizen but actually an agent of the government, one does not have to strain hard to view his conduct as a governmental invasion of privacy.

Whether a court, balancing the interests at stake, would consider such an intrusion justifiable would probably turn upon the nature of the investigation. It would be entirely reasonable to hold that if the investigation seeks to ferret out the perpetrator of a specific crime, the conduct is permissible; but if the purpose is to seek general political intelligence, the invasion of privacy is not warranted. Thus, the right of privacy is applicable in the same general circumstances as the First Amendment.

3. Entrapment

On its face, the concept of entrapment would appear to introduce important restrictions upon the FBI's use of informers. To the extent that an informer operated as an *agent provocateur*, it would seem that the government itself was in part responsible for any illegal conduct in which the informer participated. It would appear to follow that such use of an informer could be enjoined or otherwise prevented, and that the government would have waived its right to punish anyone for the offense in which its agent joined.

In actual practice, however, the law of entrapment has not functioned that way. The doctrine has never been held to rest on constitutional foundations; rather it is considered either a rule of statutory interpretation or a rule originated by the courts and applied by them as a matter of judicial policy. In part for this reason, the entrapment doctrine has never served as grounds for obtaining an injunction against improper use of informers or for a civil remedy against the police for violation of individual rights. Entrapment has thus been limited in its use to a defense against criminal prosecution. Even here its scope and effect have been drastically curtailed.

In the first place, most courts hold that entrapment can be invoked as a defense only by admitting the offense charged. Thus, it is normally used only as a last resort in an otherwise hopeless case. Second, the courts have adopted very strict rules about what constitutes entrapment. The view accepted by a majority of the Supreme Court is that the defense of entrapment is available only when "the criminal design originates with the officials of the Government, and they implant in the mind of an innocent person the disposition to commit the alleged offense and induce its commission." Thus, the offense must be procured from an otherwise wholly innocent defendant. The prosecution thus has the opportunity to make an "appropriate and searching inquiry into [the defendant's] conduct and predisposition" as bearing on his claim of innocence. The result is that the defense of entrapment can rarely be proved to the satisfaction of a jury and is seldom attempted.

The doctrine of entrapment evolved largely out of prosecutions of sumptuary laws—narcotics, prostitution and gambling —where use of informers and solicitation was considered imperative and where the rights of the defendants were submerged under a tide of morality. The law should be reconstructed, at least when applied in other contexts, to take into account the realities of FBI practices in national security investigations.

An important beginning would be to persuade the courts to place the law of entrapment in a constitutional framework. Such a foundation could readily be found in the Fourth Amendment or in the due process clause. The way would then be open for the use of the right against entrapment as an affirmative instrument to enjoin improper police practices or to penalize police who engage in them.

Another significant reform would be to allow the claim of entrapment as an alternative defense, not dependent upon an admission of guilt. This would probably require a pre-trial determination by the court of whether entrapment had in fact occurred.

A further change would be to impose upon the police the obligation to establish probable cause that a law violation was taking place as a condition of planting an informer in an organization or group. This would have the advantage of eliminating the use of informers altogether except in situations subject to check by the courts, rather than trying to pick up the pieces after the damage had occurred.

Most important of all would be the development of a new definition of entrapment. A suggestion of the lines this might take appears in the minority position of the Supreme Court in its entrapment decisions. According to this view the basic question should be "whether the police conduct revealed in the particular case falls below standards . . . for the proper use of governmental power." The test would then be whether the government agent went beyond the proper degree of encouragement. The acceptance of such a theory would go far to make entrapment doctrine a major obstacle to the excesses of the Bureau in using informers in the national security field.

4. The Fourth Amendment

The Fourth Amendment provides that the "right of the people to be secure in their persons, houses, papers, and effects, against unreasonable searches and seizures, shall not be violated." One of its primary purposes, as revealed by both English and American history, was to protect the right of political opposition against unwarranted intrusions by official authority. Moreover, the employment of informers and infiltrators has always been recognized as "dirty business": informers are likely to be unsavory characters; the product of their labors must be viewed with distrust; the practice requires the government to engage in gross deceptions in dealing with its citizens; the whole process is associated with a totalitarian type of secret police. In view of this background, one would expect the Fourth Amendment to be an important factor in curbing the use of informers in political surveillance. But, surprisingly, this is not the case.

The legal issues that the courts must consider in dealing with the Fourth Amendment revolve around three major problems. First, does the government's action that is challenged constitute a "search" or "seizure"—is the Fourth Amendment applicable at all? Second, if the conduct falls within the terms of the amendment, was the search or seizure "unreasonable"? Third, if the search or seizure would be reasonable, what procedures are required; is a warrant necessary and upon what basis should it be issued? The development of Fourth Amendment law with respect to informers has been hung up on the first problem.

In its first major decision on the scope of the Fourth Amendment the Supreme Court gave the constitutional mandate a broad application. *Boyd* v. *United States* in 1886 held that a legal proceeding to compel a defendant to produce books and papers violated both the Fourth and Fifth Amendments. The Fourth Amendment, said the court, applied to "all invasions on the part of the government and its employees of the sanctity of a man's home and the privacies of life. It is not the breaking of his doors and the rummaging of his drawers, that constitutes the essence of the offence; but it is the invasion of his indefeasible right of personal security, personal liberty, and private property."

Later decisions, however, drastically curtailed the Fourth

Amendment's application. Thus, in *Olmstead* v. *United States*, and in subsequent cases, mostly involving forms of electronic surveillance, the court majority came to accept a property theory of the Fourth Amendment. In that view only those government intrusions that infringed lawfully held property rights were within the coverage of the amendment. Such a position left no room for application of the Fourth Amendment to the use of informers (apart from a situation where the informer's methods involved a trespass upon property) and in three cases in 1966 the court in effect took this position.

Meanwhile, as we have seen, the property theory of the Fourth Amendment was abandoned in two cases decided in 1967—*Berger* v. *New York* and *Katz* v. *United States*. The *Berger* and *Katz* cases, overruling *Olmstead*, held that the Fourth Amendment did apply to wiretapping and other forms of electronic surveillance, regardless of whether trespass or other invasion of physical property had occurred. At this point the Supreme Court seemed on the verge of returning to the *Boyd* theory—that any intrusion by the government upon personal security and liberty would be subject to the Fourth Amendment. That hope was dashed in *United States* v. *White* when the court reaffirmed its position that the activities of an informer (using a concealed radio transmitter) were not within the scope of Fourth Amendment limitations. The Supreme Court has never squarely faced the question, however, whether the Fourth Amendment applies to the use of informers for political surveillance.

The current position of the Supreme Court seems wholly inconsistent with the original purpose and present function of the Fourth Amendment. A government informer, acting as a government agent to obtain information from unsuspecting citizens, is surely engaged in a search and a seizure. His conduct plainly constitutes an intrusion by the government into the personal privacy and liberty of those upon whom he reports. The fact that the information is obtained by deception rather than by forceful entry would not seem to be a decisive factor. The whole process violates the basic right the Fourth Amendment was designed to protect—the right to be let alone. Moreover, it seriously interferes with the right of political opposition: dissenting activities cannot be carried on with the government looking over the citizen's shoulder.

The Supreme Court is undoubtedly reluctant, for practical reasons, to place controls over the ancient police practice of employing informers. The record of the FBI to date, however, and the possibility of greater abuse in the future make it imperative that the court return to the original premises of the Fourth Amendment, and make that guarantee applicable to the use of government informers, at least in the area of national security investigators.

Once the informer system is brought under the control of the Fourth Amendment, other problems could be faced and resolved. The next issue would be to determine what kinds of informer practice constitute an "unreasonable" search or seizure and so are totally forbidden. Two points of reference in drawing the line between "reasonable" and "unreasonable" are important.

First, for reasons already stated, the use of informers for the collection of general political intelligence or data pertaining to prevention of possible political offenses in the future would fall into the category of an unreasonable search and seizure. Use in direct crime investigation, on the other hand, would be prima facie reasonable. Second, the delineation between unreasonable and reasonable would be marked by various factors relating to the methods used. Some of the considerations would be: the degree to which the government took the initiative in placing the informer, the kind of controls the government exercised over the informer, the manner in which the informer obtained information and especially the extent to which the informer participated in the activities of the persons or organizations he was assigned to watch.

Finally, in those cases where the use of informers would not constitute an unreasonable search or seizure, important questions of procedure would arise. Under the Fourth Amendment a warrant would be mandatory, at least in all but exceptional situations, before the government could employ an informer. This would require the government to make a showing of "probable cause," supported by oath, and to describe "particularly" the scope of the informer's activities and the nature of information he was to obtain. The warrant procedure could also be used to compel a statement of the duration of the operation and the kind of deception contemplated.

Again, there are many practical problems. Experience has shown that the role of the judicial officer in issuing a warrant may be merely to rubber-stamp the whole process. There are signs, however, that the Supreme Court will rigorously insist that the judicial officer make a more knowledgeable decision in warrant cases. Hence, the requirement of judicial supervision could become a more useful control. Furthermore, the warrant procedure would produce a better record than we now have of how much and where the FBI uses the informer system.

D. CONCLUSIONS

The conclusion to be drawn from this survey is that our judicial system is capable of affording a much more effective protection than it now does against infringements of the Bill of Rights by the FBI and other police agencies. The fundamental principles embodied in the Bill of Rights were designed to safeguard the citizen against the very dangers now confronting us. But the courts have failed to adapt the ancient principles to the new conditions. Particularly, they have failed to apply constitutional guarantees to the civil liberties threats that are justified in the name of "national security." Unless the courts bring the Bill of Rights up to date in this area, judicial protection against improper Bureau practices will remain weak.

III: Protective Measures: Legislative and Executive

The role which can be played by legal principles and legal institutions is limited in itself and ineffective without support from the whole community. It is, therefore, necessary to look to other institutions and other methods as well. Two prime elements are involved. One is the overriding importance of access to information about the FBI operations. The other is the development of techniques for scrutiny and supervision of those operations.

Access to information is essential for any control because there is no other way by which the issues can be known, understood, confronted and solved. There are, of course, many difficulties. A police force, especially a security police force, cannot operate altogether in the open. Yet this fact simply makes the problem harder; it does not lessen its significance. Uncontrollable strength and power grow out of secrecy. Not only does concealment permit and encourage abuses of authority and prevent rectification, but it feeds the rumors, ignorance and myth-making which envelop a security police. Secrecy permits the police force to play upon fear, manipulate public opinion and further aggrandize its power.

Scrutiny and supervision by outside agencies are equally important. James Madison and the founding fathers rested their hopes of an open society on a system of checks and balances, and history has confirmed their theories. Yet the FBI is virtually unique in its isolation and independence. It is a self-perpetuating, ingrown institution shielded from any supervision and even from criticism.

In seeking greater visibility and greater supervision, it should be possible to rely to some extent upon existing institutions. The President and the Attorney General owe an obligation to the American people to establish control over the FBI. Congress, through its appropriation committees, judiciary committees and special investigating committees, should begin to treat the Bureau like any other agency in the executive branch. And the Bureau itself should be reshaped in ways that have been proposed, not the least of which is to have as its Director a person who is not by profession a policeman.

But it seems clear that this will not be enough. The FBI is not any ordinary institution, and it has not reached its present entrenched position by accident or by the work of one man. There is need for some special machinery designed to meet the special problem of controlling a security police force.

The form this machinery should take grows out of two basic considerations. First, a security police can never be controlled without mobilizing power outside the governmental apparatus. The government is so obsessed with its law-and-order function, so ridden with bureaucratic loyalties, so vulnerable to its own investigators that it cannot be trusted to curb its police force. The way must be shown by independent forces in the community who represent the long-range aspirations of the society and are less committed to the immediate fortunes of the administration in power.

Second, individual citizens must have a direct, assured method, separate from the cumbersome judicial process, for airing complaints that the Bureau has abused its authority.

These two requirements are not met by the same kind of machinery. The first calls for a board of overseers, composed of distinguished private citizens who are committed to the principles of an open society and see the problems in a different way from the Bureau and the government. Such a board would have access to all Bureau records and activities. It would review the Bureau's policies, scrutinize its programs and inspect its operations. It would make periodic and special reports to the President and the Attorney General, to Congress and to the public. Recommendations of the board would not be binding on the government but probably they would let in some light and be influential. The power of the board would rest upon its understanding of the ground rules of a democratic society and its appeal to the democratic conscience of the nation.

The other type of machinery calls for an ombudsman, having authority to receive and investigate citizen complaints. He too would have access to Bureau materials, power to obtain information necessary to his inquiries and authority to recommend remedial action.

No mere reform of present institutions or establishment of new ones will, of course, solve the basic problem of holding a security police within the boundaries of the Bill of Rights. Ultimately, the only solution rests on an understanding of the dangers, a commitment to watch for their appearance and the courage to demand their correction. Such a solution must be found in the attitudes and actions of the nation's leadership, official and non-official. But even more it demands a positive acceptance of the principles of an open society by the community as a whole.

IV: Conference Discussion

MR. NAVASKY: Mr. Emerson, how much of the ideology that you identify, such as the equation of national security with the traditional American way of life, do you feel is conscious and emanates from the top and trickles down through the

Bureau and how much is built into the mission of the FBI and into the systems, the internal systems, of the Bureau?

MR. EMERSON: I would say both contribute. I would say that the present Director, who is not the first Director but the sixth, but who has been Director since 1924, was brought up in the Red scares of World War I and was imbued with that messianic anti-Communist philosophy that has permeated the Bureau. The nature of the Bureau would be somewhat different under another Director.

On the other hand, almost any national security police would tend to approach its job in this same way. It attracts persons who have those feelings about the problem. It has a job to do. Any bureaucracy tends to develop further and further in the direction in which it is originally set, so any security police will attempt to solve national security problems by enforcing law and order and by ignoring a solution that responds to social conditions. That can be expected and that's why any organization needs to be kept under surveillance itself, and needs to be supervised.

My feeling about the problem of supervision is that the government itself does not have the independent power really to deal with its own national security police force—that the only forces that are sufficient are those independent, nongovernmental, enlightened forces, represented by the press, the media, the university, the dissonant groups themselves and so forth. These will insist upon an adherence to the right of freedom of expression. That's why I feel that something outside the government, some board of overseers outside the government, must exist to counteract the inevitable effect of both the Bureau as it now exists and a Bureau as it is likely to exist in the future.

MR. WRIGHT: A question of Mr. Emerson. You said that the FBI conceives of itself as an instrument to prevent "radical social change in America." Is that a fair comment? Isn't the

FBI really involved in working against groups and individuals who threaten democratic processes in this country, and openly so? Today the FBI views itself as protecting the democratic decision-making processes for the rest of us. I guess we have a basic disagreement between us on this point. I think that the FBI and the government in general have the duty to see that the radicals don't get away with this process of intimidation of the rest of us.

I think that too often in this country discussion centers on the rights of the radicals, of their free expression, and we tend to ignore the right of the rest of us to resist what they intend for this country. I think that the government has the right and the duty to resist, and I think that we should recognize the difference between influencing the democratic processes by means of free speech, and other rights that are protected under the Constitution, and the revolutionary attempt to effect change in this country.

MR. EMERSON: I simply disagree with your conclusion that the Bureau confines itself to the area you have in mind. It's obviously the function of the Bureau to enforce the ground rules of the democratic process, and one of the ground rules of the democratic process is that you solve problems by expression and not by violence and similar illegal means. There's no doubt that we need a police force to enforce those ground rules.

The problem, as I see it, and I think it's a fair comment— you may disagree—but it's my conclusion that the Bureau goes far beyond that. They start perhaps from that position, but then they extend themselves into areas of opinion and beliefs and associations that are differently related or have no connection with the use of undemocratic methods. I would also add that the basic principle of freedom of expression is that the rights of everyone are interlocked, that persons who engage in violence are still nevertheless to be protected when they don't engage in violence, and, in fact, are to be encouraged not to engage in violence by being protected when they use peaceful methods of persuasion. Consequently, they have rights too that must be protected. The Bureau doesn't recognize that sort of a distinction, and in its zeal it goes far beyond any limitation on legitimate law-enforcement operations.

Mr. Broderick: I don't quite understand, Professor Emerson, where you are drawing the line on the FBI's proper function. Do you say under no circumstances it should involve itself in intelligence gathering, or are you saying that political intelligence gathering is impermissible but that criminal intelligence gathering is permissible and we need some supervision to see that the line is adhered to?

Mr. Emerson: That's a question on which I hope to get help from this conference. That is, I believe, the key question with respect to the analysis and proposals I've made. It is very difficult to draw that line between legitimate enforcement operations and general political intelligence or general preventive measures. In its extremes, I think the line can be drawn. When the Federal Bureau of Investigation first started, it started under a mandate of that sort, that it was to investigate only violations or suspected violations of specific federal laws, and Attorney General Stone, in appointing Mr. Hoover to the directorship, gave him explicit instructions with respect to that. Later, the Bureau branched far beyond that, and it is very difficult to draw the line. The line I attempt to draw is, yes, between criminal activities and information directly related to that, and political non-criminal activities and general intelligence of a political nature, the building of dossiers about millions of citizens, operations of that sort.

It seems to me also that the Bureau has adopted a policy of limiting its operations to strictly legal violations in the civil rights field, and probably in other fields. It has consistently said that its function in the civil rights field was merely to investigate violations, and it has tended to confine itself to that. Now, even there, of course, it has infiltrated the Ku Klux Klan, and that's a kind of problem. I would say that the Ku Klux Klan is probably an organization that is not only violence-prone but violence-directed. The surveillance is probably correct. I would draw the distinction perhaps between the Ku Klux Klan and the John Birch Society. But the Bureau did infiltrate, as the Media papers indicate, every black student organization. That is roughly the difference and I hope the conference will help me build the particulars.

MR. H. H. WILSON:* Perhaps I didn't understand Mr. Emerson, but did you say the FBI should be able to investigate, collect dossiers and so on, where there was suspicion of illegal action?

MR. EMERSON: Reasonable cause to suspect a criminal activity.

MR. WILSON: Doesn't that leave the whole thing wide open again?

MR. EMERSON: It does open it, and I think the only way to solve that is by a much more intensive survey of specific situations than I have undertaken. Again, I say that the outlines of the principle involved are to my mind fairly clear. The application of it becomes very difficult. This is in part because every dissonant political organization that is at all militant is likely to have overtones of law violations, or law violators, on its fringes, or be suspected of possible law violations. If you add, so far as the younger groups are concerned, the problem of drug violations, you get into a very difficult situation in enforcing a rule that you only investigate criminal violations.

I admit those difficulties and, as I say, it would be a major step forward if we could specify how to draw that line, but

* Professor of Politics, Princeton University.

I think the line must be drawn. Also, this is the advantage of having supervision. It's not a line that one can attempt to draw on paper and then leave up to the organization itself to enforce. No bureaucracy could possibly be held within that kind of general principle. It's a general principle that has to be enforced from outside the bureaucracy, by the Attorney General, by congressional committees and by some board of public citizens with access to the information.

MR. CARRINGTON: Professor Emerson, in May of this year a national magazine commissioned a Gallup poll to study the reactions of the American people to the FBI. The poll showed an 80 per cent favorable to 4 per cent unfavorable opinion of the FBI. But on the specific areas to which you address yourself, tapping telephones and using electronic bugs, the poll showed that 52 per cent approved while 25 per cent were opposed. Seventy-one per cent approved investigating political and protest groups while 12 per cent were opposed. Seventy-four per cent approved having the agency attend protest demonstrations while 7 per cent were opposed.

Now, this seems to me to be an overwhelming mandate by the American people for the FBI to engage in the investigative practices that you have opposed so vigorously here.

MR. EMERSON: Well, suppose you try the Gallup poll on the question: Should the FBI investigate political groups in such a way as to give the impression that there is an FBI agent behind every mailbox? This is what the Media documents indicate was a Bureau point of view. Suppose you asked, in a Gallup poll: Should the FBI infiltrate groups with persons who will teach members how to make bombs, encourage members to bomb buildings and participate in actual illegal activities? How do you think the public would respond to that?

The issue is, of course, given the FBI's version of its operations and its account of the dangers that are involved, the public has been led to believe that the FBI performs an important function. And it does.

But our job here, it seems to me, is to make the people aware of what the facts are, and if the people, when fully aware of the facts, take the position that infiltrators should encourage people to bomb buildings, I will at that point go along with it, but not until I'm convinced that we understand what the real issues are.

I think that, for the first time in many years, the public is beginning to understand what the problem is, and how far the Bureau has gone beyond its original purposes and beyond its proper purposes.

MR. NEIER: There's a reference in your paper, Professor Emerson, to the possibilities of placing some of the FBI's surveillance practices under the Fourth Amendment. I think that is a hopeful way of having some determination made before the FBI conducts surveillance on whether a particular situation falls into the criminal activity realm or only that of political activity.

But there's a practice of the FBI, hinted at in the Media papers, which was made more explicit by a certain FBI surveillance and has come into the open because of a court proceeding. The surveillance was of the November 15, 1969, moratorium. The practice is, in essence, this.

An FBI agent visited a bank to look at the bank records of a group sponsoring buses to Washington, D.C., for the moratorium. The Media papers indicate that the FBI also obtained the unlisted telephone number of an individual associated with a black economic development group in Philadelphia. The FBI, in pre-trial examinations in the moratorium case, said they had obtained the bank records. In case they ever wanted to sue them in court, they had listed on their own records the bank officer who would have to be subpoenaed in order to obtain the same bank records they already had. In the Media papers, the Bureau noted the telephone company official who would have to be subpoenaed in order to obtain the unlisted telephone number they already had.

In essence, what the FBI is doing is relying on the fact that the only control the courts have fashioned for protection of Fourth Amendment rights is an exclusionary rule. They engage in surveillance without any kind of restraints by the Fourth Amendment or anything else. Only if they should happen to need the material in court do they go back and follow proper procedures, with judicial supervision, in order to get the same material in a way that makes it legally admissible.

It seems to me that, in essence, this nullifies any capacity of the Fourth Amendment, at least under its present application by the courts, to control the FBI system of political intelligence. The political intelligence first takes place; then, if the information is ever needed in court, the Bureau will follow Fourth Amendment rules.

MR. EMERSON: That's correct, and that's also one of the major problems. A large part of what is done, in terms of the collection of political intelligence, never comes under the scrutiny of the courts because it remains in the FBI files or is used in a different way; it never comes to be used as evidence. An extension of the Fourth Amendment to require a court warrant prior to placing an informer in an organization, for instance, or prior to engaging in certain kinds of investigatory activities, would be helpful and would, in the course of time, draw the line between what is legitimate and what is illegitimate for the FBI to do. But it would not by itself be a solution. The only solution I see is to open FBI operations to greater scrutiny.

MR. ELLIFF: Since it seems the FBI intelligence operations are based neither on statutory authority nor constitutional authority, I'd like you to comment on two particular issues.

First, the statutory authority of the FBI was changed in the mid-1960s to authorize the FBI to specifically assist in the protection of the President. This was done after the Warren Commission held hearings, of which the transcripts were made public, where the FBI Director and other officials testified that the Bureau's intelligence included "gathering information about subversives, ultra-rightists, racists and fascists whose prior acts or statements depict propensity for violence and hatred against organized government."

Now, this was on the record before Congress authorized the FBI to assist in the protection of the President. These procedures and methods, sweeping intelligence methods, were acknowledged by the Bureau in its open testimony before the Warren Commission, and this was there for Congress to see when it made that explicit authorization.

Second, on the constitutional power, I would like you to comment on the argument that's asserted, by Mr. Rehnquist and others, that the inherent power of the President, based in part on the guarantee clause, and perhaps more importantly, on the power of the President to enforce the laws, would be sufficient to authorize intelligence gathering on any subject relevant to the President's governmental responsibilities.

MR. EMERSON: On your first suggestion of statutory authority by virtue of the obligation to protect the President, it seems to me quite clear that a statute of that sort would not authorize the FBI to maintain dossiers on 2 million people just on the off-chance that they may be around when the President comes to make a speech sometime. It clearly has never been intended to extend that far, and if it did, it would be unconstitutional.

The protection of the President is not something that can be solved by keeping an index of every potential subversive. That's a philosophy the FBI indulges in far too much—that you can maintain a complete system of scrutiny, that you can have 100 per cent security. It's impossible. Everybody knows that except the FBI. There has to be a certain laxness in the system, a certain looseness, or you'll have a police state. Protection of the President, which incidentally is the main function of the Secret Service, not the FBI, could not possibly be used as a basis for the kind of political intelligence gathering that the FBI now engages in.

On the constitutional point, Mr. Rehnquist is completely wrong, and I think his colleagues will show him that he's wrong when it comes up before the Supreme Court. The inherent power of the President, as the steel seizure case indicates, does not allow the President to do whatever is necessary, in his opinion, to safeguard the security of the country. He is bound by constitutional limitations.

Mr. Rehnquist, I'm sure, would agree that the President cannot violate the First Amendment. He cannot violate the Fourth Amendment no matter what he thinks is necessary to protect the security of the country. In my judgment, the Fourth Amendment does not allow the President to tap wires in national security cases without a warrant. Any theory of emergency or inherent presidential powers just carries us into a whole area of dictatorship which is entirely foreign to our constitutional system.

MR. LEWIN: Professor Emerson, is the important problem you focused on presented whenever excessive governmental action impinges on constitutional rights as a result of the unilateral authority of a government official? Specifically, there have been charges in recent months of excessive use of grand jury investigations to impinge on First Amendment rights. There have been charges of mass arrests. Is the FBI problem in any way different in kind from those presented in these other areas?

MR. EMERSON: Yes. It's different in kind. It's very similar, of course; that is, there are many other areas in our national life today where there are serious infringements on the Bill of Rights, or possibilities of them. And the FBI situation is only one aspect of that. But it is different in the sense that here you have an organization of several thousand agents in a highly disciplined, highly centralized, highly organized institution that is devoting a large part of its activities to recording and surveying the political activities of American dissenters. I think that nowhere else do you find that concentration of power, that potentiality. The political police of any state is a major problem far beyond that of most other problems.

Let me add one other thing. I agree with you that one cannot solve these issues by looking solely at the Federal Bureau of Investigation. For one thing, we have to look at some of the statutes on our books now which infringe on political rights because, if a statute, such as the Smith Act, authorized punishment for expression of opinion, then the FBI can investigate expression of opinion because that's a violation of law. So to some extent we need to look at some of the laws on our books to see that they are brought into line with a system of freedom of expression.

Mr. Dorsen: I wanted to pick up a point Mr. Carrington made in connection with the results of the poll he quoted. I'm not personally familiar with that particular poll but, as Professor Emerson pointed out, I'm sure we would all agree that the results of any poll depend in large measure on just the way the question is framed. And the questions concerning the FBI can be framed in a variety of ways.

But even apart from that, it seems to me pretty clear that polls cannot determine the rights of the people of the United States under the Constitution.

I am familiar with the results of a poll taken about a year or two ago in which those questioned were asked if they approved of certain individual provisions of the Bill of Rights with the source not identified. And when those provisions were put to the people, a majority of them voted against the Bill of Rights.

It's important to recall, I think, that someone as conservative as Justice Robert Jackson, who was formerly Attorney General of the United States, in the famous flag salute case went out of his way to point out that the rights of the people cannot depend on any poll. They cannot depend on any majority.

The kind of issues that Professor Emerson has raised, while very difficult, do obviously touch upon First Amendment rights. And the people here today, and ultimately the courts and the Supreme Court, are going to have to determine those rights, and I don't think they can be determined by what a majority, a shifting and vague majority of the people, think at any one time.

The whole purpose of the Bill of Rights was to protect minorities, not majorities.

PART V
CONCLUSIONS

CHAPTER SEVENTEEN

LESSONS OF THE CONFERENCE

BY PAT WATTERS AND STEPHEN GILLERS

The participants at the Princeton FBI conference did not attempt to reach a consensus or formulate resolutions. That was not their goal. The conference was intended to provide a forum for a thorough citizen review of the Bureau and of the relationship between its activities and the well-being of the nation. But in editing the conference papers and discussion, we have discovered certain recurring themes. Among them:

Performance. Is the FBI's performance in law enforcement as efficient and effective as the public interest demands?

Control. How secret are Bureau operations and policy formulation? To what extent are these subject to public control?

Rights. To what extent do the Bureau's activities threaten the civil rights and civil liberties of Americans?

The conference participants made a number of suggestions with regard to each of these and related topics. These suggestions are appropriate starting points for further public debate. For convenience, a summary of the conference suggestions, all of which have been discussed in this book, are collected here.

We do not analyze the merits of any of the following

proposals—that is the job of the preceding chapters—but only summarize the important ones. The accompanying page citations refer to the major places in the book where the suggestion was made and related matter discussed.

FBI Investigative and Information-Gathering Powers. "The most important single step which should be taken to safeguard the Bill of Rights is to limit the statutory authority of the FBI to the narrow function of assisting directly in the enforcement of those federal laws over which it is given jurisdiction" (p. 418, Ch. 16 generally). This limitation should apply to the accumulation of dossiers, the use of informers, including the infiltration of private organizations, and electronic surveillance (pp. 349–50, Ch. 13). The test for the use of these information-gathering techniques should be Fourth Amendment standards (pp. 202–5, 434, 444). To the extent that national security interests permit electronic or informer surveillance without traditional protection, standards should nevertheless be established to control such activity and protect against the unchecked consequences (pp. 364–65, 366).

Counterespionage and Anti-Subversion Intelligence. A separate agency, inside or outside the Bureau, should have responsibility to investigate espionage and subversive activities (pp. 116–18, 216, 288–89). There are several reasons for this. The Bureau's defensive functions have clashed with the CIA's offensive ones; this conflict has caused mutual resentment and non-cooperation (pp. 116–17). Also, routine police activities demand skills different from the specialized and complex ones needed in counterespionage work (pp.116–18).

A separate intelligence service subject to review by a permanent domestic intelligence advisory board, empowered by the President to review all aspects of domestic intelligence, might also be established (pp. 288–89).

Loyalty-Security Investigations. There should be further study of the FBI's responsibilities in the loyalty-security area because the "chain of inquiry which starts with searching out 'loyalty' and 'subversive activities' is an endless one" (p. 240). Keeping the names of individual informers secret while publicizing the existence of an informer network whose purpose it is to discover loyalty-security threats is intimidating and demoralizing (pp. 52–53, 350, Ch. 13). Questioning a person's neighbors and friends about that person "leaves a very strong impression that somehow or other this guy is really a bad guy and you should watch out for him too" (p. 104). The Bureau's responsibilities here must be narrowly defined and carefully weighed against competing societal interests in privacy and freedom (pp. 412–14).

Reassertion of Executive and Legislative Policy and Budgetary Controls. In general, the Bureau should be subject to periodic scrutiny (p. 288). Congress should exercise its legitimate supervisory function and undertake a full-scale review of the Bureau's policies and budget (pp. 62–63, 288). Congress should require that the FBI, like other federal agencies, submit an itemized rather than a block budget (p. 64). The budget should be subject to thorough Justice Department as well as congressional review (pp. 65–66, 78, Ch. 3).

The Bureau should not be permitted to lend agents to Congress, including the House Appropriations Committee. This allows the Bureau to "serve" both the executive and legislative branches simultaneously (p. 82).

It was also suggested that the Bureau should withdraw its opposition to allowing agents to work under Justice Department task force attorneys (p. 210). Task force attorneys are competent to assume responsibility for agents. The Bureau's slight loss of control is not a sufficient reason to prohibit this innovation.

Finally, in appointing a new Director, the President might reassert executive control by appointing someone from outside the Bureau who would bring fresh ideas and talents to the position (pp. 107–8).

Democratic Control. Two other suggestions to make the Bureau responsive to democratic control, especially on a day-to-day basis, are (a) the creation of a board of overseers composed of public and private persons with power to review Bureau policy-making, guard against threats to civil liberties and keep the public informed; and (b) the appointment of a Bureau ombudsman with power to respond to individual citizens' claims of abuse or denial of rights (pp. 436–37).

Dissemination of Derogatory Information. Dissemination of derogatory information about individuals should generally be limited to the fact of conviction and not mere arrests (pp. 135–36, 228, 234, Ch. 9). The fact of conviction should be disseminated only for law-enforcement purposes, narrowly construed (pp. 136, 223, 234, Ch. 9). The Bureau should not become a "national credit bureau," dispensing derogatory information to private organizations (e.g., banks, insurance companies, credit card companies) (p. 291).

Purging of and Access to Files. Individuals should have the right to see and challenge any information the FBI has accumulated about them. Rational guidelines for purging outdated and misleading information should be formulated (p. 235).

Civil Right Enforcement. There were suggestions pertaining to the Bureau's responsibilities to investigate violations of federally protected civil rights. The Bureau should consider training a special group of agents to have primary responsibility in this field (p. 201). The Bureau should hire more minority group agents and abolish its unwritten policy to place few or no black agents in the South (pp. 187, 193, 201). The number of women agents should be significantly increased (p. 97–98). The Bureau should also consider the creation of a separate FBI division to handle police misconduct cases so that the agents who work with local police will not also have the responsibility to investigate charges against them (p. 217). These actions would provide more effective protection to minorities from local police abuse and increase Bureau sensitivity to racial problems.

Organized Crime. There was a feeling at the conference that the Bureau has inexplicably failed to give organized criminal activities the attention our national interests require. Such attention should include greater cooperation with local police (p. 120, Ch. 6).

Local Police. The FBI should give more official cooperation to other law-enforcement agencies, especially local police. A free exchange of information between the Bureau and local police is hampered by the Bureau's lack of reciprocity (p. 118).

It was suggested that local police should control the central fingerprint file because they use it 99 per cent of the time, and that the International Association of Chiefs of Police or a similar group should administer a federally funded National Crime Information Center (p. 122).

The conferees discussed the FBI's role and effectiveness in training local police. The Bureau should not have central authority in this area because it hasn't the expertise. There are fundamental differences between the jobs of FBI agents and of policemen (pp. 124–31). Also, central FBI authority here gives the appearance and creates the risk of a national police force (p. 122). The Bureau should be encouraged, however, to provide technical aid to local police departments and assist them in institutional reforms (p. 127, Ch. 4).

Propagating a Political Ideology. The Bureau Director should be prohibited from propagating a political ideology in books and articles. If a prohibition is undesirable, then the President should appoint, and the Senate confirm, a Director sensitive to the problems raised by such activity (pp. 30, 201, 202).

Statistics. The FBI has brought some order to crime statistics, but it has used these figures to prove extraordinary success and to influence congressional budgetary decisions. As a result, the Bureau has concentrated on statistic-producing crimes (e.g., stolen cars) to the detriment of other areas (e.g., organized crime) (pp. 78–79, 132–33). An independent agency, charged with collecting and analyzing national crime data according to approved statistical techniques, could provide neutrality and greater accuracy (p. 135).

Less Concern for Image. The FBI's obsession with self-image has had a number of undesirable effects. Innovation and reform within the Bureau has been hampered (p. 106). The Bureau has "lulled" the public "into a false sense of security" (p. 88). It has created a "megalomania in the leadership." Agents are not permitted to criticize the Bureau (pp. 106–7) and are punished for "embarrassment to the Bureau" (p. 88). Misleading statistics concerning the racial, ethnic and sexual composition of the FBI are propagated (pp. 96–97, 97–98). The Bureau has fired agents and other employees who have participated in political activities disapproved of by the Bureau (p. 99).

Protection of Agents' Rights. The FBI should be open to agents' criticisms (pp. 103–6). Furthermore, agents should be able to challenge the Bureau's policies without fear of reprisal (e.g., demotion, assignment to undesirable locations or expulsion) (pp. 89, 107).

At the conclusion of the FBI conference, Norman Dorsen, speaking for himself and his two co-chairmen, Duane Lockard and Burke Marshall, said:

> We were initially reluctant to hold a conference on the FBI because we were concerned that in the past even constructive criticism of the Bureau had been misconstrued to be an attack against it.

This was not our purpose. The level at which this conference has progressed is the best answer to such a charge. None of us denies the need for effective law enforcement but each of us wants to see that job performed in the best way possible.

Perhaps the most important lesson of this conference is that the American people need more information about an institution that has played so instrumental a role in their lives during the last half century. We have raised many questions these last two days and answered a few. But the scarcity of information available to the public about the Bureau has necessarily limited our inquiries.

Still it is as important to ask the right questions as it is to have the answers. And, of course, the questions must be asked before answers are even possible.

Further study is needed. We urge our legislative representatives to consider a national commission of inquiry that would answer the many questions raised here. The Senate itself, which now has the power to approve the next FBI Director, might assume this responsibility. The important point is that such an inquiry should seek neither to vindicate nor condemn the Bureau. It should seek only to improve it.

For fifty years a powerful federal agency has not had the thorough review that we believe freedom and good government require in a democracy. Public officials have not conducted such a review. And private citizens find themselves unable to do so thoroughly for lack of public information. We have made a start here, but it is only a start. We urge the Congress to continue.

The FBI conference was conceived and conducted to be an examination of the institution, the Federal Bureau of Investigation. This book reflects that intention. Whatever may be the views of future Directors, conservative or liberal, the powers and structure of the Bureau should not be theirs alone to determine. These threshold issues are fundamental to the quality of life in a democracy and should be answered only after a full public debate. The question of who watches the watchers will always test democracy's commitment to freedom, but it is a question that must be answered. In the case of the FBI, the nation has so far answered it by looking the other way.

APPENDIX

CALL TO THE CONFERENCE

AND CORRESPONDENCE WITH

J. EDGAR HOOVER

CALL TO THE CONFERENCE

The Committee for Public Justice and the Woodrow Wilson School at Princeton University are co-sponsoring a Conference on the FBI at *Corwin Hall* on the Princeton campus, October 29 and 30.

The Conference chairmen are Burke Marshall, deputy Dean of the Yale Law School, Duane Lockard, chairman of the Princeton Politics Department, and Norman Dorsen, Professor of Law at New York University Law School.

The Conference is conceived and planned as a scholarly effort to understand the structure of the FBI and its powers and role in American society. Apparently, no private or public body has before attempted such a study. This fact, we think, provides sufficient reason to do so now.

There are, however, two other reasons. First, public debate about the Bureau has increased in recent years, but this debate has been piecemeal and of mixed quality. Perhaps it has confused more issues than it has cleared up. Furthermore, it lacks the over-all framework that the current Conference can provide. A new law giving the Senate power to approve the next FBI Director is the second additional reason to hold this conference. This law provides an excellent opportunity for a Congressional evaluation of the Bureau. The co-sponsors believe that facts developed and issues highlighted at the current Conference will aid that evaluation.

The FBI has frequently been the subject of the type of public discussion that is calculated more to have a political effect than to contribute to an intelligent understanding of the Bureau and its work. The co-sponsors are aware of this and have conceived, and are determined to conduct, the Conference on the FBI in a non-partisan and scholarly manner. Accordingly, we have invited men and women of different disciplines and points of view to participate in the discussion. We have asked the Attorney General of the United States and the Director of the FBI to send representatives. We have invited the press and the public. Finally, to assure that the proceedings are fully exposed to the test of public opinion, we have arranged to publish portions of them.

We intend to explore the structure, role and powers of the FBI. Since we are private citizens, without access to all relevant information, this goal is difficult, but not impossible. We approach it in three ways: First, we have asked a number of men and women to prepare and deliver papers on the Bureau's activities in particular areas; second, we have formed panels of individuals who have had experience with the Bureau; third, we have invited other knowledgeable persons to attend the Conference and actively participate in the roundtable discussion of the papers and the panels.

We have arranged for papers and panels in those areas where the Bureau's responsibilities are most evident. These include civil rights, organized crime, the Bill of Rights, and the Bureau's relationship with local police departments. In addition, we will explore whatever role the Bureau may have as a political police force.

We will hear papers and panels on the methods the Bureau uses to achieve results and conduct its business. These include the collection and dissemination of data, the use of informers, and the use of electronic surveillance. In addition, we will study the ways in which the Bureau maintains a positive public image; how, in short, it sells itself. This, too, is an element of its power.

Finally, papers by former agents and a panel of former agents will tell us something about the internal structure of the Bureau and how that structure relates to the Bureau's operation.

Other papers include a historical analysis of the Bureau, an examination of the Bureau's counterparts in Great Britain, and an examination of the Bureau's budget and its relationship with Congress in this area.

Finally, and perhaps one of the more important sources of analysis and information, a panel of former Justice Department lawyers will examine the role, power, and structure of the Bureau by discussing their own experiences with it.

PRINCETON UNIVERSITY
Department of Politics
Princeton, New Jersey 08540

September 28, 1971

The Honorable J. Edgar Hoover
Federal Bureau of Investigation
Washington, D.C.

Dear Mr. Hoover:

The Woodrow Wilson School at Princeton University, in collaboration with the Committee for Public Justice, is conducting a Conference on problems of national police agencies focusing primarily on the Federal Bureau of Investigation. We have commissioned a number of what we hope will be excellent papers analyzing the Bureau and its experience. These papers will be made available prior to the Conference and will be the basis for discussion in the actual sessions.

Since it would be useful to the Conference to have persons present who would strongly defend the Bureau and its role, I hope you will send a representative to attend as an active participant.

The Conference will be held on the Princeton University campus on October 29–30, 1971. If you wish to send a representative please let us know and he or she will be sent the Conference papers in advance.

For your information, I am suggesting to Attorney General John Mitchell that he too send a representative.

Sincerely,

/s/ Duane Lockard

UNITED STATES DEPARTMENT OF JUSTICE
Federal Bureau of Investigation
Washington, D.C. 20535

Office of the Director   *October 7, 1971*

Mr. Duane Lockard
Department of Politics
Princeton University
Princeton, New Jersey 08540

Dear Mr. Lockard:

Thank you for your letter of September 28, 1971, extending to me an invitation for a representative of the FBI to "strongly defend the Bureau and its role" during the forthcoming October conference which will, in your words, focus "primarily on the Federal Bureau of Investigation." We were aware of the plans for the conference, having read the announcements in the press, and some related remarks, critical of the FBI, attributed to persons who apparently will be among the "judges" hearing this case. For example, the press reported, and attributed to persons who appeared to be both spokesmen for your group and "judges" at the inquiry, that ". . . the study could be criticized as being stacked against the FBI," that the FBI is not a "disenthralled seeker of truth," and that "the FBI for reasons I find unfortunate became ideological some time back and this put a scale over its eyes."

While I should like to believe that the correlation between your own words casting us in the role of a defendant, and the critical remarks made by some of the "judges" before the fact-finding inquiry had even begun is one of pure coincidence only, you will understand from that coincidence why I immediately recalled with some amusement the story of the frontier judge who said he would first give the defendant a fair trial and then hang him.

We acknowledge and appreciate your invitation to "defend," but we are declining in view of our serious doubt that any worthwhile purpose could be served by an FBI representative attending an inquiry casting him in the role of defendant before even the first fact is brought out, and condemned by the "judges" before trial begins. It simply is asking too much that any FBI representative appear personally under those circumstances. For that reason I shall try to explain briefly in this letter some of the facts of the FBI "defense," hoping that they will be considered material during the deliberations of your group and in any public reports which you may issue later.

Basically, our position is that the FBI need tailor no special "defense" of its own for this occasion. The basic facts on how the FBI is organized and how it discharges its duties have been so well known for so long, and to so many responsible persons, that they are obvious to all except those who are so blind that they do not wish to see.

The duties assigned to us seem as good a place as any to start. We are well aware that some complain of these claiming infringement on what they contend to be their rights and liberties. There are bank robbers who believe that we should not investigate bank robberies, and thieves and others charged with crimes after investigation who condemn us in court and out. More recently there are those who bomb, riot, and destroy both human life and property for what they claim to be more sophisticated reasons and who resent our investigations as an intrusion into what they esteem to be matters of their own conscience only. We frequently are the targets of personal abuse, of the most vile invectives at the command of both the totalitarian right and the totalitarian left. Yet, neither these nor those who appear to sympathize with them seem willing to publicly admit the basic and obvious fact that our investigative duties are not of our own choosing. They were delivered to us, with the requirement that we take all necessary action, by laws passed by the Congress and by rules and regulations laid down by the President and the Attorney General. We are forever in the unenviable position of the policeman being assaulted by the mob. He neither enacts the law nor judges the legality of it, but it usually is he, and he alone, who must dodge the brickbats hurled by those protesting against it. Any genuine fact-finding inquiry concerning the FBI will admit and underscore these facts.

In performing the duties assigned to us, we are not at all a law unto ourselves as some of our critics would have the American people believe. There are many who monitor us in some way or other; they are a system of checks and balances on the manner in which we perform our duties. Senators and Representatives are interested in how we work. They are free to express their interest and they often do so, individually or collectively. We must investigate our cases to the satisfaction of the Department of Justice, and within the context of such rules as it lays down for us. Our work must satisfy the United States Attorney, who makes an independent decision on whether the case we bring before him will or will not be prosecuted. The United States Magistrate exercises a supervisory authority to accept or reject the adequacy of our reasons shown for asking for an arrest warrant or a search warrant. Our cases which pass the inspection of our monitors up to this point then go before the Federal courts in the uncounted thousands. I am sure you will agree that our work is carefully evaluated in those forums.

In sum, we say that there are many who exercise some official vigilance over the manner in which the FBI performs its duties, that they are to be found in each of the three branches of Government, and that our performance has won the approval of the great majority of them. If your group doubts that the FBI has performed so well, we suggest a fact-finding poll of all living Presidents, Attorneys General, United States Senators, United States Representatives, United States Attorneys, United States Magistrates (and former Commissioners), and Federal judges, with all questions and all answers spread upon the public record so that the people of this nation might see for themselves. Perhaps we are mistaken, but we do believe that if this were done the "defense" of the FBI would be made by others highly qualified, and that it would be one on which we could rest our case.

If it be thought inappropriate to question some, such as the Federal judges, because they must remain impartial at all times, your group could accomplish the same fact-finding results by conducting a review of all reported Federal court decisions in cases investigated by the FBI during the past decade, or as far beyond that as you wish to go to make certain that your study has the necessary depth. You can list and cite for public view all such decisions, calling particular attention to those in which the courts have disapproved our action, and showing the percentage of those cases against the total of all that we have brought to the courts. I assume here that you would also call public attention to those decisions in which the courts have spoken well of FBI work. Further, we suggest that you consider, and report on, the Miranda Rule, the Mallory Rule, the Jencks Rule, the rule on fair lineups, the arrest and search and seizure requirements of the Fourth Amendment, and all the many other rules laid down for control of the Special Agent or other law enforcement officers investigating a criminal case. You will find that we have set an excellent record for obedience to them. With relatively few exceptions our work has met with the approval of the Federal judges. The few exceptions concern us for we know that law enforcement, dealing constantly with those human rights held most sacred, theoretically has no tolerance for error. We know, of course, that we do err, but it is our request that the error be viewed in context and that we be granted the same tolerance extended to others for an occasional mistake.

We venture to suggest one condition which should be set on such polls. If one person in a group is to be polled, *all* should be polled and all should be reported openly and completely. Honest fact-finding admits of nothing less. If the FBI, investigating a criminal case, were to bring a witness against the accused and in any manner deliberately hide the many who would testify in his favor, you would be outraged and justifiably so. We would feel a sense of outrage at similar conduct directed against us. The technique of making one dissenter appear to be representative of a large group which, in fact, is not in agreement with him is a technique of deception and one which any court of inquiry ought to abhor.

I have been speaking of the fact that we try hard to merit the approval of the many who officially monitor our work, and apparently with a reasonable degree of success. We do more than that; we try to improve the investigatory process in those areas in which we are allowed some discretion. Examples of our innovation in this direction are in the public record and should be among the facts of official interest to your group. I shall call a few to your attention.

For centuries the common law which we brought with us from England has held that an officer lawfully may shoot a fleeing felon to prevent his escape. We found that power unnecessary for our particular purposes, and rejected it. The FBI rule now is, and long has been, that a Special Agent or other FBI officer may shoot only in self-defense or the defense of others. If the observance of this rule allows a fleeing felon to escape, we hopefully will apprehend him another day. The rule innovated by the FBI, on its own initiative, raises the sanctity of a human life a notch above that required by the law. We consider this to be significant and hope that you agree.

We have innovated improvements in other areas. During the past decade, Presidents, Governors, Attorneys General, legislators, and others have emphasized the need for police training and education. The FBI saw that need a long time ago. Our FBI National Academy, a 12-week course for selected police officers from states, counties, and cities, and some from friendly foreign nations, opened in 1935 and has been in continuous operation since that time. It is now being substantially expanded. More than 5,000 officers have received this instruction and we have been led to believe that at least the great majority consider it a contribution to better law enforcement.

In a quite different area, the FBI Laboratory has innovated for more effective and humanitarian law enforcement. During recent years, the Supreme Court and the lower courts have emphasized the humanitarian approach toward proving criminal cases more by physical evidence and less by confessions taken from the accused. We like to believe that they have done so on learning that the FBI Laboratory, established in 1932, proved that in many cases it can be done. Scientific examination of evidence leads to proof of guilt or innocence quite independent of anything said by the accused. We are as proud of the cases showing innocence as of those showing guilt and have not been reluctant to say so. That fact should be of interest to your group, for it is another example of professional and humanitarian law enforcement at its best.

Possibly even more important, we have innovated our own rules to better protect the constitutional rights of the accused. I am sure that at least most of those who attend your conference hailed as a great step forward the decision of the Supreme Court in the *Miranda* case which, briefly stated, grants the accused in custody a right to say nothing and a right to a lawyer. Do they know, also, that for decades prior to the Supreme Court edict in *Miranda,* all Special Agents of the FBI were, by our own house rule, over and above the requirements of the courts, advising criminal subjects of those same rights? The Supreme Court willingly took cognizance of the fact in the text of the *Miranda* decision in remarks quite lauda-tory of the FBI. Please note those remarks in *Miranda v. Arizona,* 384 U.S. 436, at 483 (1966), where the Court, speaking through Chief Justice Warren, stated, in part, that "Over the years the Fed-eral Bureau of Investigation has compiled an exemplary record of effective law enforcement. . . ." I suggest that no fact-finding in-vestigation of the FBI would be complete without calling public attention to those words of the Supreme Court.

We have innovated other rules which should commend them-selves to you. For example, in recent years the Supreme Court has strongly emphasized the desirability of making arrests and searches by warrant, a protection for the citizen (and the officer) against over-reaching by the officer whether by honest mistake or otherwise. That rule has been the FBI rule and practice for decades.

In short, we in the FBI have ourselves innovated on our own initiative, above and beyond the legal and administrative require-ments laid down upon us, rules and practices designed for more lawful and humanitarian enforcement of the criminal law. This is a part of our "defense" and we hope that your group will consider it a fact worthy of being brought to public attention.

To do the work of the FBI we have assembled a staff which I believe is so capable that any deep and fair fact-finding study will find it to be one of outstanding honesty and ability. We have sought to develop and enforce work rules to guarantee the taxpayer a day's work, and even a little more, for a day's pay. We have tried to keep our employees free of the corrosive influence of bribery which sometimes has weakened an otherwise honest and effective law enforcement agency. We have admittedly demanded of FBI employees a standard of morality which could be approved by the majority of the American people. On a few occasions we have been told by those who officially monitor us that we have been too strict, but I submit to public judgment the view that in a law enforcement agency, a tax-supported institution, if there is to be error it should be on the side of being too strict rather than being too loose.

It is precisely in this area of employee relations that we have had a few of our most vocal critics. I think it inevitable in any large organization; some will disagree with the rules and some will disobey them. Yet, in our view, discipline is an absolute necessity. An undisciplined law enforcement agency is a menace to society. And discipline, I should add, must have many facets, not the least of which is to curb the enthusiasm of an overzealous Special Agent or official who, in his pursuit of the alleged criminal or subversive, tends to rationalize toward the belief that the end justifies the means, bitterly condemning the curbs on his zeal as a handcuff on what he alleges to be modern and efficient law enforcement. I trust that you will agree.

Here I may as well frankly recognize the fact that your group probably will hear criticism from former Special Agents of the FBI. I trust that you will review that criticism, and report it in proper context. Neither you nor I, nor any other person, can manage a large organization to the total satisfaction of all employees. You have the opportunity of placing this criticism in proper balance if you will take full note of the evidence favorable to the FBI. There is an organization known as The Society of Former Special Agents of the FBI, wholly private and in no way a part of the Government, whose members number in the thousands. It is unique, I believe, in the annals of Government employment. The organization exists, or so I have been told, because its members are proud of having served in the FBI. If your scales of justice are well balanced, I am sure that you will find that the views of these many greatly outweigh those of a dissident few, and I think that fairness requires that the views of the many be so well represented in your inquiry that the difference in weight is made obvious.

Somewhat related to these problems is that of decision making. I believe it my duty to encourage a full expression of employee views on FBI problems, and I do so encourage, quite contrary to statements made by some of the critics. I believe it my duty, as the appointed head of the FBI, to review all views and make the final decision, except where it should be referred to higher authority. I believe it the duty of the employee, once the final decision is made, to either faithfully carry out the directive or marshal convincing proof that it is in error. I submit for judgment the belief that there is no other way to operate an efficient law enforcement organization.

Perhaps the earlier reference to enforcement of the law within the strictures of the law brings up the subject of wiretapping. Being sure that it will come up at your conference, I would like to ask a favor of your group in the interest of fairness. I would think they would wish to show in their report, if such be issued, the Federal law permits wiretapping under controlled circumstances. Further, that in each and every wiretapping, regardless of circumstances, the FBI first obtains the written approval of the Attorney General. Also, that with respect to the wiretapping which occurred before passage of the present Federal statute, the FBI followed the opinions of a long line of Attorneys General that wiretapping was legal. Your attention is called to 63 Yale Law Journal 792, where the then Deputy Attorney General of the United States said, in part, that "It has long been the position of the Department of Justice that the mere interception of telephone communications is not prohibited by Federal law . . . every Attorney General, commencing with William D. Mitchell in 1931, has endorsed the desirability and need for the use of wire tapping as an investigative technique in certain types of cases." All these facts may be well known to your group, but for some reason they often are omitted in public charges that wiretapping by the FBI is without lawful basis. Some critics would have the public believe that the FBI has acted totally outside the law, when the fact is that we simply followed the legal advice given to us by the Attorney General. Your group can set the record straight for all to see, and I hope that you will do so.

These remarks cover the salient points of our "defense" and perhaps not so briefly as either of us might have wished. Obviously they do not cover everything. The ingenuity and the tenacity of our critics preclude a total answer. Were I to attempt to answer all charges I would be debating in this forum or that every day of the year, to the neglect of my duties. If I were to attempt to so answer, any critic could make any charge, even one totally fabricated and force me into a forum of his own choosing. The result is that many charges must go unanswered. Some are false on their face, some are false by twisted innuendo, and some could be proved false only by the use of information which must be kept in confidence for legal or investigative reasons. This is not to deny that we, and I, have made mistakes. The judges and others sometimes have so advised us. We are only human.

One final thought. No remarks in our "defense" will still the voices of the critics, and these are not intended to do so. The critics have their rights of free speech under the First Amendment and I am sure they will continue to use those rights to the hilt. In at least many cases, we are denied an effective answer. As the Supreme Court has said so preceptively, ". . . it is the rare case where the denial overtakes the original charge. Denials, retractions, and corrections are not 'hot' news, and rarely receive the prominence of the original story." *Rosenbloom v. Metromedia,* 39 L Ed 2d 296, 313 (1971). I hope that in bringing charges against us, if such be the case, you will bear in mind this handicap under which we must labor and bring it to public attention. Elementary fairness seems to so require. Moreover, a public official such as myself cannot successfully sue for libel or slander, even when the charges made against him are totally false, unless he can prove that those charges were made with actual malice. This is extremely difficult to prove, as anyone familiar with the recent court decisions on libel and slander well knows. The result is that in so many cases of criticism my only recourse is that of taking some personal pleasure in knowing that the critics have abundantly proven, in the reams and volumes that they have published, that one of their principal charges—that I am beyond criticism—is totally false.

I suggest that if evidence like that which I have briefly described here is fully developed and exposed to public view, the ultimate "verdict" must be that the FBI is a lawfully composed and operated public agency, staffed by honest and reasonably intelligent citizens doing a difficult job in the best way they know how and, moreover, doing it quite as well as it could be done by anyone else. While it may be quite true that we deserve some criticism, I think we also deserve an "acquittal." I think any deep and fair inquiry will command this result, and I remain hopeful of it despite the obviously partisan statements made by some of your group in announcing that the inquiry would be held.

Very truly yours,

/s/ John Edgar Hoover
Director

PRINCETON UNIVERSITY
Princeton, New Jersey 08540

October 21, 1971

The Honorable J. Edgar Hoover
Federal Bureau of Investigation
United States Department of Justice
Washington, D.C. 20535

Dear Mr. Hoover:

I appreciate your reply to my invitation of September 28, 1971, but you may have misunderstood the purpose of our October 29th and 30th Conference. I apologize if I contributed to that misunderstanding; allow me to clear it up and ask you to reconsider your decision.

Apparently the major factor in the Bureau's decision not to participate is your belief that the Conference and its participants had already prejudged the result. This is not the case. We have invited a number of highly respected participants and observers to the Conference. These people, and the organizers of the Conference have many differing views on the FBI's work and have no vested interest in reaching a particular result. They are professionals who will bring to this study the careful, reasoned analysis the sponsors will insist on. In addition, to assure that our conclusions and suggestions receive a test of public scrutiny, we have invited the press and the public to attend the Conference.

Our invitation was issued in the spirit of a serious inquiry in which a representative of the FBI itself would have much to contribute to an understanding of the Bureau's operation. The sponsors of the Conference do not feel they are competent to sit as "judges" of the FBI, and do not intend to do so.

Rather, the Conference was conceived and planned as a scholarly effort to improve our understanding of the functioning of an important American institution. We believe this effort reflects the Constitutional tradition of private citizen participation in the operation of Government and the consideration of public questions. We think such an investigation appropriate because in the history of the FBI there has never been this kind of thorough examination.

The oversight of federal institutions provided by Congress and the courts does not seem to us to rule out the need for a citizen-scholar inquiry of the kind we envision.

In sponsoring this Conference, we have been strongly aware of criticism from responsible citizens and officials of (1) the Bureau's failure adequately to deal with organized crime; (2) the extent and nature of use of informers; (3) the collection of vast quantities of data on private citizens; (4) the Bureau's budget; (5) its efficiency in enforcement of federal civil rights laws; and (6) its public relations activities. None of these areas is mentioned in your letter. This makes it all the more appropriate to have your representative present to assure the fullest exploration of these questions.

I thank you for your suggestion that we invite a member of the Society of Former Special Agents of the FBI. We have sent that invitation. Nevertheless, we hope you will reconsider and send in addition, a current member of the Bureau.

In any event, I assure you that we have duplicated and will make available to the participants your letter of October 7 which you hoped would be "considered material during the deliberations" of the Conference.

Thank you again for your response; I hope you will reconsider.

Sincerely,

/s/ Duane Lockard

FOOTNOTES

CHAPTER ONE
THE SELLING OF THE FBI
by Robert Sherrill

Page 5; for Nash story:
Fred J. Cook, *The FBI Nobody Knows* (New York: Pyramid Books, 1964), pp. 153–54.

Page 7; favorable books on the FBI:
Courtney Ryley Cooper, *Ten Thousand Public Enemies* (Boston: Little, Brown, 1935). Herbert Corey, *Farewell, Mr. Gangster! America's War on Crime* (New York: Appleton-Century, 1936; also published in Buenos Aires, Imprenta Lopez, 1939, as *¡Adiós, Señor Bandido!*). Irving Crump and John W. Newton, *Our G-Men* (New York: Dodd, Mead, 1937). John Joseph Floherty, *Inside the FBI* (Philadelphia: Lippincott, 1943), and *Our FBI, An Inside Story* (Philadelphia: Lippincott, 1951). While Hoover may have been more profligate with his forewords and introductions in those salad days, he continued the practice, of course, in his later life. Already mentioned as having benefited thereby is Don Whitehead's *The FBI Story* (New York: Random House, 1956). Others are *The FBI in Peace and War* by Frederick Lewis Collins (New York: Putnam, 1963); *Youth and the FBI* by John J. Floherty and Mike McGrady (Philadelphia: Lippincott, 1960); *The Story of the FBI; an Official Picture History of the FBI* by the editors of *Look* (New York: Dutton, 1954). All have Hoover forewords.

Page 7; for Hoover letters:
Cook, op. cit., p. 166.

Page 10
A. C. Millspaugh, *Crime Control by the National Government* (Washington: Brookings Institute, 1937).

Page 10
William W. Turner, *Hoover's FBI: The Men and the Myth* (Los Angeles: Sherbourne Press, Inc., 1970), p. 290.

Page 11; Hoover and Hollywood:
Whitehead, op. cit., p. 336.

Page 15
Masters of Deceit: The Story of Communism In America and How to Fight It (New York: Pocket Books, 1968), p. 314. (Emphasis in original.)

Page 16
Ibid., p. 265.

Page 17; requests to do TV shows:
Washington *Star*, April 21, 1965.

Page 18; De Loach quote:
Ibid.

Page 20; Kitman quote:
Washington *Post*, July 20, 1971.

Page 20
Washington *Star Sunday Magazine*, June 20, 1971.

Page 20
Potomac, March 19, 1967.

Page 20; security checks:
New York *Times*, June 2, 1965.

Page 25; Graham report:
New York *Times*, September 8, 1971.

Page 26
James Boyd, *Above the Law* (New York: New American Library, 1968), p. 110.

Page 27; FBI Crime Records Division:
James Phelan, "Hoover of the FBI," *Saturday Evening Post*, September 25, 1965.

CHAPTER TWO
THE HISTORY OF THE FBI:
DEMOCRACY'S DEVELOPMENT OF A SECRET POLICE
by Vern Countryman

Page 33; hearings:
Hearings of House Appropriations Committee on Deficiency Appropriations for 1907, 59th Cong., 2d Sess. (1907), 202–3; Hearings of House Appropriations Committee on Sundry Civil Appropriations for 1909, 60th Cong., 1st Sess. (1908), 773–80.

Page 33; Sherley quote:
Hearings for 1909, op. cit., 778–79.

Page 33; Smith quote:
Hearings for 1909, op. cit., 778–80.

Page 34; Sherley quote:
42 Cong. Rec. (1908), 5555, 5558.

Page 34; authority for FBI:
16 Stat. 162 (1870). Section 8 of this statute authorized the Attorney General to make "all necessary rules and regulations for the government of

said Department of Justice, and for the management and distribution of its business." Section 9 provided that the Solicitor General and certain assistant Attorneys General and Solicitors General should be appointed by the President with the advice and consent of the Senate and that "[a]ll the other officers, clerks, and employees in the said Department shall be appointed and be removable by the Attorney-General."

Page 34; Bonaparte's case for the FBI:
Annual Report of the Attorney General of the United States (1907), 9–10 (hereinafter cited as Atty. Gen. Rep. for indicated year).

Page 34; Secret Service jurisdiction:
33 Stat. 1169 (1905). The limiting language was introduced by 20 Stat. 384 (1879).

Page 34; protection of the President:
34 Stat. 708 (1906).

Page 35; Tawney proposal:
35 Stat. 328 (1908). See also 35 Stat. 968 (1909).

Page 35; hiring of 9 agents:
Hearings of House Appropriations Committee on Sundry Civil Appropriations for 1910, 60th Cong., 2d Sess. (1909), 235–36, 1006.

Page 35; Bonaparte report:
Atty. Gen. Rep. (1908), 7–8.

Page 35; Bonaparte on merger:
Hearings . . . for 1910, op. cit., 1006.

Page 36; Roosevelt message:
43 Cong. Rec. (1908), 24–25.

Page 37; limitations to frauds, etc.:
Hearings . . . for 1910, op. cit., 1012, 1032, 1035, 1036, 1038, 1041, 1046.

Page 37; "crimes against the United States":
35 Stat. 1013 (1909).

Page 37; exception for congressmen:
43 Cong. Rec. (1909), 3128.

Page 37; "for such other investigations":
36 Stat. 748 (1910).

Page 37; "Bureau of Investigation":
Atty. Gen. Rep. (1909), 8.

Page 37; name "Federal Bureau of Investigation":
34 Stat. 77 (1935).

Page 37; ". . . and to land frauds":
Atty. Gen. Rep. (1908), 5–6; Atty. Gen. Rep. (1909), 17.

Page 37; ". . . immoral purpose":
36 Stat. 825 (1910), now 18 U.S.C. Sections 2421–24 (1970).

Page 37; "immorality in general":
H.R. Rep. 47, 61st Cong., 2d Sess. (1910), 9–10.

Page 38
Johnson v. *United States,* 215 Fed. 679 (7th Cir. 1914).

Page 38
Caminetti v. *United States,* 242 U.S. 470 (1917).

Page 38; 1932 Mann Act convictions:
Atty. Gen. Rep. (1932), 108.

Page 38; Mann Act convictions since 1922:
Atty. Gen. Rep. (1939), 157, 160.

Page 38; brothel raid:
Max Lowenthal, *The Federal Bureau of Investigation* (New York: William Sloane Associates 1950), pp. 19–20.

Page 38; Miami raid:
Fred J. Cook, *The FBI Nobody Knows* (New York: Pyramid Books, 1964), pp. 60, 248.

Page 38; "commercialized vice":
Atty. Gen. Rep. (1941), 183.

Page 38; Mann Act convictions since 1965:
FBI Ann. Rep. (1951), 3a; Atty. Gen. Rep. (1961), 344; FBI Ann. Rep. (1965), 20; (1966), 20; (1967), 20; (1968), 20; (1969), 19; (1970), 19.

Page 38; Dyer Act:
41 Stat. 324 (1919), now 18 U.S.C. Sections 2311–12 (1970).

Page 38; 1970 Dyer Act convictions:
FBI Ann. Rep. (1970), 18–19.

Page 38; FBI appropriations:
83 Stat. 409 (1969). (In fiscal 1971 Congress authorized $294 million for the FBI. In fiscal 1972 the equivalent figure was approximately $334 million. *Congressional Quarterly,* January 29, 1972, p. 185. Editors.)

Page 39; kidnapping:
47 Stat. 326 (1932); 48 Stat. 781 (1934), now 18 U.S.C. Section 1201 (1969).

Page 39; extortion through mails:
47 Stat. 649 (1932); 48 Stat. 781 (1934), now 18 U.S.C. Section 875 (1969); 18 U.S.C. Sections 876–77 (1971 Supp.).

Page 39; interstate theft:
47 Stat. 773 (1933), now 18 U.S.C. Section 2117 (1970).

Page 39 ". . . avoid state prosecution":
48 Stat. 782 (1934), now 18 U.S.C. Section 1073 (1971 Supp.).

Page 39; bank robbery:
48 Stat. 783 (1934), now 18 U.S.C. Section 2113 (1971 Supp.).

Page 39; stolen property:
48 Stat. 794 (1934), now 18 U.S.C. Section 2314 (1970).

Page 39; firearms:
48 Stat. 1239 (1934), now 18 U.S.C. Sections 921–28 (1971 Supp.).

Page 39; extortions:
48 Stat. 979 (1934), now 18 U.S.C. Section 1951 (1970).

Page 39; 1970 convictions:
FBI Ann. Rep. (1970), 18–19.

Page 39; carry firearms:
48 Stat. 1008 (1934), now 18 U.S.C. Section 3052 (1970).

Page 39; Civil Rights Act investigations:
FBI Ann. Rep. (1955), 6.

Page 40; civil rights convictions:
Atty. Gen. Rep. (1961), 336, 343; FBI Ann. Rep. (1964), 9, 17; (1966),
10, 19; (1967), 12, 19; (1968), 19; (1969), 9, 18; (1970), 11, 18.

Page 40; "World War I":
Don Whitehead, *The FBI Story* (New York: Random House, 1956), p. 25.

Page 40; Bielaski quote:
Atty. Gen. Rep. (1916), 62.

Page 40; Gregory quote:
Atty. Gen. Rep. (1917), 80.

Page 41; draft arrests:
Whitehead, *The FBI Story,* op. cit., p. 38, puts the total number of arrests as "some 50,000." Lowenthal, *The Federal Bureau of Investigation,*
op. cit., p. 27, asserts that 75,000 were arrested in the New York metropolitan area alone.

Page 41; "1 out of 200":
Lowenthal, op. cit., p. 28.

Page 41; "1,505 inducted":
Whitehead, op. cit., p. 39.

Page 41; ". . . express instructions":
Lowenthal, op. cit., p. 35.

Page 41; "bomb scare":
Lowenthal, op. cit., Ch. 7; Whitehead, op. cit., Ch. 5; L. Post, *The Deportations Delirium of Nineteen-Twenty* (New York: Plenum Pub., 1923),
Ch. 4. There had also been an earlier bombing of the federal building
in Chicago in September, 1918, in which four persons were killed, and
there was a later one in New York City, in September, 1920, in which
thirty were killed.

Page 41; General Intelligence Division:
Atty. Gen. Rep. (1919), 15. There is some confusion whether the General
Intelligence Division was within the Bureau or outside it. Whitehead
reports that the GID was a part of "the administrative staff" of an
assistant attorney general in charge of all investigations into radicalism.

Whitehead, op. cit., p. 41. But the Bureau in its annual reports consistently designated the GID as "a division of" the Bureau. Atty. Gen. Rep. (1919), 15; (1920), 172; (1921), 129; (1923), 69.

Page 41; Flynn quote:
Atty. Gen. Rep. (1919), 15.

Page 42; number arrested:
Attorney General Palmer reported "approximately 300." Atty. Gen. Rep. (1920), 174. Whitehead, op. cit., p. 48, puts the figure at "more than 250." Cook, *The FBI Nobody Knows*, op. cit., p. 97, asserts that 200 were seized in New York alone, of whom all but 39 were released.

Page 42; basis for deportation:
40 Stat. 1012 (1918), now 8 U.S.C. Section 1182 (28) (1970).

Page 42; "Soviet Ark":
Whitehead, op. cit., p. 48. Whitehead's further claim, accepted by Cook, op. cit., p. 97, that "the Supreme Court affirmed the decision" to deport Goldman and Berkman is a slight exaggeration. Apparently Goldman had sought relief in the courts from the deportation order and had lost, in judicial proceedings not officially reported. She appealed to the Supreme Court but on December 18, 1919, withdrew her appeal. *Goldman* v. *Caminetti,* 251 U.S. 565 (1919).

Page 42; Senate resolution:
S. Res. 213, 66th Cong., 1st Sess. (1919).

Page 42; Palmer report:
S. Doc. No. 153, 66th Cong., 1st Sess. (1919), 5–6, 10.

Page 43; nighttime raids:
Post, *The Deportations Delirium* . . . , op. cit., pp. 78, 80, 167.

Page 43; instructions to agents and results:
Hearings before House Committee on Rules on Charges Made Against Department of Justice by Louis F. Post and others, 66th Cong., 2d Sess. (1920), 215.

Page 43
Hearings before House Committee on Rules to Investigate Administration of Louis F. Post, Assistant Secretary of Labor, in the Matter of Deportation of Aliens, 66th Cong., 2d Sess. (1920), 72.

Page 43; Colyer v. *Skeffington:*
265 Fed. 17 (D. Mass. 1920).

Page 43; reversal on appeal:
Skeffington v. *Katzeff,* 277 Fed. 129 (1st Cir. 1922). See also *United States ex rel. Abern* v. *Wallis,* 268 Fed. 413 (S.D.N.Y. 1920).

Page 44; court quote:
265 Fed. at 43.

Page 44; Post analysis:
Post, op. cit., pp. 152, 156, 171.

Page 44; Church report:
C. Panunzio, *The Deportation Cases of 1919–20* (1931), reprinted in Hear-

ings of Senate Judiciary Committee on Charges of Illegal Practices of the Department of Justice, 66th Cong., 3rd Sess. (1921), 308–24.

Page 45; Post charges:
Hearings, note 63, *supra,* 41–43, 48–51, 71.

Page 46; Palmer quote:
Hearings, note 62, *supra,* 5–8, 49, 209.

Page 47; Hoover-Walsh exchange:
Hearings before Senate Judiciary Committee on Charges of Illegal Practices of the Department of Justice, 66th Cong., 3rd Sess. (1921), 17, 19–20, 50, 95.

Page 47; Palmer reference to Hoover:
Ibid., 7, 9, 10, 15, 35.

Page 48; the two reports:
64 Cong. Rec. (1923), 3004–27.

Page 48; Burns quote:
Atty. Gen. Rep. (1921), 129, 131.

Page 48
O. Fraenkel, *The Sacco-Vanzetti Case* (New York: Knopf, 1931), pp. 20, 126–29.

Page 49; Hoover's promotion:
A. Mason, *Harlan Fiske Stone: Pillar of the Law* (New York: Viking Press, 1956), pp. 149–53.

Page 49; Roosevelt order:
Atty. Gen. Rep. (1939), 8; (1940), 152. Whitehead, op. cit., Ch. 18, reports, on the basis of Hoover's recollection, that Roosevelt in 1936 had orally directed Hoover to undertake an investigation of "Communist and Fascist activities."

Page 49
Ex parte Quirin, 317 U.S. 1 (1942).

Page 49; sentences of saboteurs:
R. Cushman, "Ex parte Quirin et al.—The Nazi Saboteur Case," 28 *Cornell Law Quarterly,* 54, 58 (1942).

Page 49; FBI takes credit:
FBI, *The Story of the Federal Bureau of Investigation* (1955), pp. 8–9.

Page 49; Coast Guard involvement:
See C. Bernstein, "The Saboteur Trial: A Case History," 11 *George Washington Law Review,* 131 (1943).

Page 50; Hoover report:
Atty. Gen. Rep. (1941), 178.

Page 50; espionage convictions—number:
None from 1940 through 1941, thirty-seven in 1942, nineteen in 1943, eleven in 1944, ten in 1945 and three in 1946. Atty. Gen. Rep. (1940),

177; (1941), 198; FBI Ann. Rep. (1942), 23; (1943), 24; (1944), 27; (1945), 25; (1946), 23.

Page 50; explanation for low convictions:
FBI Ann. Rep. (1942), 3.

Page 50; Hoover quote:
FBI Ann. Rep. (1950), 11.

Page 50
Coplon v. *United States,* 191 F. 2d 749 (D.C. Cir. 1951), *cert. den.* 342 U.S. 926 (1952).

Page 51
United States v. *Coplon,* 185 F. 2d 629 (2d Cir. 1950), *cert. den.* 342 U.S. 920 (1952).

Page 51; FBI claim:
See e.g., FBI Ann. Rep. (1948), 23; (1969), 21; (1970), 21.

Page 51; Roosevelt's order:
See text at page 49 *supra.* This claim of enduring effectiveness for a presidential request that other law-enforcement agencies turn over national security information to the FBI seems as farfetched as the FBI's later claim of perpetual authority to engage in bugging based on an ad hoc memorandum from Attorney General Brownell in 1954. Victor S. Navasky, *Kennedy Justice* (New York: Atheneum, 1971), pp. 92, 451–52.

Page 51; Smith Act:
54 Stat. 670 (1940), now 18 U.S.C. Section 2385 (1970).

Page 51; wartime conviction:
Dunne v. *United States,* 138 F. 2d 137 (8th Cir. 1943), *cert. den.* 320 U.S. 790 (1943).

Page 51; ". . . prepared by the FBI":
FBI Ann. Rep. (1951), 6.

Page 51; convictions upheld:
Dennis v. *United States,* 341 U.S. 494 (1951).

Page 51; Hoover report:
FBI Ann. Rep. (1952), 11–12; (1953), 11–12; (1954), 13–14; (1955), 16–17; (1956), 20–21; (1958), 17–18.

Page 51; membership clause:
FBI Ann. Rep. (1956), 21. There were only five convictions altogether under the membership clause. Atty. Gen. Rep. (1960), 347.

Page 51; convictions by 1957:
Atty. Gen. Rep. (1957), 18.

Page 51; "second string" convictions:
Yates v. *United States,* 354 U.S. 298 (1957).

Page 52; Hoover report on Smith Act:
FBI Ann. Rep. (1959), 25.

Page 52; Hoover 1960 summary:
Atty. Gen. Rep. (1960), 347.

Page 52; Truman order:
Executive Order 9835, 12 Fed. Reg. 1935 (1947), as amended by Executive Order 10241, 16 Fed. Reg. 3690 (1951).

Page 52; Eisenhower order:
Executive Order 10450, 18 Fed. Reg. 2489 (1953).

Page 52; 1958 study:
Ralph S. Brown, Jr., *Loyalty and Security* (New Haven: Yale University Press, 1958), p. 181.

Page 52; "16 million today":
U. S. Bureau of the Census, Statistical Abstract of the United States (1970), 213.

Page 53; transfer to Civil Service Commission:
The present practice is that where the preliminary screening by the commission indicates that the loyalty of the subject is questionable, the commission is to "refer the matter to the Federal Bureau of Investigation for a full field investigation." But in any case the President may direct that the preliminary investigation be made by the FBI and so may the Secretary of State with respect to positions "of a high degree of importance or sensitivity." 5 U.S.C. Section 1304 (b) and (c) (1967).

Page 53
See pp. 33–7, *supra.*

Page 53; Internal Security Act:
64 Stat. 987 (1950).

Page 53; 1954 amendment:
68 Stat. 777 (1954).

Page 53; printing press inventory:
68 Stat. 586 (1954).

Page 53; "22 witnesses presented":
FBI Ann. Rep. (1952), 14.

Page 53; Supreme Court reversal:
Communist Party v. *Subversive Activities Control Board,* 351 U.S. 115 (1956).

Page 53; Supreme Court affirmance:
Communist Party v. *Subversive Activities Control Board,* 367 U.S. 1 (1961).

Page 53; registration provisions:
Albertson v. *Subversive Activities Control Board,* 382 U.S. 70 (1965). See also *Communist Party* v. *United States,* 384 F. 2d 957 (D.C. Cir. 1967).

Page 53; ". . . patch up the old statute":
81 Stat. 765 (1968), now 50 U.S.C. Sections 781–98 (1971 Supp.). By 1960 the board had ordered thirteen organizations to register as Communist fronts, but none of them had done so. FBI Ann. Rep. (1959), 27; Atty. Gen. Rep. (1960), 348.

Page 54; constitutional infirmities:
See *Boorda* v. *Subversive Activities Control Board,* 421 F. 2d 1142 (D.C. Cir. 1969), *cert. den.* 397 U.S. 1042 (1970).

Page 54; ". . . sinecures in Washington":
In Appropriation Committee hearings in July, 1971, board Chairman John W. Mahan admitted that the board had only two cases pending before it —to label the Young Workers' Liberation League and the Center for Marxist Education as Communist fronts—and that in the first six months of 1971 the board had sat for only ten days to hear three witnesses. Senator Ellender's inquiry about how the board spent the rest of its time provoked the following colloquy:

> *Mr. Mahan:* I have spent some time, as much as possible, in the House and the Senate trying to correct the laws so they will work more efficiently and effectively.
>
> *Sen. Ellender:* That is not your job. You are doing that to kill time . . .

Hearings before Senate Appropriations Subcommittee on SACB Appropriations for 1972, 92nd Cong., 1st Sess. (1971), 905–8.

Page 54; Nixon order:
Executive Order 11605, 36 Fed. Reg. 12831 (1971).

Page 54; Internal Security Act:
64 Stat. 1021 (1950).

Page 54; repeal of Title II:
85 Stat. 347 (1971).

Page 55; pre-FBI fingerprinting:
Atty. Gen. Rep. (1908), 50; (1909), 69, 345.

Page 55; move from Leavenworth:
Atty. Gen. Rep. (1924), 71; (1925), 122.

Page 55; Hoover report:
Atty. Gen. Rep. (1930), 80; (1931), 92.

Page 55; ". . . virtually complete":
FBI, *The Identification Facilities of the FBI* (1941), pp. 33–35.

Page 55; international exchange:
Atty. Gen. Rep. (1932), 106.

Page 55; "82 countries":
FBI Ann. Rep. (1970), 33.

Page 55; "200 million prints":
Hearings before House Appropriations Subcommittee on Department of Justice Appropriations for 1972, 92nd Cong., 1st Sess.(1971), 695–96.

Page 56; Hoover report:
Hearings before Senate Appropriations Subcommittee on Department of Justice Appropriations for 1972, 92nd Cong., 1st Sess. (1971), 208; Hearings, note, "200 million prints," *supra,* 707–9.

Page 56; computerization:
Hearings before Senate Appropriations Subcommittee on Department of Justice Appropriations for 1972, 92nd Cong., 1st Sess. (1971), 195–97; Hearings, note, p. 487, "200 million prints," 700.

Page 56; statistics function:
Atty. Gen. Rep. (1931), 92.

Page 56; Brookings study:
A. Millspaugh, *Crime Control by the National Government* (Washington, D.C.: Brookings Institute, 1937), 274.

Page 56; ". . . statistics remain deficient":
National Commission on the Causes and Prevention of Violence, Staff Report, *Crimes of Violence* (1969), 16–38; President's Commission on Law Enforcement and Administration of Justice, Task Force Report, *Crime and Its Impact—An Assessment* (1967), 128–36. Ward, "Careers in Crime: The FBI Story," 7 *Journal of Resources in Crime and Delinquency* 207 (1970); Robinson, "A Critical View of the Uniform Crime Reports," 64 *Michigan Law Review* 1031 (1966); Wolfgang, "Uniform Crime Reports: A Critical Appraisal," 111 *Univ. Pennsylvania Law Review* 709 (1963).

Page 56; "the heart of FBI operations":
FBI Ann. Rep. (1967), 48.

Page 56; number of name checks:
Hearings, note, p. 487, "200 million prints," 670.

Page 56; number of names on file:
FBI Ann. Rep. (1970), 44.

Page 56; Justice Department directive:
J. Hoover, "The Confidential Nature of FBI Reports," 8 *Syracuse Law Review* 2, 11, n. 10 (1956) (citing Supp. No. 4 [revised] of departmental order 3464, January 13, 1953). See also *United States ex rel. Touhy* v. *Ragen,* 340 U.S. 462 (1951). This order is still in effect. Letter from Helen W. Gandy, Office of the Director, FBI, March 23, 1971.

Page 57; number of employees:
Hearings, note, p. 487, "200 million prints," 675.

Page 57; initiation of training school:
Atty. Gen. Rep. (1921), 128.

Page 57; "perfected":
Atty. Gen. Rep. (1929), 68.

Page 57; "West Point" reference:
FBI Ann. Rep. (1970), 30.

Page 57; training increase:
Hearings, note, p. 487, "200 million prints," 661, 724–25. See also 42 U.S.C. Section 3744 (1970).

Page 57; tourist number:
Hearings before House Appropriations Subcommittee on Justice Department

Appropriations for 1970, 91st Cong., 1st Sess. (1969), 504. But only 531,370 took the tour in 1970. FBI Ann. Rep. (1970), 45. And in 1971 Hoover made no report to the subcommittee on the FBI tours.

Page 58; "Hoover is the FBI":
Whitehead, op. cit., p. 119.

Page 58; civil service exemption:
28 U.S.C. Section 536 (1969). See also Executive Order No. 10987, 27 Fed. Reg. 550 (1962), par. 5(a).

Page 58; "Director is head":
80 Stat. 616 (1966), now 28 U.S.C. Section 532 (1968).

Page 58; ". . . responsible only to the Attorney General":
Whitehead, op. cit., p. 67; Mason, *Harlan Fiske Stone,* op. cit., p. 151.

Page 58; "greatest single problem":
Navasky, *Kennedy Justice,* op. cit., p. 7.

Page 59; Hoover on crime:
Hearings before House Appropriations Subcommittee on Justice Department Appropriations for 1961, 86th Cong., 2d Sess. (1960), 348–49.

Page 60; Hoover on juvenile delinquency:
Hearings before House Appropriations Subcommittee on Justice Department Appropriations for 1963, 87th Cong., 2d Sess. (1962), 332–33.

Page 60; Hoover on probation and parole:
Hearings, note, p. 487, "200 million prints," 719–23.

Page 61; Hoover on the Communist party:
Ibid., 737–39.

Page 61; Hoover on the New Left:
Hearings before House Appropriations Subcommittee on Justice Department Appropriations for 1970, 91st Cong., 1st Sess. (1969), 522.

Page 62; Hoover on combined menace:
Ibid., 532–33.

CHAPTER THREE
THE BUREAU'S BUDGET: A SOURCE OF POWER
by Walter Pincus

Page 66
Following the conference at Princeton, the "official [work] schedule" of "members of our headquarters staff who are qualified to discuss the topic [the FBI budget]" precluded FBI assistance, according to John Mohr.

Page 72
In the 1940s, then-Attorney General Francis Biddle recommended to President Roosevelt that FBI agents not be provided to the House committee in response to an earlier request by Representative Cannon.

CHAPTER FOUR
THE INSIDE STORY: AN AGENT'S DILEMMAS
by *William W. Turner*

Page 89
The Shaw letter was published in *The Nation*, February 8, 1971. Shaw was forced to resign, and the resignation was accepted "with prejudice" on grounds of "atrocious judgment." A suit on his behalf by the ACLU eventuated in an out-of-court settlement giving him back pay and striking the "with prejudice."

Page 89; on Kathryn Kelly:
The recommendation was made in a memorandum from Grapp to the Director, dated October 15, 1959. The document is reproduced in the appendix to *Hoover's FBI: The Men and the Myth* by this author (New York: Dell, 1971).

Page 95
Nevertheless, the FBI nurtures the image that all agents are lawyers or accountants. At the time the requirements were loosened in 1961, Assistant Director Nicholas Callahan was quoted in the June issue of *National Geographic Magazine:* "An applicant for appointment as special agent must be . . . a graduate of a State-accredited resident law school or a four-year resident accounting school with at least three years' practical accounting experience." For the 1970 edition of the Encyclopaedia Britannica, Hoover wrote that agents "must be graduates of an accredited law school . . . or must have graduated from an accredited four-year college with a major in accounting and have had three years' personal experience in that field."

Page 97
Lewis resigned from the FBI several years ago.

CHAPTER FIVE
THE FBI AND OTHER POLICE FORCES
by *William W. Turner*

Page 113
A second-line power, Canada, has the Royal Canadian Mounted Police doing both.

Page 113
Quite often the terms "intelligence" and "espionage" are used interchangeably, and they frequently overlap in practice. There is a distinction. Intelligence is generally accepted as the gathering, evaluation and dissemination of information, much of which comes from open, accessible or published sources. Espionage has a more clandestine connotation, being the procurement by one means or another of secret or undisclosed information. Espionage is the more complex and specialized.

Page 115; Hoover quote:
Don Whitehead, *The FBI Story* (New York: Random House, 1956), p. 305. A number of eminent scientists have scoffed at the idea that the crude drawings presented in evidence conveyed secrets of the atom bomb.

Page 115; Hoover quote:
Whitehead, op. cit., p. 312.

Page 119
The origins are obscure. A source close to the situation says Hoover took exception to being followed by Parker's intelligence squad while in Southern California on his annual sojourn to the Del Mar racetrack.

Page 120
For instance, the situation was exacerbated by the FBI's move to take over presidential protection from the Secret Service following the Kennedy assassination. For example, the FBI has jurisdiction over homicide only when it occurs on an Indian or government reservation.

CHAPTER SIX

ORGANIZED CRIME: THE STRANGE RELUCTANCE
by Fred J. Cook

Page 142
For a description of this first Mafia meeting in Cleveland, see Hank Messick, *The Silent Syndicate* (New York: Macmillan, 1967), p. 39.

Page 144
This description of the accomplishments of the Atlantic City conference is based on a summary given me by a former high official of the Federal Bureau of Narcotics. See Fred Cook, *The Secret Rulers* (New York: Duell, Sloan & Pearce, 1966), pp. 77–79.

Page 144
Ramsey Clark, *Crime in America* (New York: Simon & Schuster, 1970), p. 75

Page 144
Mayer, "Myth of the G-Men," *The Forum,* September, 1935.

Page 145
Seagle, "The American National Police," *Harper's Magazine,* November, 1934.

Page 146
Burton B. Turkus and Sid Feder, *Murder Inc.* (New York: Permabooks, 1952), pp. 69 and 80.

Page 148
William W. Turner, *Hoover's FBI: The Men and the Myth* (New York: Dell, 1971), p. 178.

Page 149
For an account of the Apalachin raid and the record of the sixty who were arrested there, see Frederic Sondern, Jr., *Brotherhood of Evil: The Mafia* (New York: Farrar, Straus & Cudahy, 1959). The details concerning those who escaped were given to me by officials of the Federal Bureau of Narcotics.

Page 150
This description of Wessel's activities and subsequent quotes attributed to him are all the result of numerous conversations between Wessel and the author over several years.

Page 151
McCormack's testimony is from the record of hearings held by the New York State Commission of Investigation in 1960. I covered it in greater detail in *A Two-Dollar Bet Means Murder* (New York: Dial Press, 1961).

Page 152; FBI cooperation with Special Group:
Goettel, "Why the Crime Syndicate Can't Be Touched," *Harper's Magazine,* November, 1960.

Page 152; Hoover and Special Group:
Interview with Harry Singer and Gerald Duncan, the New York *Mirror,* April 3, 1961.

Page 153; Hoover quote:
From the widely disseminated text of the address by Hoover before the International Association of Police Chiefs, October 3, 1960.

Page 154
These Hoover quotes are taken from a special release put out by the FBI publicity bureau after Hoover testified, evidently in a determination to make certain that no one missed his testimony.

Page 154
Turner, *Hoover's FBI,* op. cit., p. 173.

Page 156; surrender of Lepke:
Turkus and Feder, *Murder Inc.,* op. cit., 269–370.

Page 156; agents assigned to organized crime:
Turner, op. cit., p. 176. Tom Wicker in "What Have They Done Since They Shot Dillinger?" in the New York *Times Magazine,* December 28, 1969, wrote that Hoover had only two agents assigned to organized crime in the New York office when Robert Kennedy became Attorney General.

Page 157; Kennedy and organized crime:
Turner, op. cit., p. 179.

Page 157; Kennedy quote:
The Wall Street Journal, October 10, 1968.

Page 157; FBI and electronic surveillance:
Interview with E. Silberling, New York *World Journal Tribune,* January 1, 1967.

Page 158; another 76,000 pages of transcript:
New York *Times,* June 30, 1971.

Page 158
Clark, *Crime in America,* op. cit., pp. 80–81.

Page 159; organized crime indictments:
Ibid., pp. 81–82.

Page 159
The Graham quote is from Turner, op. cit., p. 185.

Page 160
The Wall Street Journal, October 10, 1968.

Page 160
Jack Anderson, New York *Post,* September 2, 1971.

Page 162; Wessel quote:
Cook, *A Two-Dollar Bet Means Murder,* op. cit., p. 11

CHAPTER SEVEN
CIVIL RIGHTS: TOO MUCH, TOO LATE
by Arlie Schardt

Page 167
The paper "Racial Tensions and Civil Rights" (March 1, 1956) was presented
by the FBI Director at a Cabinet briefing, March 9, 1956; located in file
144-012. It is cited in John T. Elliff, "Aspects of Federal Civil Rights
Enforcement: The Justice Department and the FBI, 1939–1964," *Perspectives in American History,* Volume V: *Law in American History* (Cambridge: Charles Warren Center for Studies in American History, Harvard
University Press, 1971), pp. 643–47.

Page 169; Elliff quote:
Ibid., p. 645.

Page 171; FBI memo:
U. S. Commission on Civil Rights, "Law Enforcement: A Report on Equal
Protection in the South" (1965), p. 166 (hereafter "Law Enforcement").

Page 172; Vivian quote:
From the notes of author Paul Good re interviews for his book *The American
Serfs* (New York: G. P. Putnam's Sons, 1968).

Page 173
"Law Enforcement," p. 143.

Page 174
Ibid., pp. 142, 167.

Page 175
Howard Zinn, *SNCC, The New Abolitionists* (Boston: Beacon Press, 1964),
pp. 199–200 (emphasis Zinn's).

Page 175
"Law Enforcement," p. 151.

Page 178
"CBS Morning Report" transcript from series of January 12–16, 1970.

Page 178
"Law Enforcement," p. 164.

Page 179
Ibid., p. 165.

Page 181
Mississippi Advisory Committee to the U. S. Commission on Civil Rights, "Report: Administration of Justice in Mississippi" (Washington, D.C.: 1963), pp. 24–25.

Page 181
"Justice," 1961 U. S. Commission on Civil Rights Report, Book 5, p. 110.

Page 183
Jack Nelson and Jack Bass, *The Orangeburg Massacre* (New York: World Pub., 1970), pp. 165–70.

Page 186; Hoover letter:
"CBS Morning Report" transcript, January 12–16, 1970.

Page 187; Hoover quote:
Washington *Post,* November 26, 1964, and *Time,* December 14, 1970.

Page 189
Time, December 14, 1970.

Page 190; FBI investigation of King beating:
Victor Navasky, *Kennedy Justice* (New York: Atheneum, 1971), pp. 121–22, Navasky interview with C. B. King.

Page 191
"Civil Rights in Texas," A Report of the Texas Advisory Committee to the U. S. Commission on Civil Rights, February, 1970, p. 7 (hereafter "Civil Rights in Texas").

Page 191; Ruiz quote:
Ibid., p. 18.

Page 191; Uvalde, Texas, incident:
Ibid., p. 19.

Page 192
Ibid., p. 35.

Page 193; Ruiz quote:
Ibid., p. 41.

Page 193; on Mexican-American employment:
"Mexican-Americans and the Administration of Justice in the Southwest," Report of the U. S. Commission on Civil Rights, March, 1970, pp. 85–86.

Page 194; Fuentes incident:
Ibid., pp. 29–33.

Page 194
"Civil Rights in Texas," p. 47.

Page 198
Los Angeles *Times,* February 13, 1970.

CHAPTER NINE

DISSEMINATION OF DEROGATORY INFORMATION:
A WEAPON AGAINST CRIME OR PART OF THE
PROBLEM?
by Aryeh Neier

Page 220; legislative history of § 534:
72 Cong. Rec. 1989 (71st Cong., 2d Sess.), June 20, 1930.

Page 221; Menard v. Mitchell:
328 F. Supp. 718, 726 (D.D.C. 1971), *on remand* from 430 F. 2d 486
(D.C. Cir. 1970). *Menard* v. *Mitchell* is the leading case relevant to this
paper and will be referred to frequently. The case is sponsored by the
National Capital Area ACLU. The plaintiff had been arrested by the Los
Angeles police, never accorded a judicial hearing on the legality of his
detention and finally released when the police were fully satisfied that there
was no basis for charging him with a crime. The FBI obtained his fingerprint record and the suit was brought to purge these records from the FBI
files.

Page 221
The ordinance exempts employees of local retail or wholesale merchants. It
applies specifically to photographers, appliance salesmen, household furnishing salesmen, novelties and confections, home improvements (storm win-
dows, insulation, painters), vendors of service or merchandise, haulers and
solicitors.

Page 223; Nader quote:
"The Dossier Invades the Home," *Saturday Review,* April 17, 1971.

Page 223; Hogan prosecutions:
New York *Times,* September 18, 1970.

Page 227; Bible quote:
Congressional Record, September 20, 1971, at S14558.

Page 228; Bureau quote:
F.B.I. Law Enforcement Bulletin 4 (January, 1946).

Page 229; confidentiality of juvenile arrest records:
See Alan Sussman, "The Confidentiality of Family Court Records," *New York
Law Journal,* January 6–8, 1971.

Page 231
Gregory v. *Litton Systems, Inc.,* 316 F. Supp. 401 (1970).

Page 232
A. Hess and F. Le Poole, "Abuse of the Record of Arrest Not Leading to Conviction," 13 *Crime and Delinquency* 494 (1967).

Page 232
See Alan F. Westin, *Privacy and Freedom* (New York: Atheneum, 1967).

Page 232; ex-convict quote:
William R. Coons, "An Attica Graduate Tells His Story," New York *Times Magazine,* October 10, 1971.

Page 233; arrest statistics:
Crime in the United States, F.B.I. Uniform Crime Reports, 1969.

Page 235; N.Y. fingerprinting law:
New York State Laws 1969, Ch. 1071, N. Y. Gen. Bus. Law Section 359-e (12) (McKinney Supp. 1969).

Page 235; results of N.Y. law:
New York *Times,* February 5, 1970.

CHAPTER TEN
THE FBI AS A POLITICAL POLICE
(A portion of the conference paper delivered by Thomas I. Emerson)

Page 239; 2,000 agents investigating political activity:
American Civil Liberties Union, *Surveillance: Is This the Law?* (1971).

Page 240; ". . . the interests of national security":
Executive Order 10450, 3 C.F.R. 936 (Supp. 1953).

Page 240; Hoover description:
Society of Former Special Agents of the FBI, *J. Edgar Hoover on Communism* (New York: Random House, 1969), p. 123.

Page 241
See Elliff's paper, Ch. 11, for a discussion of the Bureau's claims of authority to investigate in the national security area.

Page 241
"Report on Certain Alleged Practices of the FBI," 10 *Lawyers Guild Review* 185, 189 (1950).

Page 241
On its face the document might have been a conscientious objector report, but contact with the subject himself indicates it was not.

Page 242; Hoover testimony (1960):
Quoted in I. F. Stone's *Weekly,* November 2, 1959, p. 2.

Page 242; Hoover testimony (1962):
Ibid., October 14, 1963, p. 4.

Page 242; Earth Day surveillance:
New York *Times,* April 15, 1971.

Page 242; Mitchell defense:
New York *Times,* April 17, 1971.

Page 242; Bureau on campus:
See, e.g., Fred Cook, *The FBI Nobody Knows* (New York: Pyramid Books, 1964), pp. 394–404; Media documents.

Page 243
"Report on Certain Alleged Practices of the FBI," 10 *Lawyers Guild Review* 185, 189 (1950).

Page 244; anti-war activist summary:
Summary taken from the New York *Times,* April 25, 1971.

Page 244
Other accounts of the character of Bureau national security investigations may be found in Thomas I. Emerson and David Helfeld, "Loyalty Among Government Employees," 58 *Yale Law Journal* 1, 70–72 (1948); Eleanor Bontecou, *The Federal Loyalty-Security Program* (Ithaca: Cornell University Press, 1953), Ch. III; Alan Barth, "How Good Is an FBI Report?", *Harper's Magazine,* March, 1954, p. 25; Ralph S. Brown, Jr., *Loyalty and Security* (New Haven: Yale University Press, 1958), pp. 24–30.

Page 245; on methodology:
See Elliff's paper, Ch. 11.

Page 245; Coplon reports:
"Report on Certain Alleged Practices of the FBI," 10 *Lawyers Guild Review* 185, 191–92 (1950).

Page 245; ". . . rarely be documented":
See Max Lowenthal, *The Federal Bureau of Investigation* (New York: William Sloane Associates, 1950), pp. 319 *et seq.;* Cook, *The FBI Nobody Knows,* op. cit., pp. 26–27.

Page 247; Hoover use of previously unpublished material:
See, e.g., Ch. 11, *Masters of Deceit* (New York: Pocket Books, 1968). In his later writing Mr. Hoover seems to have abandoned the practice.

Page 247; Brownell reading:
For an account of this episode see Francis Biddle, " 'Ethics in Government,' and the Use of FBI Files," *The Reporter,* January 5, 1954, p. 13.

Page 247; Truman policy:
New York *Times,* October 27, 1954.

Page 247; Eisenhower policy:
New York *Times,* March 25, 1954.

Page 247; Nixon use:
New York *Times,* October 27, 1954.

Page 248; McCarthy access:
I. F. Stone's *Weekly,* November 9, 1959, p. 3; Tom Wicker, "What Have They

Done Since They Shot Dillinger?", New York *Times Magazine,* December 28, 1969, pp. 4, 15.

Page 248; Morris reading:
Alan Barth, "How Good Is An FBI Report?", op. cit., p. 25.

Page 248; Gillette use:
Ibid., New York *Times,* March 24, 1953.

Page 248; Huac use:
See I. F. Stone's *Weekly,* November 9, 1959.

Page 248; loyalty-security program:
See, e.g., the material transmitted to the Federal Communications Commission, as reported in Cook, op. cit., pp. 391–94.

Page 248; state legislative use:
See, e.g., I. F. Stone's *Weekly,* November 9, 1959; Vern Countryman, *Un-American Activities in the State of Washington* (Ithaca: Cornell University Press, 1951), pp. 153, 158–59.

Page 248; Van Deman files:
New York *Times,* September 7, 1971. The *Times* also reported: "A spokesman for the FBI contended, however, that these reports could not have come directly from the Bureau." Ibid.

Page 249; King and Alioto material:
On Martin Luther King see, e.g., Victor Navasky, *Kennedy Justice* (New York: Atheneum, 1971), pp. 35, 137–38, 153–54. On Mayor Alioto see, e.g., New York *Times,* March 3 and 18, 1971.

Page 249; Hoover on Berrigans:
New York *Times,* November 28, 1970.

Page 249; federal judge rebuke:
The Nation, May 19, 1956, p. 421.

Page 249; Hoover on TWA pilot:
New York *Times,* April 20, 1971.

Page 250; surveillance at meetings:
See Wall's paper, Ch. 14.

Page 250; use of informers:
See Donner's paper, Ch. 13.

Page 250; Hoover on McCarthy:
Quoted in *The Progressive,* February, 1960, p. 30. For other accounts of the Hoover-McCarthy relationship see Wicker, "What Have They Done Since They Shot Dillinger?", op. cit., p. 28; Cook, op. cit., p. 422.

Page 250; Hoover on Mundt:
William V. Shannon, "He May Be the Man Who Stayed Too Long," New York *Times,* April 18, 1971.

Page 250; Hoover on Eugene McCarthy:
Quoted in Wicker, op. cit., p. 19.

Page 251; fear of blackmail:
New York *Times,* April 19, 1971.

Page 251; Hoover's effect on Congress:
See, e.g., "J. Edgar Hoover and the FBI," *The Progressive,* January, 1960, p. 25; James A. Wechsler, "The Decline of J. Edgar Hoover," *The Progressive,* January, 1965, pp. 12, 16–17; Wicker, op. cit., pp. 14–15; Cook, op. cit., p. 415; William W. Turner, *Hoover's FBI: The Man and the Myth* (New York: Dell, 1971), pp. 95–97.

Page 251
Frank Donner, "The Theory and Practice of American Political Intelligence," *The New York Review of Books,* April 22, 1971, pp. 27, 29.

Page 251; FBI and counterinsurgency:
See Anne Flitcraft, *Police on the Home Front* (1971).

Page 252; autonomy of FBI:
See, e.g., Cook, op. cit., Ch. 12; Turner, *Hoover's FBI,* op. cit., Ch. VIII.

CHAPTER ELEVEN
THE SCOPE AND BASIS OF FBI DATA COLLECTION
by John T. Elliff

Page 256; Mitchell quote:
Interview on "David Frost Show," Justice Department (JD) press release, April 8, 1971.

Page 257
Muskie press release, April 14, 1971.

Page 257
Nelson press release, April 15, 1971.

Page 258; "National Environmental Actions, April 22, 1970":
This is the heading of the report, on FBI letterhead stationery, dated June 10, 1970, Washington, D.C., obtained by Senator Muskie's office. Muskie press release, April 14, 1971.

Page 260; ". . . Further requests":
SAC, WFO (105-91485) (P) to Director, FBI (105-148456), February 16, 1970.

Page 261; FBI's statement of objectives:
Hearings of House Appropriations Subcommittee on Department of Justice Appropriations for 1972, 92nd Cong., 1st Sess. (1971), 651.

Page 261; Totten v. *United States:*
92 U.S. 105 (1875).

Page 262; Justice Department position:
Brief for the United States in *United States* v. *Keith* 444 F. 2d 651 (6th Cir. 1971).

Page 262; In re Neagle:
135 U.S. 1, 64 (1890).

Page 262; ". . . to enforce the laws":
Assistant Attorney General William H. Rehnquist, Statement Before the Senate
Subcommittee on Constitutional Rights, JD press release, March 9, 1971.

Page 262; the President "has no power . . .":
Brief note, p. 499, Justice Department position.

Page 263; Mitchell policy
Federal Handling of Demonstrations, Hearings of Senate Subcommittee on
Administration Practices and Procedure, 91st Cong., 2d Sess. (1970), 52–
53.

Page 264; Justice Department belief:
Rehnquist, *supra,* note, ". . . to enforce the laws": (emphasis added).

Page 265; ". . . respecting subversive organizations":
1955 Annual Report of the Attorney General, p. 57; *Report of the Commission
on Government Security* (Washington: GPO, 1957), p. 654.

Page 265; Addressograph plates:
LHM, March 10, 1966, Philadelphia, Pennsylvania. (Much of the subsequent
text is based on analysis of the Media documents, which are footnoted
throughout. These were given to the author by journalists who had received
them.)

Page 266; WILPF memo:
SAC, Philadelphia (100-9882), to Director, FBI (61-1538), September 24,
1965.

Page 266; Haverford College inquiry:
SAC, Philadelphia (100-50737), to SA Thomas F. Lewis, August 1, 1969.

Page 267; Old Left/New Left distinction:
SAC, Philadelphia. To Designated Employees (100-49107), September 16,
1970.

Page 267; informant's report:
SA John T. Blair to SAC, Philadelphia (100-46556), September 24, 1970.

Page 268; Sullivan quote:
"Extremism and the Churches," Address to Community Christian Service,
Clarksville, Indiana, February 11, 1970.

Page 268; Minutemen surveillance:
Hearings Before House Appropriations Subcommittee on Justice Department
Appropriations for 1966, 89th Cong., 1st Sess. (1965), 325–26.

Page 268; JDL:
SA Edward A. Smith to SAC, Philadelphia (105-18173), October 21, 1970.

Page 269; informant's report:
SAC, San Francisco, to Director, FBI (100-68441) (P), February 26, 1971;
see William Greider article, Washington *Post,* June 13, 1971, for interviews
with former agents and department officials regarding Security Index.

Page 269
Title II, Internal Security Act, 64 Stat. 987 (1950)

Page 269; informal memo:
"New Left Notes-Philadelphia," Edition #1, September 16, 1970.

Page 270; Hoover quote on Secret Service:
New York *Times, The Witnesses: Selected and Edited from the Warren Commission's Hearings* (New York: McGraw-Hill, 1965), pp. 600, 605, 607.

Page 271; Hoover testimony:
1972 Appropriations Hearings, note, p. 499, FBI's statement of objectives, 733–35.

Page 271; Hoover on right-wing groups:
The Witnesses, op. cit., p. 595.

Page 271; Belmont quote:
Ibid., pp. 611–12.

Page 272; "police report form":
SA William S. Betts to SAC, Philadelphia (100-49715), June 7, 1968.

Page 272; Mitchell quote:
Campus Unrest, Hearings Before the Special Subcommittee on Education, House of Representatives, 91st Cong., 1st Sess. (1969), 857, 883.

Page 273; Hoover quote on quidelines:
1972 Appropriations Hearings, note, p. 499, FBI's statement of objectives, 755.

Page 273; interview instructions:
SAC, WFO (105-97600) (RUC), to Director, FBI, November 11, 1969.

Page 274; Cohen and Curry:
Institute of Living Law, "*Combating Totalitarian Propaganda—The Method of Exposure . . .*" 10 University of Chicago Law Review, pp. 107, 139 (1943).

Page 274
President's Committee on Civil Rights, *To Secure These Rights* (Washington, 1947), p. 52.

Page 275; "hatemongers":
Annual Report of the Attorney General (1960), 328.

Page 275; Hoover quote on extremists:
"Racial Tension and Civil Rights," March 1, 1956, enclosed in Director, FBI, to Executive Assistant to the Attorney General, March 9, 1956.

Page 275; Bureau and racial extremists:
Hearings for 1966, op. cit., 342–43; Annual Report of the Attorney General (1965), 363.

Page 276; nine city survey:
Text of FBI report on recent racial disturbances, New York *Times,* September 27, 1964.

Page 277
Clark to Hoover, September 14, 1967, portions in *Time,* May 3, 1971.

Page 277; report on Black Student Congress:
Supplemental Intelligence Report, Troop "J," Lancaster station, Code 421, Pennsylvania State Police, October 17, 1967.

Page 278; instructions on ghetto informants:
SAC, Philadelphia (170-6), to All Headquarters Agents, February 26, 1968; SAC, Philadelphia (170-6), to All Resident Agents, March 29, 1968.

Page 279; instructions on infiltration of black groups:
SAC, Philadelphia (170-6), to All Agents, August 12, 1968.

Page 280; summary of informant report:
SA Richard E. Logan to SAC, Philadelphia (170-708), January 27, 1971.

Page 280; ". . . indexing purposes":
SA James I. Halterman to SAC, Philadelphia (157-3852), February 4, 1971.

Page 280; report on possible Chairman:
SA Edward M. Cole to SAC, Philadelphia (157-3852), February 9, 1971.

Page 280; report on checking accounts:
SA Thomas F. Lewis to SAC, Philadelphia (157-3852), June 18, 1970; SE Raymond J. Bott (PH 157-3852), July 13, 1970.

Page 281; report on 1970 Convention:
SAC Joe D. Jamieson (PH 157-4954) to All Agents, October 12, 1970.

Page 282; obtaining printed literature:
Initial Report Re: Student Protest, January 27, 1969.

Page 282; "list of black students":
"List of Current Black Students," May 1, 1969.

Page 282; Wayne State University:
SA Kenneth K. Smythe (PH 157-4250) to All Agents, June 17, 1970.

Page 283; DID instructions:
Director, FBI (157-3550-3), to SAC, Albany, etc., November 4, 1970.

Page 283; investigations of thirteen groups:
SAC, Philadelphia (157-3562), to Director, FBI, December 2, 1970.

Page 284; internal memo:
SAC, Philadelphia (157-5663) (C), to Director, FBI, February 26, 1971.

Page 285; LHM quoted:
LHM, "Black Student Union," February 26, 1971.

Page 285; high school "background data":
SAC, Newark (157-5183) (P), to SAC, Philadelphia, February 22, 1971.

Page 286; chancellor's quote:
SAC, Baltimore (157-5119), to Director, FBI, February 17, 1971.

Page 286; Klan informant quote:
SA Donald G. Cox to SAC, Philadelphia (157-1646), December 1, 1970.

Page 287
Francis Biddle, *In Brief Authority* (Garden City, N.Y.: Doubleday, 1962), p. 261.

Page 288; ". . . fifty years without accounting":
Similar views appeared under the title "FBI Inspection" in *The New Republic*, May 29, 1971.

Page 288; Justice Department position:
Rehnquist testimony, note, p. 500, ". . . to enforce the law."

Page 289; domestic intelligence advisory council:
Harry Howe Ransom, *The Intelligence Establishment* (Cambridge: Harvard University Press, 1970), pp. 229, 300.

CHAPTER TWELVE
ELECTRONIC SURVEILLANCE
by Victor Navasky and Nathan Lewin

Page 298
Text of letter sent December 17, 1971, by Senator Edward M. Kennedy to members of Administrative Practice Subcommittee, U. S. Senate, regarding non-court-ordered electronic surveillance.

Page 298; "informed sources":
Russell Sacket, "Insiders Say . . . ," Atlanta *Journal*, p. 24-B, Newsday News Service, December 15, 1971.

Page 299; Hoover testimony:
Hearings Before a Subcommittee on Departments of State, Justice and Commerce, etc. Appropriations for 1971 of the House Committee on Appropriations, 91st Cong., 2d Sess. (1970), 754; Hearings Before a Subcommittee on Departments of State, Justice, and Commerce, etc. Appropriations for 1972 of the House Committee on Appropriations, 92nd Cong., 1st Sess. (1971), 752.

Page 300; Hoover testimony on wiretaps:
See Hearings Before a Subcommittee on Department of State, Justice and Commerce, etc. Appropriations for 1970 of the House Committee on Appropriations, 91st Cong., 1st Sess. (1969), 544; Hearings on 1971 Appropriations, 754; Hearings on 1972 Appropriations, 752.

Page 302; Schwartz reference:
Cited in Tom Wicker, "A Cross Invasion," New York *Times*, Sec. IV, p. 11, col. 6, December 19, 1971.

Page 304
Brief for the United States, *United States* v. *United States District Court*, No. 70-153, p. 10.

Page 310
Schwartz v. *Texas*, 344 U.S. 199 (1952).

Page 310
Irvine v. *California*, 347 U.S. 128 (1954).

Page 311; Hoover quote:
Hearings on Appropriations (1931), 63–64.

Page 312
53 *Harvard Law Review*, 863, 870, n. 53 (1940).

Page 312
58 *Yale Law Journal*, 422, 423 (1949).

Page 312; Stone order:
86 Cong. Rec. App. 1471 (1940). The order stated: "Unethical tactics: Wire tapping, entrapment, or the use of any other improper, illegal, or unethical tactics in procuring information in connection with investigating activity will not be tolerated by the Bureau."

Page 312; Sargent order:
New York *Times*, June 7, 1928, p. 19.

Page 312
Olmstead v. *United States*, 277 U.S. 438 (1928).

Page 313; Mitchell justification:
Hearings Before a House Committee on Expenditures in the Executive Departments, 71st Cong., 3rd Sess. (1931), 2.

Page 313; Justice Dept. 1933 Approf.:
47 Stat. 1381.

Page 313; Nardone v. *United States:*
302 U.S. 379 (1937).

Page 314; Nardone v. *United States II:*
308 U.S. 338 (1939).

Page 315; Hoover quote:
Quoted in Hearings Before Subcommittee No. 1 of the House Committee on the Judiciary on H.R. 2266 and H.R. 3099, 77th Cong., 1st Sess. (1941), 222–23.

Page 315; "flagrant white slavery":
Washington *Star*, March 13, 1940, p. A-3 [emphasis added].

Page 315; ". . . the fruit of wiretaps":
The *Nardone* brief's quotation of the description of the "Pascuzzi-Goldberg gang" case says: "The principals in this combine were convicted as the result of a wire-tap investigation, one of whom was Joe Moceri, listed as a public enemy in Detroit . . . Another defendant also convicted in the same case was Sam Goldberg, former New York confidence man . . ." Brief, p. 21.

Page 315
Goldman v. *United States*, 316 U.S. 129 (1942).

Page 316; Jackson press release:
86 Cong. Rec. App. 1471–72 (1940).

Page 319; Jackson rationale:
Hearings Before Subcommittee No. 1, note, p. 504, 2nd Hoover quote, 18.

Page 319; organized bar condemnation:
See, e.g., Committee on Federal Legislation, Report on Pending Wiretap Bills of the Association of the Bar of the City of New York (1954), p. 17, n. 9 ("We believe that the Department's view is a misconstruction of the statute as it has been interpreted by the Supreme Court").

Page 320; Ryan dismissal:
United States v. *Coplon*, 88 F. Supp. 921, 925 (S.D.N.Y. 1950).

Page 322; Theoharis quote:
The Nation, June 14, 1971, p. 745.

Page 323; ADA demand:
New York *Times*, April 1, 1949, p. 48.

Page 323; McGrath announcement:
New York *Times*, January 9, 1950, p. 15; April 16, 1950, Sec. VI, p. 33.

Page 323
Irvine v. *California*, 347 U.S. 128 (1954).

Page 324; Solicitor General quote:
Supplemental Memorandum for the United States, No. 1029, O.T. 1965, p. 3.

Page 329; taint by tresspassory eavesdrop:
See *Schipani* v. *United States*, 385 U.S. 372 (1966).

Page 329; procedural issues:
See, e.g., *Alderman* v. *United States*, 394 U.S. 165 (1968).

CHAPTER THIRTEEN
POLITICAL INFORMERS
by Frank Donner

Page 344; Donnelly quote:
Yale Law Journal (1951), p. 1126.

Page 349; Hoover Quote:
Cited in J. K. Skolnick, *The Politics of Protest* (New York: Bantam Books, 1969), p. 263.

Page 355; "20-year-old high school dropout":
Washington *Post*, April 24, 1971.

Page 356
All documents are replete with indications of the FBI's elephantine bureaucracy and its jungle of paper work. My favorite is a memo to the resident agents from a special agent directing them to develop ghetto informants. But what if there are no ghettos in the area in question? In that case, they are to file a memo to that effect with the special agent "with a copy for the RA's error folder, so they will not be charged with failure to perform."

Page 359
The informer prospect is amazed that the FBI should have learned so promptly that he is planning to or has already joined the target group. The knowledge comes to the Bureau agent through an informer already in the organization.

CHAPTER FIFTEEN
THE BRITISH ANALOGY
by C. H. Rolph

Page 390
L. Brandeis and S. Warren, "The Right to Privacy," 4 *Harvard Law Review* 193 (1890).

Page 390; "35 states":
W. Prosser, "Privacy," 48 *California Law Review* 383 (1960).

Page 390
Conservative Political Centre, "Price of Privacy," London, 1971.

Page 404
Vance Packard, *The Naked Society* (New York: David McKay, 1964), p. 24.

CHAPTER SIXTEEN
THE FBI AND THE BILL OF RIGHTS
by Thomas I. Emerson

Page 413; ". . . uninhibited, robust, and wide-open":
New York Times v. *Sullivan,* 376 U.S. 254, 270 (1964).

Page 418; Stone restriction:
Max Lowenthal, *The Federal Bureau of Investigation* (New York: William Sloane Associates, 1950), Chs. 1 and 27; Fred J. Cook, *The FBI Nobody Knows* (New York: Pyramid Books, 1964), pp. 50–55; Vern Countryman, "The Illegal FBI," *The New York Review of Books,* July 31, 1969, p. 34.

Page 419
Youngstown Sheet & Tube Co. v. *Sawyer,* 343 U.S. 579 (1952). The broad language of the Supreme Court in *In re Neagle,* 135 U.S. 1 (1890), and *In re Debs,* 158 U.S. 564 (1895), upon which the government position relies, was drastically curtailed by the decision in the *Youngstown* case.

Page 420; Hoover quote:
New York *Times,* December 5, 1964. See also "J. Edgar Hoover and the FBI," *The Progressive,* February, 1960, pp. 28–29; Cook, *The FBI Nobody Knows,* op. cit., pp. 404–11.

Page 421
Lamont v. *Postmaster General,* 381 U.S. 301 (1965); *Talley* v. *California,* 362 U.S. 60 (1960); *N.A.A.C.P.* v. *Alabama,* 357 U.S. 449 (1958); *Bates* v.

Little Rock, 361 U.S. 516 (1960); *Gibson* v. *Florida Legislative Investigation Committee*, 372 U.S. 539 (1963).

Page 421
Shelton v. *Tucker*, 364 U.S. 479 (1960); *United States* v. *Robel*, 389 U.S. 258 (1967); *Schnieder* v. *Smith*, 390 U.S. 17 (1968).

Page 422
For a discussion of the legal doctrines and how they might be applied, see Frank Askin, "Police Dossiers and Emerging Principles of First Amendment Adjudication," 22 *Stanford Law Review* 196 (1970); Note, "Chilling Political Expression by Use of Police Intelligence Files: *Anderson* v. *Sills*," 5 *Harvard Civil Rights-Civil Liberties Law Review* 71 (1970); and Notes in 65 *Northwestern University Law Review* 461 (1970); 83 *Harvard Law Review* 935 (1970); and 58 *Georgetown Law Journal* 553 (1970).

Page 423
Griswold v. *Connecticut*, 381 U.S. 479 (1965); see also *Stanley* v. *Georgia*, 394 U.S. 557 (1969).

Page 427; secret informers:
Hoffa v. *United States*, 385 U.S. 293, 311 (1966).

Page 427
For discussion of the application of the First Amendment to the use of informers see Note, "Police Undercover Agents: New Threat to First Amendment Freedoms," 37 *George Washington Law Review* 634, 659–65 (1969); Note, "Present and Suggested Limitations on the Use of Secret Agents and Informers in Law Enforcement, 41 *University of Colorado Law Review* 261, 278–81 (1969); Peter Buschbaum, "Police Infiltration of Political Groups," 4 *Harvard Civil Rights-Civil Liberties Law Review* 331 (1969).

Page 429; availability of entrapment defense:
Sorrells v. *United States*, 287 U.S. 435, 442 (1932). The other leading decision, which reaffirms the rule, is *Sherman* v. *United States*, 356 U.S. 369 (1958).

Page 429; "defendant's conduct":
287 U.S. 451; see also 356 U.S. 373.

Page 429
For discussion of the law of entrapment see Richard Donnelly, "Judicial Control of Informants, Spies, Stool Pigeons, and Agent Provocateurs," 60 *Yale Law Journal* 1091 (1951); Note, "The Serpent Beguiled Me and I Did Eat: The Constitutional Status of the Entrapment Defenses," 74 *Yale Law Journal* 942 (1965); Rotenberg, "The Police Detection Practice of Encouragement: *Lewis* v. *United States* and Beyond," 4 *Houston Law Review* 609 (1967); Lester B. Orfield, "The Defense of Entrapment in the Federal Courts," 1967 *Duke Law Journal* 39 (1967).

Page 430; minority view:
Sherman v. *United States*, 356 U.S. 369, 382 (1958).

Page 431
Boyd v. *United States*, 116 U.S. 616, 630 (1886).

Page 432; property rights analysis:
Goldman v. *United States,* 316 U.S. 129 (1942); *On Lee* v. *United States,* 343 U.S. 747 (1952); *Lopez* v. *United States,* 373 U.S. 427 (1963).

Page 432; Fourth Amendment and informers:
Lewis v. *United States,* 385 U.S. 206 (1966); *Hoffa* v. *United States,* 385 U.S. 293 (1966); *Osborn* v. *United States,* 385 U.S. 323 (1966).

Page 432; Berger v. *N.Y.; Katz* v. *U.S.:*
388 U.S. 41 (1967); 389 U.S. 347 (1967).

Page 432; U.S. v. *White:*
401 U.S. 745 (1971).

Page 433
There is clear authority for applying the Fourth Amendment with greater stringency when First Amendment rights are involved. *Marcus* v. *Search Warrant,* 367 U.S. 717 (1961); *A Quantity of Books* v. *Kansas,* 378 U.S. 205 (1964); *Stanford* v. *Texas,* 379 U.S. 476 (1965).

Page 436
For discussion of proposals for internal reform of the Bureau, see H. H. Wilson, "The FBI Today: The Case for Effective Control," *The Nation,* February 8, 1971, p. 169.

INDEX